HOODWINKING HITLER

Also by William B. Breuer

An American Saga
Bloody Clash at Sadzot
Captain Cool
They Jumped at Midnight
Drop Zone Sicily
Agony at Anzio
Hitler's Fortress Cherbourg
Death of a Nazi Army
Operation Torch
Storming Hitler's Rhine
Retaking the Philippines
Devil Boats
Operation Dragoon
The Secret War with Germany
Sea Wolf
Hitler's Undercover War
Geronimo!

HOODWINKING
HITLER

THE NORMANDY
DECEPTION

WILLIAM B. BREUER

PRAEGER

Westport, Connecticut
London

Library of Congress Cataloging-in-Publication Data

Breuer, William B.
    Hoodwinking Hitler: the Normandy deception /
    William B. Breuer.
        p. cm.
    Includes bibliographical references and index.
    ISBN 0-275-94438-7 (alk. paper)
    1. World War, 1939–1945—Campaigns—France—Normandy.
    2. Deception (Military science)—History—20th century. 3. World
    War, 1939–1945—Military intelligence. 4. Strategy—History—20th
    century.   I. Title.
    D756.5.N6B74   1993
    940.54'2142—dc20   92–31714

British Library Cataloguing in Publication Data is available.

Library of Congress Catalog Card Number: 92–31714
ISBN: 0-275-94438-7

First published in 1993

Praeger Publishers, 88 Post Road West, Westport, CT 06881
An imprint of Greenwood Publishing Group, Inc.

Printed in the United States of America

The paper used in this book complies with the Permanent
Paper Standard issued by the National Information Standards
Organization (Z39.48—1984).

10 9 8 7 6 5 4 3 2 1

Dedicated to
Anthony Carder Stout,
founder and president of
The Battle of Normandy Foundation,
whose devotion and energy
have kept burning brightly
the flame of American heroism
in World War II

There is required for the composition of a great commander not only massive common sense and reasoning power, but also an element of legerdemain, an original and sinister touch, which leaves the enemy puzzled as well as beaten.

—Winston S. Churchill

Contents

Maps

Photo essay follows page 108

HOODWINKING
HITLER

I

A Plot to Murder
President Roosevelt

An icy wind was blowing in from the Atlantic Ocean across Hampton Roads, Virginia, as a black Cadillac limousine, its blinds pulled to conceal the passenger in the rear seat, edged along the dock and came to a halt beside the new battleship USS *Iowa*. Two husky Secret Service men lifted President Franklin D. Roosevelt from the vehicle and carried him up the gangplank and into the cavernous bowels of the 45,000-ton vessel, America's most modern and speediest. It was the evening of November 12, 1943.

Inside his wardroom, the 61-year-old Roosevelt, who had been crippled by polio at age 39, let out a sigh of relief as he eased the straps holding a 15-pound metal brace to each leg.[1]

Roosevelt, who had served as assistant secretary of the Navy in World War I, shared the sailor's superstition that Friday is an unlucky day on which to start a long voyage. So the huge *Iowa* remained at her berth that night and did not shove off until 12:01 A.M., Saturday, November 13. Roosevelt had no qualms about the number "13" being an ill omen.

Also on board were silver-thatched General George C. Marshall, the Army chief of staff; Admiral Ernest J. King, the chief of naval operations; General Henry H. "Hap" Arnold, commander of the Army Air Corps; Admiral William D. Leahy, chief of staff to the president; Lieutenant General Brehon Somervell, chief of the Army Services of Supply; and 51 subordinate staff officers, aides, analysts, and figure-filberts.

President Roosevelt and his entourage were bound for Oran, a port in North Africa, on the first leg of one of the most crucial meetings of World War II, a summit of the Grand Alliance (the United States, Great Britain, and the Soviet Union) at Teheran, Iran. The Big Three were Roosevelt, British Prime Minister Winston S. Churchill, and Soviet Premier Joseph Vissarionovich Dzhugashvili (known to the world as Joseph Stalin).

Code-named Eureka, the Teheran conference promised to be both a showdown between the Americans and the British, who had been squabbling for months over grand strategy, and an effort to hammer out a Big Three agreement for the invasion of Adolf Hitler's *Festung Europa* (Fortress Europe).

Roosevelt and General Marshall were committed to launching a massive frontal assault from Britain directly across the English Channel against German-held France in the early spring of 1944. At a Roosevelt-Churchill conference in Quebec in August 1943, the British, while making no firm commitment, had agreed in principle to that operation, code-named Overlord.[2]

Eureka was a closely guarded secret, as was President Roosevelt's journey. Although the *Iowa* had a possible speed of 33 knots, she would be cutting through submarine-infested waters. Some ambitious German U-boat skipper could gain immortality in the Third Reich should his torpedoes sink the battleship carrying the president of the United States and nearly the entire military high command. A strict radio silence was maintained. It was hoped that Roosevelt, with his staff, could reach Oran before the Germans learned of his whereabouts and intentions.

While the *Iowa* was knifing through the rollers of the wintry Atlantic on a course for Gibraltar and beyond, the HMS *Renown*, a British battlewagon, slipped out of a harbor in southern England and also headed for the Mediterranean Sea. On board the *Renown* were Winston Churchill and his top military advisor, Field Marshal Alan Brooke, chief of the Imperial General Staff.

Before arriving in Teheran, Roosevelt and Churchill would meet in Cairo, where they would try to thrash out their differences over grand strategy. Verbal explosions were likely, replete with pounding tables and hurling expletives for George Marshall and his opposite number, Alan Brooke, who were cordial in public, detested and did not trust one another.

Both antagonists, Marshall and Brooke, were capable, intelligent, and tough. Almost since their first strategic meeting early in 1942, friction had developed between the pair that resulted in making each succeeding conference a tension-racked affair. Marshall, low-key but forceful, resented what he considered to be Brooke's patronizing attitude toward American generals—"newcomers to war from the Colonies." Following an especially rowdy session in early 1943, Brooke penned in his daily log: "[Marshall's] strategic ability does not impress me at all."

Alan Brooke, who emerged from World War I as the most decorated British soldier since Wellington and Marlborough, felt that Marshall, who had never commanded as much as a platoon in combat, was largely a "political general." Brooke had once confided to his diary that General Douglas MacArthur ("a real soldier") should be the United States Army chief of staff instead of Marshall. Word of such views got back to Marshall and served to pour more oil on burning waters.

Brooke's grand design for victory, which he had clung to almost since America became England's war ally on December 9, 1941, was to continue to bomb the Third Reich day and night, keep a naval blockade of German ports, keep Adolf

Hitler off-balance with commando raids and clever, diabolical deceptions that would force the *Oberkommando der Wehrmacht* (OKW; the German high command) to garrison some 2,000 miles of western European coastline, strike at German morale with a relentless propaganda blitz, encourage enemy rebellion from within, and conduct military operations on the lightly defended fringes of the fuehrer's empire. When these combined pressures indicated a weakening of German strength and morale, then—and *only* then—should the Anglo-Americans launch a prodigious assault across the Channel and aim for the heart of the Third Reich.

Now, on the battleship *Renown* and sailing toward Gibraltar, Field Marshal Brooke scrawled in his diary: "I wish our [Cairo] conference was over. I despair of getting our American friends to have any strategic vision."[3]

On the *Iowa*, General Marshall was aware that Brooke was a vocal advocate of drawing German forces away from northern France by launching a campaign in the Balkans, a large peninsula in southeastern Europe that included Albania, Greece, Bulgaria, Romania, portions of Turkey, and most of Yugoslavia. The American chief of staff considered such a scheme to be indecisive and costly—more Allied nibbling on the fringes of the Greater Reich. Marshall had his own pet tactic for splitting German units in France when the Anglo-Americans struck across the Channel against Normandy: Operation Anvil, an invasion of the Riviera to tie down the *Wehrmacht* (armed forces) on D-Day.

Alan Brooke bitterly opposed Anvil, convinced that an intricate deception and feint campaign could pin down the Germans along the Riviera and that Anglo-American forces earmarked for Anvil could be used better in diversionary operations in the eastern Mediterranean, especially in the Balkans.

In recent months, Marshall had become so angry as a result of his strategy differences with Brooke that he even threatened to resign from the Army should the field marshal's views prevail. Privately, the American general told aides that he would not be a party to any campaign in the Balkans and charged that Brooke was acting in an "underhand way" in trying to get U.S. armed forces "sucked into that remote region."[4]

On November 22, 1943, President Roosevelt and his entourage, having disembarked from the *Iowa* at Oran, touched down at the Cairo airport in the *Sacred Cow*, the chief executive's personal aircraft. A caravan of Buicks drove the president and his group to their quarters, a collection of comfortable villas, where, under the keen-eyed scrutiny of the Great Sphinx and Field Marshal Brooke, they were greeted effusively by Winston Churchill, who was nattily dressed in a white suit, brandishing his ever-present cigar.

On the following morning, the American and British delegations gathered around a highly polished mahogany conference table in Cairo's fashionable Mena Palace Hotel. The participants hardly had settled into their chairs when verbal fireworks erupted. Alan Brooke grew angry when the Americans promptly seized the initiative: instead of discussing Overlord and Anvil, George Marshall proposed an operation to aid General Chiang Kai-shek, the Chinese strongman, by landing British and American troops in the Bay of Bengal, in the Far East, halfway around the world.

Brooke felt that Marshall was stalling, intent on avoiding a discussion of Overlord and Anvil until the meetings with Joseph Stalin in Teheran. Stalin, Brooke knew, favored Overlord. Tempers flared. Sharp-tongued Brooke snorted that the Bay of Bengal operation was a waste of time and effort. One word led to a thousand—and then came the explosion.

General Joseph W. "Vinegar Joe" Stilwell, the tough, bespectacled American commander in the CBI (China-Burma-India) theater, who long had been battling the Japanese on a shoestring, recalled: "Brooke got good and nasty and [Admiral Ernest] King got good and sore. King almost climbed over the table at Brooke. God, he was mad! I wish to hell King had socked him!"[5]

For three more days, accusations flew back and forth, with Marshall and Brooke the principal combatants. When the two groups prepared for the flight to Teheran, nothing had been accomplished and storm warnings were still aloft.

Harry Hopkins, Roosevelt's closest civilian advisor, who had met with Joseph Stalin several times during the war, was deeply concerned that the cunning Soviet dictator would get the best of Roosevelt. But the president merely shrugged. "Don't worry about Uncle Joe—I can handle him," Roosevelt said with typical self-confidence.

Winston Churchill held a more pragmatic view: "Joe Stalin has all the charm of a cobra snake—and is just as deadly!"

Churchill and Roosevelt agreed on one point: the meeting with Stalin would be a delicate one. Stalin had long been convinced that the United States and Great Britain had conspired to let the Germans and the Russians bleed each other into impotence before the Anglo-Americans struck in western Europe.

Winston Churchill did not trust the Soviets and would have to choose his words carefully. Through British intelligence, the 69-year-old, cherubic prime minister knew that while the Russian and German armies were slaughtering each other on the Eastern Front, there were clandestine contacts between members of the Soviet and Reich general staffs. If it served Stalin, Churchill was convinced, secret British and American plans for invading Europe would not be long in reaching Adolf Hitler's ears.

Meanwhile at the Russian embassy in Teheran, a bustling ancient city of some 600,000, Joseph Stalin and his aides were discussing means for dealing with the Americans and British. Stalin's eyes, like those of Churchill, were cast on the eastern Mediterranean and the Balkans, fertile grounds for postwar Communist expansion. Stalin was bent on halting any British insurgence into those regions.

Hardly had Franklin Roosevelt been lifted from the *Sacred Cow* and into a wheelchair at Teheran airport on November 27, 1943, than Stalin took the president aside. Three days earlier, the dictator told him, Soviet intelligence had uncovered a Nazi plot to murder Roosevelt during his stay in Teheran. Code-named Long Pounce by the Germans, the assassination was being masterminded by swashbuckling *Obersturmbannfuehrer SS* (Lieutenant Colonel) Otto Skorzeny, who had the sinister label of "The Most Dangerous Man in Europe."

Skorzeny, one of Adolf Hitler's favorites, was an imposing figure, six feet five inches tall and looking like Hollywood's version of an evil Nazi assassin—complete with a dueling scar on one cheek from his Vienna university days. Only a few months earlier, Skorzeny had gained worldwide fame by leading a daring commando raid with gliders to rescue Benito Mussolini, who had been ousted as the dictator of Italy and was being held for trial on top of an Abruzzi mountain named Gran Sasso.[6]

The president thanked Stalin for the warning and showed no outward concern. Not so Michael Riley, the conscientious chief of the U.S. Secret Service whose job it was to protect the life of America's chief executive—Riley quickly bundled Roosevelt into a limousine that had been waiting at the airport and rushed across Teheran and inside the protecting high walls of the U.S. embassy.

Roosevelt had hardly the time to remove his brutal leg braces and nip at an aperitif when a breathless delegation dispatched by Stalin arrived at the embassy. Since the American legation was two miles across the city from the Soviet and British embassies, which were side by side, would it not be more prudent for Roosevelt to occupy one of the comfortable villas on the tightly guarded Russian embassy grounds where the Big Three summit would convene? This would eliminate the risk of assassination while Roosevelt was traveling through the crowded streets at least twice each day, the emissaries stressed.

Roosevelt was noncommittal.

Mike Riley was in favor of accepting the offer, so the invitation was accepted. Now the wily Uncle Joe Stalin would have the ear of the president of the United States without Churchill and his vision of invading the Balkans being around to join in "unofficial" discussions.

Whirlwind Mike Riley rapidly arranged for the transfer of the president. It appeared that at least half of the American and Soviet armies were mustered to jointly line the major avenue to be taken. A heavily guarded caravan—armored cars with GIs manning machine guns, military policemen on motorcycles, three automobiles carrying alert Secret Service men with Tommy guns cradled in their arms—drove out through the gates of the American embassy. In the middle of the convoy was the presidential limousine.

Actually, the caravan was an elaborate piece of deception, complete with a "clay pigeon" posing as President Roosevelt in the back seat of the shiny black limousine. The dummy presidential convoy had just left the embassy grounds when a lone, somewhat decrepit and dusty old Ford slipped out through a back gate and raced away. In the back seat, clutching his straw hat, was President Roosevelt, who seemed to be enjoying the cloak-and-dagger scenario. Harry Hopkins sat beside the president and Admiral Bill Leahy, Roosevelt's personal chief of staff, held down the passenger side in front.

At the wheel was a grim-faced Secret Service man, who was determined to follow Mike Riley's stern instructions to "get the Boss there as fast as you can—don't halt or slow down for anything!" Lying on the seat between Leahy and Riley's man was a sawed-off shotgun—fully loaded.

Leahy and Hopkins were striving to appear unmoved by the high speeds over a circuitous and devious route, which part of the way consisted of an unpaved road and stretches that would have been little more than dingy back alleys in the United States. So fast did the Secret Service driver go that, despite the much greater distance, the car sped through the Russian embassy gates before the heavily guarded dummy presidential caravan finished its two-mile trek. When the driver jolted the old Ford to a halt, Roosevelt grinned widely, considering the episode more of a lark than anything as serious as foiling a murder plot by dedicated Nazi hit men.

After a larger part of the dirt and grime that must have collected for years was cleaned out, reasonably comfortable quarters were arranged for the president in a villa on the Russian property. Mike Riley was far from enthused about the situation, as Harry Hopkins would recall years later:

> The servants who made the President's bed and cleaned his room were all members of the highly efficient OGPU [Stalin's secret police], and expressive bulges were plainly discernible in the hip pockets under their white coats.
>
> It was a nervous time for Mike Riley and his own Secret Service men, who were trained to suspect *everybody* and who did not like to admit into the President's presence anyone who was armed with as much as a gold toothpick.

A few members of the president's entourage grumbled that this yarn about a Nazi murder plot might well be a Stalin trick to achieve some self-serving goal. "Don't worry about that," Roosevelt replied. "I can handle Uncle Joe."

Buildings on the Soviet embassy grounds and the surrounding park were patrolled around the clock by a large number of Russian special agents armed with automatic weapons who stopped *everybody*. All of Roosevelt's entourage were furnished with passes made out in Russian, with only their names being recognizable.

America's highest brass—four-star generals and admirals and top civilian officials—were advised to stop instantly if challenged by the Russian agents. The "advice" was observed meticulously.

President Roosevelt had just settled into his villa when a suitor came calling—Joseph Stalin. In an amiable tone, the Soviet dictator assured Roosevelt that he firmly backed a cross-Channel invasion of France by the Anglo-Americans and, in essence, expressed the hope that the president would persuade Churchill and the British to keep out of the Balkans.

When Field Marshal Alan Brooke learned of the secret Stalin-Roosevelt confabulation, he wrote gloomily in his diary: "This conference is over before it even begins."[7]

Three weeks before the Teheran summit, a young American parachuted in the vicinity of Dohuk, about 100 miles south of Baghdad, the ancient capital of Iraq, which bordered Iran on the east. Known as C–12, the parachutist was an agent of the Office of Strategic Services (OSS), America's cloak-and-dagger agency.

C–12 spoke Kurdish fluently and his assignment was to live among the tribesmen there, just as other undercover OSS agents were doing in many remote locales of the world. One day, word reached the Kurdish village that several men had "fallen from the sky" in a valley a few miles away, so the American, clad in Kurdish garb, and a few of the tribesmen mounted ponies and rode to the site.

It soon became evident to C–12 that the parachutists were Germans, and, through a mixture of high school French and pigeon English, the American learned that their mission was to go to Teheran, in neighboring Iran, and kill President Roosevelt. (Apparently these German commandos were the vanguard of Otto Skorzeny's Long Pounce operation.)

The commandos had with them a heavy container of a substance that C–12, through his OSS training, was able to identify as trinitrotoluene, popularly known as TNT, a powerful explosive. When the Germans indicated they wanted a guide to take them on the long, mountainous trip to Teheran, C–12, whom the strangers thought was a native Kurd, volunteered. To allay any suspicions the assassins may have felt, C–12 haggled over the fee he was to receive and insisted that he be paid handsomely with dinars and rials.

That same day, the tiny group set out for Teheran with C–12 at the wheel of a wheezing, dilapidated truck of undetermined pedigree and vintage. As the American steered along the narrow, winding gravel road that wound over and alongside the steep mountains, he rejected a fleeting idea: when going over the peak of a high elevation and gathering speed on the descent, he would leap out on the driver's side and let the truck take the Germans to their deaths as it plunged off the road and down the mountain.

If C–12 was racked with curiosity about how Nazi assassins knew details about where the Allied Big Three would meet and when, he made no inquiry of his employers, fearful of arousing their suspicions. He decided to bide his time and do what he could to thwart the Germans or report their goal to American authorities in Teheran.

After a journey of three days, C–12 and the Nazi assassins arrived in Teheran. In keeping with the Nazis' instructions, the swarthy American, who spoke Farsi, had no trouble in renting a one-story house on Ferdousi Avenue, the heavily traveled thoroughfare along which President Roosevelt presumably would ride while going back and forth between the U.S. and Soviet embassies.

Almost at once, the Germans began digging a tunnel from the basement of their house, which rested virtually on the sidewalk, to what they judged to be the center of Ferdousi Avenue, just below the surface. As C–12 watched, the Germans placed their entire load of TNT at the end of the tunnel—to be detonated when Roosevelt's limousine passed over it. C–12 grasped enough of the Germans' chatter to know that they were conjecturing over how high in the sky the president would be blown by the blast.

But the Germans became frantic. They could not find the detonators they had brought along. C–12 knew where the blasting caps were: he had carefully hidden them. While his employers desperately searched the house, the OSS operative slipped away and hightailed it on foot to the American embassy. Clad in his flea-infested, billowy pants and tasseled turban, C–12 had a difficult time persuading the gate sentries that he was an American on an urgent mission, but they finally allowed him to be escorted inside.

A squad of American soldiers promptly surrounded the house where the Germans were holed up and captured them. Two GIs crawled into the tunnel and removed the TNT.[8]

A few hours later, C–12 was told that Franklin Roosevelt wanted to see him. In a borrowed uniform (he was a genuine U.S. Army officer) and clean-shaven for the first time in weeks, C–12 had visions of a high decoration for saving the life of the president. Instead, a presidential aide would reveal years later, Roosevelt angrily accused the OSS agent of needlessly risking the president's life. Why hadn't C–12 reported the plot the minute the group crossed the Iranian frontier? It did no good for C–12 to explain that Iran and Germany were not at war with one another, and until the Nazi infiltrators had provided evidence of their illegal intentions by digging the tunnel, they had done nothing with which they could be charged. Be that as it may, C–12 was ordered to return to Baghdad, there to meditate on the unfairness of life.[9]

2

An Ingenious Stratagem
Is Unveiled

Outside the Russian embassy sharp-eyed sentries stood guard as the Big Three summit convened in a large drawing room at 4:30 P.M. on November 28, 1943. Seated around a highly polished mahogany conference table was a strange set of allies: Winston Churchill and Franklin Roosevelt, both aristocrats born to wealth and staunch pillars of capitalism, and Joseph Stalin, the son of a cobbler and fervent missionary for the spread of communism.

It had been a shotgun wedding, one entered into to bring about the downfall of a common deadly foe—Adolf Hitler and Nazism. Churchill, known to American leaders as "The Prime," once explained to his confidential secretary why he, an arch-anti-Communist, had climbed into bed with Stalin: "If Herr Hitler invaded Hell, I would make at least a favorable reference to the Devil in the House of Commons."[1]

Stalin was resplendent in a field marshal's uniform that appeared to have been tailored precisely for the summit. Lord Moran, Churchill's personal physician, later observed: "Stalin's outfit looked as if the tailor had put a large shelf on each shoulder, and on them dumped a lot of gold lace and stars."[2]

Every American and British eye and ear were focused on the Russian leader. Most of them were hearing and seeing him for the first time. Churchill was the exception. He had had one-on-one confrontations with Stalin numerous times and described those sessions as being "as pleasant as having your teeth pulled."

Churchill, eloquent and calculating, and Stalin, often blunt and equally calculating, did most of the talking, although Roosevelt kicked off the discussions by reminding them that the Americans and British had agreed on May 1944 as the period for a cross-Channel invasion of France.

After the British prime minister spoke at length about his determination to carry out that operation, in the next breath, he launched into a lengthy plea for expanded military actions in the Balkans and eastern Mediterranean. Then he asked Stalin what Russia would like to see the Western Allies do. Attack over the English Channel against France was the reply.

When the first session broke up, the talk among Roosevelt's aides at dinner centered on Stalin. Prior to the first session, most of them thought that Stalin was a bandit leader, a thug, who had slashed his way to the top of his government. While there may have been merit to their description, they now knew that they were dealing with a highly intelligent and cunning figure who knew what he wanted and was ruthlessly determined to get it.

Stalin, the Americans found, was largely agreeable and considerate of the viewpoints of Roosevelt and Churchill—until one of them proposed some action that the Russian leader thought was detrimental to his country's interests. Then he could be brutally blunt to the point of rudeness.[3]

Bright and early the next morning, Winston Churchill, having heard of the private, 45-minute Roosevelt-Stalin talk and perhaps believing that the two men were ganging up on him, sent a courier with a note to the American president. Would Roosevelt be his guest at lunch? Sorry, the president replied, he had an important meeting scheduled with his staff. Actually, Roosevelt was going to hold another secret meeting with Stalin.

When the summit was resumed that afternoon, General George Marshall argued that Anvil, an invasion of the French Riviera, was crucial toward the goal of dispersing German divisions in France. Anvil, according to American plans, would hit about a month after the cross-Channel attack, or as soon as sufficient landing craft was gathered in the eastern Mediterranean. It would be folly to get "bogged down interminably" in the Balkans, Marshall declared, in an apparent jab at Field Marshal Brooke. Joe Stalin grunted his agreement.

That night at dinner, Brooke knew that he and Churchill were fighting a rearguard action and that their battle to invade the Balkans had been lost. He was in a black mood, convinced that Roosevelt and Marshall were incredibly naive and mere pawns in the hands of the wily Stalin.

Pecking at his salad in a private dining room, Brooke looked at Lord Moran and muttered: "Doc, I shall come to you to send me to a lunatic asylum. I cannot stand much more of [these talks]. Seven hours' conference today, and we are not an inch further along."[4]

The final session, on November 30, was heated. At one point Stalin turned to Churchill and growled: "Do you really believe in [the cross Channel attack] or are you stalling on it?"[5]

Churchill's face turned crimson. An awkward hush fell over the room. Even in supercharged climates, the leader of a major power does not publicly infer that the head of an allied nation is a double-dealer and a liar. The prime minister puffed on his cigar and replied that he did indeed support Overlord, but he felt that the other operations he was proposing in the Balkans would help insure the success of the invasion of France.

It appeared that Churchill was indeed stalling. He proposed that the political aspects of his Mediterranean and Balkans proposals be referred to the three nations' foreign ministers present at Teheran for their advice.[6] Stalin barked back: "Why do that? We are the chiefs of government. We know what we want to do. Why turn the matter over to some subordinates to advise us?"[7]

Stalin proved that he himself was an expert "staller" when such a tactic served his purpose. When confronted with specific requests by Roosevelt or Churchill that required Russian cooperation, Stalin always replied that he would have to wait until he returned to Moscow and consulted his government before giving the answers. "I cannot always act without reference to Moscow," the premier who ruled the Soviet Union with an iron fist declared.

Despite the barrage of harsh charges and countercharges that had rocked the drawing room for three days, the Big Three finally agreed on their next strategic operations. American, British, and Canadian forces would assemble in England and strike across the Channel against northern France in May 1944, and Anvil would hit the French Riviera in the south as soon as possible afterward. The Overlord invasion would coincide with a massive Soviet offensive in the East in order to pin down German divisions there until the Western Allies were solidly ashore in northern France.

Still Joe Stalin was not satisfied and demanded to know precisely where the blow across the Channel would hit. Churchill lied that a specific locale was "still under study." Actually, Normandy had been selected months earlier as the site of the landing beaches.

Now the Russian leader confronted President Roosevelt with a blunt question: Who was going to command Overlord? It was an odd query; never had Roosevelt or Churchill asked Stalin which of his generals he would appoint to command certain operations on the Eastern Front. Hedging, the president replied that he had not decided whom he would name. Moments later, Roosevelt leaned over to Admiral Bill Leahy, who was seated beside him, and whispered: "That Old Bolshevik is trying to force me to give him the name of our supreme commander."[8]

Now that the Big Three had reached agreement on Overlord, Winston Churchill took to the floor to brief the gathering on Plan Bodyguard, an incredibly intricate and devious deception scheme created largely by ingenious British minds to hoodwink Adolf Hitler on the location and date of the cross-Channel invasion.[9] Never had warfare known the scope and complexity of this colossal stratagem which, in essence, would be a Trojan horse to mask Allied intentions. Despite the mighty invasion force the Allies would muster in England, Overlord would be a success only if Bodyguard kept D-Day secrets from the Germans.[10]

Privately, many Allied generals doubted if that could be achieved. A few weeks before the Teheran conference, British General J.F.M. Whitely, who had been involved in planning cross-Channel operations, told confidants that he was "not prepared to bet a pound sterling" on the chances of keeping the place and date secret. "How does one 'hide' an invasion?" he asked.

Winston Churchill, now that he was ready to unveil Bodyguard for Stalin and his generals, was in his element. The prospect of baffling and bluffing the fuehrer appealed to his pixieish, creative intellect.

"It was the prime minister who had all the ideas," recalled Lieutenant Colonel Ronald E. L. Wingate, one of Britain's foremost deception artists. "It was his drive, his brilliant imagination, and his technical knowledge that initiated all these ideas and plans."[11]

Back on May 10, 1940, after Great Britain had been at war with Nazi Germany for eight months, King George VI summoned Winston Churchill to Buckingham Palace. That morning, 70-year-old Neville Chamberlain, who for two years had been trying to appease Adolf Hitler, resigned as prime minister—on the same day that the fuehrer unleashed his powerful war machine that would overrun France, Belgium, and the Netherlands in a *blitzkrieg* that lasted only an astonishing six weeks. King George asked Churchill, the First Lord of the Admiralty, to take over the reins of government, an offer he eagerly accepted. The two men held a brief discussion of the bleak war picture, and Churchill, in a series of bows, withdrew.

At that time, England was an island under siege. It was England's blackest hour. Across the Channel was coiled the powerful Wehrmacht, ready to leap to England and conquer that virtually defenseless nation. Unknown to the new prime minister, he was on a secret *die Sonderfahndungsliste, G.B.* (Special Search List, Great Britain) compiled by the German Military Government of England. It contained the names, occupations, and addresses of 2,300 statesmen, clergymen, educators, and other "undesirables" who were to be seized at once and turned over to the Gestapo for "processing." Names were in alphabetical order. Number 49 on the list was "Churchill, Winston Spencer, Ministerpresident, Westerham/Kent, Chartwell Manor."

Meanwhile, Churchill reached an inescapable conclusion: if Great Britain were to survive as a nation against the threat of history's greatest military juggernaut, Churchill would have to rapidly mount a campaign of subterfuge of unprecedented scope and ingenuity. Moving with typical alacrity, Churchill began mobilizing the intellectual brains of England into a clandestine force, warriors whose weapons would be intrigue, deceit, fakery, lies, deception, and stealth.

These men and women were to conceive and implement devious, always elaborate and delicately subtle, and sometimes brutal schemes to mask Britain's glaring military deficiencies. As the months rolled past and the course of the war began to tilt toward the Allies, the ghost warriors turned their weapons toward confounding and confusing the fuehrer on Allied offensive operations, while continuing to ferret out enemy capabilities and plans. In this duel of wits with Nazi Germany, a war within a war, there would be no holds barred.

Now, as Churchill began his Bodyguard briefing at Teheran, he was confronted by a challenge that would sorely test his widely recognized guile and skills as an orator. He did not trust the Russians, so he would give only sufficient details for Stalin and his generals to grasp the deception's theme in order that they could play their assigned roles in the plan. At the same time, he would keep the Russians in the dark about specific techniques to be used.

Churchill's qualms about Soviet trustworthiness harkened back to December 20, 1941, when British and Russian delegations, meeting secretly in Moscow, had signed a pact that provided for an exchange of all intelligence against Germany collected by both nations. In theory, the agreement was admirable. In reality, it only deepened long-held suspicions. Little, if any, information ever changed hands.

Prior to negotiating that 1941 agreement, the British and Russian secret services had been battling one another for decades—murders, kidnappings, mayhem. Now, Churchill conjectured, would these two blood enemies suddenly drop their animosities and work closely toward deceiving Adolf Hitler on Overlord?

Weeks before Teheran, Churchill concluded that he would have to risk the definite possibility that disclosing Bodyguard information to Stalin might boomerang. In the postwar years, the savage rivalry between the British and Russian secret services might erupt again and the Soviets would use the Bodyguard deception techniques against England.

Premier Stalin, inscrutable as always, puffed on a pipe and listened intently as Churchill described Bodyguard, a witch's brew of plots, subplots, and counterplots—a tangled web of spoofs, spooks, fraud, deceit, camouflage, stealth, misdirection, skulduggery, fakery, lies, and occasional mayhem—collectively known to the British as "special means."

"The plan has to be just close enough to the truth to seem credible to Herr Hitler, but will mislead him completely," Churchill explained. "Hopefully, Bodyguard will catch the Germans off-guard on D-Day and gain a thin extra edge that could mean the difference between a glorious triumph and a bloody debacle for the Allies." With a twinkle in his eye, Churchill added: "If we pull this off, it will be *the greatest hoax in history!*"

Bodyguard consisted of five major arenas of secret activities:

1. *Deception.* Its function was to plant upon the enemy, through every channel available, tens of thousands of bits and pieces of information. These would be allowed to reach German intelligence in such a subtle way as to convince the enemy that he himself had discovered them through his own herculean efforts and infinite powers of deduction. When assembled by German intelligence, these splinters of information would create a highly plausible—but false—big picture of Allied capabilities and intentions.

2. *Security and counterintelligence, handmaidens of deception.* This element was designed to deny the Oberkommando der Wehrmacht (OKW) the secrets of Overlord. This required outwitting the *Abwehr* and other German intelligence services.

3. *Offensive intelligence.* Its purpose was to divine German intentions, a painstaking and extremely difficult procedure. This required creating a detailed order of battle (the disposition and identity of German forces).

4. *Political warfare.* Designed to pierce the German mind through a sustained barrage of clever, but plausible, propaganda, lies, and fictions, all intended to lower enemy morale, to drive a wedge between the Nazi leadership and the *herrenvolk* (people), and to create in the Third Reich intensified war-weariness and defeatism.

5. *Brutal, unadulterated mayhem.* To be inflicted upon the Wehrmacht by constant stealthy commando raids and through other machinations, and to organize, arm, and control the French, Belgian, and Dutch underground groups in acts of sabotage and guerrilla warfare that would slow down, or even halt in some instances, the German reaction to the invasion of northern France. Even the lives of Allied agents and resistance members would be "expendable" if needed to achieve some important covert objective.

Crucial to the Western Allies getting ashore in France and staying there on D-Day and beyond would be influencing Adolf Hitler and his generals to disperse widely their combat divisions, so the Germans could not rush overwhelming firepower and numerical superiority to the landing beaches and drive the invaders back into the sea. Toward reaching that objective of keeping German forces scattered throughout Europe, Scandinavia, the Mediterranean, and the Balkans, Bodyguard contained five erroneous strategical considerations that would be foisted off on the fuehrer and his generals:

FAKE SCENARIO 1. That the Allies were convinced that the heavy bombing against the Third Reich had nearly demolished its war production potential, and, if increased, bombing alone would force the surrender of Germany. Therefore, the Allies had given a high priority to bringing bombers from the United States, resulting in slowing the ground forces buildup in England so that any invasion, if needed, could not possibly hit before mid-July 1944.

FAKE SCENARIO 2. That the Allies would continue land warfare in May or June 1944, with a coordinated American-British-Russian attack on German-held Norway. An objective of this operation would be to force neutral Sweden to join the Allies, after which Swedish ports and airfields would be used to support an Anglo-American attack against Denmark (occupied by the Wehrmacht) from England in mid-summer 1944.

FAKE SCENARIO 3. That a series of major Allied operations would be launched against the Balkans in May or June 1944. These would include an Anglo-American landing in the vicinity of Trieste, a British assault on German-held Greece, and a British-Russian invasion of Romania from the Black Sea to threaten the Reich's chief source of oil at Ploesti.

FAKE SCENARIO 4. That the Soviet Army planned to launch a mammoth offensive on the Eastern Front in July (two months after the genuine Overlord D-Day).

FAKE SCENARIO 5. That the Anglo-Americans were convinced that German forces defending northwest Europe were so formidable that 50 divisions would have to be gathered in Great Britain and that these forces would not be trained and ready until at least mid-July 1944.

Joseph Stalin, certainly no amateur in the fine art of deceit, conniving, and double-dealing, seemed to be fascinated by the machinations of the deception plan, and he readily agreed to Churchill's proposal that members of British and American cloak-and-dagger agencies fly to Moscow in February to coordinate deception operations with their opposite numbers on the Soviet general staff.

The melding of the three Allied secret intelligence services to bring about the downfall of Adolf Hitler and his Nazi regime became official when Churchill, Roosevelt, and Stalin signed a document that said "it is agreed that a cover plan to mystify and mislead [the Germans] as regard these impending operations in Europe should be concerted between the [three] staffs concerned."

There was a fourth secret service not mentioned—the German Abwehr. All through the war, Admiral Wilhelm Canaris, chief of the Abwehr, had been covertly feeding a stream of top-secret reports on the military and political situation in the Third Reich to MI-6, the British secret service branch responsible for collecting intelligence outside the Commonwealth.

November 30 was the final night of the summit and Winston Churchill's 69th birthday. In order to celebrate both milestones, Churchill played host at a lavish dinner party in the British embassy. It was a gala affair. Russian custom was followed, which meant that toasts were consumed to nearly all of the 34 persons at the banquet table. Roosevelt, Churchill, and Stalin made speeches. Churchill, the arch-anti-Communist, droned on about Britain's abiding friendship with the Soviets.

After enduring the speeches, the revelers turned to idle repartee. Suddenly, Stalin grew serious and declared (through his interpreter) that after the war 50,000 German officers would be rounded up and shot.

Silence descended on the room. Roosevelt drew on his cigarette and said nothing. Rising from his chair, an irritated Churchill paced about the banquet room and replied: "The British government and people will never tolerate mass executions. Even if in war passion they allow them to begin, they would turn violently against those responsible after the first butchery had taken place!"[12]

Unmoved, Stalin growled, "Fifty thousand must be shot!" Even more angry, Churchill retorted: "I would rather be taken out into the garden here and now and be shot myself than sully my own and my country's honor by such infamy!"[13]

Again a strained silence. Then Franklin Roosevelt broke out his famous lop-sided grin and tried to quiet the air with a remark he thought was a joke, suggesting that, as a compromise, not 50,000, but only 49,000 be shot.

The president's attempt at humor fell flat on its face. So Air Corps Colonel Elliott Roosevelt, his son, tried to smooth over his father's remarks. Unsteadily, a glass of champagne in his hand, the younger Roosevelt said that he was in agreement with Premier Stalin's proposal and that he was confident that the U.S. Army would back it.

Winston Churchill grew even more livid. He detested Elliott Roosevelt, who, he felt, was a "pompous, spoiled brat." The prime minister was astonished that the president would remain silent while his offspring "committed" the U.S. Army to executing 50,000 German officers.[14] Churchill stomped out of the room, slamming the door behind him. Allied "harmony" had reached the breaking point.

Joe Stalin apparently realized how serious the discussion had become, so he and Vyacheslav Molotov, his young foreign commissar, rushed after the prime minister and caught up with him in an anteroom. Stalin assured Churchill that it had all been a big joke and asked the Brit to return to the party, which he agreed to do.

Festivities reigned into the early morning hours, when, in a haze of champagne and vodka, old pals Churchill, Stalin, and Roosevelt swore undying friendship and bid one another goodnight.

At noon the next day, Franklin Roosevelt, no doubt nursing a throbbing head, and his aides lifted off from the Teheran airport in the *Sacred Cow* and headed for Cairo and five more days of talks with Winston Churchill and his military leaders.

While in Cairo, Roosevelt began serious reflection on which general would command Overlord. Since the Americans would be providing two-thirds of the manpower, the president could pick the man he wanted. In the inner circles in Washington, it had been a foregone conclusion that 63-year-old Chief of Staff George Marshall, who had been General John J. "Blackjack" Pershing's aide in World War I, would be given this historic command. Perhaps Marshall agreed, for his wife had even begun packing for the trip to London.

Marshall, a cool and distant figure, with whom hardly anyone could claim to be on intimate terms, impressed those who knew him with his brilliance as an organizer, total unselfishness, and impartiality of judgment—a sort of Roman nobility of character.

One of those convinced that George Marshall was a shoo-in for the Overlord command was his protégé, 53-year-old Dwight D. Eisenhower, known as Ike since childhood. Less than four years earlier, in 1940, Eisenhower was an obscure staff lieutenant colonel. When the Japanese launched their sneak attack to wipe out the United States Pacific Fleet at Pearl Harbor, Colonel Eisenhower was called to Washington by General Marshall, who made him chief of the war plans division.

Eisenhower quickly impressed Marshall with his incisiveness, energy, poise, and grasp of intricate problems. Perhaps to the astonishment of Eisenhower, Marshall leaped him over scores of generals senior in rank (Eisenhower was then a major general) and appointed the self-styled Kansas farm boy commander of all American forces in Europe in the summer of 1942.

When a high-level Anglo-American decision was made to invade North Africa in November 1942, Eisenhower was given command of the operation (code-named Torch). After the successful invasion, he led the assault against Sicily (which was overrun in six weeks) in July 1943 and the invasion of southern Italy in September 1943.

Ike Eisenhower soon felt that he was in the backwash of the global war, even though the fighting in Italy was as brutal as encountered anywhere during the global conflict. So he wrote to George Marshall, pleading for the command of a corps (two or more divisions) in Overlord.

Now in Cairo on the morning of December 5, 1943, Franklin Roosevelt and Winston Churchill were driven out to view the pyramids. Almost as if in passing, the president said that he felt George Marshall was both "invaluable and indispensable to the successful conduct of the global war" and that he could not spare him from Washington. Would the prime minister agree to the appointment of Dwight Eisenhower to lead Overlord?

Churchill responded by saying that "he had the warmest regard for General Eisenhower, and would trust our fortunes to his direction with hearty good will." However, the prime minister said that it was a decision for the president himself to make.[15]

At the beginning of his return trip to Washington from Cairo, Roosevelt summoned Ike Eisenhower to meet him in Tunis, a port city in Tunisia. Eisenhower's headquarters, from which he was directing operations in the Mediterranean, was at Algiers, Algeria. Hardly had Eisenhower entered the president's car than Roosevelt turned to him and, in an offhand tone, said, "Well, Ike, you are going to command Overlord."[16]

Eisenhower struggled to mask his surprise and astonishment, having felt that General Marshall would gain the command plum. "Mr. President," Ike finally said, "I realize that such an appointment involved difficult decisions. I hope that you will not be disappointed."[17]

At the British embassy in Cairo that night, Field Marshal Alan Brooke was crushed by news of Eisenhower's appointment. During the Roosevelt-Churchill conference in Quebec in late summer 1943, the prime minister had promised Brooke the coveted Overlord post.

Brooke confided to his diary after Roosevelt's choice of the supreme commander became known: "Ike has a very limited brain"; "Eisenhower has only the vaguest grasp of strategy and tactics."[18]

Eisenhower's appointment as Commander of Supreme Headquarters, Allied Expeditionary Force (SHAEF) in London, was to be a closely guarded secret. So at about 4:45 A.M. on New Year's Day 1944, the four-star general, his rank insignia carefully covered, slipped aboard an airplane at Marrakech (West Africa) and winged toward Washington, D.C., for consultations with George Marshall and other top figures in the Pentagon.

Eisenhower almost failed to reach his destination. While flying along the edge of one of the Azores Islands in the Atlantic, his plane was fired on by trigger-happy Portuguese gunners, but the shells missed their mark.

3

The "Santa Clauses" Duel
with the "Blacks"

With the arrival of New Year's Day 1944, the fate of the Third Reich, which Adolf Hitler had boasted a decade earlier would last for 1,000 years, rested largely in the hands of two of the Nazi regime's quaintest figures, Admiral Wilhelm Canaris and *Brigadefuehrer SS* Walther Schellenberg. Each headed a competing intelligence agency, and it was their crucial task to pinpoint the time and place of the looming Anglo-American invasion of Fortress Europe.[1]

Thirty-three-year-old Schellenberg, bright, energetic, and ambitious, was head of the *Sicherheitsdienst* (SD), the political intelligence branch of the *Schutzstaffel* (SS). Canaris, 56 years old, was a small, nervous, intense man who talked with a slight lisp. He was chief of the Abwehr, with 16,000 agents sprinkled around the world.

Spymasters Wilhelm Canaris and Walther Schellenberg could have been a father and son, for they seemed to be devoted to one another. Early every morning, Schellenberg left his Berlin home near the Kurfurstendam to meet Canaris at the riding stables in the Tiergarten, where they mounted sleek thoroughbreds and, impeccably clad in riding outfits, cantered along the tree-shrouded paths.

Berlin, once a majestic city of some 4 million industrious people, was now drab and gray, only a skeleton of its former glory. Always there was the eerie wail of air-raid sirens. Big Halifax and Lancaster bombers of the Royal Air Force (RAF) came by night, as many as 1,000 of them at a time in a stream stretching for 100 miles. They showered the German capital with thousands of high-explosive and incendiary bombs, obliterating huge areas and reducing rubble piles still further to powder.

Buried under tons of debris after each raid would be hundreds of Berliners—dead, half-alive, mutilated. A short respite followed. With daylight the sirens would moan again, a warning that a seeming conveyor belt of American Flying Fortresses and Liberators was renewing the bombings.

Herrenvolk, their clothes threadbare after more than four years of war, faces haggard and worried, no doubt felt twinges of bitterness as they hurried to work and passed Canaris and Schellenberg trotting peacefully along under the trees. Many had sons and husbands who had "Fallen for the Fuehrer," as the heading stated on the long, black-bordered lists of Wehrmacht war dead that appeared in German newspapers each day.

Walther Schellenberg never missed the morning ride with the fatherly Wilhelm Canaris, after which they breakfasted together at a ritzy restaurant that, despite the deprivations endured by most Berliners, still had a staff of waiters outfitted in tuxedos. Even when Schellenberg's home had been hit by an RAF bomb one night and his young son's bed was covered by debris, the SD intelligence chief left his wife to clean up the mess and hurried to rendezvous with Admiral Canaris.

Schellenberg admired the older man's cunning and notable achievements. Canaris, who called the other man "my young friend," appreciated Schellenberg's deference to him and his enormous vitality and keen mind.

Actually, they were mortal enemies, and the morning horseback rides through the Tiergarten were merely a means for them to feel out one another to try to get clues as to what kind of attack the SD planned to launch against the Abwehr, and vice versa. Above all else, Schellenberg hungered to be the hero who could go to the fuehrer and tell him the true secrets of the Allies' D-Day, an intelligence bonanza that could skyrocket Schellenberg into a post as head of all intelligence agencies—including Canaris' Abwehr.

Schellenberg had long suspected that his "good friend" Canaris was passing German secrets to British intelligence agents. The little admiral was a key leader in the *Schwarze Kapelle* (Black Orchestra), a tightly knit secret group of prominent German military officers, government officials, church and civic leaders, who, for several years, had been conspiring to get rid of Adolf Hitler and his Nazi regime.

In the eyes of Schellenberg and his young SS officers, the "Santa Clauses," as they derisively called Canaris and his elderly Abwehr aides, were traitors and should be hanged. Even a more serious offense, in Schellenberg's view, was that the Abwehr leaders were rivals for power—an unforgivable crime.

Canaris and his key Abwehr men, all officers of the old school with a strict code of honor, did not regard themselves as traitors to the Fatherland; they were merely dedicated foes of Adolf Hitler and his Nazi hierarchy, which, they felt, were taking Germany hell-bent down the road to total destruction.

Fortunately for the Allied agencies whose job it was to hoodwink the fuehrer on D-Day, the SD and the Abwehr were devoting more energy and time in trying to discredit one another than they were spending in seeking to unlock the secrets of the looming assault on Fortress Europe.

Since 1933, *Reichsfuehrer SS* Heinrich Himmler, Minister of the Interior and Schellenberg's boss, and his "Blacks," as they were called by Canaris and the Abwehr from the color of their uniforms, had built a police empire that stopped only at Adolf Hitler's door in the Reich Chancellery. But Himmler and Schellenberg were irritated by the one remaining enclave—the Abwehr.

Himmler, who was also commander of the elite SS, an army within an army, and the dreaded *Geheime Staatspolizei* (Gestapo), was the second most powerful man in the Third Reich. His head was filled with loony ideas, one of which was that he believed he was the reincarnation of King Heinrich I, who had ruled the Germanic people in the 11th century.

Himmler's brain seethed with unorthodox schemes. In one of these, he had a plan for his SS troops to live in communities in the Soviet Union based on the ancient Teutonic order of chivalry, once the Red Army had been smashed. Modern technology would be banned from these towns; airplanes, trains, and automobiles would be replaced by a special breed of animals, "steppes horses," which were being developed by a renowned German biologist, Professor Erik Schaeffer.

Himmler, a thin, laconic man whose facial contours and pince nez eyeglasses gave him an owlish appearance, held great faith in astrologers, magicians, fortune tellers, and spiritualists—although in 1941, he blamed them for the defection to Great Britain of the number-three Nazi, Rudolf Hess. It was a carefully guarded joke in Walther Schellenberg's inner SD circle that Himmler planned to convene a council of magicians in order to learn where and when the Anglo-Americans would land on D-Day.[2]

During the ongoing dueling with the Abwehr, Himmler ordered his Gestapo to keep watch on everything the Santa Clauses did or said. This included tapping Abwehr telephones, "tailing" Canaris himself, covertly interviewing the kennel owner who kept the admiral's beloved dachshunds on occasion, and cracking an Abwehr safe. In vain, the Blacks tried to infiltrate the Abwehr but were thwarted because they were up against sly professionals.

As far back as June 1942, Walther Schellenberg tried to get his friend Wilhelm Canaris arrested, charged with treason, and no doubt hanged—a surefire expedient for eliminating the main obstacle to the SD intelligence chief's towering ambitions. One morning, shortly after his customary horseback ride through the Tiergarten with Canaris, Schellenberg called on Heinrich Himmler and turned over a bulging file that he said held proof of the many "treacheries" committed by the Abwehr leader.

Himmler's reaction was certainly not the one Schellenberg expected. The SS chief merely thumbed through the thick set of papers, then said, "Leave the file here and I'll show it to the Fuehrer when an opportunity occurs."[3]

Schellenberg departed convinced that the fate of Wilhelm Canaris and the Abwehr had been sealed. Months passed, however, and nothing happened. When Schellenberg brought up the matter a few times, Himmler always responded vaguely. Then it struck the ambitious SD officer: the wily Canaris had a hold over Himmler himself, perhaps some odious episode in the reichsfuehrer's background or ancestry.[4]

In any event, the redoubtable little admiral continued to ward off Himmler, Schellenberg, and the other Blacks who were out to get his scalp and those of the other Santa Clauses. Canaris still thought that he could survive the defeat of Hitler's regime, that the Abwehr could remain impregnable.

Walther Schellenberg lived the high life. Even his ornate office in Berlin would have turned Chinese potentates of old green with envy. The floor was covered with thick Oriental rugs, and valuable ornaments and accessories decorated the premises. Next to his desk was a battery of telephones that kept him in constant touch with the fuehrer's Chancellery. A bevy of heel-clicking aides, bright-eyed, eager young SS officers, were on hand to gratify his every whim or wish.

Yet Schellenberg worked as though he were a warrior under siege. Highly sensitive microphones, which picked up and recorded the slightest murmur, were concealed in the walls, ceiling, and furniture. Sturdy iron grills covered the windows. An electric warning system on the doors and windows was linked to a general alarm circuit. The safe, desk, and filing cabinets were similarly protected.

If an intruder approached Schellenberg without his prior knowledge, an alarm automatically sounded, guards blocked all the exits, others rushed to the office with drawn Schmeisser machine pistols, and a company of black-uniformed SS troops surrounded the building. His seemingly innocent mahogany desk had two machine guns built into it. They were pointed at the visitors' chairs—without the visitors' knowledge. The guns could be fired by pressing a button on the side of the desk.

Schellenberg wore a ring with a large blue stone, and under the stone was a gold capsule of cyanide, to be taken in the event he was kidnapped or otherwise hopelessly trapped. When he traveled outside the Third Reich, he had a false tooth fitted that contained another dose of poison.

Cunning and decisive, the SD intelligence chief was a workaholic, putting in 17-hour days on the job. His favorite relaxation, along with early morning horseback rides in Berlin's historic Tiergarten, was his vast collection of pornographic photos, some of which had been posed especially to gratify his specific fantasies.

The old militant Nazis, those going back to the Munich *bierstube* (beer hall) bombings by thugs in Hitler's fledgling party in the 1920s, detested Schellenberg. Behind his back, they sneeringly called him *Märzveilchen* (March violet), because he had not joined the party until after it came to power in March 1933.

But even his critics conceded that Schellenberg had qualities that endeared him to Heinrich Himmler—total lack of scruples and an inborn capacity for intrigue. Schellenberg was sort of an intellectual gangster. For 11 years, he had been clawing and scratching to get to the top of the Nazi hierarchy.

Unlike his SD rival, Admiral Wilhelm Canaris had a simple lifestyle. Headquarters of the Abwehr's worldwide espionage apparatus was located at 74–76 Tirpitz Ufer, overlooking Berlin's famed Tiergarten and its spreading chestnut trees. "The old fox's den," his men called it. Canaris and a few hundred Abwehr people worked in two former townhouses, where creaking old elevators ran to the fifth floors. Canaris' personal office was far from pretentious. On the wall behind his chair was an inscribed photograph of Adolf Hitler. On his desk was a symbol that could have represented the secret service of any nation: three brass monkeys, one looking over its shoulder, one cupping his ear and listening, and the third with its hand over its mouth.

Despite having spent his adult life as an officer in the *Kriegsmarine* (navy), the five-foot-four, white-haired Canaris detested martial trappings. He bristled at the sight of military decorations, so his staff and anyone wanting a favor from him were careful to remove all medals and ribbons before entering his office. He wore his uniform only when the occasion so demanded.

Canaris was moody but, when so inclined, was described by an aide as "lively and talkative as an old lady."

When he took his two dachshunds with him on inspection trips, Canaris always reserved a room with two beds so the dogs did not have to sleep on the floor. When traveling without his pets, whether in Germany or abroad, he telephoned his office in Berlin each day to inquire about the state of health of his beloved dachshunds. From an aide at Tirpitz Ufer, he received a detailed rundown on the dogs' eating habits and bodily functions.

No doubt it was puzzling to Walther Schellenberg's SD agents, who were tapping Abwehr telephone lines, to hear this curious conversation. Perhaps they felt that the foxy Canaris was engaging in some sort of coded talk, the dogs' names actually meaning certain unidentified persons.

When his dogs were ill, the admiral plunged into deep depression. At Abwehr headquarters, an ambitious officer's chances for promotion would be squashed if Canaris only heard that he had talked disparagingly of dogs. Consequently, 74–76 Tirpitz Ufer was crammed with outspoken and prodigious canine lovers.

Canaris detested violence. And while duty occasionally took him to lively nightclubs along the Unter den Linden, his idea of a delightful evening was cooking a sumptuous meal for himself at his modest quarters.

Wilhelm Canaris' very name conjured visions of mystery and intrigue. During World War I, he had been one of the kaiser's most devious and productive spies. One of his subagents was a seductive Dutch dancer, Mata Hari, who was executed by a French firing squad when her espionage activities for Germany were detected.[5]

Canaris had been Germany's supreme spymaster since December 1933, when Adolf Hitler, who had just seized power, summoned him to the Reich Chancellery, appointed him chief of the moribund Abwehr, and ordered him to energize and greatly expand the intelligence service.

Canaris had been an unlikely figure to become the eyes and ears of a mighty war machine that the fuehrer even then was starting to build. In addition to his loathing of violence, he was not a member of the Nazi party (nor would he ever become one). In fact, he detested the unprincipled brutes with whom Hitler had surrounded himself, people like Hermann Goering, Heinrich Himmler, Reinhard Heydrich, and Julius Streicher.

Since Canaris held such fervent anti-Nazi views, it was only natural that, within a few years of his appointment to head the Abwehr, he would make secret contacts with British intelligence and become a key leader in the Schwarze Kapelle, the German conspiracy to oust (or kill) Adolf Hitler.

For several years now, Admiral Canaris had been engaged in a dangerous high-wire balancing act—with no safety net. Should he slip, it would mean torture and a hideous death at the hands of the Gestapo. Now, with an Allied invasion of Fortress Europe clearly looming, it was Canaris' job to provide the intelligence Hitler needed to smash the enemy landings. At the same time, the admiral was conniving to keep the fuehrer from achieving that objective, preferably before the invasion bloodshed began.

Through secret channels, British intelligence learned that Schellenberg, Himmler, and other Blacks were diligently striving to destroy Canaris by challenging his loyalty to Adolf Hitler. It was crucial to the British to keep the admiral alive and at his Abwehr post. So in one of the most curious operations of its kind, the Brits conceived a scheme to strengthen Canaris' standing with the one man who counted—the fuehrer.

Over BBC (British Broadcasting Company), in the London press (copies of which reached the Reich Chancellery daily), and various other means, a bitter campaign was launched to vilify Admiral Canaris. Among the nicer things the Brits had to say about the Abwehr chief was that he was a "brutal assassin," an "evil genius," and a "rat with a human face."

4

Machinations at Herrengasse 23

During the first week of January 1944, Walther Schellenberg was poring over an astonishing document that had just arrived at his immense office by courier from Ankara, the capital of Turkey. The ambitious SD intelligence chief felt a surge of exhilaration. In these photographed copies of authentic British papers he saw what he thought might be the key to unlocking Allied strategic intentions. He thought this amazing discovery might be the springboard to catapult him into control of all Reich intelligence services, including the Abwehr.

Marked "Most Secret" (the highest British security rating), these documents had been pilfered from a black metal dispatch box belonging to Sir Hughe Montgomery Knatchbull-Hugessen, His Britanic Majesty's Ambassador Extraordinary and Plenipotentiary to Turkey. Only Schellenberg, Heinrich Himmler, and a few others in the SD and Foreign Ministry knew that the theft had been perpetrated by Knatchbull-Hugessen's trusted valet, whose true name was Elysea Bazna.

One of the photographic copies of the original documents was headed the *Declaration of Teheran*, and it bore the signature of Franklin D. Roosevelt, Winston S. Churchill, and Joseph Stalin. "We shall work together in war and in peace," it stated, and it pledged to crush Nazi Germany as rapidly as possible.

Other papers from the Teheran conference hinted that the Allies were planning on invading Fortress Europe, not across the Channel from England, but rather through the Balkans and other points in the eastern Mediterranean. Anglo-American forces, already fighting in Italy since September 1943, would join in the offensive by driving northward through Vienna, Munich, and on to Berlin, the pilfered papers indicated. Schellenberg quickly passed copies of the Teheran documents to his boss, Heinrich Himmler, who shuttled them on to Adolf Hitler.

Bazna, Walther Schellenberg's ace spy (German code name Cicero) in Ankara, was a 39-year-old native of Yugoslavia, a swarthy egomaniacal adventurer and petty thief. He had been employed by Knatchbull-Hugessen as his *kavass* (the

Turkish name for a manservant in a diplomatic household) only since September 1943.

Knatchbull-Hugessen was a remnant of the stately life of British imperial power. A product of Eton and married to the daughter of a distinguished general, he had been ambassador to China before being posted to Ankara. Knatchbull-Hugessen's task was to destroy German influence in neutral Turkey and to bring that country into the war on the side of the Allies. He would also play a leading role in Operation Zeppelin, a component of Bodyguard. Zeppelin would suggest that the Allies planned to make their invasion of Fortress Europe in the Balkans, somewhere along the hundreds of miles of Adriatic shoreline in southeastern Europe.

Shortly after going to work for Ambassador Knatchbull-Hugessen, Bazna learned that the diplomat was in the habit of taking to his quarters a black dispatch box with secret telegrams and documents, which he read late at night in the privacy of his bedroom. Bazna waited for the right moment, which came in late October, and he made a wax imprint of the ambassador's dispatch box lock. From the impression, a key was crafted.

Then, with Knatchbull-Hugessen in a deep sleep at about 2:00 A.M. one morning, Bazna slipped into the ambassador's quarters, removed a handful of most-secret documents, scurried back to his own room, and photographed the papers with an old 35-millimeter Leica camera. Tiptoeing back up the creaking stairs, Bazna replaced the papers in the dispatch box and locked it.

Twenty-four hours later, under cover of darkness, Bazna contacted Ludwig C. Moyzisch, a quiet, diligent Austrian who was the SD station chief in Ankara. Bazna (who did not give his name) offered to sell most-secret documents direct from the files of the British ambassador.

Moyzisch was deeply suspicious and regarded the valet as an *agent provocateur*, sent by an unknown enemy of Germany to get the SD man involved in some devious Allied machination. Despite his misgivings, Moyzisch was reluctant to pass up the chance to obtain crucial enemy documents, so he asked the visitor his price for the film. Bazna, no piker, demanded the Turkish equivalent of 80,000 American dollars or 20,000 British pounds.

Moyzisch, a cautious veteran of countless undercover meetings, told Bazna to hand over the first roll of film at 10:00 P.M. on October 30 in the dark toolshed in the German embassy garden. If the SD station chief was satisfied that the documents were authentic, he would give the valet the hefty payoff he demanded.

Early the next morning, Moyzisch rushed to see Franz von Papen, who had been the kaiser's World War I spy in the United States and now held the crucial post of German ambassador to Turkey. It was the crafty von Papen's main task to coerce Turkey into the war on the side of the Third Reich. The SD station chief told the ambassador of the mystery man who had called on him the previous night.

Although uneasy about Bazna's *bona fides*, von Papen fired off a telegram to Foreign Minister Joachim von Ribbentrop in Berlin, explaining Bazna's proposition—secret documents in return for big money. A copy of the signal also went to Walther Schellenberg at SD headquarters.

Schellenberg suspected that Bazna might be an enemy agent, but an intuitive feeling, based on years of cloak-and-dagger machinations, convinced him that the man might be able to steal genuine documents from the British embassy. So the SD officer recommended to von Ribbentrop that the valet's offer be accepted. In a "Personal Most Secret" telegram, the foreign minister advised von Papen that he was dispatching the funds that Bazna was demanding.

At the designated time, 10:00 P.M., Ludwig Moyzisch and Bazna held a *treff* (German name for a secret rendezvous) at the Reich embassy's toolshed. Bazna handed over a roll of film, Moyzisch himself processed it in his darkroom, and a quick analysis indicated that the film indeed contained copies of authentic, highly secret British diplomatic "print." So Moyzisch entered an embassy room where Bazna was waiting and handed him his fee—more money than Cicero (as he was code-named by the Germans) ever expected to see in a lifetime.

Ludwig Moyzisch received strict orders from Schellenberg not to show the microfilms of the purloined British documents to Ambassador von Papen, but to send them directly to the SD in Berlin. This was a routine security measure to protect Cicero, one that any secret service would have taken. Cicero had fallen from heaven with his stacks of most-secret documents and was in a better position than any German spy to discover the secrets of Allied D-Day.

For whatever his reason, Moyzisch chose to disobey the order, and he showed the documents to Franz von Papen. Included in the papers was a record of talks between Ambassador Knatchbull-Hugessen and the Turkish government. These confabulations seemed to indicate that Turkey was on the brink of abandoning its neutrality and joining the Allies—the very action that von Papen was supposed to prevent.

Diminutive von Papen charged into the office of the Turkish foreign minister, ranted, raved, and threatened massive reprisals against Turkey by the Wehrmacht and the Luftwaffe. Hardly had von Papen stomped angrily out of the office than the Turkish foreign minister notified Knatchbull-Hugessen of the encounter. Within the hour, the British ambassador fired off a cable to London: "Von Papen obviously knows far more than he should."

Hearing of Franz von Papen's outburst, Walther Schellenberg was furious. The impetuous German ambassador could have alerted the Allies and sacrificed the SD's best chance to learn their strategic intentions.

Meanwhile at the Foreign Ministry in Berlin, a copy of Ambassador von Papen's telegram about Hughe Knatchbull-Hugessen's valet reached the desk of Fritz Kolbe, an obscure, mild-mannered career bureaucrat. A short, wiry man of about 40 with a few remaining strands of blond hair, Kolbe had been in government service since the mid–1920s, and his reputation was that of a dedicated civil servant who plugged along without complaint on dreary administrative details.

In 1940, Kolbe, a devout Catholic, was appointed assistant to Karl Ritter,

Foreign Minister Joachim von Ribbentrop's liaison to the Reich military high command, a position of great trust. It was Kolbe's job to sift through the hundreds of cables that poured into the Foreign Ministry each day from German diplomatic and military posts around the world, then place the important ones on the desk of his boss, Karl Ritter.

Early in 1943, Fritz Kolbe, long anti-Nazi but now convinced that the fuehrer was taking the Fatherland down a road to destruction, felt that the only way to bring about the defeat of Nazism would be by an Allied victory. On a pretext, Kolbe traveled to neutral Switzerland, met secretly with an official of England's MI–6 (foreign intelligence) and offered to supply the Brits with stacks of secret papers from von Ribbentrop's ministry. In order to show his good faith and that he had direct access to top secrets, Kolbe told the MI–6 man that a German agent was "working close to Winston Churchill" and was funneling information to Berlin by way of neutral Stockholm, Sweden.[1]

The British were suspicious of Fritz Kolbe and regarded him as an agent provocateur who had been sent by the shifty Joachim von Ribbentrop to penetrate the extensive British espionage network in Switzerland. Kolbe was rapidly given the heave.

Dejected, but undaunted, Kolbe returned to Berlin, pondered his situation, and decided that the Americans were his last hope. So in mid-August 1943, Kolbe sent a Swiss friend, a German-born doctor, to visit the U.S. legation in Berne. There he made contact with Gerald Mayer, an Office of Strategic Services (OSS) operative, who was told by the doctor that he represented an "important official" in Berlin who was eager to pass secret information to the Allies. Mayer, like the Brits had been, was highly skeptical, but he made arrangements for the Berlin mystery man to meet directly with the OSS station chief in Berlin.

Again Fritz Kolbe wrangled a temporary assignment in Berne, this time as a diplomatic courier. On August 23, 1943, under cover of night, the German bureaucrat stole up to a building at Herrengasse 23 in the picturesque, medieval section of Berne. Squinting in the dim glow of a street light, Kolbe discerned the lettering on a small sign next to the door:

ALLEN W. DULLES
SPECIAL ASSISTANT TO THE
AMERICAN MINISTER

The sign was merely part of the games that those involved in international intrigue play. Allen Welsh Dulles, as nearly all of the hundreds of German and Allied spies roaming about Switzerland knew, was actually the OSS station chief in Berne, a hotbed of espionage.[2]

Dulles was fond of tweed jackets and bow ties, wore rimless spectacles, and was seldom caught without his briar pipe—a stereotype of Hollywood's version of a kindly college professor. Despite his deceptively mild appearance, Dulles was tough-minded and cagy. During World War I, he had been stationed in Berne, ostensibly as an employee of the U.S. State Department. Then he was doing the same job he was doing a war later—collecting intelligence from inside neighboring Germany.

Dulles was unwittingly on the brink of his biggest espionage bonanza of the war as bespectacled Fritz Kolbe was escorted into the spacious clubroom by Gerald Mayer. Several years earlier, Mayer had fled his native Germany to avoid Jewish prosecution, settled in Berne, and was recruited by Dulles.

While Dulles and Mayer looked on in awe, Kolbe opened his briefcase and pulled out nearly 200 German top-secret cables, spreading them out on the floor until they nearly covered the entire room. Dulles, who had had a lifetime of shocks and surprises in the volatile and unpredictable world of global intrigue, could not mask his astonishment. "Where did you get *those*?" the OSS man asked. "I smuggled them out of the Foreign Ministry a few at a time, strapped to my legs," Kolbe replied softly.[3]

Dulles and Mayer spent the night examining the documents. They appeared to be genuine. But as a hedge against the German being a foxy double-agent, Dulles asked Major General William J. "Wild Bill" Donovan, the OSS director back in Washington, for an investigation of Fritz Kolbe's background. Back came word: "He is authentic."

Fritz Kolbe agreed to become an OSS agent, a direct pipeline into the heart of the Third Reich, and was given the code name George Wood by Dulles. Kolbe returned to his job in the Foreign Ministry and eventually would deliver to Dulles in excess of 1,600 top-secret cables and documents.[4]

Fritz Kolbe's documents provided Allied intelligence with an enormous amount of secret information on Nazi military and espionage affairs. However, in London, Colonel Claude M. Dansey, the irascible, sharp-tongued assistant chief of MI–6, promptly denounced the authenticity of Kolbe's papers. Described by friends as "crusty" and by his British enemies as "that cantankerous old son of a bitch," Dansey was known to be critical of anything American.

Colonel Dansey had what was described as a "fierce proprietary obsession" about any intelligence operations carried on in Switzerland. Back in 1934, as a member of the British Secret Intelligence Service and acting largely on his own, he created a remarkable network of spies in Germany, Switzerland, Belgium, the Netherlands, and Austria. Dansey attached a succinct name to his network— Z.

As the years passed, Dansey's secret organization grew particularly strong in Switzerland, so with the arrival of Fritz Kolbe, Dansey railed that it was impossible for Allen Dulles to pull off such a spectacular intelligence coup "right under my nose," as the MI–6 official put it. Obviously, the Kolbe materials were a plant, and Kolbe was a slick German agent. Worse, Dulles had fallen for it "like a ton of bricks."[5]

When the documents were compared with British intercepts of German wireless messages and appeared to be genuine, Claude Dansey refused to budge an inch. "I won't let OSS run riot all over Switzerland and foul up the whole intelligence field," Dansey snorted. God only knew what amateurs like Allen Dulles might do. If Dulles was not careful, he would blow the whole Z network in Switzerland in a few days.[6]

Nine months before his dramatic meeting with Fritz Kolbe, Allen Dulles secretly had slipped into Berne in November 1942, on the same day that Allied forces under General Dwight Eisenhower invaded North Africa. In order to keep his presence unknown, Dulles did everything but don a false beard. Two days later, Swiss newspapers carried front-page stories about the arrival of Dulles, whom they identified as "a personal representative of President Roosevelt."

Dulles soon learned that he was a one-man gang. There was no OSS staff and none could be brought in through the enemy-held regions that surrounded Switzerland. So he began to build up his espionage network from scratch. American businessmen stranded in Switzerland when the Germans suddenly closed the French border were recruited, and a local banker secretly purchased foreign currency for Dulles' clandestine operations.

Eventually, the OSS station chief approached nearly every American living in Switzerland, and most agreed to join up. For a few it was a pocketbook motivation: their families had major business interests in German-occupied Europe.

An early recruit was 40-year-old Gero von Schulze Gaevernitz, a German-born naturalized American citizen, who had first come to the United States in 1924 to launch a career in international banking. Later, he returned to the Fatherland and established a high niche in elite circles of banking and industry.

Adolf Hitler came to power, and Gaevernitz' father, who had been a prominent German legislator, fled to Switzerland with his Jewish wife. When war broke out, their son Gero joined them in Berne.

Another early Dulles recruit was Hans Bernd Gisevius, a bear of a man, six feet four inches and 260 pounds, who was an Abwehr agent with a stiff Prussian bearing assigned to the Nazi consulate in Zurich. Gisevius, an attorney, had joined the Gestapo in 1933, only to be ousted six months later because of his lack of enthusiasm for the Nazi cause. Then he became a member of the Berlin police, but he was fired for criticizing the SS. In 1939 he joined the Schwarze Kapelle and was accepted as an Abwehr agent. Wilhelm Canaris sent him to Zurich where he would be the eyes and ears of the German anti-Hitler conspiracy.

Gisevius first tried to establish clandestine contact with the British secret service in Berne, but had been rejected in the belief that he was actually an agent provocateur. However, Allen Dulles decided to take a chance on him.

In a scenario reminiscent of a Hollywood spy thriller, Dulles and Gisevius rendezvoused on a black night on the steps of the World Council of Churches building in Berne. The German told about the anti-Nazi group in the Third Reich and how it hoped to throw the fuehrer out of power and sign a separate peace treaty with the Western Allies to keep the Russians out of Germany.

Dulles was impressed by Gisevius' sincerity and his reasons for seeking the destruction of the fuehrer and his Nazi regime. A few more covert meetings were held between the two men, and plans were worked out for Gisevius to furnish couriers for bringing information out of Berlin to Berne. Among those who would perform this crucial but perilous task were Theodor Struenck, a director of a large insurance firm in Frankfurt, and Eduard Waetjen, a Berlin lawyer.

Meanwhile, the OSS station chief opened up a second line of communications inside the Nazi government in Berlin. In a secret rendezvous, Dulles and Adam von Trott zu Solz, an official of the German Foreign Ministry and former Rhodes scholar, discussed at length the "Opposition" (as Dulles called it) to Hitler in the Reich. Von Trott said he represented a young intellectual faction called the Kreisau Circle, most of whose members worked for the Nazi government. Von Trott knew precisely what he wanted and told Dulles that if the OSS did not aid the Kreisau Circle and the Schwarze Kapelle, the German conspirators would "turn to the East"—making a deal with Joseph Stalin for a postwar government in Germany.

Fritz Kolbe, as important as he was to the American secret intelligence service, was a small fish compared to the huge shark that Allen Dulles had been trying to haul in—Heinrich Himmler, Nazi Germany's second most powerful man. Dulles knew that agents representing Himmler, the SS and Gestapo head, had approached the OSS station chief in Stockholm with a startling proposal.

Himmler, through his emissaries, suggested that the United States and Great Britain "sanction" a coup that would oust the fuehrer (presumably by killing him) and then sign a separate peace treaty with Germany and its new head of state—Heinrich Himmler. When the reichsfuehrer's "peace feeler" to Stockholm seemed to be stalled, he directed his protégé, the ambitious Walther Schellenberg, to pursue the matter with other sources.

So Schellenberg dispatched Prince Max Egon von Hohenlohe-Langenburg-Rothenhaus to meet secretly with Allen Dulles, who the SD intelligence chief regarded as the "most influential White House man in Europe." Von Hohenlohe, who sprang from a prominent German aristocratic family, lived in Spain with his wife, a Spanish marquise. He had known Allen Dulles in New York and Berlin in the 1920s, and during the current war, he had chiefly been engaged in flitting about Europe as "a society favorite" in most of the capitals. So he was a natural to act as an emissary to Dulles.

Von Hohenlohe met with the OSS station chief at a tiny inn perched on the side of a mountain some ten miles outside Berne. Seated at a dining hall table next to a huge window, Dulles could see any stranger who might be approaching the inn. The reunion between the two old friends, on February 16, 1943, was a joyous one.

Allen Dulles, aware that there was not one iota of a chance that the governments of the United States and Great Britain would accept a Germany with Heinrich Himmler as its leader, feigned interest in the proposal. If the Gestapo and SS head was encouraged, in his ruthless grasp for power, to believe that the United

States was sympathetic to his goal, then Himmler might be energized into launching a coup that would "dispose" of the fuehrer. This action might shatter the Wehrmacht's morale and cause it to revolt.

A month later, startling evidence reached the OSS in Berne that Dulles' ploy may have produced results in the Third Reich. An unknown party had placed a time bomb in Adolf Hitler's personal airplane, but it failed to explode. A second attempt on the fuehrer's life four weeks later also ended in failure. Presumably, Heinrich Himmler, who may have been the figure behind the deeds, spearheaded the Gestapo investigation into these two assassination efforts.

It appeared that Allen Dulles' scheme to provoke Himmler into taking "direct action" was an OSS orchestration conducted by General Bill Donovan in Washington. In the fall of 1943, Felix Kersten, Himmler's Finnish physician and trusted confidant, met secretly in a dimly lit cafe in Stockholm with Abram Stevens Hewitt who, like Dulles when the situation so demanded, billed himself as President Roosevelt's "personal representative in Europe." In reality, Hewitt, a wealthy New York blueblood, an Oxford and Harvard product and grandson of a New York City mayor, was an OSS agent.

As had been the case with Dulles in Berne, Hewitt feigned interest in pursuing Himmler's proposal that he, Himmler, succeed the "deposed" fuehrer. As a result of this covert rendezvous, Kersten contacted Himmler on October 24 and suggested that Walther Schellenberg be rushed incognito to Stockholm to meet with "Roosevelt's personal representative," Abram Hewitt.

Wearing civilian clothes (and reportedly a false beard), Schellenberg flew to Sweden on November 9 and met secretly with Hewitt, who assured the German that negotiations for a "compromise peace" could be launched as soon as Himmler "took action." Schellenberg, who presumably could envision himself as Germany's number two leader as soon as Himmler elevated himself to head of government, rushed back to Berlin and eagerly reported to his boss, the reichsfuehrer.[7]

Much to the dismay of Schellenberg, who thirsted for power even more than did Himmler, the reichsfuehrer flip-flopped and declared that he would not "betray my fuehrer." In American jargon, the Gestapo chief had apparently been afflicted with a severe case of "cold feet."[8] Schellenberg, one of only a handful of Nazi bigwigs who dared to argue with Himmler, pursued the matter, and his boss finally agreed to meet face to face with Hewitt, but only if the American was willing to fly to Berlin.

In Washington, Bill Donovan concluded that the *ruse de guerre* had reached a dangerous stage. Should Hewitt manage to slip into and out of Berlin (a highly doubtful feat), there was deep concern in OSS headquarters that the Soviets might learn of the United States secret contacts with Himmler and conclude that a deal was in the works that did not include the Russians.

Donovan felt that a smart blacksmith knew precisely when to take his iron out of the fire. So Felix Kersten was tersely informed that Abram Hewitt had been called back to Washington for "consultation." The Himmler project, and possibly the last chance to overthrow Adolf Hitler and his regime without a massive invasion of Continental Europe, had been canceled.

Meanwhile in Switzerland, a tiny, mountainous enclave surrounded entirely by German troops in Germany, France, Italy, and Austria, Allen Dulles had an unexpected visitor—Fritz Kolbe (OSS code name George Wood). On November 14, 1943, Kolbe, some three months after their initial meeting, brought Dulles copies of three telegrams. Two of them were dated November 3, 1943, and the other was dated November 4. Stamped top-secret, these were Ambassador Franz von Papen's messages to Foreign Minister Joachim von Ribbentrop concerning Elysea Bazna, the valet of the British ambassador to Turkey.

These telegrams were blockbusters, for they disclosed the shocking fact that the Germans had a spy in a sensitive position where he could conceivably learn the secrets of Allied intentions for the pending invasion of Fortress Europe. Since this security breach was a British matter, Dulles promptly contacted Vanden Huyvel, his British colleague in Berne, and set up an urgent meeting.

At a small *gasthaus* outside the city, Dulles told Huyvel what he had learned about the leak in the embassy in Ankara. Deeply alarmed, Huyvel quickly alerted London. Three days later, the two men met again. Huyvel was quite excited and pleaded with Dulles to forget about the von Papen telegrams and to not get involved in the Cicero (Bazna) affair. London was "aware" of the situation, Huyvel explained.[9]

Indeed London was aware. British agents had been supplying the ambassador's valet with selected documents to photograph and feed to the SD in Berlin. In order to establish Bazna's credentials with the Germans, a few of the papers were genuine and provided forewarning of an occasional actual secondary Allied military operation. These accurate documents, intended to build Cicero's credibility with his German controllers, masked a flow of fictitious documents that falsely hinted of Allied plans for invading the Balkans in the spring of 1944, part of the Bodyguard scheme to keep German divisions far from northern France on D-Day.

A few weeks later, Walther Schellenberg grew suspicious of Cicero, who had continued to send copies of top-secret British documents to Berlin. Cicero, the SD intelligence chief learned, had lied about his ability to speak English. With this language handicap, along with the fact that Cicero had a minimal formal education and no knowledge of British diplomatic procedures, how had the valet been able to select certain documents from the hundreds that reached the British embassy?[10]

Through Fritz Kolbe in the Foreign Ministry, Allen Dulles in Berne learned of Schellenberg's misgivings, and the OSS man passed the word to his British colleagues. MI–6 took steps to boost Cicero's credibility, and the valet sent Berlin a genuine top-secret document that revealed the Allies were planning to bomb Sofia, Bulgaria (a German ally), on January 14, 1944.

Deception was often a brutal game, one demanding that certain information concerning Allied operations be played into German hands in order to deceive the fuehrer about other, far more crucial operations—most significantly Overlord, the cross-Channel invasion of northern France.

On January 14, in order to check on the accuracy of Cicero's report, Ludwig Moyzisch, the SD station chief in Ankara, telephoned the German embassy in Sofia. A Turkish operator said that the line had been cut. Moyzisch tried again the next morning and was told by an embassy official in Sofia: "We've had a terrific air raid. The whole town's in flames! There are heavy casualties!"[11] Walther Schellenberg had his proof. Bulgarian corpses bore mute testimony to Cicero's skills and credibility.

By January 1944, pipe-puffing, low-key Allen Dulles had built a far-reaching espionage network that stretched throughout Europe and pierced the heart of the Nazi government and military hierarchy in Berlin. Dulles had arranged with OSS chief Bill Donovan for a special distribution system for the highly sensitive intelligence he was obtaining from the Opposition to Hitler in Germany. These cables to Washington were code-named "Breakers" to ensure that they would be read only by those in the highest places with a "need to know."[12]

Breakers went to a selected few: President Roosevelt's personal map room in the White House, Secretary of State Cordell Hull, Executive Assistant to the Assistant Secretary of State Fletcher Warrent, and a handful of others. Between September 1943 and May 1944, Dulles dispatched 146 Breakers to Washington. One of them was a 200,000-word history of the Schwarze Kapelle conspiracy, compiled by the hulking Prussian Hans Gisevius at enormous risk to his life.

As it developed, the Breakers apparently had not even been distributed, Allen Dulles would learn to his dismay. He suspected that a Soviet agent burrowed into the federal government, or a Communist sympathizer in Washington, had blocked circulation of the Breakers to prevent an agreement between the Schwarze Kapelle and the Anglo-Americans that would halt the war short of the total destruction of Germany.[13]

5

Istanbul Intrigue

Istanbul, neutral Turkey's largest city and long a center for splendor and corruption, was World War II's foremost listening post in the eastern Mediterranean. Because of its strategic location which linked Europe and Asia, Turkey was coveted as an ally by both the Allies and the Third Reich.

With the arrival of 1944 and the Allies preparing to invade Fortress Europe, Istanbul had acquired a Byzantine underworld in which foreigners outspied the natives, although the Turks were no pikers in the espionage trade. Nearly every secret service in the world held forth in this ancient city on the Bosporus. Swarms of spies roamed daily through plush hotel lobbies, elegant restaurants, and trendy nightclubs.

Between enemies and neutrals alike, there were no barriers in Istanbul. At cocktail time in the evening or at swinging parties that lasted until the early morning hours, American, German, British, Soviet, French, Yugoslavian, Polish, Japanese, and Greek agents sat at adjacent tables or bumped into one another on crowded dance floors. In Istanbul, there was nothing secret in the secret services: every spy knew the identities of the other spies.

Comely, shapely young women were in great demand in the Turkish city: there was a limited number of them to go around. So swains of rival clandestine agencies scrambled not only for the same secrets but for the same dark-eyed beauties.

A glamorous femme fatale might be snuggled up to a British agent at a soirée and the next night be clinging to the arm of a Nazi spy. Not only would she be a desired source of diversion, but the secrets she might gain from one spy (usually while in bed) could be valuable to a future bed partner.

Seldom, if ever, had secret services operated so openly as they did in Istanbul. Hardly a day passed without some incident involving these supposedly covert matters. As usual, the Russians had the largest contingent—and were the most conspicuous. Firm believers in "direct action" (meaning murder and sabotage), the Soviets were forever blowing up things and people.

Strongly represented in Istanbul were the Germans—Walther Schellenberg's Sicherheitsdienst; Wilhelm Canaris' Abwehr; the *Reichssicherheitshauptamt* (RSHA), Adolf Hitler's internal security agency; and the *Auslandsorganization*, whose function was cloudy. Great Britain's secret service also was well represented. German agents knew who the British agents were (and vice versa), but not always what clandestine schemes in which they were engaged. The Brits would vanish for a few days, perhaps going to another country to organize an underground network. Then they would return to Istanbul for a few days of relaxation, often in the company of Hungarian girls in the chorus line in the Taxim Kasino.

Enrico Vasco, the congenial Portuguese bartender at the popular Taxim Kasino, kept his ears alert to pick up tidbits of information which he would peddle to the German, British, Russian, or American embassies for whatever price the market would bear. High-priced call girls used the casino as a base of operations. They were experts at rifling the pockets of sleeping clients and selling any pertinent papers to whichever spy would pay the most money.

Personal loyalties and national allegiances crisscrossed. The bureau chief of a Berlin newspaper cozied up to the British. An American broadcaster aided the Soviets. Turkish officials were supposed to keep tabs on the doings of foreign spies and choke off their antics. But the chief of the Turkish secret service reportedly was cooperating with the Germans (for a hefty monthly payoff), while his deputy allegedly kept the British informed (also for a large retainer). Two of their aides worked for both the British and the Germans while picking up extra money moonlighting for the Russians.

Keeping the highest profile among the American operatives in Istanbul was George Howard Earle III, who had cut a dashing figure since arriving in the city in mid–1943. A wealthy Philadelphian and former governor of Pennsylvania, Earle held the rank of lieutenant commander and was an assistant naval attaché.

Burly, ruggedly handsome, and in his mid-forties, George Earle's real assignment was to penetrate the German espionage network and to enhance Operation Zeppelin, the Bodyguard stratagem to influence Adolf Hitler into believing that the Allies planned to launch a major invasion of the Balkans in spring 1944, thereby pinning down Wehrmacht divisions hundreds of miles from the true landing sites in Normandy.

Earle had long been near the top of the Nazi's most-dangerous list. In Berlin, Schellenberg's SD had a thick file labeled "George Howard Earle the Third." Among the most damaging charges against him (in the eyes of the SD) was that he was a close friend and political crony of President Roosevelt.

While serving as a diplomat in Austria in 1934, George Earle's reports from Vienna to Washington were far more blunt than was customary from a State Department representative abroad. He warned that the new German leader, Adolf

Hitler, was planning to rearm the Third Reich and that his intentions were to conquer Europe.

Striped-pants bureaucrats in the State Department were horrified and refused to explore the validity of this outrageous accusation. Earle was frowned upon as a man with an inflated ego hankering for notoriety, a congenital troublemaker, and a disgrace to diplomatic drawing rooms.

A few years later, however, George Earle was assigned as an envoy to the court of King Boris in Sofia, Bulgaria, where his strident anti-Hitler views created one incident after another, details of which were scrupulously recorded in his Berlin file. Once he found a German spy poking around in his quarters and handled the situation in a most undiplomatic manner—by beating the intruder until he confessed his mission was to obtain derogatory information on the outspoken anti-Nazi, Earle.

On another occasion while Earle was posted to Sofia, a Nazi-orchestrated demonstration against the United States erupted in front of the American embassy. Infuriated, Earle whipped out a pistol from a drawer, rushed to a second-floor window, and was prevented from firing at the demonstrators only after a struggle with his aide.

Two months later, Earle provoked a brawl with German agents in a Sofia nightclub. A few Nazis in the place asked the orchestra to play the *Horst Wessel Lied*, a sort of Hitler regime national anthem. Seated at his table, Earle seethed. When the rendition concluded, Earle rushed to the bandstand and demanded that the musicians play *Tipperary*, a nostalgic British ballad dating back to World War I. With the strains of *Tipperary* echoing through the crowded nightclub, an empty whiskey bottle was flung from the direction of a table occupied by the Nazi agents and crashed on the floor near George Earle and his three male companions, two Americans and one British. A Pier Six brawl erupted. Fists flew. Furniture was used in supporting roles. The nightclub was largely wrecked. Earle proclaimed his side victorious.

Back in Washington, some members of Congress were upset by the barroom brawl. One legislator took to the House floor to denounce George Earle's "unseemly behavior" and demanded that he be promptly recalled and sacked.

If a few in Congress were mad, State Department bureaucrats were livid. A short time later, in December 1941, after Uncle Sam was bombed into global conflict and after Bulgaria joined with Hitler in the war, Earle returned to the United States and was blackballed by the State Department. So Franklin Roosevelt, who was politically indebted to the former Pennsylvania governor and was fond of him personally, searched for a likely locale from which Earle could productively resume his vendetta against Adolf Hitler and the Nazis.

Turkey struck the president as the ideal post for the rambunctious George Earle, since most of the secret intelligence reports reaching the White House seemed to come from that hotbed of international intrigue. Although Earle would have been hard put to tell the difference between an aircraft carrier and a battleship, Roosevelt commissioned him a lieutenant commander in the Navy and dispatched him to Turkey as his personal agent.

As soon as Earle reached Istanbul in mid–1943, he sent a telegram to "Adrienne," an old flame, in Budapest, Hungary, advising her that he was staying in the Park Hotel and inviting her to join him there. Adrienne was a beautiful Hungarian woman who had danced in the chorus at a fashionable Sofia nightclub. Earle had struck up an acquaintance with her when he had been posted in Bulgaria, and the pair developed a close friendship.[1]

Adrienne was thrilled by the invitation from the charismatic American, but was awed by the international undertones of the situation. Hungary was at war with the United States on the side of Nazi Germany; Turkey was a neutral nation. So she sought the counsel of a trusted friend, Asta Matzhold, the wife of an Austrian journalist assigned to Budapest.

Frau Matzhold agreed that the complexities were vast and said she would get the advice of her husband Louis, who represented the *Berliner Boersen-Zeitung*, a large daily in the Third Reich and one controlled by Hitler's propaganda minister, Joseph Goebbels (as were all German media). Louis Matzhold was also an agent of the SD (code-named Michael).

Correspondent Matzhold quickly fired off a coded communication to Berlin, telling of the despised George Earle's invitation to Adrienne and declaring that this might be a chance for an intelligence bonanza. A few days later, Rudolf Likus, an SS officer, flew from Berlin to Budapest, held a treff with "Michael," and hatched a scheme whereby Adrienne would be the pawn and Earle the dupe in order to establish a pipeline directly into President Roosevelt's Oval Office and conceivably uncover Allied plans for the invasion of Fortress Europe.

Matzhold would go to Turkey as the first part of the machination, get in touch with George Earle (whom he had known back in Washington when the Austrian was a correspondent there), project himself as Adrienne's sympathetic guru, and pump the Navy officer for information about Allied strategic intentions.

A day later, Matzhold was in Istanbul, contacted Earle at the Park Hotel, confided that he was a secret anti-Nazi involved in the German internal movement to oust the fuehrer. As the evening wore along and the grape flowed, Earle told Matzhold that he had learned from his good friend Franklin Roosevelt that the Allies planned to land at several places in the Balkans and in Spain. Matzhold felt a surge of exhilaration over this juicy intelligence coup, so he flew to Berlin to give a firsthand report to the SD on what the former governor had disclosed.

Could George Earle, a shrewd man and an experienced politician, have been so stupid as to reveal to a casual acquaintance intelligence of such enormous significance? Hardly. Earle had been well aware that Matzhold was a Nazi spy and privately regarded him only one notch above an ignoramus. Earle arranged to be with Matzhold on a number of social occasions in the weeks ahead and seized on these chances to continue to subtly plant the fiction that the Allies would invade the Balkans and other locales in southern Europe.

The scheme hatched by the SS officer, Rudolf Likus, and Matzhold to use the sultry Adrienne as a pawn from whom to extract information presumably given to her by George Earle moved ahead when Likus, who was well connected in Berlin, arranged with Hungarian authorities to permit her to travel to Istanbul for a reunion with her American friend. Unwittingly, Earle threw a monkey-wrench into the works when he realized he had tired of Adrienne, even before she arrived, and began courting a Belgian beauty.

Meanwhile, after Adrienne settled in Istanbul, nearly every secret service in the city focused on her in order to tap the pipeline leading from her through Earle and directly into the White House. Each clandestine agency assigned its most dashing lady-killer to woo Adrienne. Using money provided by their agencies, eager suitors showered her with gifts, including a six-karat diamond ring.

Only Wilhelm Hamburger, a handsome, personable young Viennese doctor who had been delegated by the Abwehr to do the courting and snooping, had not been furnished with funds with which to purchase expensive baubles for Adrienne. All Hamburger could give her was love. But he seemed to be an expert in that field, and Adrienne soon became infatuated with her debonair suitor.

A few weeks later, Hamburger learned a shocking secret: Adrienne was performing her cooing with assorted secret agents at the behest of George Earle in order to extract intelligence to be passed on to Washington. By now, Hamburger had been struck with a quiver of Cupid's arrows and was deeply in love with the vivacious Adrienne. George Earle aided him to defect from the Abwehr so that the German could remain with the woman he adored.[2] Through Hamburger, Earle was able to get a detailed rundown on the extensive Abwehr espionage apparatus in Turkey (some 350 agents) and, therefore, knew which operatives to target for dispensing fictitious information on Allied strategic plans.

In Berlin, hundreds of miles from the high jinks in Istanbul, *Generaloberst* Alfred Jodl was expected by Hitler to draft German countermeasures to rapidly crush any attempted Allied invasion of Fortress Europe. The customary contingency plans, which all military staffs draw up in advance to meet any eventuality, would not suffice. Jodl was burdened by a severe handicap: how could he create a plan to smash the landing when the hard strategic intelligence was lacking?[3]

Since the beginning of the war more than four years earlier, General Jodl had been *Chef des Wehrmachtfuhrungsstab* (chief of the high command's operations staff). He was the officer designated by Adolf Hitler to translate the fuehrer's strategic decisions into precise orders for distribution to combat commanders in the field.

On January 6, 1944, Jodl summoned Wilhelm Canaris, leader of the Abwehr, and Colonel Alexis von Roenne, to the rambling complex of bunkers at Zossen, south of Berlin, to which the Wehrmacht's general staff had moved to escape the relentless pounding of the German capital by British and American bombers.

If any one intelligence officer could be singled out as the key figure in the preinvasion drama, it was Baron von Roenne.

As the army's senior intelligence chief of *Fremde Heere West* (FHW; Foreign Armies West), it was his mission to provide the fuehrer with the definitive hard intelligence he needed to make troop deployments. In essence, the spies of all the German secret services, the intelligence analysts, the code-breakers, the couriers, and the hangers-on, worked indirectly for von Roenne. Buck-passing screeched to a halt at his desk. His incredibly complicated and frustrating task was to produce a *Feindbild*, or picture of the enemy, including the Anglo-American order of battle for the pending invasion.

Colonel von Roenne came from the aristocracy, and his family was one of the oldest in the Reich. Their baronetcy had been bestowed upon them by Frederick the Great for the heroic roles they had played in the great battles of the 18th century. They were patricians of old Prussia, and Alexis von Roenne's character had been shaped by a strict code of etiquette. Even more severe was his old Prussian code of discipline and loyalty. If an officer violated that code, he would be expected to shoot himself in the head rather than live in disgrace.

Baron von Roenne, a tall, slender officer known for his ability to make decisions with lightning speed, had been an Adolf Hitler favorite since mid–1939, when the fuehrer was preparing to invade woefully weak Poland. Hitler had been bedeviled by an agonizing question: would France, with a huge army reputed to be the world's best, and Great Britain, with its enormous seapower and first-rate general staff, leap into the conflict?

Hitler knew that he could not, at the same time, attack Poland and maintain a formidable defense in the West to ward off French and British armies. So he asked for a special study, and the task was given to Baron von Roenne, regarded as one of the Wehrmacht's brightest young officers. In his report, von Roenne said that the two Western powers would only assemble their armed forces, conduct saber-rattling, and do nothing.

That report confirmed the fuehrer's viewpoint, and the world was introduced to a frightening new warfare technique, the blitzkrieg, as German panzer-tipped columns crushed the Polish army in only six weeks. In the West, as von Roenne had predicted, the French and British assumed the role of spectators to the Polish catastrophe. Euphoric, Hitler summoned then Major von Roenne to the Reich Chancellery and decorated him with the *Deutsches Kreuz*.

Now, in early January 1944, Colonel General Alfred Jodl, in Zossen, was reading the riot act to Baron von Roenne and Admiral Wilhelm Canaris. The fuehrer was demanding solid strategic intelligence about Allied intentions, Jodl declared. Then Jodl gave indications that his strategic views had been influenced by Plan Zeppelin, the Bodyguard component intended to infer that the Allied invasion would take place in the Balkans and elsewhere in the eastern Mediterranean. "I want you to give the Balkans far greater attention than has hitherto been the case," Jodl said. "What happens there is not only indicative of the enemy's intentions, but is likely to supply valuable indices for the sum total of the Anglo-Americans' strategic intentions elsewhere."[4]

Jodl said that the Allies apparently had ceased to withdraw landing craft from the Mediterranean region, and a number of major infantry and tank units in Italy had "vanished without a trace." Both conclusions were accurate. "As I see it," Jodl concluded, "these moves indicate that the main effort of the Allies will be in the general area of the eastern Mediterranean and the Balkans."[5]

Baron von Roenne was dismayed when he left Jodl's office, convinced that the Anglo-Americans would not waste their manpower, resources, and time conducting landings and raids on the fringes of the Nazi empire in the Balkans and eastern Mediterranean, but rather would strike hard directly across the English Channel.

On December 16, 1943, only three weeks before von Roenne and Wilhelm Canaris had been taken to the woodshed for a sound thrashing by General Jodl, the FHW intelligence chief had discovered a crucial Allied secret—the code name Overlord, which bore all the earmarks of a major Anglo-American assault across the Channel. The highly capable German Y-Service, whose job it was to intercept British and American radio traffic, had picked up a report by a careless U.S. colonel in London, who mentioned a pending operation called Overlord.

A few days later, documents pilfered by the SD spy Cicero, from the British ambassador's dispatch box in Ankara reached von Roenne's desk. These papers contained strategic decisions reached by the Allied Big Three in Teheran and also used the code word Overlord.

So even though General Jodl seemed to believe that the major Allied thrust would be in the Balkans, von Roenne was convinced that the northwest coast of Europe would be the target. Wireless intercepts continued to reveal that a huge Anglo-American force was assembling in southern England, but two questions gnawed at von Roenne's innards: exactly where on the long coast of France, Belgium, and the Netherlands did the Allies plan to land, and on precisely what date would the mammoth operation be launched?

With Adolf Hitler breathing heavily down his neck, Baron von Roenne intensified his efforts to unlock the secrets of D-Day. In his Mercedes Benz, the FHW officer raced up and down the Channel coast, conducting a personal reconnaissance of vulnerable areas, consulting with local commanders and intelligence officers in the field.

No detail or chance remark by Wehrmacht officers defending the Channel coast escaped the cerebral von Roenne, who had a perception of military matters seldom found in staff officers in any army. For the baron himself had been a combat leader in brutal battles on the Russian front, had been critically wounded, and was hospitalized for months in early 1943.

By mid-January 1944, von Roenne concluded that the cross-Channel attack would hit at the Pas de Calais, the largely rural region of Picardy and Artois across from England's famed White Cliffs of Dover. He told Major Ludwig Soltmann, his chief of the British desk, "Why should the Anglo-Americans risk the long crossing from Portsmouth, for example, when they can dash across to [the Pas de] Calais from Dover where the Channel is only 20 miles wide?''[6]

That was the precise conclusion that Plan Bodyguard intended to have the German high command draw. However, von Roenne had made only a preliminary analysis, largely based on his gut instincts. Before a final conclusion could be reached, the FHW head would require countless bits and scraps of intelligence to paint an accurate Feindbild.

6

Eavesdropping on the Fuehrer

During the drab, melancholy days of January 1944, Field Marshal Karl Rudolf Gerd von Rundstedt, the 69-year-old *Oberbefehlshaber West* (or OB West), was quietly enjoying the courtly life of a country gentleman in Saint-Germain-en-Laye, a suburb of once glamorous Paris, which had been under the Nazi heel since mid–1940. Few Frenchmen knew that the most powerful field marshal in the West lived in an unpretentious villa behind the high school at 28 Rue Alexandre Dumas. The grounds were surrounded by a high wall, and the huge iron gates were kept permanently shut. Entrance to the villa was through a corridor that had been cut into its side. OB West was located nearby at 20 Boulevard Victor Hugo. It was a gigantic, three-storied blockhouse, 100 yards long and 60 feet deep, and imbedded in the side of a slope.

Known as the "Last of the Prussian Knights," von Rundstedt had grown increasingly dispirited over Adolf Hitler's vague and often meaningless orders from far-off *Wolfsschanze* (Wolves' Lair), the fuehrer's command post near Rastenberg in East Prussia, behind the Russian front.[1] Von Rundstedt did little to conceal his contempt for the man he contemptuously called "the Bohemian Corporal," from the fuehrer's World War I service as an infantry lance corporal in France. Yet the ramrod-straight, dignified field marshal held Hitler's respect—and his command in the West—due to von Rundstedt's exceptional performances in leading the German legions to smashing victories in Poland and France and in the early days of the 1941 invasion of the Soviet Union.

In late 1943, von Rundstedt asked the fuehrer for additional troops. Instead, a famed German field marshal, Erwin Rommel, 17 years von Rundstedt's junior, arrived in France and was given direct command of repelling any invasion of northwest Europe. Dignified old von Rundstedt was humiliated and suspected that it was the first step toward retiring him from the Wehrmacht.

Field Marshal Rommel was armed with a *Gummibefehl*, a flexible directive ordering him to inspect the Atlantic Wall and report back directly to Adolf

Hitler's headquarters. Being bypassed in the chain of command so upset von Rundstedt that he began referring to Rommel as *der Marschall Bubi* (the Marshal Laddie, or the Boy Marshal).

Although shown on Wehrmacht command charts as leader of Army Group B (the Seventh Army in Normandy and the Fifteenth Army in the Pas de Calais) and subordinate to von Rundstedt, Rommel would pay lip service to the commander-in-chief-west and maintain direct contact with the fuehrer. By January 1944, von Rundstedt nearly abandoned interest in the war and slipped into almost figurehead status.

"See that guard at the front gate?" a philosophical von Rundstedt said to a visitor to his villa. "I cannot move him to the other side of the house without the Bohemian Corporal's personal permission."

Despite his indifference, von Rundstedt was convinced that he knew where the Allies would strike. He often would scan a large wall map and tell his staff: "If I were the enemy, here's where I would land." His pointer touched the Pas de Calais.

Erwin Rommel had received his jewel-studded, gold-encrusted marshal's baton personally from Adolf Hitler two years earlier at age 49, to become the youngest field marshal in German history. Blessed with boundless energy and determination, Rommel had hardly arrived at his Army Group B headquarters at La Roche-Guyon, north of Paris, when he set out in his chauffeur-driven Mercedes 230 sedan for a hectic inspection trip around the perimeter of the Western European fortress, from Denmark to the Mediterranean. The Boy Marshal swept down like some avenging angel upon the somnolent Wehrmacht units, where the principal preoccupation was often to avoid being transferred to the dreaded Russian front.

Erwin Rommel was appalled by what he saw. In a few places, around the major ports, the huge concrete and steel fortifications were completed, and they were menacing indeed. But in most places, especially along the open beaches, the defenses were almost negligible. Rommel growled to his 36-year-old aide, Captain Hellmuth Lang, that the vaunted Atlantic Wall was "a figment of Hitler's *Wolkenkuckucksheim* [cloudy cuckoo land]!"

When von Rundstedt heard of Rommel's denunciation of the Atlantic Wall, he agreed entirely, possibly the only time he had concurred with the youthful field marshal on anything—particularly on how *der Grossinvasion* should be defeated. If the Anglo-Americans charged across the Channel, Rommel was convinced that they would have to be met head-on at the water's edge. With the Western Allies' almost total control of the air, he concluded that the crack panzer divisions being held far inland would be destroyed before they could reach the beachhead. So these panzers, in his view, had to be positioned along the coast or directly behind it.

Standing on a Normandy beach being swept by icy blasts of wind off the Channel, Rommel pointed with his "informal" marshal's baton (a two-foot-long black stick with a white tassel) and told Captain Lang: "Reserves will never get up to the point of the attack. . . . The *Hauptkampflinie* [main line of resistance] must be right here!''

Rommel's doctrine of defending every yard of shoreline was precisely contrary to the theory of von Rundstedt. Nurtured in the traditions of the old Prussian armies, the aged field marshal subscribed to the doctrine of Frederick the Great: "He who defends all, defends nothing. . . . Little minds want to defend everything, sensible men concentrate on the essential."

Von Rundstedt was convinced that the Anglo-Americans would get ashore in Western Europe at any point and time of their choosing. His plan was to hold most of his troops back from the coast and to rush them forward to strike at the time the invaders were most vulnerable—just after they landed, disorganized and without adequate supplies and weapons.

Adolf Hitler generally endorsed Erwin Rommel's anti-invasion plan, although he did not advise Field Marshal von Rundstedt of that fact. Instead, the fuehrer dispatched an aide to break the news to Major General Günther Blumentritt, chief of staff of OB West (von Rundstedt's headquarters).

With Gerd von Rundstedt's reluctant backing, Erwin Rommel plunged into the mammoth task of shoring up defenses along the Atlantic Wall, a barrier of bunkers, strong points, and other fortifications stretching from Norway westward to the Spanish border, a distance of more than 2,000 miles. For weeks, he dashed up and down the long coastline, at all hours of the day and night, seven days a week. His stocky figure, wearing an ankle-length leather greatcoat and a woolen scarf around the neck, became a familiar sight.

Rommel talked with the generals and privates, praised, cajoled, badgered, and criticized, supervised the construction of beach obstacles, helped set up artillery fields of fire, and shuffled troop dispositions. Along the sands, in paths and gullies leading from the beaches, Rommel ordered 5 million mines planted. Before the Anglo-Americans came, he hoped to have 60 million mines of all shapes and sizes strung along the coast: Pancake types capable of blowing off tank treads; ones attached to wooden stakes and concrete cones which would be covered from sight at high tide and could demolish landing craft; types the Americans called "Bouncing Betsys"—when stepped upon they would leap up to a man's midriff, then explode and blow him to smithereens.

Lieutenant Arthur Jahnke, the young commander of Strongpoint W–5, along the Dunes of Varreville at the base of the Cherbourg peninsula, was one of those who felt Erwin Rommel's wrath. Looking up from his work one January day, Jahnke saw the field marshal's mud-spattered vehicle speed toward his position and lurch to a halt. Out hopped Rommel, who briskly strode toward a nearby blockhouse overlooking the English Channel. Neither Rommel nor Jahnke had any way of knowing that this precise locale was marked "Utah Beach" on secret maps at the Allied high command in London.

In the trunk of Rommel's car were several accordions. It had been his custom to present these musical instruments to outstanding Atlantic Wall units that had prepared their positions with great energy and determination. It soon became evident to Lieutenant Jahnke that he and his men would receive no accordion. The field marshal was in a foul mood.

Rommel traipsed up and down the dunes with his omnipresent aide, Hellmuth Lang, and the unlucky Arthur Jahnke struggling to keep pace. The field marshal's criticism fell like hail: not enough obstacles on the beach, too few mines around the strong point, not sufficient barbed wire entanglements. What had Lieutenant Jahnke been doing to occupy his time—sleeping?

At the latter remark, Jahnke bristled. A decorated veteran who had been seriously wounded on the Russian front, the young officer was not awed by the presence of the legendary Rommel. "Marschall, sir, I string all the wire I'm sent, and I plant all the mines, but I can't do more than that," Jahnke protested in a firm yet respectful tone. "As to the obstacles, we put them in the water but it takes only one strong tide to drag them out to sea. The sand doesn't hold."

Rommel was not accustomed to such forthright responses from junior officers. For several moments Rommel stared stonily at Jahnke, then barked: *"Die Hande, Lieutnant! Ich will die Hande sehen!"* ("Your hands, Lieutenant! I want to see your hands!")

Puzzled by this curious order, Jahnke removed his heavy-duty leather gloves. At the sight of the deep cuts and scratches that disfigured the lieutenant's hands, Rommel visibly softened. "Very well, Jahnke, I expect my officers to get out there and string barbed wire with their men," he said with a trace of approval. "The blood you lost building the fortifications is as precious as what you may have shed in combat!"

Just before Rommel departed for his next inspection, Captain Lang trotted up to Lieutenant Jahnke. Holding out an accordion, he said to the Strongpoint W–5 commander, "The field marshal is presenting this to you and your men."[2] There was a clicking of heels and a rash of saluting (Rommel never gave the Nazi salute of an upraised arm); the field marshal climbed into his vehicle and sped away, trailing a plume of dust.

Returning to his headquarters in La Roche-Guyon, on January 16, 1944, Rommel wrote a lengthy report on his conclusions and dispatched it to Adolf Hitler at Berchtesgaden, the fuehrer's Alpine retreat in Bavaria. Part of Rommel's analysis said:

> The center of gravity of the enemy landings will probably be the sector held by the Fifteenth Army [Pas de Calais]. . . . It is quite likely that the enemy's main effort will be directed against the sector between Boulogne and the mouth of the Somme [River], where he will derive maximum advantage from the support of his long-range guns, from the shortest crossing for the assault, and later supply operations.[3]

Even before Field Marshal Rommel's assessment of Anglo-American intentions reached Hitler's desk, it was being intercepted and decoded by a British special intelligence operation code-named Ultra. The nerve center of Ultra—referred to as Station X by those in the know—was a large, stone Victorian mansion located 40 miles north of London, just outside the town of Bletchley Park, hard by the tracks of the London Midland and Scottish Railway.

Ultra had evolved over a period of years. Prior to Hitler's invasion of Poland in September 1939, the Wehrmacht had adopted an encoding machine called Enigma, whose ciphers were considered unbreakable. Even if an enemy were to steal or capture an Enigma, it would be of no use to him without knowledge of the keying procedures, which were changed almost daily.

In 1938, Polish intelligence, which had been working closely with its opposite number in London against Germany and Russia, stole an Enigma. A British naval officer, Commander Alistair Denniston, smuggled the device to London from Warsaw in an exceptional feat of derring-do.

Leading British scientists, mathematicians, and cryptanalysts concluded that there was but one way to penetrate Enigma: develop another machine that could imitate the changes in keying procedures that the Germans were making. Intelligence gained from Enigma would be of little value if it had to be painstakingly deciphered by humans, a function that could consume many weeks or months for a single German message.

So the envisioned British machine also would have to be capable of making an almost infinite series of intricate mathematical calculations within the space of a few minutes. Could such a machine be built? It existed only in theory.

Work on the project began in 1938 in the Bletchley Park mansion. A team of Britain's foremost thinkers labored under the most intense security month after month, never knowing if the job could be done. The development team was headed by Alan Turing and Alfred Knox, a pair of mathematical geniuses who were as eccentric as they were brilliant.

The specialists at the old mansion referred to the apparatus to which they were struggling to give birth as "the Bomb." As time rolled past, they began to despair. Then, on the eve of Great Britain's going to war, they hit pay dirt. The Bomb was able to match the electrical circuits of Enigma, permitting the device to imitate each change in keying procedure by the Germans. But it was not until April 1940 (eight months later) that bugs were eliminated from the Bomb and the first significant Wehrmacht wireless intercepts were unbuttoned.

Development of the Bomb would prove to be an intelligence bonanza of unprecedented magnitude. Information deciphered by it was code-named Ultra. From this point onward, the British (and later the Americans) would know the precise strength and location of German units and be advised in advance of enemy moves and intentions.[4]

Shortly after Ultra became operational, British Rear Admiral John H. Godfrey, chief of the Naval Intelligence Division (NID) of the Admiralty, sent for Commander Ewen Montagu. Always known as Uncle John, Godfrey was energetic and inquisitive and was a ruthless and impatient taskmaster. His technique was to drive everyone under him to the limit—and beyond. But it worked. And those serving under Godfrey admired and respected him.[5]

Commander Montagu entered Godfrey's office with a degree of concern, wondering if he was going to be rebuked for some delinquency. To the contrary, Uncle John advised Montagu that he was to handle all nonoperational special intelligence, and to get the full picture he was to go to Bletchley Park. The NID boss warned him that Station X was an extremely secret operation, so he was not to go in uniform.

Montagu went home and dug out an old civilian suit, reeking of mothballs. Then he caught a train for the short ride and hailed a taxicab at Bletchley Junction.

"Take me to Bletchley Park," Montagu told the drive.

"Oh, the cloak-and-dagger place!" the cabbie responded.[6]

That day, Commander Montagu had lunch with an old friend, Denys Page, an Oxford don, who had been involved in developing the Bomb. No sooner had the two men been seated than Page began sniffing the air and wondering aloud about the source of the overpowering aroma of mothballs.

Montagu related the warning he had received from Admiral Godfrey about the critical need to keep the utmost secrecy and how the cab driver at Bletchley Junction knew that some clandestine operation was being carried out in the old mansion. Page conceded that probably everyone in Bletchley Park knew about the mysterious goings-on, even though the precise nature of actual work did not leak to the townsfolk.

Page was convinced that it would require a near miracle to keep the Abwehr from learning about the true nature of the secretive events taking place at the old Victorian mansion. Presumably, there were German spies roaming England—maybe even ones that had been "planted" right there in Bletchley Park years earlier. Only a week before Commander Montagu arrived, the chief of the Imperial General Staff and a large entourage, riding in a long, noisy convoy of vehicles with two motorcycle soldiers in the lead, roared into peaceful Bletchley Park to look over the top-secret Ultra operation.

"All the bloody party came in wearing full uniforms, red tabs, cars flying the Union flag and all!" Page told his friend. "So much for secrecy!"[7]

By January 1944, between 2,000 and 4,000 top-secret German wireless messages were intercepted and unbuttoned daily at Bletchley Park. Despite Denys Page's realistic concerns about Ultra security nearly four years earlier, the Germans had disclosed not the slightest clue that they suspected that their wire traffic had eavesdroppers on it.

Among these intercepted signals were Field Marshals von Rundstedt's and Rommel's daily reports to one another and to Berlin of the strengths and dispositions of all German units in the West—often down to company levels. Although recording and deciphering this mass of enemy signals was incredibly dull and boring, the information provided the most priceless intelligence of the war.

Across the Atlantic, a small group of Americans working under intense secrecy also was eavesdropping on the fuehrer. Under Colonel W. Preston Corderman, the Signals Security Agency (SSA) was operating at Vint Hills Farms, a secluded estate in the horse country of Virginia 46 miles west of Washington, D.C., and at Arlington Hill, a short distance west of the capital.

This wireless operation was so secret that few in Washington even knew it existed. It was said that at a Pentagon meeting of top generals, one brought up the Signals Security Agency. "What in the hell is that?" asked a three-star general.

SSA's listening post was a half-world away in a most unlikely spot—Asmara, Ethiopia, in North Africa. Staffed by 300 Americans, Asmara rushed its raw intercepts, mostly those from Berlin, on an on-line radioteleprinter to Colonel Corderman's facilities near Washington. There the intercepts were deciphered, then flashed back across the Atlantic to an American signals center deep underground in the heart of London. From there, the pilfered German messages were distributed to a select group of American and British military leaders preparing for Overlord. Perhaps no more than 20 persons in all England knew how the material had been obtained—or that an SSA even existed.

While Field Marshal Erwin Rommel was preparing feverishly to "Dunkirk" the Allied invaders when and if they came, he called on two old friends during mid-January 1944. Unknown to the Desert Fox, Colonel General Alexander von Faulkenhausen, the German military governor of Belgium, and Colonel General Karl-Heinrich von Stuelpnagel, Hitler's military governor of France, were key leaders in the Schwarze Kapelle conspiracy.

During these visits, Rommel spoke at length about his deep concern over the future of the Fatherland and dropped clues that those in the know would have recognized unmistakably as meaning the field marshal was in sympathy with any responsible group seeking to conclude the war with the Anglo-Americans—with or without the knowledge and consent of the fuehrer.

A fuzzy winter sun was peeping over Hamburg, Germany, casting its timid glow on a city that was largely rubble and ashes after a frightful five days and nights of an apocalyptic rain of explosives and incendiaries a few months earlier by heavy British and American bombers based in England. It was January 14, 1944.

Seated in his office in the Abwehr branch on Sophien Terrace was Major Hermann Sandel, a reserve officer in his late forties, who had lived in the United States for several years before the war. Sandel was regarded as the Abwehr's foremost authority on the United States and Great Britain.

An aide entered Sandel's office and handed him a decoded, unsigned radioed message: *"Hoerte, dass Eisenhower am 16 Januar in England eintreffen wird."* (Heard that Eisenhower will arrive in England on January 16.)[8]

The sender of the important message was A.3725, Sandel's best spy in Great Britain who always came up with significant military information of a higher grade than did most of the other Abwehr agents. A.3725 was Hans Hansen, a young Danish draftsman. This was his 935th secret message to Hamburg since the summer of 1940, when he had parachuted near Salisbury, England. Miraculously, for three and a half years, A.3725 had avoided capture by Britain's Secret Intelligence Service (SIS).

Hansen had learned of Eisenhower's arrival even as the four-star American general was inside his private railroad coach, *Bayonet*, which was carrying him through thick fog from Prestwick Airport in Scotland to SHAEF headquarters on fashionable Grosvenor Square in London. A.3725 had radioed the news to Hamburg 48 hours before the official Allied announcement was due.

So eager were the Abwehr and the Oberkommando der Wehrmacht for even scraps of information from the enemy camp in Great Britain that apparently no one thought to question how a 25-year-old Danish national in an obscure job as a draftsman could have obtained such top-secret Allied information.

Good old A.3725. Again he had outwitted the British and come through. Major Sandel was so delighted that he put the Eisenhower message on the *G-Schreiber*, the direct-line cipher teletype for distribution to Group 1 at "Belinda," the super-secret Abwehr post in a Berlin suburb.

The professorial Hermann Sandel then drafted a message to his star spy in England and it went out at 8:30 P.M. on the regular schedule of Hamburg's daily radio contact with Hans Hansen: "Many thanks for excellent number 935. Keep us posted on Eisenhower's movements in context of invasion preparations."[9]

Hans Hansen never saw the accolade. The British had been outfoxing the German espionage apparatus almost since England went to war against the Third Reich on September 3, 1939. Within hours, agents of MI–5 (Britain's counter-espionage agency) and Scotland Yard men had fanned out over the British Isles in a mammoth roundup of German spies.

Before hostilities erupted, the Abwehr had 256 agents in Great Britain, and they were organized into two networks. One was called the R-chain, consisting of mobile agents who traveled in and out of England collecting intelligence on what seemed to be legitimate business ventures. The other network was the S-chain of "silent" or "sleeper" agents—Germans, citizens of neutral nations, and British renegades who had blended into the population and everyday life years earlier.

As a result of the big spy roundup during the first ten days of war, the Abwehr's espionage operation, which had been built up painstakingly over the years, was in shambles. Most German agents were hauled from their homes or places of work, and a few, seeing the handwriting on the wall and hoping to save their necks, turned themselves in to authorities.

Within a few months, seven captured German spies had gone to the gallows and many more were awaiting execution. What a waste to the British Empire, thought 30-year-old Major Thomas A. "Tar" Robertson, a handsome, articulate officer in MI–5. He conceived the idea for a deception scheme whereby captured German spies, instead of being hanged, buried, and forgotten, would be put to work double-crossing their former Nazi masters. Already the British had used this technique a couple of times, but only on an unorganized basis.

Tar Robertson finagled an appointment with Colonel John H. Bevan, who was in charge of the London Controlling Section (LCS), a super-hush-hush global deception operation in the Cabinet Office under Prime Minister Winston Churchill's military advisor, General Hastings "Pug" Ismay. Using his ample powers of persuasion, Major Robertson convinced Bevan that a live double-crosser would bolster the war effort far more than a dead German spy.

Colonel Bevan, a quiet, yet incisive officer and son of a prominent and wealthy London stockbroker, bought the concept. He promptly set the wheels in motion to create the finely tuned deception instrument with which double-crossers, stage-managed by MI–5, would mislead and confound Adolf Hitler and his generals.

Quite appropriately, the British named their new apparatus the Twenty Committee. Twenty in Roman numerals is XX, so the panel was usually called the XX-Committee or Double-Cross Committee. John C. Masterman, a tall Oxford intellectual, was appointed to mastermind the fledgling operation. A former member of the British Olympic soccer team and once a Wimbledon tennis player, Masterman was 49 years old and possessed a keen, innovative mind.

When collared, the German spies were taken to the XX-Committee's interrogation center at Latchmere House, a former convalescent home for "shell-shocked" British officers in World War I, in Surrey. There, Hitler's minions were given a choice: they could either become double-agents and radio back misleading information concocted by the Double-Cross, or they could be hanged. All of them chose to "turn" on their Abwehr masters and eagerly told their British controllers (also known as case officers) where they had hidden their Afu shortwave radios and disclosed their secret Abwehr codes.

Through the Latchmere House interrogations, the pending arrival of Hans Hansen had become known, and when he parachuted over England in mid–1940, he came down into the arms of a British reception committee. Hansen, aware that the jig was up, was quickly "turned" and given the code name "Tate" by the British. In January 1944, his signal to his Hamburg controller that Eisenhower would soon reach London was calculated to strengthen his credibility with the Abwehr. What harm would result from the disclosure? Two days later, the entire world would be let in on the secret anyhow.

7

A Conspiracy in Lisbon

Otto John, a prominent German lawyer, stepped from a Swedish civilian airliner at an airport on the outskirts of Madrid. Clutching a bulging briefcase, John hailed a taxicab which drove him through the Puerta del Sol in the heart of the thriving city and dropped him off at a fashionable hotel. It was January 9, 1944.

John was on urgent business: he would hold clandestine meetings with American and British officials in an effort to establish firm communications between the Schwarze Kapelle and Allied headquarters in London. Like other leaders in the German conspiracy to oust or assassinate Adolf Hitler, John had long been convinced that the fuehrer was leading the Fatherland to a catastrophe.

Otto John was aware that he was in an especially dangerous place, for Madrid was infested with German spies, stringers, Peeping Toms, sleepers, strap-hangers, go-fors, cut-outs, and go-betweens. This large contingent of Nazi agents operated without fear of arrest by Spanish police, for *El Caudillo* (leader) Francisco Franco years earlier had passed word to his government and military that they were to turn a blind eye toward German covert capers.

Generalissimo Franco had been deeply indebted to the fuehrer since 1936, when Franco's Rebel forces and the Loyalist army of the existing regime began a bloody, savage civil war that would last for three years. During that time, Abwehr chief Wilhelm Canaris, as Hitler's emissary, under the cover name "M. Guillermo," flew to Spain repeatedly to provide Franco with arms, funds, and intelligence.[1]

Early on the morning after his arrival in Madrid, Otto John cautiously left his hotel for a meeting with Colonel William Hohenthal, the U.S. military attaché in Madrid. John disclosed that "we" (no names were given) planned to eliminate Adolf Hitler soon in order to end the war. Could the Schwarze Kapelle remain in touch with the Americans? Colonel Hohenthal readily agreed and provided John with his secret telephone number in the U.S. embassy.

Delighted that the Americans were interested in establishing direct contact with the Schwarze Kapelle, John caught a train for Lisbon, where he would try to make a similar arrangement with the British secret service. There should be no doubt about the German conspirators' dedication, John reflected. Four times during the previous four months, the Schwarze Kapelle had made efforts to kill Hitler.

On the first occasion, in September 1943, 47-year-old German General Helmuth Stieff stashed explosives near the fuehrer's battle headquarters in East Prussia, but the blast went off prematurely. Security around Hitler became so tight that the scheme could not be resumed.

Two weeks later, a young German officer (whose identity would remain unknown) volunteered to smuggle a pistol into a staff meeting at the *Berghof*, the fuehrer's mountaintop retreat in Bavaria, and shoot Hitler pointblank. However, being so junior in rank, the conspirator was placed far in the back of the conference room next to an SS guard.

Undaunted, the conspirators tried again in November 1943. *Hauptmann* (Captain) Axel von dem Bussche planned to conceal two grenades underneath a new army overcoat he was to model for Hitler. When the fuehrer approached, he would pull the pins and blow himself and the head of the Third Reich into smithereens. Shortly before the modeling was to be held, an Allied bomber attack struck and the army-overcoat demonstration was postponed, never to be revived.

Then, just over two weeks before Otto John left Berlin for his mission to Madrid and Lisbon, 36-year-old Lieutenant Colonel Klaus Philip Maria Count von Stauffenberg, a German aristocrat who had lost an eye, an arm, and part of the other hand while fighting in North Africa, agreed to make yet another effort. When the fuehrer called a manpower conference, von Stauffenberg, a staff officer in the high command, got as far as the anteroom with a bomb in his briefcase, then was told that the session had been canceled.[2]

Reaching Lisbon, Otto John set up a nighttime rendezvous with a female British agent in a parked car on a dark side street. The woman was cold to his overtures for establishing contact with the Schwarze Kapelle, and as the pair drove through the city, she told the German that strict instructions had been received from London for British agents to have no further contact with the Schwarze Kapelle. "The war will now be settled by force of arms," she declared.

John was dejected. The Schwarze Kapelle's hopes of preventing a bloodbath on both sides in an Allied invasion of Europe had been blunted curtly. No one would ever know for certain the reason for the British refusal to work with the German anti-Hitler conspirators, but a finger could be pointed at an arch-traitor who held a high post in MI–6—Harold Adrian Russell Philby, known to his friends as Kim.[3]

While ostensibly serving his country in a highly sensitive intelligence post, one whose functions included the manipulation of double agents, Kim Philby himself was a double agent—and his primary allegiance was to the Soviet Union. Since the outbreak of the war, Philby had been feeding England's defense secrets to the Russians. One of his assignments from the NKVD (Soviet secret service) was to try to convince the upper circles in Great Britain that there was no practical way to deal with the Germans short of total destruction of the Third Reich.[4]

Impeccably groomed, handsome, and reeking with charm that many ladies found irresistible, Philby was chief of the Iberian subsection of Section V, a vital department that dealt with MI–6 counterespionage operations in Portugal and Spain. Stewart Menzies, the astute MI–6 chief who was responsible for his appointment, trusted the gifted Philby completely—the major blunder of Menzies' otherwise distinguished career in the cloak-and-dagger business.[5]

Kim Philby was born on New Year's Day 1912 in Ambala, India, the only son of Harry St. John Bridger Philby, at that time a civil servant in the government of India. In the decade after Kim's birth, the father had become a top-level British official and served as an advisor to Winston Churchill in the Admiralty during World War I. Later, the senior Philby became an advisor to the king of Arabia, wearing the flowing Arab costume, and became a Moslem, assuming the name Haj Abdullah.

St. John Philby was also a brute and terrorized his young son Kim, whose lifelong stutter may have been derived from an intense fear of his father. St. John Philby also was known for his rampages against British policy in the Mideast, and in 1940 he was imprisoned for his outspoken disapproval of the Allied war effort. Perhaps from his father, Kim inherited a secret bitterness toward the British establishment.

The disdain for anything British was accelerated after Kim Philby entered elite Cambridge Trinity College in England in 1931. There he was exposed to the depth of feeling against the establishment by most of the British intellectuals of that period. Antipatriotism was not just tolerated, it was fashionable. Marxism was not only respectable, membership in the Communist party was considered a badge of honor. It was widely believed that Philby was recruited covertly into the Communist party while at Cambridge.

As the war continued to rage in Europe in the years after his appointment to MI–6, Kim Philby's star rose steadily, and it was even predicted that it was just a matter of time until Stewart Menzies' fair-haired boy became chief of British intelligence.

Each month, Philby met secretly with "Ernst," his NKVD controller, who held a menial job as a front in London and lived in the attic of a rooming house in London's Maida Vale. Ernst, whose real name was Nicholas Rostov, was a German Jewish refugee whom Philby had met in Vienna while the Communists were fomenting bloody political riots in the mid–1930s. Ernst by then was already a hard-core Communist agitator and organizer, trusted by Moscow first as a talent scout for new recruits for the party and later in the more demanding job of control for Soviet spies.

Ernst's physical appearance was that of a classic sinister spy: heavyset, furtive mannered, and wearing thick eyeglasses that seemed to have come from the bottoms of Coca-Cola bottles. Underneath the shabby exterior was a cool, calculating brain and an unswerving belief in communism and its methods that never failed to reinforce Philby in his moments of doubt and panic over the double life he was leading.

Ernst spoke French, Spanish, English, German, and Italian with a heavy accent. Since the hectic days in Vienna a decade earlier, he had been Philby's friend, advisor, inspiration, and conduit to the NKVD. The Brit was said to have once confided to a close friend that he admired Ernst more than any man alive.[6]

Soviet intelligence was eager to obtain from Philby any information concerning the looming cross-Channel invasion that he could get his hands on, for the Anglo-Americans secretly had decided to tell Joseph Stalin as little as possible about Overlord. Suspicions were deep among the Western Allies that the Russians might tip off the Germans about the locale to be assaulted. Stalin, who Winston Churchill had once told a confidant had "the morals of a snake," might see an advantage of Overlord being a bloody failure, for it could create a power vacuum in Europe—a void that the Soviets would quickly fill once the German armed forces were destroyed.

At the same time that Otto John was dickering with Allied agents in Madrid and Lisbon, John Masterman, the chief of the Double-Cross Committee, which long had been convinced that every one of the 260 or so German spies in Great Britain had been captured, turned, or hanged, became highly alarmed when Radio Security Service intercepts indicated that three or more of Hitler's agents were now operating in England outside of British control. They appeared to be members of an Abwehr network called Ostro and were mailing intelligence reports to their Lisbon controller, who radioed the information to the Third Reich.

Masterman and others involved with Bodyguard spent sleepless nights over the Ostro apparatus. Success of the Normandy landings could depend on deceiving the Germans, so the Ostro agents on the loose in England had to be rapidly uncovered and arrested to prevent factual Allied invasion secrets from flowing to the German high command. Since the Ostro spies maintained no contact with the double agents already being manipulated, they would have to be traced back through their control in Lisbon, whose identity MI–6 did not know.

So it was decided at the highest levels of British intelligence that an agent who knew Lisbon well would be dispatched to the Portuguese capital to locate and identify the Ostro network controller. Stewart Menzies picked Kim Philby for the critical sleuthing job.

While Philby was preparing to leave for Lisbon, Dusko Popov (code-named Tricycle), a wealthy Yugoslavian playboy and double agent, flew unescorted from England to the Portuguese capital to report to his Abwehr control, Luduvico von Karsthoff, and hand over a large batch of papers dealing with the Anglo-American military buildup in the British Isles. These documents had been carefully concocted by the Double-Cross Committee to boost the Fortitude deception scheme, which was designed to convince the Germans that the Allies would land at the Pas de Calais.

Through Ultra intercepts, it was known that Berlin was starving for information on the American units that were flowing like conveyors from ports in the United States to England, Scotland, and Ireland. So the information Tricycle brought revealed (accurately) that the crack U.S. 82nd Airborne Division (which had fought in Sicily and Italy) was now in Britain and that three other American divisions (all of them fictitious) were billeted in southeastern England directly across from the Pas de Calais.

Luduvico von Karsthoff, an Austrian, was a major in the Abwehr and his real name was Erik von Auenrode. His wife, Elizabeth, a black-haired beauty, was a society lioness in Lisbon. She was fond of tossing gala parties at which the elite—and spies—of many nations were guests.[7]

After his treff with Major von Auenrode, Tricycle met with Johann Jebsen, an old university chum from Vienna, who drove between Lisbon and his villa in Estoril in a Rolls-Royce. Jebsen held the rank of captain in the Abwehr.

Jebsen had been sent to Lisbon by Wilhelm Canaris in early 1943, possibly to give the Schwarze Kapelle an outpost in that cosmopolitan city. Later in 1943, during a reunion with Dusko Popov, his tongue was loosened by whiskey and he dropped sufficient hints to convince Popov that he was disenchanted with the Hitler regime. Popov reported the encounter to the Double-Cross in London and was given instructions to recruit Jebsen, which he did. Jebsen was code-named Artist.

Now, in January 1944, Popov and Jebsen were celebrating with drinks, and the Abwehr captain mentioned that an individual named Paul von Fidrmuc, who lived in Lisbon, was thought to be head of a network of German agents in England. That organization was code-named Ostro, Jebsen added.

Tricycle, unaware that MI–6 was desperately seeking to identify the Ostro controller in Lisbon, radioed the information to London, which, in turn, flashed it back to Kim Philby, who had just arrived in the Portuguese capital. Philby advised his Russian masters, who already knew Paul von Fidrmuc and provided Philby with a wealth of background information on the suspected Ostro network chief.

Von Fidrmuc's mistress, Philby was told, was Gertrude "Trudy" Körner, a tall, shapely blonde in her late twenties, who worked as a secretary in the German embassy as a cover. She was actually one of Walther Schellenberg's spies, having joined the SS while still in her teens. Trudy was cheating on Paul von Fidrmuc—with another woman—and her love partner was the beautiful Elizabeth von Auenrode, the wife of Tricycle's Abwehr controller in Lisbon.

Philby promptly hatched a scheme to track down the Ostro controller through the two women. Four Portuguese men, who worked as subagents for the British, were assigned to stake out a secluded villa in Estoril (used as an SD hideout) where Trudy Körner and Elizabeth von Auenrode were known to conduct night-time frolics.

On the second night of the vigil, the two women drove up and entered the villa. Moments later, a light came on in a first-floor bedroom. Waiting for about 20 minutes, the stakeout men crept up to the window (whose blinds had not been drawn) and silently snapped several pictures of Trudy and Elizabeth cavorting on the bed.

Then the four men slipped into the house, burst into the bedroom, identified themselves as Portuguese detectives, and told the panic-stricken women that they were under arrest for trespassing on property that did not belong to them. Since Trudy was masquerading as a secretary, she could not reveal that she was actually an SD agent and therefore entitled to be in the villa.

Skilled in the art of intrigue, the Portuguese men went into their planned skit. Two of them shouted loudly that the women were going to be thrown in jail, but one of the men said soothingly that matters could be straightened out then and there only if Trudy and Elizabeth would provide a little information.

Explaining that the Portuguese police were anxious to obtain background about foreigners in the country, the pleasant "detective" brought up the name of Paul von Fidrmuc, Trudy's boyfriend, who lived in luxury, spent a great deal of money, yet never seemed to be gainfully employed. Were the rumors that the British were spreading true, that von Fidrmuc was the mastermind behind a widespread espionage network, which included several agents reporting to him from England?

Despite her embarrassing predicament, Trudy Körner burst out laughing. Von Fidrmuc had no spy ring, she exclaimed loudly. Rather he was the biggest fraud in the history of espionage. Talking rapidly now, Trudy said that her boyfriend of four years culled items from newspapers and magazines, embellished three fictitious Ostro spies in England, and was paid handsomely by the Abwehr for his services.

Apparently intent on extricating herself from arrest for trespassing, Trudy also disclosed where von Fidrmuc lived and agreed to make arrangements for a British agent to hold a late-night meeting with him. That agent would be Kim Philby.[8]

Forty-eight hours later, Philby was behind the wheel of a spiffy Jaguar driving toward a Lisbon suburb for his meeting with Paul von Fidrmuc. It was 2:00 A.M., and the streets were eerily still. The Brit was determined to find out whether von Fidrmuc was head of a genuine Ostro network with three spies running loose in England.

Philby climbed out of his Jaguar in front of a stylish, secluded villa, rang the door chimes, and was admitted by a tall, tanned man with bushy, gray-flecked brown hair—Paul von Fidrmuc. The Abwehr agent greeted his visitor with Old World cordiality and the two men sat down for a round of cocktails and idle chit-chat.

It was a strange confrontation: one of Britain's top intelligence figures and a German spy who may have had the means to unlock Allied invasion secrets. For perhaps a half-hour, Philby and his host sipped drinks. Just as a cuckoo clock struck three, Philby suddenly blurted that von Fidrmuc was a world champion phony and that the Ostro network was a fraud. Von Fidrmuc, a cool customer, never blinked an eye and merely took a swallow of whiskey. Even when the Brit threatened to make certain that the Abwehr in Berlin was informed that their Lisbon agent had been cheating them out of vast sums of money, unless he came clean about the Ostro network, von Fidrmuc simply replied that the Germans would regard such a denunciation as a devious British trick.

Philby sensed that his foe was cracking and said that he had proof that the Ostro network was a fake. Then he produced the compromising snapshots of von Fidrmuc's long-time mistress, Trudy Körner, and Elizabeth von Auenrode in the SD villa. Pointing to Trudy's likeness, Philby said that she was the one who had unmasked him.

Von Fidrmuc seemed to be drained of his will to resist. Yes, he said resignedly, the Ostro network was fictitious, a creature of his fertile imagination. Then, as though to redeem himself in the eyes of his opponent, he swore that he was in contact with a genuine Germany spy, code-named *Der Druide* (Druid) that even Trudy Körner did not know about.

Philby did not know if he should believe von Fidrmuc's tale. Perhaps he had invented Druid as a face-saving gesture. However, British intelligence would take nothing for granted, and for weeks they scoured England for the mysterious Druid, but their efforts were in vain.

Druid had lived in Germany for two years while attending college there and had been recruited by the SD and sent into England on May 10, 1941. Since he belonged to the SS, Druid had never had contact with any of the rival Abwehr spies, which may have accounted for the fact that he had never been captured. For nearly three years now, Druid had been reporting to Berlin through Paul von Fidrmuc's wireless set in Lisbon.

Druid was a 28-year-old Welshman named Gwyn Evans, who had become infatuated with Nazism and hated the British with a passion. As he roamed England, he had in his possession an official British identity card, ample food and clothing coupons, and, most important, a radio for transmitting information to Lisbon.[9]

Druid, as it developed, would be the only German agent at large in Britain as D-Day approached. Could he upset the delicate intricacies of Plan Bodyguard by alerting his German masters to the precise landing beaches?

8

A Flip-Flop by the Russian Bear

Hardly had Supreme Commander Dwight Eisenhower stepped down from his private railroad car *Bayonet* in London just after midnight on January 16, 1944, than the invasion of Fortress Europe began to dominate every aspect of the war against Nazi Germany. Within days of taking command at SHAEF headquarters in Grosvenor Square, Eisenhower was figuratively staggering under the tremendous burden.

A week after his arrival, Ike was seated at a small desk he used for personal correspondence at his private quarters in a townhouse known as Hayes Lodge in Mayfair. It was past 1:00 A.M. Outside, a thick fog stole through the blackness. Although he disliked writing in longhand, the general now took up a pen to reveal to his wife, Mamie, waiting out the war in Washington, D.C., the exhausting scope of his task: "If I could give you an exact diary account of the past week, you'd get some idea of what a flea on a hot griddle really does."

During 16-hour workdays, seven days a week, General Eisenhower was wrestling with tangled problems, from trivial to gargantuan, that no commander ever had been called on to solve. Code-named Neptune, the assault phase of the invasion would be the most complex and dangerous operation of its kind that history had known. On D-Day alone, if all went well, the equivalent of 300 trainloads of soldiers—150,000 of them—along with 19,500 vehicles would be ashore by nightfall. Neptune's printed operational order was five inches thick. Even the typed list of American units alone—1,403 of them, from two-man photography teams to divisions—came to 31 pages.

Despite this gigantic Allied strike force, Neptune would be a highly dangerous operation—almost a gamble. Amphibious assaults are the most precarious of military maneuvers. Field Marshal Gerd von Rundstedt had at his disposal in France, Belgium, and the Netherlands five field armies numbering about a million and a half men, including 350,000 SS troops, grouped into two paratroop, 17 first-rate, and 31 mediocre infantry divisions.

Neptune planners were at the mercy of the English Channel tides and the weather. Only twice each month did tidal conditions and the moon meet the requirements of a combined amphibious and airborne assault. The Germans knew these facts of life as well. They also were aware that in an operation of such enormous scope as Neptune, geographical considerations would limit the number of locales in Western Europe where the invader could land.

It was clear to Ike Eisenhower and to other Allied commanders that, if things went right for the Wehrmacht, von Rundstedt and his subordinate, Field Marshal Erwin Rommel, were more than capable of inflicting a catastrophe on the invaders.

Late one night after an especially hectic and frustrating day, the bald Eisenhower remarked dryly to his aide and confidant Lieutenant Commander Harry C. Butcher, a peacetime radio network executive, "If I had any hair left, I'd be tearing it out by now!"

The enormous load on the supreme commander's shoulders was made even heavier by the behind-the-scenes sniping at him from a few top British generals. They doubted his qualifications and experience to lead this mightiest of military operations. There were those on the Imperial General Staff, most notably Field Marshal Alan Brooke, who regarded the American as one who had risen to a position of great power through his deft political capabilities and sheer good fortune.

Brooke, still sulking over failing to get the supreme commander's job, wrote in his diary: "It must be remembered that Eisenhower never commanded a battalion in action when he found himself commanding a group of armies in Africa. . . . I have little confidence in his ability to handle the military situation confronting him . . . tactics, strategy and command [are not] his strong points."[1]

Eisenhower, of course, heard of the sniping and was quite sensitive to the accusations. In one of his personal diary entries, he wrote: "It wearies me to be thought of as timid, when I've had to do things that were so risky as to be almost crazy. Ho hum!"[2]

Within a week of his arrival in London, Eisenhower met at Norfolk House, SHAEF's planning center on St. James Square, with British Major General Frederick Morgan, the architect of the original Overlord plan, and Colonel Noel Wild, an expert in clandestine and unorthodox warfare. Wild, also a Brit, was chief of SHAEF's Committee on Special Means (CSM), the group responsible for implementing Overlord deception stratagems.[3]

The two British officers were to brief Eisenhower on Bodyguard, for part of the supreme commander's duties would be to coordinate and control the execution of the cover and deception plans that would support the invasion. Ike was, in fact, in charge of invasion plans in all their dimensions, and he demanded that he be kept fully informed of anything that was done in his name.

Standing before a large wall map, Colonel Wild told the supreme commander of Bodyguard's two functions. Through a tangle of intrigues, Bodyguard was designed to compel Adolf Hitler to disperse his panzer and infantry divisions throughout Europe so he could not concentrate sufficient power in Normandy to smash Neptune, and to delay the fuehrer's response to the Allied landings by disrupting and confusing the entire Wehrmacht command apparatus.

D-Day in Normandy would be crucial, but not more so than the succeeding four weeks in which a race would ensue between the invaders, pouring in more forces by sea, and the Germans in France, rushing by land to the beachhead. Neptune's success or failure might well depend upon Hitler keeping Colonel General Hans von Salmuth's Fifteenth Army idle along the Pas de Calais until the Allies had built up sufficient strength to hold onto the Normandy enclave.

Eisenhower was fascinated by the wily machinations in Bodyguard. While he would retain executive responsibility for the deception project, operational control would remain in the hands of Colonel John Bevan, chief of the London Controlling Section (LCS) and with Colonel Wild at the CSM.

Winston Churchill, back in 1940, had established the LCS, a top-secret bureau within his Cabinet Office at 10 Downing Street, to plan and execute stratagems to deceive and mystify Adolf Hitler about the real intentions of the then beleaguered British armed forces.

Great Britain's experience in the use of "special means" had existed for 500 years, during which British statesmen and generals had used them to establish and defend a kingdom, then an empire. Special means had played a major role in adversely affecting Adolf Hitler's strategies during the early years of the war, and now they were to be harnessed by clever minds to cloak and protect the invasion of Normandy.

Although only a colonel, John Bevan's position was unique in British history. His power extended throughout the world. He coordinated all British military, political, and civil agencies to make certain that they conformed to the multitude of Bodyguard deception schemes. Even Winston Churchill was, in essence, "controlled" by John Bevan and his LCS. It would be Bevan's operatives who would plant questions in the House of Commons, then direct Churchill to refuse to reply—thereby enhancing some hoax to mislead the Germans.

Bevan's influence even reached across the Atlantic, where he was responsible for coordinating what was said and done by President Franklin Roosevelt and Pentagon leaders with regard to actual operational cover plans. The LCS representative in the United States was Colonel H. M. O'Connor, who worked through the U.S. Joint Security Control (JSC). Under the Joint Chiefs of Staff (Army, Navy, and Air Corps), the JSC members were the directors of intelligence for the three services. As with the LCS, the JSC's function was to spread the Bodyguard hoaxes and to coordinate the activities of American agencies so that they would say or do nothing that would torpedo Bodyguard and tip off the fuehrer that he was being hoodwinked.

When their services were required, a vast army of agents in the field—Britain's MI–5, MI–6, and SOE (Special Operations Executive), and America's OSS— were at the beck and call of John Bevan's LCS. Also available to Bevan when needed were the cover and deception sections of the British and Allied armies;

the U.S. State Department and its opposite number in England, the Foreign Office; and the economic and political warfare agencies of both nations. By 1944, Allied deception and deceit had definitely become a growth industry, the like of which history had never known.

Late on the afternoon of January 29, John Bevan and U.S. Colonel William H. Baumer lifted off from Prestwick Airport outside Glasgow, Scotland, bound for Moscow to coordinate Russian participation in Bodyguard. Two months earlier, at the Teheran summit, Roosevelt, Churchill, and Stalin had agreed that the Anglo-Americans would send a delegation to Moscow for that purpose.

Baumer, a native of Omaha, Nebraska, and a product of West Point, was the Pentagon's representative on the LCS. Also on the flight was Archibald Clark Kerr, who was returning to his post as British ambassador to the Soviet Union.[4]

When the four-engine airplane rolled to a halt at a snow-blanketed Moscow airfield, a low-level Soviet delegation, none of whose members were known to Bevan or Baumer, greeted the visitors with all the warmth one would muster to hail the arrival of the bubonic plague. Complicating matters was that none of the Russians spoke English. Passports were scrupulously inspected. A series of mysterious telephone calls were placed. Then the visitors were escorted to a mess hall for "breakfast," which consisted mainly of vodka and cognac. "The Russians like to get their visitors stinko," Ambassador Kerr whispered to his companions.

Finally, an old Rolls-Royce drove up with a British official who rescued Bevan, Baumer, and Kerr and took them to the British embassy, located near the Kremlin, Joseph Stalin's seat of absolute power in the Soviet Union.

It immediately became apparent that more stumbling blocks had been put into place when British embassy officials had to take steps to ensure that Bevan and Baumer were given access to Soviet military officers and government officials, even though the joint conference had been in the works for 60 days. Then the two deceptionists were left cooling their heels for four days. On February 3, an angry John Bevan fired off a coded telegram to London: "I have not yet met the Russian representatives, but I am living in hope."[5]

Finally, on February 7, the Soviets informed the irritated Bevan and Baumer that they were now ready to confer. Dilapidated Russian cars came to collect the two men. When the tiny caravan arrived at a weather-beaten building, Bevan and Baumer were hustled up creaking stairs to the "conference room"—a small, dingy chamber reeking with odors and illuminated by a single, naked lightbulb attached to a frazzled cord hanging from the ceiling. A few Soviet Junior officers greeted their allies with cool reserve. Bevan and Baumer recognized none of them but believed that the two men who huddled in a dark corner with hat brims pulled down over their eyes were no doubt OGPU (secret police) men. Nothing substantial was discussed. Thirty minutes after it began, the conference broke up.

Six days later, the Soviets sent word to the British embassy that they were ready to resume discussions. This time a burly, square-jawed Russian appeared;

he identified himself as General Feodor Kuznetzov. He was accompanied by another Soviet general and a third man in civilian clothes who was introduced as belonging to the Foreign Ministry.

Neither John Bevan nor Bill Baumer knew who these Russians were or what they did. Nonetheless, Bevan launched into a lengthy briefing on Bodyguard. It was a delicate task: the LCS chief had to provide sufficient facts so that the Soviets would grasp the essential plan, yet he was careful not to disclose details concerning techniques that the Anglo-Americans would use in implementing the stratagems to mask Overlord. Like Winston Churchill, Bevan was fearful that these stratagems might be turned against England by the Russians once the war was concluded.

In his desire to be vague and reveal only the parts of Bodyguard that the Russians needed to know in order to conduct their part in the deception strategy, Bevan confused the Russians—primarily the result of the unfamiliar espionage terms that had to be filtered through a Soviet interpreter.

After three sessions, Bevan seemed to have put over to the Soviets their part in Bodyguard. First, the Russians were to mislead the fuehrer into believing that the Red Army's huge summer offensive could not possibly be launched until July (more than a month after the true D-Day in Normandy), in order to pin down Wehrmacht divisions on the Eastern Front. Actually, the Soviet assault would kick off ten days after D-Day.

Second, the Russians, in concert with the Americans and the British, were to imply to the Germans, through assorted schemes, that joint Allied operations would hit Norway and the Balkans. A variety of special means would be used by all three Allies to impress upon Adolf Hitler that these full-scale invasions would take place in May or early June. Again, the objective was to keep German troops in place throughout Scandinavia and southeast Europe.

Both of these proposed stratagems for the Russians would be elements of Zeppelin, the deception plan for the eastern Mediterranean, and would be geared to the phony concept that the Anglo-American D-Day for invading Fortress Europe would be about July 15.

General Kuznetzov, who never once changed expression during the long hours of discussion, finally ventured the view that the Soviets would do their part in the Scandinavian hoax, which largely would involve the massing of landing craft to threaten German-held Norway and its neighbor, neutral Sweden. But he dug in his heels against Russian involvement in Zeppelin, the implied threat against the Balkans.

Tension between the two delegations increased when Kuznetzov and his colleagues failed to show up for another scheduled session. Bevan complained vigorously about the snub and was told that it had resulted because Stalin was ''inspecting the front lines,'' and it was essential to consult him before further discussions.

While the American and British delegates holed up in the embassy and fumed, a thick blanket of silence fell over the schedule. Repeated efforts by Bevan and Baumer to reach Soviet officials by telephone resulted in the lines going dead. No doubt the OGPU had the British embassy wiretapped.

On February 29, a month after Bevan and Baumer had taken off from Prestwick in Scotland, the LCS chief sent a telegram to London: "No meeting since February 14. However, Stalin is back from the front and I am hoping for a decision soon."[6]

Despite the deeply pessimistic mood of Bevan and Baumer toward reaching an agreement on Bodyguard in light of the Russians' curious and secretive antics, Major General John R. Deane, head of the U.S. Military Mission to Moscow, was upbeat. "Kuznetsov is very enthusiastic over Bodyguard," Deane told the doubting Bevan and Baumer.[7]

It seemed clear that the reason for the Russians' prolonged silence was that the Red hierarchy was vigorously debating the implications of Bodyguard, for Joseph Stalin had his covetous eyes on the Balkans as fertile grounds for postwar Communist expansion.

Not only were Bevan and Baumer angry and frustrated, they had to get back to London to direct Bodyguard. D-Day in Normandy was only four months away. In Bevan's absence, the deception plan was being stage-managed by his highly capable deputy, Lieutenant Colonel Ronald Evelyn Leslie Wingate, who was an architect of the original Bodyguard plan and a cousin of Lawrence of Arabia. If they did not hear from the Russians within 24 hours, Bevan and Baumer agreed, they would pack up and go home.

At 10:30 P.M. on March 1 the telephone rang in the British embassy, where a cocktail party was in progress. A Russian officer, speaking in flawless, unaccented English, said General Feodor Kuznetsov would hold an important meeting at 1:30 A.M.—only three hours away.

Hardly had Baumer and Bevan entered the conference room than a beaming Kuznetsov nearly bowled them off their feet: the Soviets were accepting Bodyguard as a deception stratagem to help defeat Adolf Hitler and would go all-out to perform their role in the plan. What was more, the Russian general declared, an official document would be ready for both delegations to sign in 36 hours.

Bevan and Baumer were elated, puzzled, amazed—and suspicious. The Russian bear had been dancing around the Bodyguard issues for five weeks. Why the sudden flip-flop?

There were two possible reasons, the two men conjectured. After scrutinizing Bodyguard in great detail, Stalin and his inner clique had decided there would be no harm in going along with the deception plan. Or the Communist chieftains may have concluded that their contribution to Bodyguard would have minimal effect on the war in the long run, so to convey the facade of harmony between the Allies, they would agree to the deception plan with the intention of doing nothing to implement it.[8]

At the appointed time—4:00 P.M. on March 3—the delegations gathered at

Karl Marx Place to put their signatures to the Bodyguard agreement. Within hours, John Bevan and Bill Baumer were in an American B–24 bomber, converted for civilian passenger use, winging back toward London. Each wondered if the lengthy mission to Russia had been a total waste of valuable time.

9

"Wild Bill" and His OSS

While the machinations between the Allied representatives were being conducted in Moscow in early 1944, Major General William J. Donovan, chief of the Office of Strategic Services (OSS), was directing the secret operations of the global espionage and sabotage apparatus which he had built from scratch in less than three years.

Donovan gained the moniker "Wild Bill" in his youth, and he enhanced it with his exploits against the Germans in the muddy, bloody battlefields of France in World War I. As a colonel in command of the famed "Fighting 69th" Infantry Regiment, he had been awarded America's top three decorations for valor, including the Congressional Medal of Honor.[1] Born in 1883, Donovan was a stocky, gray-haired man, a Herbert Hoover Republican (a "blemish" that Democrat Franklin Roosevelt overlooked), a devout Catholic, and a millionaire Wall Street lawyer with global connections in numerous fields of endeavor.

Bill Donovan plunged into the espionage business on July 11, 1941, when President Roosevelt signed an executive order designating him as Coordinator of Information (COI). It was an intentionally vague title. Privately, in order not to touch off an uproar from American isolationists demanding that the country be kept out of "other nations' quarrels," Roosevelt instructed Donovan to launch political warfare against Uncle Sam's enemies. The president would use unvouchered funds to cover Donovan's expenses.[2]

Establishing the covert COI was a landmark in U.S. history and was designed to fill a crucial need for a worldwide intelligence agency. Until Donovan's appointment, the United States was the only major power that did not have such a clandestine agency. In an often hostile and volatile world, Uncle Sam was stumbling around without eyes and ears.

Almost at once, Bill Donovan became a mystery man in Washington. Charles A. Lindbergh, the "Lone Eagle" who had earned enduring fame when he became the first person to fly the Atlantic Ocean solo in 1927, was a vocal voice in

America First, an organization whose goal was to keep the United States out of the war in Europe. He declared that the COI was "full of politics, ballyhoo, and controversy."[3]

At the War Department, hidebound generals snorted that the COI was a "fly-by-night civilian outfit headed up by a wild man who was trying to horn in on the war." West Pointers scoffed at the COI staff as "Donovan's Dragoons."

From across the Atlantic was heard the strident howl of Paul Joseph Goebbels, Adolf Hilter's propaganda minister, who shrilled that the COI had "a staff of nine Jewish scribblers, two cows and a goat."[4]

Curiosity about the COI turned to deep suspicion in Washington. As if on cue from an unseen director, a host of predatory government bureaucracies forgot about their internecine animosities and joined forces in an effort to strangle this unwanted newcomer at birth. The grumbling grew so intense that President Roosevelt loaned his son James to the COI as a "liaison officer" to prevent other agencies from demolishing Donovan's outfit before it even got started.

Suspicion among a sizeable segment of the American population grew into abhorrence when word leaked out that Bill Donovan was to be Uncle Sam's masterspy. Secure in their belief that two wide oceans protected the nation, tens of millions of Americans were obsessed with Uncle Sam minding his own business. A decade earlier, when the U.S. Army Signal Corps was on the verge of cracking supersecret foreign codes, a horrified Secretary of State Henry L. Stimson (later secretary of war) fought its request for funds, exclaiming, "Gentlemen simply do not open other people's mail." Had the sleeping giant America "opened other people's mail" at that time, the debacle at Pearl Harbor on December 7, 1941, might well have been avoided.

Shunned by much of official Washington as though he were a leper, Bill Donovan had to scratch for COI office space, and finally he was able to move his tiny staff into three small rooms in the old State Department Building on Pennsylvania Avenue, next to the White House. He "borrowed" a few pieces of office furniture from other places in the building. There was but one telephone in the COI cubicles, and each time it rang, which was seldom, Donovan and his two aides all leaped to answer.

Donovan's task was mind-boggling. Within months, he was expected to create a global apparatus that would engage in espionage, sabotage, "black" propaganda, guerrilla warfare, and related subversive antics. He would have to catch up with the secret service operations of Germany, Russia, Japan, Great Britain, and other major powers whose covert organizations had been steeped in the trade for centuries.

Two months after President Roosevelt established the Coordinator of Information, Bill Donovan had some 100 employees and was embroiled in disputes with several federal agencies involved to one degree or another with collecting intelligence. These included the FBI, Army intelligence (G–2), Office of Naval Intelligence (ONI), and the State Department security section.

J. Edgar Hoover and Donovan, two of Washington's most strong-willed figures, became especially bitter foes. The famed FBI chief was apparently convinced that Donovan and his band of amateur upstarts were trying to poach on his private preserve.

Back in mid-September 1939, two weeks after Adolf Hitler's war juggernaut plunged into Poland, President Roosevelt called in Hoover, a square-jawed, black-haired bachelor, and instructed the FBI to take charge of handling all matters involving espionage, sabotage, and subversive activities in the United States. For the first time in its 163-year life, America would have a single agency designated to fight insidious forces seeking to subvert the nation.

When the Japanese bombed a woefully unprepared United States into global war on December 7, 1941, Roosevelt was burdened with countless problems, and the ongoing hassles between intelligence services and Bill Donovan had begun to irritate him during the dark early months of the war. The president was on the verge of resolving the situation by abolishing the COI.

One day at lunch, Roosevelt confided to Adolph Berle, who was in charge of the State Department's intelligence function, that he was thinking of getting reserve Colonel Bill Donovan promoted to brigadier general, then "put him on some nice Pacific island where he can have a scrap with some Japs every morning before breakfast."[5]

Within days, however, Roosevelt had a change of heart, and on June 13, 1942, he issued an Executive Order that, in essence, abolished the COI and established in its place the Office of Strategic Services—although Donovan would have to wait eight months to get his general's star.

If anything, the creation of the OSS stirred up the fussing-and-feuding pot in Washington. The Army's chief of intelligence refused to speak to a *reserve* officer and communicated with Donovan through an intermediary only when absolutely necessary. J. Edgar Hoover and the head of Navy intelligence were embroiled in a squabble of their own, but they managed to find time to take potshots at Bill Donovan and the OSS.

Part of the problem was the Army and Navy intelligence were grossly unprepared for the new kind of world war that had suddenly been thrust upon them. "The G–2 men could not see over the hill to the necessity of establishing an agency for securing the new kind of information needed," General Henry H. "Hap" Arnold, commander of the Army Air Corps and a member of the Joint Chiefs of Staff, said.[6]

During the early months of 1942, Bill Donovan, like a demon possessed, conducted a personal recruiting campaign for his fledgling cloak-and-dagger outfit. At posh cocktail parties in Washington, D.C., and New York City, in Wall Street law firm suites, in the cloistered halls of Ivy League universities, in multibillion-dollar banks and investment companies, on military bases, and along countless byways and highways, the indefatigable OSS boss gave his sales pitch.

Earlier, a friend, British Navy Commander Ian Fleming, a renowned spy novelist who was involved in the Double-Cross Committee manipulations, urged Donovan to recruit mainly men and women in their forties and fifties, for they presumably would possess sounder judgment. But such conservative advice did not suit Donovan. For his field agents—those who would spy, conduct sabotage, slit throats, organize guerrillas, and wreak mayhem behind enemy lines–the OSS chief preferred younger men (and women). He described those he was seeking as "hellraisers who are calculatingly reckless, of disciplined daring, and eager for aggressive action." This breed of field agents he labeled "Cowboys."

Flocking to Bill Donovan's siren call was a curious mixed bag: multimillionaire bluebloods and union organizers, missionaries and bartenders, a former Russian general, a big game hunter, a former advisor to a Chinese warlord, a customs collector. Then there were professors, corporate executives, lawyers, editors, athletes, scientists, labor leaders, ornithologists, code experts, anthropologists, wild-animal trainers, bankers, safecrackers, remittance men, paroled convicts, circus acrobats, a bullfighter, and scores of average citizens.[7] In defense of his recruiting Wall Street lawyers and bankers, Bill Donovan, with a twinkle in his eye, explained: "They make excellent second-story men!"

In mid-January 1942, six weeks after the United States went to war, Bill Donovan's officers penetrated (that is, broke into at night) the Spanish embassy in Washington, D.C., and began photographing the top-secret codebooks and assorted documents of Generalissimo Francisco Franco's pro-Nazi government. When J. Edgar Hoover learned of the caper, he was infuriated but did not register a formal protest.

Three months later, in April, when Donovan's boys made another periodic nocturnal visit to the Spanish embassy to practice their photographic skills, they were tailed by FBI agents in two squad cars. Waiting for the intruders to get inside the building, the FBI vehicles pulled in front of the embassy and parked. A few minutes later, they turned on their sirens, whose strident sounds pierced the stillness. For blocks around, citizens ran into the streets to locate the source of the shrill noise. Then the FBI cars sped away, just before the "burglars" scurried hell-bent out of the building.

Now it was Bill Donovan's turn to be angry. Unlike Hoover, he protested the FBI antic to the White House, where presidential aides solved the squabble by ordering the Spanish embassy penetration project turned over to the FBI.[8]

Meanwhile, the feud between the hidebound diplomats in the State Department and Bill Donovan and his footloose operatives continued to simmer. In April 1942, Assistant Secretary of State Breckenridge Long wrote in his diary: "Donovan has been a thorn in the side of a number of the regular agencies of the government—including the Department of State. He is into everybody's business—knows no bounds or jurisdiction—tries to fill the shoes of each agency charged with responsibility for a war activity. He has almost unlimited money and a regular army at work and agents all over the world."[9]

The State Department soon objected to issuing passports to OSS men bound for assignments at locales all over the world. Ruth Shipley, who ran the State Department's passport division as though it were her own personal fiefdom, insisted that Donovan's agents travel with their passports clearly marked OSS.

That triggered a grim joke at OSS headquarters: agents also should go abroad with a sign hanging on their backs. On the sign, painted in large letters, would be the word SPY. Discussions were held at high levels before the State Department was convinced that espionage operations could not be conducted in the glare of a spotlight—nor were they compatible with Shipley's whims.

Standard operating procedures were almost taboo in OSS. Productive action was the lone objective. Louis Ream, a peacetime executive for United States Steel; Atherton Richard, a Hawaiian pineapple magnate; and other top OSS administrators would walk into Donovan's office loaded down with dozens of charts of every known shape and size. Donovan would glance at them, smile, approve them with a slight wave of the hand—and promptly forget about them.[10]

Shortly after the United States went to war in December 1941, Navy Lieutenant Commander John ''Pappy'' Ford, a Bill Donovan OSS recruit, set up a small temporary office in Washington, D.C. A famed Hollywood movie director, Ford had been acclaimed with Academy Awards for directing such blockbusters as *The Grapes of Wrath*, *Stagecoach*, *Young Mr. Lincoln*, and *How Green Was My Valley*.

Back in mid–1940, with America starting to partially mobilize in the wake of the threat of Adolf Hitler's powerful military juggernaut, Pappy Ford, then 45 years old and holding the reserve rank of Navy lieutenant commander, formed Field Photographic, an ad hoc unit without official Navy status. He signed up some of the biggest names in Hollywood: cameramen, soundmen, special effects wizards, film editors, and script writers. Ford organized his talented cinema civilians into a martial-type unit, taught them the basics of military discipline, then tried tenaciously to get Washington naval brass to absorb Field Photographic into the official reserves. For more than a year, Ford pleaded his case, but he was given the cold shoulder.

Ford was about to give up on his crusade as a lost cause when, just before Pearl Harbor, lightning struck from an unexpected source. Field Photographic was swept up intact by OSS boss Bill Donovan, who felt that the combat moving-picture unit would be a valuable tool for deception and intelligence purposes.

A few weeks later in Washington, Commander Ford called in two of his young petty officers, Robert Parrish and Bill Faralla, who had labored in the vineyards of the Hollywood movie industry. Ford instructed them to test a new type of combat camera that had been developed by Ray Cunningham, a technician at RKO Studios. The revolutionary moving-picture camera was mounted on a .30-.30 rifle stock; all the photographer had to do was point the camera and squeeze the trigger.

Rising from his desk, Pappy Ford spit in the direction of a wooden box he kept in the corner for that function, lit his pipe, and said to Parrish and Faralla, ''Give me a complete photographic report on the State Department Building next to the White House. Cover it from all angles, outside, inside, what have you. Don't take any crap from anyone. If they give you a hard time, show them your OSS card.''[11]

Parrish and Faralla, wearing their Navy uniforms, entered a hospital across from the White House, climbed to the roof, and were accosted by a nurse. "Who are you men and what are you doing here?" she demanded to know, suspiciously eyeing the gunlike camera and other paraphernalia the strangers were carrying.

"We're here on official business, Mam," Parrish responded as Faralla flashed his OSS card. "We're from the OSS."

"Oh, yes," the nurse replied. "The OSS. Well, continue with your work."[12]

Faralla and Parrish were convinced that the dedicated nurse had no clue as to what OSS even stood for, much less what its function was. They set up a tripod, attached the odd-looking camera to it, aimed what appeared to a Marine on the roof of the Old State Department Building to be a machine gun. The sentry waved furiously, but the pair kept shooting moving pictures, including footage of a World War I machine gun "guarding" the White House.

Glancing back toward the State Department roof, Parrish froze as he saw a squad of Marine reinforcements dash into line and point their old bolt-action rifles at the unknown intruders on the hospital roof. With their first "combat photography" under their belts, Parrish and Faralla surrendered. They were locked up in the basement of the old State building for 40 hours until Bill Donovan learned of the episode and sent an emissary to spring them.[13]

Pappy Ford and Bill Donovan hit it off from the beginning; each was a rugged individualist with a touch of the maverick in him. They would have been failures as diplomats for each said precisely what was on his mind. In mid–1943, Donovan called a meeting at OSS headquarters in Washington for precisely 8:00 A.M. Hard-driving, hard-drinking Ford had been carousing the city until daylight, and when he walked silently into the conference room, his eyes concealed behind dark glasses, the others had already taken their seats.

"Commander Ford," Donovan barked. "If you can see well enough, we'll get started!"

"General," Pappy replied evenly, "I can see one thing—you've got that ribbon for your Congressional Medal of Honor on the wrong place on your uniform!"[14]

Donovan joined in the chorus of laughter.

Once over a drink or 20, John Ford described Bill Donovan as "the sort of guy who thinks nothing of parachuting into France, blowing up a bridge, pissing in Luftwaffe gas tanks, then dancing that night with a German female spy!"[15]

For two years, Ford and units of his Field Photographic roamed the world on secret assignments for Bill Donovan. Then, in March 1944, Ford and a team of his peacetime Hollywood civilians were in London to collect information for Overlord planners and to help deceive the Germans on the true invasion site in Normandy. Their effort was a kernel of Fortitude South, an element of Bodyguard.

Each day for weeks, Ford's camera teams climbed into twin-engine B–25 bombers and flew low-level sweeps along hundreds of miles of the French shoreline. Their mission was to get moving pictures of the coves, bays, inlets, beaches, and adjacent terrain along the 60-mile strip of Normandy targeted for the cross-Channel assault.

To mask the true landing beaches, the Field Photographic teams placed particular emphasis on taking footage of the Pas de Calais shoreline. Since the OSS men were not in the know either about the true landing beaches or the deception plan masking Overload, they presumed that the Pas de Calais would be the target. Otherwise, why had they been ordered to devote so much effort and time photographing that region?[16]

Meanwhile back in Washington, OSS chief Bill Donovan had long been concerned over the fact that the United States had no inside knowledge of what was taking place behind the towering gray walls of the Kremlin in Moscow. With the Soviets expected to play a role in the deception plan Bodyguard, Donovan felt that this critical void must be filled. So in early January 1944, he sent President Franklin Roosevelt a scheme to penetrate the Russian hierarchy.

Bill Donovan's plot to plant American eyes and ears in the Kremlin began a few weeks earlier when he went to the White House to see Roosevelt. During the past two years, the Soviets had greatly expanded their embassy staff in Washington, D.C., which meant that Russian espionage activities in the United States were accelerating, Donovan reminded the president. While the Soviets were gathering a wealth of information about U.S. war production and armed forces, American and British commanders in Europe had to rely on German wireless intercepts to know where the Russian army was and what it was doing. While constantly demanding information on American and British war plans and troop positions, the Soviets stonewalled requests for intelligence from the Western Allies.

Donovan's plan was for him to fly to Moscow and arrange for an agreement whereby an OSS mission would be stationed in Moscow and a Soviet NKVD (intelligence) contingent would set up shop in Washington, D.C. Donovan stressed that the NKVD already had penetrated vital American military facilities, defense contractors, and even the federal government, so Uncle Sam would gain far more than he would lose by such an exchange.

Roosevelt approved Donovan's approval, and two days before Christmas 1943, Bill Donovan's aircraft landed at a Moscow airport piled high with snow. There he was greeted by an old friend, W. Averell Harriman, the ambassador to Russia.

On December 27, General Donovan arrived at the NKVD headquarters in a drab, ancient building at 2 Dzerzhinsky Street and was escorted to a large conference room where a bevy of Russian generals were arrayed. Silently, they studied the American; he studied them. One chair was situated so that whoever sat in it would have to stare into a strong light. It was an old police trick to put the "culprit" at a psychological disadvantage. Donovan noticed that the Soviets cast quick glances at the "hot seat" and apparently hoped that he would take it. Perhaps as an impish response to their tactics, he passed a few other chairs and sat down on it. Glaring into the bright light, Donovan remarked evenly: "I'm ready for the fifth degree!"[17]

Doing most of the questioning was Lieutenant General P. M. Fitin, head of the Soviet External Intelligence Service. Donovan quickly noted that Fitin was very "un-Russian." Soft-spoken and polite, Fitin had long blond hair and blue eyes and appeared to be totally out of character as a spymaster.

On the other hand, his colleague, Major General A. P. Ossipov, chief of subversion in foreign countries, was a blunt, stone-faced man with a threatening manner. Ossipov spoke fluent English and acted as interpreter. Fitin asked numerous questions about the OSS, particularly about how its agents were infiltrated into and behind enemy lines. Donovan answered all queries frankly.

Finally, Bill Donovan sprang his unique proposals: exchanging intelligence liaison missions. Suspicious, the Russian generals wanted to know if the OSS head had some devious reason in mind. Donovan fixed them with a withering stare and made no reply. Cautiously, the Soviets agreed that the exchange might be beneficial to both countries.

When Donovan was ready to leave Moscow, Ambassador Averell Harriman offered to let him fly in the four-engine airplane that was kept by the U.S. government at a Moscow airport for Harriman's use. Permission was required from the Russians to take off, Harriman explained, but that would be but a routine matter.

The Americans were angered and chagrined when Foreign Minister Vyacheslav Molotov refused to permit Donovan to fly to Cairo in the aircraft. "It's only for the use of the ambassador," Molotov explained.[18] Pleas to get Molotov to change his mind were fruitless. However, the foreign minister said Donovan could fly out in a Soviet two-engine job. The offer was rejected. There would be little chance for a light aircraft to survive the tornadolike wind blasts that swirled around Moscow in mid-winter.

Donovan told Harriman that the Soviet official was trying to throw his weight around to show who was boss. "Averell, you leave this one to me," the OSS head exclaimed. "I know how to deal with Russians!"[19]

Donovan, Harriman's pilot, and Charles "Chip" Bohlen, a U.S. embassy official who spoke Russian, drove to the Moscow airport where the four-engine plane was being kept under guard. Through Bohlen, Donovan told the officer of the guard, a young captain, that he was an American general and it would be an unfriendly act between Allies if he refused to let Harriman's pilot see the weather report.

The Soviet captain had his orders and was quite frightened to find himself in such a delicate situation. Donovan kept hammering at the Russian until he finally agreed to let the Americans see the weather report. It showed the weather was horrendous and that there was no possibility of flying that night. Had there been, Donovan was quite prepared to hijack the Americans' own four-engine plane, gambling that the flustered Soviet guards would not dare shoot down an American general. Or would they?

During the early morning hours, the Russians moved the American aircraft to another airfield. Donovan did not know where. For the next 11 days, Harriman and Molotov bickered. Finally, the Russian was worn down and agreed to allow the OSS chief to fly out of Moscow—in the American four-engine aircraft.

When J. Edgar Hoover, the director of the Federal Bureau of Investigation learned of this pending American-Soviet exchange of spies, he hit the ceiling and fired off a hand-carried letter to Harry Hopkins, President Roosevelt's right-hand man in the White House. Hoover declared that "this situation is highly dangerous and most undesirable," adding that the "admitted goal of the NKVD is the penetration into the official secrets of the United States government."[20]

The president was hardly anxious to take on "the Director," as Hoover liked to be called. Not only did the FBI chief have great power in his office, but he was an American folk hero, as popular as anyone in the nation. It was Hoover and his G-men (as FBI agents were called) who had wiped out John Dillinger, "Baby Face" Nelson, "Pretty Boy" Floyd, and their desperado gangs that had terrorized the country in the 1930s. It was Hoover and his FBI who had scored spectacular successes in the early 1940s that had collared a few hundred Nazi spies—homegrown and imported—in the United States.

Roosevelt knew (or so he told confidants) that, with a presidential election looming in November, it could be disastrous if J. Edgar Hoover were to raise a public furor over "importing Soviet spies," even though Russia was supposed to be an ally. So Roosevelt reversed his own course and notified Averell Harriman in Moscow that the deal was off.

10

The Old Fox Is Trapped

In late February 1944, Field Marshal Erwin Rommel was taking a short leave at his home in the Swabian village of Herrlingen, perched on a hillside four miles outside Ulm in southern Germany. Rommel had made the long trip by automobile from his battle post in La Roche-Guyon to console his beloved wife Lucie-Maria, who was lonely, in common with millions of other wives and mothers in the Third Reich in its fifth year of war.[1]

It was a particularly difficult time for Frau Rommel. The couple's only child, 15-year-old Manfred, along with others his age in a Germany rapidly dwindling in manpower, had recently been called up as Luftwaffe Auxiliary and assigned to an antiaircraft battery. Manfred and his boy comrades, together with elderly men in their seventies, were charged with shooting down the swarms of American and British bombers that had been pulverizing the Reich with increasing intensity in recent months.[2]

As a child, Erwin Rommel was weak and sickly. He took no interest in hobbies, sports, or girls, and he spent most of his time daydreaming. As a teenager, he suddenly shook off his lethargy and started a program of rigorous exercise and body development. He began playing tennis, bicycling, skiing, and ice skating.

By the time Rommel was 18, he had developed toughness, self-reliance, tenacity, and pragmatism. Strictly on his own, young Rommel decided he would become a soldier. There was no military tradition in his family, and his father, Erwin, bitterly opposed his decision—and for sound reasons. The Prussian aristocrats always had dominated Germany's armed forces and presumably always would do so. Young Rommel could hope, at best, to achieve the modest rank of captain and a small pension.

The youth stuck to his guns, and his father finally supported his decision. The young man's first army application was submitted to the engineers, and the second one to the artillery. Both were rejected, presumably because the candidate was the son of a schoolteacher. Finally, he was accepted by the infantry, the toughest and least romantic of all the services. As with many high-ranking officers in any army, the Prussian aristocrats considered infantrymen to be expendable "cannon fodder."

Three months later, Private Erwin Rommel was promoted to corporal, and in another three months, he was a sergeant. In March 1911 he was assigned to the War Academy in Danzig to undergo officer training. His Prussian commandant evaluated Rommel as "thin and physically rather awkward and delicate." He added, however, that the candidate was "firm in character, with immense will-power and mentally well endowed." In summary, he gave Rommel the lukewarm appraisal of being "a useful soldier."

At Danzig, Cadet Rommel started his first and only romance. Lucie-Maria Mollin was a slender, very pretty young lady with dark hair and an olive complexion. She had a nice figure and was an excellent dancer. She and Rommel fell in love almost immediately. However, *Lieutnant* Rommel's army assignments kept the pair apart, and it would be three years before they were married.

Now in Herrlingen 31 years after his marriage, Field Marshal Erwin Rommel greeted a visitor, Karl Stroelin, a long-time friend and *Oberburgermeister* (mayor) of the large city of Stuttgart. Unknown to Rommel, Stroelin had long been a conspirator in the Schwarze Kapelle. In the comfort of the Rommels' living room, the field marshal listened without change of expression as Stroelin outlined the work of the Schwarze Kapelle, how the conspiracy planned to seize the fuehrer, bring him to trial, and execute him, and seek a separate peace with the United States and Great Britain. Such a drastic action, Stroelin warned, could result in a civil war in the Fatherland and a bloody fight between the German army and the SS *unless* a widely respected, dominating public figure surfaced immediately to lend his name to the conspiracy.

Pausing momentarily, Stroelin then dropped a bombshell: the Schwarze Kapelle leaders had agreed that the dominating figure had to be Erwin Rommel. Old friend or not, it was a perilous proposal that Stroelin was making—high treason to the Nazi state. Had he misjudged Rommel's moral fiber, Stroelin would be in Gestapo custody by nightfall.

Rommel sat in silence, deep in thought. Clearly, he was agonizing. Stroelin continued his persuasive effort.

"You are our greatest and most popular general and more respected abroad than any other," the Stuttgart mayor declared. "You are the only one who can prevent civil war and save the Fatherland."

By now, Erwin Rommel's mind was in a turmoil. Everything he was, he owed to the fuehrer. He had taken a sacred oath of loyalty to the Third Reich and Hitler, had once commanded the fuehrer's elite bodyguard, and had received his marshal's baton personally from the German leader. Yet a statement once made by Adolf Hitler himself returned time and again to Rommel: "When the government of a nation is leading it to its doom, rebellion is not only the right but the duty of every citizen."

As the minutes ticked past and Rommel wrestled with his conscience, Stroelin looked on in silence. Finally, the field marshal stated: "I believe it is my duty to come to the rescue of the Fatherland."

Riding back to his headquarters at La Roche-Guyon on the following day, the field marshal had time to reflect upon his extraordinary situation. He would try to contact General Eisenhower and forestall the bloodbath on both sides that an invasion would bring, and he was confident that the Anglo-Americans would grasp promptly any reasonable offer of a separate negotiated peace with a German government minus Adolf Hitler. Then, Rommel felt, the United States and Great Britain would join with Germany to fight the Russian hordes that were preparing a massive summer offensive to assault the eastern gates of the Third Reich.

If the two English-speaking powers refused a separate peace, then Rommel intended to inflict the greatest carnage possible on the Anglo-American invaders. Perhaps then the Western Allies would listen to reason—and the demands of their citizens to negotiate a separate peace with the Germans.

In the meantime, the Old Fox—Abwehr chief Wilhelm Canaris—was continuing his precarious high-wire balancing act, conspiring with Schwarze Kapelle leaders on the one hand and doing business with the fuehrer and his high command on the other. But the little admiral's political schizophrenia, the wear and tear of the seemingly interminable war, and the relentless undercover duels with powerful Nazi figures long seeking to crush him, all were reflected in the declining performance of the Abwehr.

Complaints against Canaris and the Abwehr mounted steadily. Blood enemies in the SS and in the Nazi apparatus dug up old beefs. The flames of discontent were fanned by Walther Schellenberg, the leader of the SD, who was seeking to launch a lethal blow against Canaris, one that would catapult the SD chief into control of all Reich intelligence agencies.

Foreign Minister Joachim von Ribbentrop, also infected with an insatiable lust for ever more power, engaged in skulduggery aimed to topple Canaris, the man who had been his longtime foe. In fact, the pompous von Ribbentrop had no shortage of enemies. Count Galeazzo Ciano, Italian dictator Benito Mussolini's son-in-law and the Italian foreign minister before *Il Duce* was bounced from office and executed in 1943, was typical of those who despised von Ribbentrop. Count Ciano, who once had to deal with the Nazi functionary when Germany and Fascist Italy were war partners, said of him: "He is vain, frivolous and loquacious."[3] Now, in early 1944, the 51-year-old Joachim von Ribbentrop seized on a set of circumstances in far-off lands as a means to discredit or demolish Wilhelm Canaris.

Argentina, the only major nation in South America that remained a steadfast supporter of Adolf Hitler, was heavily infiltrated by Abwehr agents, including one of the slickest spies of the war, Hans Rudolf Leo Harnisch. Posing as a respectable business executive of Boker & Company, one of the largest Argentine import-export firms, the 46-year-old Harnisch (under the cover name Erich Viereck) had played a key role in the early 1943 overthrow of the Castillo regime by a military junta that put the corrupt pro-Nazi General Pedro Ramirez in power.

Wilhelm Canaris, the Old Fox, had milked this Abwehr undercover coup for all it was worth and impressed upon the fuehrer that his superspies like Hans Harnisch were working night and day around the globe for the greater glory of Nazi Germany and for victory over the Allies. Hitler was delighted.

Unknown to either Canaris or the fuehrer, British and American secret service agents also had burrowed deep into Argentina with the task of coercing (or threatening) General Ramirez into cutting his ties with the Third Reich. It was impressed upon the Argentine strongman that Nazi Germany was a sinking ship and that he would be wise to jump overboard before it was too late.

Suddenly and without prior warning, Ramirez announced that his country was breaking diplomatic relations with Germany, whose regime had kept the general in power by equipping and training his army. In Berlin, Argentina's defection triggered a wild tantrum by Adolf Hitler. He demanded a scapegoat. Joachim von Ribbentrop suggested an ideal candidate: Wilhelm Canaris.[4]

Hitler was still furious over the setback in Argentina when he received another blow, this one in neutral Spanish Morocco. There the Abwehr had been entrenched for so long and operated so openly that its headquarters there was one of the nation's best-known secrets.

Since Operation Torch, the American invasion of northwest Africa in November 1942, Spanish Morocco had been virtually surrounded by Allied troops. General Fernando Orgaz, the leader of Spanish Morocco, had been getting heavy heat from the American and British agents, who demanded that the Abwehr be booted out. In January 1944, General Orgaz finally succumbed to the Allied pressure and gave the Abwehr 24 hours to get out. With its leaders banished, the Abwehr network rapidly fell apart.

Again Hitler exploded. With an Allied invasion of Fortress Europe looming, information was needed from all over the world. Now Germany had lost its most powerful listening posts in the Western Hemisphere and in North Africa.

Admiral Canaris was fully aware that his credibility with the fuehrer had been badly tarnished due to the twin intelligence debacles. So he called on General Alfred Jodl, Hitler's closest military advisor, at Maibach One, a new concrete fortress at Zossen, south of Berlin, which sheltered the Oberkommando der Wehrmacht. It was a six-story building, three levels above ground and three below. During air raids, field marshals, generals, and staffers scrambled into the subterranean chambers and work continued.

Jodl received Canaris with frosty reserve, so the Abwehr chief knew he was in deep trouble with the fuehrer. Jodl never said or did anything unless he knew it reflected Hitler's views. In his low-key, lisping style, Canaris gave General Jodl a glowing briefing on the network of "invasion spies" that he had built in England. One agent in particular, Arabel, had been masterful, the Old Fox pointed out. Arabel was also Garbo (whose real name who Juan Pujol), who had been the Double-Cross Committee's ace operative for two years. Arabel had even recruited a raft of subagents, including one in the United States, a traveling salesman who was sending reports from the eastern half of that nation, the Old

Fox averred. Canaris said that he had divided Arabel's network into three rings, under the code names Alaric, Benedict, and Dagobert.

Hardly a day passed that the Arabel network failed to send reports on invasion preparations in England, Canaris declared. Actually, Arabel was a fictitious network, one created by the clever mind of Garbo's Double-Cross controller, an ebullient, bilingual painter–antique dealer–gourmet named Tomas Harris, whom his friends called Tommy. Most helpful in his role as Garbo's case officer was the fact that Harris spoke fluent, idiomatic Spanish.[5]

Harris' rich imagination and boundless energy were taxed creating and stage-managing the Arabel network, a two-year project designed from the beginning to deceive the Germans about the 1944 invasion. It was the most elaborate and sophisticated of the double-agent hoaxes, but the flood of information and mis-information did not in itself create a phony Feindbild for Colonel Alexis von Roenne at Foreign Armies West.

Von Roenne's "enemy picture" was being pieced together from information collected from aerial reconnaissance, intercepts by the *Funkabwehr* (wireless intelligence), captured documents, prisoner interrogations, previous data on file, and intelligence gathered from neutral diplomatic missions all over the world. Yet, because of the information from the Arabel network and other double agents in England, this source dominated all German considerations and estimates, often gaining priority over such hard intelligence as photographs from Luftwaffe reconnaissance planes that were winging daily over the British Isles.

In the wake of the Abwehr disasters in Argentina and Spanish Morocco and the rash of complaints over the lack of in-depth intelligence reports on Allied invasion plans, Reichsfuehrer SS Heinrich Himmler joined in the covert quest for Wilhelm Canaris' scalp. Himmler did not intend to hijack the Abwehr just as a bauble for his protégé, Walther Schellenberg, but to take his own secret service, the SD, off the hook.

By February 1944, the SD's high-priority project in Ankara, Turkey, the contretemps of the "superspy" Elysea Bazna (Cicero), had turned sour and was a gross embarrassment to Himmler and especially to Schellenberg, who had approved the pilfering of documents that had been planted by the British secret service. Ludwig Moyzisch, the SD station chief in Ankara and Istanbul who had handled the Cicero operation, also was badly compromised. His trusted confidential secretary, Cornelia Kapp, a pert, blonde-haired young woman, defected to the Americans and exposed the Cicero operation from the German side.

Kapp, the daughter of a German diplomat, had been working for Moyzisch since December 1943, when his regular secretary badly injured a hand and returned to Germany for extended medical treatment. While working in Sofia, Bulgaria, three years earlier, Cornelia Kapp had met and fallen in love with a handsome young American on the staff of George Earle, the rambunctious former governor of Pennsylvania and President Roosevelt's personal emissary to Czar Boris III.

When Bulgaria entered the war on the side of Nazi Germany, the U.S. delegation was expelled and returned home. Two years later, Kapp's boyfriend slipped into Turkey as an OSS agent and she joined him there. Then the young woman was called on to pinch-hit in Ludwig Moyzisch's office, where one of her tasks was to open the mail from Berlin each day.

In this flood of correspondence and documents, Kapp alertly noted that the code name "Cicero" popped up repeatedly. At great risk to herself, she slipped copies of these secret papers out of Moyzisch's office (almost every night) and turned them over to her American boyfriend, the OSS agent in Ankara.[6]

Now, in order to minimize the scandal in his own backyard, Heinrich Himmler used all of his considerable guile to magnify the Abwehr setbacks by making Wilhelm Canaris personally responsible for all of the Third Reich's intelligence disasters. No doubt Himmler called on the fuehrer and presented him with the damaging information (much of it gossip and innuendo) that ambitious Walther Schellenberg had collected about his good friend, the Old Fox, over the years.

On February 18, 1944, Wilhelm Canaris' head fell into the basket. Adolf Hilter signed a decree: "I order the creation of a unified German secret service." Brigadefuehrer SS Schellenberg and his SD "Blacks" had triumphed over Canaris and the Abwehr "Santa Clauses." Schellenberg took charge of the Abwehr and its 16,000 agents and subagents around the world.

Despite his abrupt firing of Canaris, the fuehrer broke the news to the Old Fox in as gentle a way as possible, possibly out of appreciation for the contributions the Abwehr had made to Hitler's conquests. The Third Reich's two top soldiers, Field Marshal Wilhelm Keitel and General Alfred Jodl, called on the little admiral, thanked him profusely for his service to the Reich, announced that he was to receive the *Deutsches Kreuz* (German Cross) and suggested that he take a leave to recover from his exhaustion. Then they invited the stunned Canaris to accept an "important post" with the Ministry of Economic Warfare— a hollow offer since the Reich was hardly in a position to be waging warfare of that nature. For whatever his reasons, Canaris accepted.[7]

Canaris' dismissal was more than just a change at the top in German intelligence. After his departure, the Abwehr became a ship without a rudder, drifting aimlessly. Hundreds of officers resigned from the Abwehr and volunteered for combat duty on the Russian front. Richard Protze, who was in charge of the Abwehr's office in Amsterdam, stopped sending reports to Berlin. "Without the admiral," Protze told confidants, "I have no confidence in the service."

In Western Europe, Abwehr officers, to avoid being absorbed by Schellenberg's centralized agency, formed into mobile units directly under the orders of the Wehrmacht, using the pretext that the danger of the invasion called for close liaison between intelligence officers and the *Heer* (army). For their part, Walther Schellenberg and his Blacks were deeply suspicious of the Abwehr components they had absorbed.

11

Illusions in the Balkans

General Henry M. Wilson, who had succeeded Dwight Eisenhower as Allied supreme commander in the Mediterranean, was large of frame and hearty in manner, so he had long been known by the nickname "Jumbo." His bulk alone would make it difficult for even the most myopic Nazi spy to miss him when he arrived at Cairo airport during the first week of March 1944 to welcome a Russian military delegation that had just flown in from Moscow.

Rumors in the Egyptian capital were that the high-ranking Soviet officers had come to coordinate with General Wilson arrangements for a pending Allied invasion of the Balkans. These whispers seemed to be confirmed when Cairo newspapers hinted in page-one stories that the Balkans operations would be launched no later than March 30.

Actually, Jumbo Wilson was on center stage, playing a role in Zeppelin, an element of Bodyguard, and the Cairo newspaper accounts had resulted from calculated leaks by Allied deceptionists.[1]

Since Bodyguard sought to convince Adolf Hitler that northwestern France could not be invaded from England until the summer of 1944, Zeppelin suggested that the main Allied ground effort in the spring of 1944 would be in the Balkans, thereby keeping many German divisions pinned down there, far from the true landing beaches in Normandy. Already Zeppelin had gained enormous credibility with German intelligence as a result of the false documents that had been planted on Cicero, the British ambassador's valet in Ankara, Turkey.

Zeppelin played upon Adolf Hitler's beliefs about the critical significance of the Balkans in realizing his dream of a great German empire. Not only did the Balkans provide the Wehrmacht with valuable raw materials, but Hungary, Romania, and Bulgaria had nearly 500,000 tough and well-disciplined soldiers fighting with the Germans against the Russian army.[2]

Romania, the Zeppelin deceptionists knew, was an especially sensitive region to Hitler. Mountainous and surrounded by other countries except for a 143-mile

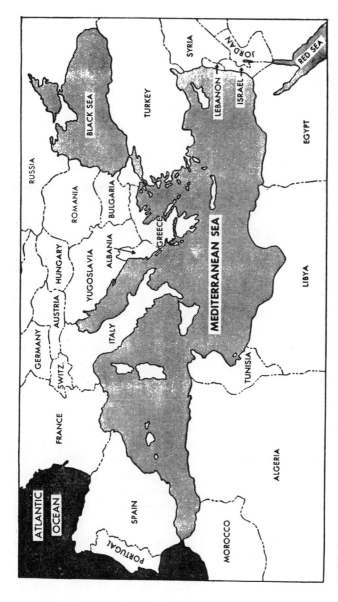

1. Mediterranean and Balkans regions.

coastline on the Black Sea, Romania had the vast Ploesti oil fields, which fueled the thirsty German war machine. Should the flow of oil from Ploesti be cut off by an Allied invasion, the Wehrmacht would be in serious trouble.

Zeppelin was being stage-managed by British Brigadier Dudley W. Clarke, a clever and remarkable officer who was in command of A-Force, the Mediterranean branch of John Bevan's London Controlling Section. Nearly four years earlier, when Great Britain stood alone against the powerful German military machine, Clarke had written a report that led Winston Churchill to create the Commandos—elite, daring, and heavily armed warriors whose specialty was swift, silent, and lethal raids in the blackness of night. Churchill called them "butcher and bolt troops."

A baffling man and an expert in unorthodox warfare, Brigadier Clarke, wearing civilian clothes, sporadically popped up in the large cities of Europe—Istanbul, in particular—on mysterious missions. Allied commanders were forever amazed at his ability to create divisions and even armies of men who did not exist. While the purpose was to confound German intelligence, Allied commanders themselves were fooled on occasion by Clarke's phantom formations.

During the early weeks of the Allied invasion of southern Italy in the fall of 1943, things were going badly and there was a serious need for infantry reinforcements. General Eisenhower, then the commander in the Mediterranean, was advised that the British had two armies—the 9th and 10th—in Levant, the countries bordering the eastern Mediterranean. Eisenhower was not happy when he learned that his staff had become confused, that the two armies were merely dummies created by Brigadier Clarke and his A-Force to fool German Intelligence.

Most of the fictitious Allied operations in the Balkans would be carried out by the fake British Twelfth Army, which consisted of six dummy divisions, five genuine divisions, and three real brigades posing as divisions. A phony timetable called for the first assaults to be launched in mid-March 1944. Since it was critical for the fuehrer to keep his divisions in and near the Balkans until long after the true D-Day in Normandy (scheduled for the last week in May 1944), A-Force would concoct plausible reasons for the Balkans invasion to be postponed several times.

A deception by-product of these fictitious amphibious operations against the Balkans was that they would take place in the middle of dark nights, a technique, it was hoped, that would fool the Germans into believing that this was standard Allied doctrine. Actually, on D-Day in Normandy, seaborne landings would be made shortly after dawn.

Back in the summer of 1943, German intelligence picked up reports that Bulgarian Czar Boris III was secretly sending peace feelers to the British. Adolf Hitler was furious and alarmed by the news and demanded that Boris meet with him at Berchtesgaden on August 21. A stormy session erupted, during which the fuehrer angrily threatened the czar and which resulted in Boris' agreement to remain an ally of the Third Reich.

A week later, Czar Boris collapsed in his palace in Sofia and died within an hour. In Berlin, Propaganda Minister Joseph Goebbels announced that the Bulgarian leader had succumbed to a rare poison, possibly snake venom—yet another mysterious tangle in the Balkans.[3]

Clearly, Czar Boris had been murdered. But who had committed the deed? The Germans, British, Americans, Soviets, or the Bulgarians themselves? Hitler suspected that the British secret service was the culprit, although he had been blaming that agency for nearly every mysterious activity that had taken place in Europe for the past two decades.

Whoever may have been responsible for the czar's demise, Brigadier Clarke intended to cash in on the ensuing unrest, turmoil, and suspicions within Bulgaria to launch against that country an accelerated combined diplomatic, political, propaganda, and sabotage campaign. Its purpose was to inflame anti-Hitler sentiment and to strengthen Zeppelin's storyline that Bulgaria was about to be invaded by the Allies.

Meanwhile in Washington, OSS chief Bill Donovan, who had been thwarted in his scheme to penetrate the Kremlin by exchanging intelligence missions, continued to communicate with the NKVD. General P. M Fitin, the "un-Russian" intelligence official whom Donovan had met during his trip to Moscow in December 1943, provided information to the OSS boss concerning the situation inside Bulgaria. In return, Donovan sent Fitin OSS field intelligence from Bulgaria, including reports by Karl von Kelokowski, a German agent who had defected to the OSS. Von Kelokowski had a direct pipeline into the upper councils of the Bulgarian government and knew that the Bulgarians were seeking a means for getting out of the war.

At the same time, Hungary became a Zeppelin target for creating a climate of looming Allied invasion by stirring up strife, discension, and unrest. Hungary had been a German ally since mid–1941, when Admiral Miklós Horthy de Nagybánya, the country's regent, had sent the 1st and 2nd Hungarian armies into Russia with the Wehrmacht on what Horthy called "a holy crusade."[4]

That noble cause soured when the fuehrer failed to make a rapid conquest of the Soviet Union by the winter of 1941–1942 and Admiral Horthy began having doubts over the wisdom of his linking arms with Adolf Hitler. So in the spring of 1942, Horthy appointed Miklós Kallay, an experienced politician and wealthy landowner, to be prime minister with the implied goal of seeking peace with the Western Allies.

Kallay made contact with the British through the Vatican in Rome, and rumors swept through Europe that Hungary was on the brink of defection. When Adolf Hitler learned of Prime Minister Kallay's action, he threw a classic tantrum and bitterly denounced the Hungarian leader as "enemy number one of the German people."[5] However, the British and the Americans turned cold shoulders to the peace overture, and Hungary had no alternative but to continue fighting.

Had the British and Americans rejected Kallay's peace feeler because it conflicted with goals of Zeppelin? Pulling Hungary out of the war might have resulted in prying loose a few divisions the Germans were keeping there to repulse the reported pending Allied invasion of that country. These divisions could then be sent to northwest France to help man the Atlantic Wall.

Whatever may have been the case, Miklós Kallay was deeply alarmed by the fuehrer's dire threats. Kallay, through contacts in Berlin, knew that Hitler had ordered his commanders to create Case Margarethe I, an operation to send 11 German divisions rapidly into Hungary in the event it tried to defect.

Prime Minister Kallay then played his trump card. Charles T. Howie, a British colonel who had fled from a German POW (prisoner of war) camp, was being held in relative comfort in Budapest. Kallay provided Howie with a radio transmitter and operator and asked him to make contact with the Royal Navy at Malta, an island in the western Mediterranean. Howie was instructed to state that Andrew Frey, a Budapest newspaperman, would be sent as an emissary with an offer for Hungary to defect from Germany. The defection would take place when the Allies landed an airborne division near Budapest.

At considerable risk to his own life, Andrew Frey sneaked out of Hungary and met with the British at Cairo. As a result of the conference, Miklós Kallay received a message from the British: "We propose that [you] send to Istanbul, as soon as possible, two senior Hungarian officers to discuss details of the proposal received."[6]

The message added that one George Paloczi-Horvath, a man of Hungarian ancestry, would deal with the Hungarian delegation. Kallay was jolted by both the need for another conference and by the British nominating Paloczi-Horvath, who, Kallay was convinced, was an undercover agent of the Russian secret service.

A few days later, Miklós Kallay was given a second jolt by an editorial that appeared in *The Times* of London. It declared that "certain states, including Hungary, should not fancy that they could save themselves by belated efforts to escape from the sinking [Nazi] ship." Kallay reasoned that the editorial had been a plant to foment bloody fighting between the Wehrmacht and the Hungarian army and people.

Could Kim Philby, the British arch-traitor high in MI-5, have arranged for the editorial in order to soften up Hungary for eventual takeover by his masters in the Kremlin? Or had Brigadier Dudley Clarke planted *The Times* article as a ploy of Zeppelin?

Despite the apparent efforts by unknown parties to have his overtures to the Western Allies brought to the attention of Adolf Hitler, Prime Minister Kallay tried again. On September 9, 1943, Ladislas Veres, an official of the press section of the Hungarian Foreign Ministry, called on J. C. Sterndale Bennett, the British minister to Turkey, in Istanbul. Under cover of night, the two men climbed aboard the British embassy's old yacht and sailed on the Sea of Mamora.

Free from prying eyes—although two members of the crew were British secret service agents—Ladislas Veres said that Hungary was willing to accept the Allies' principle of unconditional surrender but that it could not be implemented until the Anglo-American armies reached the Hungarian frontiers for fear of reprisals from the fuehrer. Bennett replied that he had been authorized by the governments of the United States and Great Britain to offer assurance that Hungary's capitulation would be kept secret until all three parties agreed that the surrender should be made public.

Prime Minister Kallay agreed to the British proposal, unaware that he was being manipulated as part of Zeppelin. The Western Allies had no intention of even approaching the border of Hungary. When Veres returned to Budapest, Kallay was jubilant, believing, in his words, that he had "brought my nation into a safe harbor."[7]

Kallay's euphoria soon turned to disillusionment. A few days later, a British and American team arrived by parachute outside Budapest in the dead of night—but it was not the secret group of liaison officers that the prime minister hoped would work covertly with the Hungarian government. Kallay had never heard of Zeppelin, but he complained that the parachuted group had been sent to organize conspiracies and create disturbances within Hungary. The deft hands of Brigadier Dudley Clarke and his A-Force seemed to have been at work.

Brigadier Clarke, the master of unorthodox warfare, was craftily bringing to bear every deception weapon in the Western Allies' arsenal to suggest that the Balkans were about to be invaded at several locales. Large numbers of bogus combat units as well as genuine elements of the Anglo-American armies, air forces, and navies, along with propagandists, saboteurs, and camouflage experts, would play roles.

One of the initial targets suggested by the Zeppelin scenario was Crete, with the operation set for the middle of March 1944. Crete is an oblong-shaped island 186 miles in length lying in the eastern Mediterranean about 150 miles southwest of Turkey. Crete had been in German hands since May 31, 1941, when Adolf Hitler conquered the Greek island with the mightiest paratroop and glider assault in history up to that time. Nearly the entire British force defending the island had been wiped out or captured.

Tobruk, a Mediterranean port in Cyrennaica, a province of Libya, was the logical selection as a base for mounting the operation. Although Tobruk's population was only some 5,000, it was noted for its fine harbor, one of the best in North Africa.

When Zeppelin was launched in late February 1944, a beehive of activity erupted as roads and railroads leading to Tobruk were improved and expanded. The Red Cross markings on the roofs of hospitals in and near the town were repainted, giving the impression that General Jumbo Wilson expected heavy Luftwaffe bombing raids to disrupt preparations for the Crete assault.

Tobruk was infested with left-behind German spies, mainly natives eager to pocket some money. So a swarm of British undercover agents, wearing civilian clothes, spent nights boozing in waterfront bars and whispering rumors that the target of all the Allied activity was Crete.

Since Crete was Greek territory, it was logical that Greek troops would participate in driving the Germans from their homeland. Therefore, British officers began giving strenuous combat training to Greek troops in Libya.

After the Wehrmacht would be driven from Crete, a temporary Allied administration would have to be set up on the island, the fourth largest in the Mediterranean. So A-Force deceptionists ordered letterheads (stationery) and office supplies from North African printers. Doubtless, German intelligence learned of these administrative acquisitions before the ink was dry.

Maps of Crete—marked "Most Secret" and "For Selective Distribution"— were printed and steps were taken to make sure that one or two copies reached the hands of locals known to be German agents. A pamphlet, *A Guide to Crete*, was printed by the thousands at firms that were sympathetic to the Germans. These pieces were for distribution to the invading troops—or so it was implied.

Wireless traffic, all of it plausible but meaningless, was accelerated in the Tobruk region for monitoring by the highly capable German Y-Service. A special U.S. Navy team and its sophisticated equipment were brought in to radio messages that indicated scores of landing craft were being brought to Tobruk through the narrow Strait of Gibraltar at the western end of the Mediterranean.

Tobruk's harbor was crammed with genuine landing craft, which earlier had been assembled for a real, but abandoned, Allied assault against Trieste, a large Italian port at the northern end of the Adriatic Sea, near the western frontier of Yugoslavia. Camouflage technicians greatly increased these genuine landing craft with scores of dummy ones constructed of wood and canvas and floated by empty oil barrels.

To support the Balkans illusion, 100 gliders suddenly appeared on airfields outside Tobruk. One hundred and fifty British Mosquitos, 58 American twin-boomed Lightnings, and 197 other genuine fighter planes were flown to airstrips in the eastern Mediterranean, within easy range of Balkans targets, and left in plain sight on the runways.

In Egypt, 12 large landing craft put on a clever show for land-based German spies (of which there was no shortage) and snooping Luftwaffe airplanes. These landing craft sailed through the Suez Canal to Alexandria by day, and then, when night fell, they retraced their route back to Suez. This ploy was intended to indicate that a steady stream of landing craft was pouring into the Mediterranean. British naval stations at Suez and Alexandria flooded the air over Egypt with wireless messages, indicating that they were controlling the passage of "hundreds" of these landing craft.

Although the phony British Twelfth Army would direct the fictitious Crete assault, real Anglo-American forces helped to create the illusion of an invasion being mounted. Tobruk's antiaircraft defenses were increased, and when Luftwaffe reconnaissance planes streaked over, they ran into a heavy concentration of fire—a fact that did not escape German intelligence.

Tough British Commandos, armed to the teeth and with faces painted black with a mixture of charcoal and olive oil, slipped ashore in Crete and at other points in the Balkans under cover of night. They carried out orders to "shoot up the place'' before retiring to submarines waiting offshore. Royal Air Force and American bombers pounded key targets in Crete and in the Balkans. Allied reconnaissance flights were stepped up, with the focus on Canea and Heraklion, the two major cities of Crete. Thousands of propaganda leaflets, designed to undermine the morale of German soldiers, were dropped over Crete and elsewhere in the Balkans. Anglo-American naval task forces increased attacks on German shipping in the Mediterranean.

A-Force deceptionists planted articles (including ones that quoted real Greek soldiers-in-exile about how eager they were to be returning to their homeland) in Mediterranean newspapers focusing on General Jumbo Wilson's deep interest in Crete and the Balkans.

A widespread whispering campaign was launched throughout the eastern Mediterranean. A lady of Greek descent (an A-Force plant) in Suez swore her bridge club to secrecy, then disclosed that she had heard from a highly reliable source that the Allied invasion target was Crete. ''Now, my dears, don't breathe a word of that to *anyone!*'' she cautioned. In teeming Alexandria, the chief port, second largest city in Egypt and a site of a heavy British naval concentration, reports circulated that the reason so many Royal Navy officers had suddenly disappeared was that they had been sent to Tobruk to help mount an invasion.

American OSS and British SOE agents accelerated the delivery of weapons, ammunition, and supplies to underground forces throughout the Balkans to make it appear that an invasion was imminent. Among those involved in this widespread operation was 28-year-old Sterling Hayden, the tall and handsome Hollywood star who had joined the OSS two years earlier because of his admiration for Wild Bill Donovan.[8]

Lieutenant Hayden was in charge of an OSS operational base at the small port of Monopoli, on the eastern coast of Italy across the Adriatic Sea from German-held Yugoslavia. Using a fleet of 14 schooners provided by the Wrigley Chewing Gum Company executive in charge of the OSS Maritime Unit in Cairo, Hayden, a merchant marine sailor before his overnight movie stardom, ran accoutrements of war through the *Kriegsmarine* (German navy) Adriatic blockade to Yugoslav guerrillas known as Partisans and led by Russian-trained Communist Josip Broz, who was called Tito by his followers.

Tito's Communist-oriented Partisans were spending half of their time fighting the Germans and the remainder battling another Yugoslav underground force named the Chetniks, named after a similar guerrilla group of World War I. Led by bearded, bespectacled Colonel Draza Mihailovic, chief of staff of a Yugoslav army unit at the time of his country's capitulation to the Germans in 1941, the Chetniks pledged their loyalty to King Peter, the teenaged monarch who fled Yugoslavia when the Wehrmacht invaded his country and established a government-in-exile in London.

Disputes between Tito's and Mihailovic's guerrillas in Yugoslavia spilled over into southern Italy, where both groups had liaison men at OSS and SOE stations in Bari. When two Chetniks who were posted to the OSS station disappeared and were never heard from again, rumors were that they had been kidnapped and murdered by Tito's men. Clashes between the two Yugoslav guerrilla groups in Bari became so heated that OSS men who had been involved with the Chetniks were cautioned not to venture into the streets of Bari unless they were armed for protection against Tito's sympathizers.[9]

Meanwhile in southern Italy, another Zeppelin illusion was being created. The bogus Polish III Corps, consisting of the dummy Polish 7th Infantry Division and the half-fictional Polish 2nd Armored Division, were pretending to get ready for an assault against Albania, with the main objective being the capital of Tirana.

Soon the fake Polish operation ran into a roadblock. Unaware that the invading force was fictional, Tito and his Yugoslav Partisans objected violently over having Poles introduced into the Balkans. In the interest of harmony, General Jumbo Wilson ordered Colonel Dudley Clarke to drop the Poles from the deception plan. However, Clarke's goal already had been reached—German intelligence knew of the Polish force that was threatening Albania.

On the night of February 22, 1944, Colonel Gardyne de Chastelain, a member of a prominent French family that long before had settled in England, was poised to bail out of a British bomber as it approached Bucharest, the capital of Romania. Before the war, De Chastelain had been an executive of the Phoenix Oil and Transport Company in Bucharest and was returning to Romania on Zeppelin deception business.

A green light flashed on in the bomber and de Chastelain dropped into the black sky. On the ground, a reception committee of Romanian underground warriors were to be waiting to collect him. But someone had squealed, and the parachutist came down into the arms of a squad of Romanian policemen.

Crashing to the ground with de Chastelain were three more British officers. They, too, were collared. Instead of being shot as spies, de Chastelain and his colleagues, much to their astonishment, were driven to a comfortable villa near Bucharest. There they were served sumptuous meals and even provided with servants.

Colonel de Chastelain suspected that he and his comrades were to be the centerpieces for some devious plot hatched by the Hungarians and their German colleagues. Then, within a few days, the real reason for this bizarre scenario surfaced: Marshal Ion Antonescu, the Romanian dictator, planned to use them as pawns in a clandestine effort to break away from Nazi Germany.

On seizing control of Romania on September 4, 1940, Ion Antonescu promoted himself to field marshal and bestowed upon himself the title of *conducator*. When Adolf Hitler's legions plunged into the Soviet Union at dawn on June 22, 1941, Marshal Antonescu sent two Romanian armies, totaling 14 divisions, to fight alongside the Wehrmacht.

Although the Romanian soldiers were skilled and tough, their ranks were steadily chopped to pieces by the Red Army meat grinder. For many months, Marshal Antonescu had been seeking a means to get out of the war. Now, through Colonel de Chastelain, the dictator felt that he had the means at hand to accomplish that goal.

Time was crucial. Through an emissary, Gardyne de Chastelain was requested to use his wireless set and operator to contact a British headquarters and arrange a reception for Antonescu's peace representative. De Chastelain made the contact, and Alexander Cretzianu, a former secretary general of the Romanian Foreign Ministry, was dispatched to Ankara, the Turkish capital. Cretzianu was instructed to inform the British and Americans that "everything was in readiness for an Allied invasion of the Balkans."[10]

Cretizanu's peace mission failed; he was stonewalled by the Anglo-American diplomats. Disillusioned, Cretzianu returned to Bucharest and took the bad news to Marshal Antonescu.

Since Zeppelin's fictitious scenario was for the Crete and Balkans invasions to hit in late March, A-Force had to create a plausible reason why the operations were being postponed for a month in order to keep German divisions pinned down in southeastern Europe. Through Double-Cross' turned agents in England, whispers, planted scraps of information, radio messages sent in easily breakable codes, and other special means, it came across that the target date had been moved ahead 30 days (to late April) because the Allied armies in Italy had failed to make expected progress, resulting in the entire strategic timetable in the Mediterranean being thrown out of kilter.

Meanwhile, Adolf Hitler, conceivably influenced by Bodyguard machinations and the real threat of defections by Balkan nations, was ready to launch Case Margarethe. Just after dawn on March 19, 1944, several Wehrmacht divisions plunged into Hungary on three sides. There was virtually no armed resistance. Prime Minister Miklós Kallay fled into the Turkish embassy where he was granted sanctuary.[11]

12

Focus on the Atlantic Wall

A handsome white palace at Wilhelmplatz 8/9, untouched by the scars of war in Berlin, was the home of the Ministry of Propaganda. It had been operating in that structure since March 1933 under the guiding genius of Paul Joseph Goebbels, the indefatigable, diminutive figure known behind his back as the Propaganda Dwarf. Inside the mansion, night and day, beat the heart of the global Nazi propaganda machine.

Goebbels, the son of a store clerk, was an educated man with literary pretensions; he joined the Nazi party in 1924. He soon was mesmerized by Adolf Hitler's leadership and became the *Gauleiter* (leader) of the party in Berlin. During the Nazi struggle to seize power in Germany, Goebbels was in charge of publicity and edited *Der Angriff* in which he relentlessly attacked Jews, Communists, and American capitalists.

When Hitler took charge of the nation, Goebbels controlled all aspects of communications in the Third Reich—newspapers, magazines, radio, book publishing, theaters, and moviemaking. A cynic and compulsive liar, he variously attributed his pronounced limp from a World War I wound or from a stretch in jail while battling for Nazism in its early years. Actually, he had been stricken with polio as a boy.

Now, in March 1944, Goebbels launched an all-out propaganda blitz designed to intimidate the Anglo-Americans and conceivably cause them to reconsider any plans to invade northwest Europe. The Nazi leader took to Radio Berlin and boasted:

> The fuehrer has fortified the coast of Europe from the North Cape [Norway] to the Mediterranean and installed the deadliest weapons that the 20th century can produce. That is why any enemy attack, even the most powerful and ferocious possible to imagine, is bound to fail.[1]

Hordes of Goebbels' photographers and moving-picture cameramen were racing up and down the English Channel coast, filming the prodigious concrete bunkers and big gun enclosures that were especially prevalent around the major ports—Cherbourg, Le Havre, Boulogne, Calais, Ostend, Zeebrugge, The Hague. A few days later, cinemas in the Third Reich showed newsreels of these mighty, "invincible" fortifications, and within weeks the same footage would be seen by theater patrons in Great Britain and the United States. Newsreel narrators in the latter two countries would describe the clips as "captured German film," but in reality the Wehrmacht deceptionists had made it possible for the clips to be pilfered by the French underground without the clandestine warriors realizing they were being duped by Nazi propaganda.

Aware that German newspapers reached neutral embassies around the world and were devoured by British intelligence in London, Goebbels plastered on the front pages dramatic five-column pictures of the heavy-caliber guns whose snouts were poked seaward. Next to these photos would be stories in which Wehrmacht junior officers defending the Atlantic Wall would be quoted about the "bloodbath" that awaited the invaders.

Goebbels' propagandists dug out old photographs of the scores of Canadian corpses strewn along the beach at Dieppe, France, after a catastrophic raid a year and a half earlier, and pointed out that this was the fate that awaited any force brash to assault the Atlantic Wall.

This relentless Nazi propaganda barrage had a certain impact at SHAEF in Grosvenor Square (called *Eisenhowerplatz* by wags). Many officers felt that Adolf Hitler was hoarding diabolical secret weapons that would be unleashed on D-Day, devices that would shatter Allied naval and air armadas and cut down the assault troops, leaving huge mounds of them on the beaches and floating offshore.

No one knew for sure what secret weapons the fuehrer had. There was no shortage of whispered conjectures in dark corners of the SHAEF headquarters. Some felt that the Germans would set fire to the Channel for two miles out to sea, just as the Allied assault waves were heading for the beaches, incinerating by the thousands those caught in the inferno.

Predictions were heard that long-range rockets would be loosed against the ports where Allied assault troops would concentrate to be ferried across the Channel for the invasion. Some of these rockets would be tipped with "freeze bombs," rumors had it, and everyone within 200 yards of impact would be frozen to death. The "freeze bomb" was one of Goebbels' pet schemes, hatched by his fertile brain.

Lethal rays and radioactive dust were other possible German secret weapons to be unleased on the invading forces, it was rumored. Speculation grew until it bordered on the neurotic—or crossed the border. Joseph Goebbels cleverly fed that neurosis with a wide variety of rumors, deceptions, and scare stories until the "secret weapons" phobia within Anglo-American ranks reached epidemic proportions.[2]

Pessimism even burrowed into the highest Anglo-American councils in England. How much of this negative mood resulted from Goebbels' relentless propaganda barrage would never be determined. At a conference in mid-March, Major General Walter B. "Beetle" Smith, Ike Eisenhower's chief of staff and alter ego, could not conceal his gloom. Smith declared solemnly that the Germans had 12 mobile divisions behind the Atlantic Wall in Normandy and suggested that a decision on bringing additional landing craft from the Mediterranean to England be held up.

This inference was not lost on those officers present: Smith was saying that Neptune might have to be called off in order to avoid an Allied holocaust on the far shore.

Smith's dark outlook was still evident a week later in conversation over a scrambled telephone with a Pentagon general in Washington. "We may find we can't do Overlord," General Smith confided. "The buffer of German divisions confronting us across the Channel is just now approaching the absolute maximum we can handle."

Most of the American, British, and Canadian troops who would spearhead Neptune were convinced that a bloodbath would engulf them when they charged ashore against the gun-studded Atlantic Wall. British commanders reported that 90 percent of their units' junior officers felt that they would not survive D-Day.

General Omar Bradley, commander of American forces for Neptune, discovered during an inspection of the 29th Infantry Division (elements of which would assault Omaha beach) that nearly all of its 14,000 men were talking of 90 percent casualties on D-Day. Alarmed by the finding, Bradley, certainly no orator, gathered division officers around him as he stood on the hood of a jeep. "This stuff about tremendous losses on D-Day is tommyrot," the soft-spoken, professorial Bradley stressed with a conviction he may not have entirely felt. "Some of you won't come back, but it'll be very few." Bradley had hoped to allay the intense fears. "I doubt if I did much good," he confided to his aide on the ride back to London.[3]

At an encampment of the U.S. 4th Infantry Division, which would strike at a beach code-named Utah, morale plummeted when one soldier went to pieces and was dragged away screaming, "We'll all be killed! They'll use our dead bodies to walk over to get ashore!"[4]

As March turned into April and the lush meadows of England were putting on their finest greenery, Prime Minister Winston Churchill exclaimed in a moment of gloom over Neptune: "Why are we trying to do *this*?"[5]

Churchill's closest military advisor, Field Marshal Alan Brooke, whose courage had been legend in World War I, scrawled in his diary: "I am very uneasy about this whole operation. At the best, it will come very short of expectations of the bulk of the people, namely those who know nothing about its enormous difficulties. At its worst, it may well be the most ghastly disaster of the whole war."[6]

While Joseph Goebbels' propaganda blitz to intimidate the Western Allies into scuttling any plans to assault the Atlantic Wall was in full bloom, the Wehrmacht in France was launching a clever deception ploy to mislead SHAEF intelligence about its troop strengths and deployments. The goal of this stratagem was to lead the Allies into believing that the German army in France was more powerful than it actually was.

Early in March, a German colonel in a staff car drove into Bayeux, a picturesque and tranquil town eight miles inland from the Channel in Normandy. The officer went to the mayor and told him that a new division would be moving into the region and that a number of Bayeux buildings would be commandeered for its use. Twenty-four hours later, three vehicles carrying perhaps ten Germans rolled into Bayeux and began reconnoitering the town. They were careless enough to tell citizens that they were the advance party for a new division that was being brought to Normandy from the Russian front.

A day later, a convoy of Wehrmacht trucks halted a mile outside of Bayeux and a company of *Feldgrau* (field gray; the average German soldier) hopped out, formed up, and marched through and out of Bayeux, hoping to give the impression that they were part of the new division. Actually, they had been garrisoned for months in another French town about 40 miles away.

That same company—and others—regularly would repeat the scenario. They would dismount, trek through a town, climb back into trucks, then march into another city 50 miles away. If a genuine Wehrmacht division actually was brought in from the Third Reich, the Russian front, or the Balkans, German officers informed local French authorities that *two* divisions were arriving.

These and other German deception measures designed to confound and mislead Allied intelligence resulted in officers at Field Marshal Gerd von Rundstedt's headquarters having to keep two lists—one real and one false—of their divisions in France. This procedure kept von Rundstedt's staff from becoming muddled. One list showed the "facts" about dummy divisions, and a second column provided accurate information on genuine divisions. As a component of the German deception plan, maps of Western Europe were created showing where all the divisions—real and fake—were located. These maps were leaked to the French, Belgian, and Dutch undergrounds and soon, as intended, reached England.

In order to convince Adolf Hitler's allies, the Japanese warlords, that Germany had overpowering forces in Western Europe that were capable of smashing any Anglo-American invasion, copies of these same phony maps were supplied to the Nipponese ambassador to Vichy, France, seat of 82-year-old French Field Marshal Henri Pétain's puppet government.

These deception stratagems to influence Anglo-American intelligence into overestimating enemy strength in France would be reported to London, the Germans knew, for they were aware that one of Europe's most productive underground networks—*Centurie*—was active in Normandy. Centurie had been founded in late 1942, one of the spy networks under gangly General Charles de Gaulle, who led the Free French in London. Soon afterward, a powerfully built former soldier named Marcel Girard, who worked as a traveling salesman for a cement firm in Caen, the historical capital of Normandy, was recruited to lead Centurie. Forty-one, graying, looking older than his years but possessing enormous energy and initiative, Girard (code-named Moureau) plunged into the prodigious assignment, using his job as a cover. Only his patriotic boss in Caen knew that the salesman never peddled a pound of cement.

Girard roamed the Normandy coast—from Ouistreham on the Calvados coast westward through Coursuelles, Arromanches, Colleville, Vierville, and Port-en-Bessein, then northward up the eastern shore of the Cherbourg peninsula to Cherbourg. Always he was under the threat of imminent arrest, but he continued to bring in new recruits for his spy network—farmers, housewives, doctors, train conductors, plumbers, mechanics, government officials, merchants, policemen, secretaries.

No one in Centurie had an inkling that one day powerful Allied forces would storm ashore along these Normandy beaches to be code-named Utah, Omaha, Sword, Gold, and Juno. Most of the amateur spies were sustained in their efforts by religious faith and a fierce resolve to rid their beloved France of the Nazi yoke.

In late 1942, the innovative Marcel Girard startled other Centurie leaders with a proposal that they create a large map of the Atlantic Wall in Normandy. He proposed that thousands of ordinary French men and women along the coast serve as the eyes and ears for the mapping project and that they pass their bits and pieces of information on the Wall to a central collecting point in Caen.

It was an "impossible" task. Yet Centurie plunged into it. A major impediment to the recruiting of operatives along the Channel coast was posed by the *Zone Interdite* (Forbidden Zone) set up by the Germans; it ran inland for several miles. An outsider had to have a legitimate reason for getting into and lingering around the restricted area. But this problem was solved when each Centurie recruiting agent was furnished with a set of official German identity papers and passes— all painstakingly counterfeited by a 38-year-old Caen housewife.

One morning in Cherbourg, the major Normandy port that would be the key objective of Neptune, several bored German sentries looked on casually as a black-cassocked Catholic priest was enthusiastically engaged in an impromptu game of kickball with several youngsters. There was much laughing and shouting. The boys were happy to have a revered man of the cloth playing ball with them in the street. How curious that a priest would be idly scampering about with the boys, the sentries guarding a casemated big-gun position near the docks may have mused to themselves.

Whatever his ecclesiastical talents, the perspiring priest obviously was not skilled at kickball. He drew back his foot and gave the oval a terrific—and errant—boot. The ball sailed past the youngsters and headed directly for the concrete-enclosed gun position some 40 yards away.

"I'll get it!" the man of the cloth shouted, apparently embarrassed that he had performed so ineptly. He chased after the ball all the way to the gun position where it had rolled. Now the German guards, who had been lulled into inattention, suddenly realized that an unauthorized person was trotting into the large-caliber gun position in pursuit of an errant ball. *"Verboten! Verboten!"* the alarmed Feldgrau shouted as they chased after the priest, frantically waving their arms.

By this time, the clergyman had reached the ball. He picked it up and started back with it, apologizing profusely for unwittingly intruding into a forbidden area. Minutes later, the priest concluded his strenuous athletic activity and began to walk away. He was approached by two strangers in civilian garb and took them to be French, but he could not be certain. They might be Gestapo agents. One of the strangers said to the man in the flowing black robe, "We know you're not a priest."

"Why, I don't know what you're talking about," the kickball player replied. "Of course I'm a priest."

"Look, we don't know who you are, but you're not a priest. You'd better get the hell out of here before the Gestapo grabs you!"

A flash of concern spread across the face of the man in black with the backward white collar. Indeed he was a bogus priest camouflaged for a mission, a member of Centurie whose assigned perilous task had been to get a closeup look at the German gun position and report the caliber of the weapon and its firing direction.

Before rapidly departing, the "priest" was curious. "Tell me, how did you *know* I'm not a priest?" he inquired of the two strangers. Pointing toward his feet, one of the men replied, "Because those bright red socks of yours stick out like two beacons in the night!"

Nearly every day, bits of information on German defenses and troops along the Atlantic Wall arrived at the central collection point in Caen. There skilled cartographers belonging to the network tediously incorporated the information on thousands of notes, rough diagrams, drawings, and other data provided by Girard's amateur spies into a series of maps of sectors along the Atlantic Wall.

These map sketches were collected by couriers and carried, usually by train, to a dingy suite of rooms in an old building located in a rundown section of Paris. These inconspicuous quarters were a central headquarters for the Battle of the Atlantic Wall, as the French underground called it.

A bespectacled, round-face young Frenchman named Jacques Piette (code-named Colonel *Personne*, Colonel Nobody) directed the spy network's Paris communications nerve center. There, dedicated checkers daily sifted through a mountain of material collected by the spies in Normandy and bundled it for transfer to London.

Lysanders, small, lumbering airplanes flown by Royal Air Force pilots, landed under the cover of night at predesignated pastures outside Paris. The planes taxied up to signaling flashlights held by French underground members, collected the bundles of Centurie Atlantic Wall maps and data, sped down the grassy field, and lifted off for England.

By far the most significant contribution to creating a detailed map of 125 miles of the Atlantic Wall came from a highly unlikely source: a daring (many said foolhardy) Centurie agent named René Duchez. A small, unimpressive Caen house painter in his mid-forties, Duchez had pulled off one of the great espionage capers in the history of warfare.

Duchez was well known to the Caen Gestapo, whose agents considered him to be grossly retarded. The house painter had a talent for putting on a convincing portrayal of an idiot seized by epileptic fists, and he loved to taunt the hated Gestapo. If Duchez spotted Gestapo agents in a cafe when he was drinking late at night (which was often), he would wobble toward their table, fall to the floor at their feet, jerking, twitching, and uttering strange gurgling noises. His eyes would bulge until they promised to burst from their sockets, and he drooled large amounts of saliva onto the highly polished shoes of the Gestapo men. The "fit" would continue for two or three minutes, until the disgusted Germans could endure no more and stalked out of the saloon.

On the night of May 13, 1943, René Duchez, feigning the wild look he used in the event the Gestapo was present, entered the Café des Touristes and sat at a table with Marcel Girard, the burly Centurie chief. Girard was alarmed; clearly Duchez had been drinking heavily, and when in this condition, he took an especial delight in mocking German customers, thereby attracting unwanted attention to himself and those with him. Girard glanced around the room and spotted two men he believed to be Gestapo agents, and the bar was filled with carousing Feldgrau.

Under the table, Duchez slipped a large envelope to Girard, and when the latter asked what was inside it, the clever painter put on his idiot face and replied casually, "Oh, it's nothing but a blueprint of the entire Atlantic Wall in Normandy."

Girard felt a chill race up his spine. René Duchez, was a great joker; was this was one of his skits for taunting the Germans in the room? "Where did you get it?" Girard whispered, convinced that the eyes of the enemy soldiers and the Gestapo men were focused on him. "Stole it from the Todt Organization," Duchez replied breezily.[7]

In a low voice, Girard swore at the grinning Duchez, and he had to fight an overpowering urge to rush out of the bar. The Centurie leader stashed the envelope in his pocket—he did not dare look at its contents—then got up, shook hands with Duchez who had gone into his drooling act, and strolled out of the cafe. Girard's legs felt like jelly, and he expected to hear a German shout, "Halt!" at any moment. If this was another of the free-spirited painter's jokes, Girard solemnly pledged to strangle him at the first opportunity.

When the Centurie chief reached home, he opened Duchez's envelope and removed a folded, six-foot-long blueprint. His heart began thumping furiously. Stamped across the top of the blueprint were the words *Sonderzeichnungen*, *Streng Geheim* (Special Blueprint, Strict Secret) and *Sofortprogramm* (highest priority construction).

In a flash, the stunned Girard knew precisely what it was: the blueprint for fortifications of the Atlantic Wall in Normandy, a 125-mile stretch between Le Havre on the east and Cherbourg on the west, depicting all bunkers, gun batteries, machine-gun and flame-thrower positions, ammunition dumps, and command posts. A week later, the priceless blueprint was in London.

Marcel Girard was racked with curiosity, and he sought out René Duchez to find out how he had pilfered the top-secret document. Over glasses of watery beer in the Café des Toristes, Duchez told his story.

Earlier that month, outside the *mairie* (police station) in Caen, Duchez spotted a notice inviting bids for a minor wallpaper job at the headquarters of Todt Organization, the German paramilitary engineering outfit that was charged with building the Atlantic Wall. The crafty Duchez recognized the notice as a chance for him to get inside a German headquarters and poke around.

Armed with his sample wallpaper book, Duchez appeared the next day at the Todt headquarters on the Avenue Bagatelle in Caen and asked to see *Bauleiter* Hermann Schnedderer. Grinning foolishly at the Germans he passed in the hallways, Duchez was escorted to the office of Schnedderer, an aging reserve colonel who had been a successful engineer in peacetime.

Seated at his desk, the colonel began thumbing through the sample book and marked several patterns that caught his eye. Duchez, trying to be helpful, leaned over the German's shoulder and purposely drooled saliva on the colonel's expensive, field gray tunic. Schnedderer selected the pattern he wanted and quickly accepted Duchez's bid price, which was ridiculously low.

Then a captain came into the room, hardly taking note of the town idiot, and piled a stack of blueprints on the colonel's desk. Moments later, Schnedderer was called out of the room and Duchez spotted the word *Atlantikwall* on the top blueprint.

Duchez's mind was spinning. Here was golden chance. Should he steal the map? Could he get out of the headquarters with the blueprint on his person without being searched? If he did pull off the coup, would not the map be quickly missed and the Gestapo sent in search of the house painter? And would he be risking his life for nothing—he had no way of knowing if the Allies even planned to invade Normandy?

Duchez took the top map off the stack, folded it carefully, and slipped it behind a wall mirror moments before the office door swung open and Bauleiter Schnedderer returned. Duchez was told to come back the following Monday and begin work.

Bright and early on the appointed day, René Duchez arrived at the Todt headquarters and learned from the gate sentry that Colonel Schnedderer had been called out of town. The guard refused to allow the Frenchman to enter the building, and the house painter began protesting loudly, while twitching, jerking, and drooling.

Hearing the racket at the front gate, a Todt officer came outside to investigate and Duchez told him about the deal he had cut with Bauleiter Schnedderer. The German knew nothing about the arrangement but allowed Duchez to enter the colonel's office and begin work.

Just before quitting time that afternoon, Duchez retrieved the Atlantic Wall blueprint from behind the mirror, thrust it into an empty wallpaper container, and strolled casually out of the German headquarters with the incriminating document under his arm. Outside two Feldgrau sentries eyed with disgust the grinning dimwit who bowed and saluted as he brushed past.

For many days, Marcel Girard expected the Germans to react with violence when they discovered that the map was missing and presumably had been stolen. But Caen remained outwardly tranquil. Royal Air Force photo intelligence in the months ahead revealed that the Wall was being built precisely to specifications. Perhaps Bauleiter Schnedderer, who had been victimized by the idiot Duchez, decided that he would report the theft to no one—as an urgent matter of self-preservation.[8]

Now, with the approach of Overlord in early 1944, a mammoth, detailed master map of the Normandy coastline had been pieced together, based on René Duchez's stolen blueprint and tens of thousands of scraps of information that had been obtained by Centurie agents. The map was being developed in a tightly guarded facility known as the Martian Room, located just outside London.

Updated daily, the Atlantic Wall map showed an amazing array of German defenses. Plotted in were the precise locations of coast and field artillery batteries, their caliber, ranges, and fields of fire and thickness of protective concrete covers; radar sites, machine-gun posts, flamethrowers, tank obstacles, and mine fields; blockhouses, command posts, tunnels, signal communications, barbed-wire entanglements, barracks, supply dumps, and vehicle parks. Even the positions of defending German units, down to platoon and squad levels, together with the names of their officers (captains and lieutenants), were being inked in.

Centurie paid an enormous price for this colossal achievement. Scores of its men and women were executed by the Gestapo. But when the Allies crossed the Channel, General Dwight Eisenhower would have more data on the Atlantic Wall at his fingertips than would German commanders in France and Berlin.

13

The Double-Cross "First Violins"

Although nearly all of Adolf Hitler's agents in the British Isles had been captured at the outbreak of war, the Double-Cross stable was swelled by an influx of "invasion spies" who began arriving in January 1944. Most of these newcomers had been dispatched from two neutral countries, Spain and Portugal, and their primary task was to ferret out and identify Allied forces.

These invasion spies were quickly collared by MI–5, which had been conveniently notified of their pending arrival through radio reports from Hamburg to their turned agents in England. Apprehended spies who refused to cooperate were bounced into Ham Commons, a former lunatic asylum, until they had a change of heart or marched to the gallows. The invasion spies were a motley crew: Spaniards, Yugoslavians, Danes, Belgians, Czechs, Dutchmen, Frenchmen, and Austrians. They were Nazi idealists, adventurers, malcontents, glory hunters, and money grubbers.

Since the first Nazi spies were hauled in by an MI–5 and Scotland Yard dragnet in September 1939, Double-Cross knew that if German intelligence were to trust and rely on them, their credibility would have to be painstakingly built up by their British case officers. This goal had been achieved largely by furnishing the Abwehr true, but harmless, information that the Germans could confirm by later events.

A true report was sent to Hamburg, for example, that a certain major British warship was sailing on the following morning for Gibraltar in the Mediterranean. Before this wireless message was dispatched by the double agent, the XX-Committee checked out Ultra intercepts to make certain that no German U-boat was in the vicinity and could arrive in time to torpedo the vessel. German spies infested Gibraltar, so when the warship arrived, they reported that fact to Hamburg—and the double agent's credibility soared with the Abwehr.

Every word a double agent radioed or wrote was carefully concocted by his Double-Cross controller. Like all planted intelligence, these reports had to contain kernels of truth mixed with fake impressions that the British hoped to foist onto the Abwehr.

When a British case officer took control of a turned German spy, his first task was to create a plausible background for him in England. In a carefully scripted scenario which was fed to Hamburg a bit at a time, a typical double agent had a job, a home, and friends—all of them fictitious. If subagents were recruited (that is, created by a case officer), they also would have to be given backgrounds and become real people.

A double agent would never be allowed to step out of character and economic status. If a turned spy was supposed to have a job waiting tables in a London restaurant, the Abwehr would have become deeply suspicious should he develop friends and contacts in London banking circles.

A turned spy's reports had to be consistent with his true educational background or technical skills. A young Belgian farmer recruited by the Abwehr and sent to England could not plausibly submit detailed reports on a new bomb the British were said to be developing.

It also was crucial that a double agent report to Hamburg from a perspective that would be plausible for a genuine spy. If the Abwehr radioed a request for a report on a closely guarded airfield in the Midlands, the case officer had to tailor the reply to reflect only what the spy could have seen while passing the facility on a train or in an automobile.

All of this required enormous concentration, skill, and a focus on microscopic detail by the Double-Cross case officers. In order not to trip themselves up and possible blow the entire Double-Cross apparatus, they had to file away in their brains the characteristics and lifestyle patterns they had created for their turned spies and nonexistent subagents.

It would be illogical for some 50 double agents, men and women, to go for months or years in England without being affected by the nagging problems of normal life. So to sustain the facade, the double agents periodically were fictionally afflicted with illnesses, losing jobs, or having to move unwillingly to another home.

By the law of averages, some of the German spies were bound to be caught, lose their nerve, get lazy, or give up spying because the Abwehr could not get their pay through to them. So periodically, the British case officers would decide to have one of the double agents suddenly "vanish"—his failure to report being interpreted by the Germans to mean that he had been captured, hit by a bus during a blackout, or otherwise no longer a productive spy. This scenario was enhanced a few times when a turned agent would send an urgent wireless signal to Hamburg in which he would say that "they" were hot on his heels and he would have to go into hiding.

British case officers had to keep current with the Abwehr's "secret language"—that is, its almost paranoiac penchant for sticking a code name on everything and everybody. The Abwehr invariably called England *Golfplatz* and the United States *Samland*. Should a case officer slip up and have his double agent inquire of Hamburg the meaning of Golfplatz, it could destroy that spy's credibility.

With the arrival of 1944, the Double-Cross prepared to use its stable of double agents in support of Operation Fortitude, a component of Bodyguard. Fortitude was divided into two parts. Fortitude North would be aimed at Scandinavian countries and designed to influence Adolf Hitler to keep the 27 divisions he had stationed in Denmark, Finland, and Norway idle on D-Day and for several weeks beyond in expectation of a combined American-British-Soviet invasion. Fortitude South involved an even more intricate fabrication, and its aim was to suggest to the fuehrer that the Anglo-American invasion against northern France would be launched across the narrow Strait of Dover against the Pas de Calais. This was intended to tie down the formidable German Fifteenth Army 170 miles northeast of the true landing beaches in Normandy.

There were subplots to Fortitude. Operation Ironside was intended to keep the German First Army stationary in the vicinity of Bordeaux, on the Bay of Biscay in southwestern France on the true D-Day and beyond by fictitious threats of an invasion at that locale, some 400 miles from Normandy. Operation Vendetta was designed to achieve the same result with the German Nineteenth Army which was defending the Riviera coast along the Mediterranean in southern France.

Yet another subplot of Fortitude was Operation Zeppelin which already had begun to influence Hitler and his high command into believing that a British-American-Soviet invasion of the Nazi-held Balkans was imminent. If all went well, some 25 Wehrmacht divisions might be tied down in the Balkans when the Allies smashed across the Channel on D-Day. Operation Diadem was the most direct of all the Fortitude machinations. It simply consisted of continuing to pin down perhaps 15 German divisions in Italy through orthodox military operations.

Fortitude, an incredibly complicated scenario, had a complex command arrangement. Although Colonel John Bevan and the London Controlling Section (working with the Joint Security Council in Washington, D.C.) maintained overall responsibility for Fortitude, the day-to-day direction of the deception plan was in the hands of U.S. Major General Harold R. "Pinky" Bull, a close operations advisor to Dwight Eisenhower at SHAEF.

The Double-Cross decided that the "orchestra" to be used to spread "facts" of Fortitude would be small. In the jargon of the espionage trade, the "first violins" would be the double agents whose credibility was high with the Abwehr. An analysis of how the Germans rated the double agents had been reached through the work of MI–5's ingenious wireless branch, the supersecret Radio Security Service (RSS).

Years earlier, the RSS had built a wireless intercept station at Hanslope Park, nine miles to the north of Station X and its Ultra operatives at Bletchley Park.

Over a period of months, a team of scholars, cryptanalysts, and academics, led by Oliver Strachey, gradually succeeded in breaking into signals flowing between the Abwehr in Berlin and Hamburg and their outposts in Madrid and Lisbon.

When an Abwehr message was intercepted and decoded by the RSS, it was passed along to the appropriate MI–5 section for evaluation and possible action or reaction. Abwehr chief Admiral Canaris, in essence, had British operatives set up directly in his personal office—even though they were wearing earphones at Hanslope Park.

A blizzard of messages between the Abwehr in the Third Reich and its outposts abroad threatened to inundate Oliver Strachey's boys at Hanslope Park. But from this deluge came numerous items that helped the British to uncover the identity of German spies in foreign countries. An Abwehr signal might state that "Moonbeam" had arrived safely in Barcelona and had checked into the International Hotel. This intelligence, intercepted at Hanslope Park, would be flashed to MI–5 agents in that Spanish city, and one or more of them would rush to the International and connive a look at the register, betraying the German agent.

Even though the first violins had been selected based on signals received by the RSS, could the Double-Cross really trust any of them? After all, they were spies. They already had renounced their allegiance to the Germans. One had switched his loyalty three times.

Utilizing the Double-Cross first violins to confound the Wehrmacht would be a delicate and risky business. No matter how elaborate the symphony, a single false note, intentional or otherwise, could destroy the illusion of an Allied invasion of the Pas de Calais. Worse, one slipup and the entire Bodyguard stratagem might be wrecked. The most horrible scenario that could evolve was that the first violins' messages might be "read in reverse" by a wily German intelligence and the true landing beaches in Normandy exposed rather than concealed.

The five first violins would be "Tate," the Danish draftsman Hans Hansen; "Brutus," a Pole who had worked for British intelligence in France and had been captured by the Gestapo and turned, or so the Germans thought; "Treasure," a Frenchwoman of Russian origin; "Tricycle," a slick Yugoslavian playboy; and "Garbo," a Spaniard who seemed to have had a lifelong ambition to become a spy and despised Nazism and communism with equal ferocity.

Brutus was Captain Roman Garby-Czerniawski, who had been assigned to the cryptanalytical service of the Polish General Staff and had been involved in smuggling the supersecret German coding machine, Enigma, out of Poland and to England. After Poland was overrun by the Wehrmacht in September 1939, Garby-Czerniawski continued his war on Hitler by slipping into Paris and becoming an agent (code-named Hubert) for Polish intelligence in London.

Then, in 1941, he was betrayed by his cipher assistant, a Frenchwoman named Mathilde Carré, who later would gain notoriety as the "Cat Woman" after squealing on many other members of *Interallié*, an underground network founded in France by Garby-Czerniawski. The Polish captain was arrested by German security police and thrown into Fresnes Prison to await execution.[1]

Colonel Joachim Rohleder, head of the Abwehr division responsible for penetrating the British secret service, offered the doomed Pole a proposition: if he would go to England as an Abwehr spy, 100 captured members of Interallié would not be executed. After lengthy meditation. Garby-Czerniawski agreed to the offer, provided that the 100 underground members were treated as prisoners of war.

A contract was struck and the Pole was given the cover name Armand. Then arrangements were made for his "escape." Two Abwehr agents picked up Armand from Fresnes Prison to go to an interrogation in Paris. When the car slowed at a sharp bend in the road, Armand, as planned, leaped out and ran into the woods. Playing their roles to the hilt, the Abwehr men gave chase and fired a few shots.[2]

As instructed, Armand fled to a certain house where he was given fresh clothes, false papers, and money. Then he made his way along a specified route to Spain, where he boarded a boat for England.[3]

Armand reached Britain in January 1943, presented himself to authorities as a Polish spy who had escaped death by fleeing in a hail of Abwehr bullets, and was routinely taken to the Royal Patriotic School for interrogation. Although leery of Armand's bona fides, the Double-Cross decided to employ him, and he received his third code name in 18 months—Brutus.

Garby-Czerniawski actually began serving as a wing commander with a Polish squadron of the Royal Air Force in England while his case officer carried on his secret work without so much as consulting him and kept a stream of reports flowing to Hamburg in Armand's name. Armand's case officer even succeeded in convincing the Germans that he had been appointed a liaison officer at the London headquarters of General Omar Bradley, who would command American ground troops in the invasion.

Treasure, the only female among the first violins, was Lily Sergeyev, a 26-year-old Frenchwoman. Free-spirited, high strung, and set in her ways, Treasure (code-named Tramp by the Germans) was judged by both the Abwehr and the Double-Cross as intelligent, resourceful, but temperamental and difficult to handle.

Adventure had always been in her blood. At 17 years of age, she had walked from Paris to Warsaw, a trek of about 900 miles, and then cycled around Europe. When war broke out in 1939, she was in Beirut, Lebanon, on a leg of a bicycle jaunt to Saigon, Indochina, halfway around the world from Paris. Instead of continuing her trip, Sergegev peddled back to Paris, determined to become a spy. Her scheme was to get enlisted in the German secret service from which vantage point she might be able to help the Allies in their war on Nazism.

In Paris, Sergegev inveigled an introduction to "Moustache," a burly Austrian she knew to be Major Emil Kliemann, second in command of the Abwehr branch in Paris. Kliemann, who fancied himself as something of a lady-killer, screened Sergegev by wining and dining her at exquisite watering holes such as Maxim's. Impressed with her sincerity (along with her physical attributes), Moustache accepted her into the fold. It was he who gave her the unflattering code name Tramp in a moment of drunken whimsy.

No one had ever accused Major Kliemann of being overburdened with brains. So now that he had recruited Tramp, he did not know what clandestine use to make of her. She suggested that she go to Lisbon, Portugal, then sneak into England as a French refugee on the lam from the Gestapo in Paris.

Sergegev's trek took her first to Madrid, Spain, where she promptly sneaked into the British embassy after dark, told her story, and volunteered to work for England as a double agent. With the connivance of MI–5 agents, she flew to London on a fake visa that indicated she had come to visit relatives. Interrogated at the secluded house in a London suburb where the clever minds of the Double-Cross hatched their schemes, Sergeyev passed with flying colors and was given the cover name Treasure.

In late February 1944, after being selected as one of the first violins in the Fortitude deception orchestra, Sergeyev told her controller that she would be far more productive if she could radio reports to her Lisbon Abwehr contact instead of relying on letters written in secret ink, as she had been doing. Double-Cross agreed: Fortitude required rapid communications. So Sergeyev, who would be going to her death if the Germans discovered her double-dealing, lured her lover, Major Kliemann, to Lisbon on the pretext of a romantic rendezvous.

Sergeyev flew to Lisbon and that night she joined the crowds strolling along the Plaza Rossio, then jumped on a streetcar that brought her back to her starting point at the Avenida Palace hotel. Convinced that she was not being tailed, Sergeyev walked to the unlit Plaza Pombal. She ambled around it twice, then glanced at the luminous dial on her watch. Her treff was set for 9:00 P.M.

Moments later, a car with dim headlights approached, drove around the plaza three times, then screeched to a halt beside Sergeyev. Quickly, the headlights were shut off, a door opened, an arm reached out, and she was yanked into the car. The vehicle leaped forward and raced off. Sergeyev did not recognize the driver. Thirty minutes later, she was in the arms of Major Kliemann in the luxurious Hotel Palacio.

Sergeyev had much exciting news. She lied about the job she had in the British Ministry of Information and how she had dated several American and British officers. She was confident that she could ferret out the secrets of the pending Allied invasion, but said that she would need a radio transmitter to send her information as rapidly as possible.

Kliemann was impressed with his girlfriend's cleverness. He provided her with a code and said that he would arrange to smuggle an Afu radio to her in England, possibly by dismantling the set and shipping it in a sacrosanct diplomatic pouch from ''neutral'' Spain.

Kliemann urged Sergeyev to be extremely cautious and to focus her attention on the region in southeastern England across from the Pas de Calais. If the Allies were going to plunge across the narrow Strait of Dover, they would be concentrating forces there. If Lily found that the Allies were collecting troops in the Salisbury-Bristol area far to the west, it would indicate the invasion would hit in Normandy.

Sergeyev returned to England and reported to her controller. She did not realize it at the time but the Third Reich had bestowed a distinct honor on her: the only woman the Abwehr entrusted to operate her own clandestine radio transmitter.[4]

Dusko Popov (code-named Tricycle) had been the XX-Committee's first double agent. Back on December 20, 1940, shortly after Major Tar Robertson had sold his concept on "turning" captured German spies rather than hanging them, Popov lifted off from Lisbon in a Dutch civilian airliner and landed at Felton Airport near Bristol, England. As soon as he had cleared customs, Popov was picked up by a stranger, driven to London, and dropped off at the Savory Hotel. In the lobby, he was met by Tar Robertson, who was wearing civilian clothes and introduced himself, and the pair went into the crowded bar for a beer or two, a sandwich, and a get-acquainted chat.

Popov had been in Belgrade at the outbreak of war. German officers suggested that Popov's family's extensive commercial interests in Europe would be "protected" if the 30-year-old man became a spy for the Third Reich. Grasping the implied threat, Popov agreed to serve Adolf Hitler, but would bide his time until he could contact British intelligence and offer his services.

When Major Robertson excused himself in the Savoy bar, he told the Yugoslavian, "We'll get down to business in the morning."[5] Indeed they did "get down to business." Not long after dawn, there was a knock at Popov's door, and he climbed sleepily out of bed to be confronted by a bevy of grim-faced men, some in uniform, others in civvies. They were from MI–5, MI–6, air intelligence, and naval intelligence.

Popov was neither accepted nor trusted. He could be a clever, genuine German spy. No one could trust anyone in the espionage profession. So in the comfort of the Savoy suite, the 12 Brits took turns grilling Popov, stopping just short of the third degree. This continued for four consecutive days. During that period, he was free to come and go at night as he wished, but Popov was aware that the shadowy figures tailing him to nightclubs were British intelligence agents.[6]

One of those boring in on Popov was the XX-Committee chief, John Masterman. His questioning—cool, calculated, incisive—"cleared" the Yugoslavian, although some of the interrogators were leery of Popov's reputation as a womanizer and a boozer.

Masterman gave him the code name Tricycle. Under the pretense of being a businessman buying goods for Yugoslavia, Tricycle was instructed to go through the motions of snooping out British secrets in the event another Abwehr agent had been assigned to shadow him. Despite the misgivings of a few on the committee, Tricycle would prove to be one of the best, and he was soon being showered with radioed praise from Hamburg for the "excellent" intelligence (nearly all of it phoney) he was sending back from Great Britain.

Among the first violins, the marquee attraction was a low-key young Spaniard named Juan Pujol, code-named Garbo. Due to the wealth of high-grade intelligence (most of it fake) that he had sent to Germany, Pujol was trusted completely by the Abwehr. Codes were often changed to thwart Allied efforts to eavesdrop on wireless messages, and each time the Abwehr sent Garbo the new cipher, the Radio Security Service could continue its snooping without missing a beat.[7]

Three years earlier, in January 1941, Pujol, who had been a poultry farmer and a manager of a small hotel, offered his services as an agent to the British embassy in Madrid. Leery of his being an Abwehr spy, Pujol was rejected. Disheartened, but refusing to be licked, Pujol hatched a scheme to strike at the Nazi dictatorship from within. He called on Gustav Lenz (real name Gustav Leisner), a former German navy officer, who was Abwehr chief in the Iberian peninsula (Spain and Portugal).

Gustav Lenz had been recruited into the Abwehr by Admiral Wilhelm Canaris back in 1937 and was sent to Madrid to run the *Abstelle*, a suboffice known in neutral countries as a *Kreigorganisationen* (war station, usually abbreviated KO). Lenz posed as a respectable businessman operating from the offices of the Excelsior Import and Export Company, a commodity brokerage firm. Actually, it was a front for Abwehr machinations in Iberia. When war broke out in Europe in September 1939, Gustav Lenz shifted his operation to the German embassy at 4 Castellana and built an espionage apparatus whose tentacles reached into almost every locale in Iberia.

In Madrid, the German embassy itself was a beehive of cloak-and-dagger machinations. There were 171 genuine diplomatic personnel, but they were far outnumbered by the 87 Abwehr operatives directly attached to the legation under cover of fake titles, along with some 230 others assigned to the intelligence staff. British wireless snoopers concluded that Gustav Lenz had some 1,500 agents and subagents sprinkled throughout Spain and perhaps 1,000 more in Portugal.

Madrid was such a critical Abwehr outpost (as it was for the British secret service) that an enormous volume of radio traffic was flowing from the German embassy to an Abwehr relay station near Wiesbaden, Germany. Lenz had working in around-the-clock shifts 33 wireless operators and ten female cipher clerks.

Almost every word being radioed from Madrid or flowing into it from the Third Reich was intercepted by the Radio Security Service in Hanslope Park. This enabled the British to identify all of the 87 Abwehr operatives permanently assigned to the German embassy in Madrid.[8]

When Juan Pujol first contacted Gustav Lenz, the old Abwehr had was wary of the young Spaniard's motives. But after investigating Pujol's background, Lenz decided to send Pujol to England in June 1941, with a questionnaire of intelligence to be collected, secret ink, $3,000 in cash, the code name Arabel, cover addresses in England, and the implied blessing of the fuehrer.

Arabel did not go to London. When he reached Lisbon, he decided to remain there and fabricate cleverly conceived intelligence reports to deceive the Abwehr. All the while, Gustav Lenz believed that Arabel was actually in the British Isles.

Using tourist guides and reference books found in Lisbon libraries, and scanning British newspapers which were in abundance in neutral Portugal, Arabel was able to create reports (purporting to come from England) that had an authentic ring. From Lisbon, the Spaniard shuffled fictitious and real troops around Great Britain—and in some instances came very close to being accurate.

It was not long until Gustav Lenz and the Abwehr in Berlin and Hamburg trusted Arabel—indeed, they came to rely on him, perhaps through their eagerness to gain any scraps of information from the British Isles. His standing with the Germans soared even higher when he "recruited" three subagents (all fictitious)—one in Liverpool, one in Glasgow, and one in western England—to supply information. This ploy cemented the Abwehr's belief that Arabel really was in London.

In February 1942, the British, through the Radio Security Service, knew about Arabel and, in the words of an MI–5 official, were "going crazy" trying to locate the Abwehr's ace spy in England. How had he slipped past British security?[9]

At the same time, Arabel decided that his hoax was on the verge of collapsing. He spoke little English, knew nothing about the composition of the British military organization, and was having a difficult time trying to furnish the Abwehr with the specific intelligence items it was demanding. So Pujol (Arabel) concluded that he could best advance his private war against Nazism by contacting British authorities in Lisbon and laying his entire story on the line.

Arrangements were made for Pujol to meet with Gene Risso-Gill, MI–6 officer in Lisbon, at a secluded inn overlooking the ocean in nearby Estoril. There the Spaniard offered his services to England. Three days later, Risso-Gill contacted Pujol and said that he had received orders to slip him into London, and the new double agent arrived there on April 25, 1942.

Pujol was given his code name Garbo and ensconced in a Victorian house in a middle-class neighborhood at 35 Crespigny Road, Hendon, in north London. Earlier, the structure had been used to keep double agents while their case officers fed false information on their behalf to Hamburg and Berlin. Pujol was provided with documents identifying him as Juan Garcia, a translator for the British Broadcasting Company.

Garbo had an intimate grasp of how the Abwehr operated, and there was no need to create a fictitious spy network for him—he had already done that while in Lisbon. Garbo was a tireless worker and dedicated to the cause of destroying Adolf Hitler and his Nazi regime. For eight hours a day, seven days a week, he laboriously wrote reports (created by his case officer) in invisible ink and mailed them to Abwehr addresses in Lisbon and Madrid. By January 1944, with the invasion of Europe on the horizon, Garbo had sent some 400 secret letters and nearly 4,000 radio messages, all of them concocted by his case officer. Meanwhile, Garbo's British controllers had fabricated an even larger phony network for their ace operative—14 agents and 11 well-placed contacts, including a key one in the Ministry of Information, where Allied secret matters were regularly handled.

Garbo's enthusiasm soared even higher when MI–5 managed to sneak his wife and young son from Lisbon to London, where they joined him at 35 Crespigny Road. He had no financial worries. A highly appreciative Abwehr was unwittingly paying his family's living expenses (plus a nest egg) to the cumulative tune of about 20,000 British pounds ($97,000), a sizeable sum at the time.[10]

These, then, were the first violins—Tate, Brutus, Treasure, Tricycle, and Garbo—who would carry the melody in the Fortitude orchestra. A host of "second violins" would provide supporting accompaniment.

Big Three summit at Teheran: Joseph Stalin (left), Franklin Roosevelt, and Winston Churchill. The decision was made to invade France and to adopt the Bodyguard deception scheme. (National Archives)

Fuehrer Adolf Hitler (right) was convinced that the Allies would strike at the Pas de Calais. Field Marshal Erwin Rommel (left) felt that the target would be Normandy. (U.S. Army)

FBI Director J. Edgar Hoover and his G-men played a key role in the phony Army Group Patton deception. (FBI)

Major General William J. "Wild Bill" Donovan, chief of the OSS. (U.S. Army)

Allen W. Dulles, OSS station
chief in Bern. (U.S. Army)

Abwehr chief Wilhelm Canaris, a leader in
the Schwarze Kapelle conspiracy against
Hitler. (U.S. Army)

Commandos of SS Lieutenant Colonel Otto Skorzeny tried to kill President Roosevelt. (U.S. Army)

Propaganda Minister Paul Joseph Goebbels. (*Signal* magazine)

Brigadefuehrer SS Walther Schellenberg. (*Signal* magazine)

Professor Reginald V. Jones pinpointed German radar sites across the Channel before D-Day. (Courtesy Professor Reginald V. Jones)

Field Marshal Rudolf Gerd von Rundstedt leaned toward the Pas de Calais as the Allied invasion target. (U.S. Army)

American Sherman tank of inflatable rubber. (U.S. Army)

American inflatable rubber liaison airplane used in Quicksilver deception. (U.S. Army)

Genuine American soldier stands beside an armored car—one of inflatable rubber— used in Quicksilver. (U.S. Army)

Wilhelmplatz 8/9, Berlin (above), was Propaganda Minister Joseph Goebbels' nerve center for directing propaganda designed to discourage looming Allied invasion. (*Signal* magazine)

INVASION

CIMETIÈRE DES ALLIÉS

Typical German propaganda (left) was aimed at the French people to keep them from an armed uprising when the Allies landed in northwest Europe. (*Signal* magazine)

General George S. Patton, Jr., was the centerpiece of Fortitude South, the scheme to convey that the invasion would hit at the Pas de Calais. An almost identical look-alike for British General Bernard L. Montgomery (inset) tried to confuse Germans on the eve of D-Day. (U.S. Army)

British Lieutenant General Frederick E. Morgan (left) laid the groundwork for Overlord in 1943. Morgan "made D-Day possible," General Eisenhower would say. (U.S. Army)

As part of Allied deceit, Supreme Commander Dwight D. Eisenhower (right) deliberately lied to Free French leader General Charles de Gaulle (far right) on invasion plans. (U.S. Army)

General Lesley T. McNair, commander of the phantom FUSAG, was killed by bombs during Cobra. (U.S. Army)

German soldier in Normandy pays final respect to fallen comrades. (National Archives)

American vehicles pick their way through the flattened town of Valognes in their attack on the port of Cherbourg. (U.S. Army)

Major General J. Lawton (Lightning Joe) Collins (center) accepts surrender of Lieutenant General Karl Wilhelm von Schlieben (left in profile), commander of Cherbourg, the primary objective of the Allied invasion. (U.S. Army)

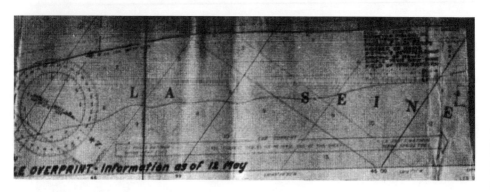

Map used by SHAEF in Overlord planning. (U.S. Army)

Field Marshal Guenther von Kluge was involved in the conspiracy to murder Hitler. He tried secretly to surrender German forces in Normandy. (U.S. Army)

Supreme Commander Dwight Eisenhower scrawled a note (right) in the event invasion met with disaster, on the eve of D-Day. (Eisenhower Library)

Major General Leland S. Hobbs, whose U.S. 30th Infantry Division suffered nearly 1,000 casualties from "friendly" bombs. (U.S. Army)

German Lieutenant General Fritz Bayerlein, whose crack Panzer Lehr Division was nearly wiped out in two hours by massive Allied bombing. (U.S. Army)

GI bazooka team firing from behind earthen hedgerow in Normandy. (U.S. Army)

German tanks blown off the road by massive Operation Cobra bombardment. (U.S. Army)

Historic Edinburgh Castle, first headquarters of the ghost Fourth Army in Scotland. A German fighter plane strafed the castle a few days after wireless network base there began operating. (Courtesy Professor Reginald V. Jones)

14

Behind the White Cliffs of Dover

Blacked-out, bomb-battered Berlin lay ghostlike and fearful the night of March 20, 1944. Citizens strained to hear the first faint hum of powerful airplane engines and the eerie wail of sirens that would foretell the nearly nightly appearance of the Royal Air Force.

Safely inside a conference room in the underground chambers of the Ober-kommando der Wehrmacht in suburban Zossen, a galaxy of the Third Reich's top military leaders in the West were chatting idly while awaiting the presence of Adolf Hitler. They were all there:

Aristocratic Field Marshal Gerd von Rundstedt, tightly clutching his gold, jewel-embedded marshal's baton. The aging Prussian was said to be having a hard time sleeping nights unless aided by generous doses of whiskey, and then he would sleep until 10 A.M.

Field Marshal Erwin Rommel, folk hero of the Fatherland. As commander of Army Group B (the Seventh Army in Normandy and the Fifteenth Army in the Pas de Calais), he was technically subordinate to von Rundstedt, but he had the authority to report directly to the fuehrer. Unlike von Rund-stedt, Rommel rarely carried his marshal's baton.

General of Panzer Troops Leo Geyr Frieherr von Schweppenburg, young, handsome, haughty. The commander of Panzer Army West, he was in charge of armored divisions in France and the Low Countries.

Bull-necked, red-faced Field Marshal Hugo Sperrle, resplendent in his powder blue Luftwaffe uniform with gold braid. Sperrle commanded Luftflotte 3, which consisted of all bombers and fighter planes in the West.

Admiral Theodor Krancke, commander of Naval Group, West, headquartered in Paris, whose job it was to alert ground forces if an Allied fleet was approaching.

Each of these leaders had an independent command. When and if the Anglo-Americans struck against northwest Europe, von Rundstedt and Rommel, unlike General Eisenhower who had almost czarlike control of all forces of the Western Allies, would have to "request" the deployment of tank, sea, and air forces. In the case of von Schweppenburg, he could not commit his crack panzer formations without the specific approval of Hitler.

The fuehrer was aware of the built-in dangers of this splintered command structure in the West, that every minute lost in rushing German forces to the point of attack would make it more difficult to repel any Allied onslaught. But he feared an even greater danger: concentrating too much military power in the hands of any one man. At this stage of the war, Hitler trusted hardly any of his generals and admirals.

Suddenly, the buzz of conversation in the conference room ceased and all leaped to their feet. Hitler strode briskly into the chamber, followed by his two confidants, Field Marshal Wilhelm Keitel and General Alfred Jodl. Many German officers, privately, called the aloof, humorless field marshal *"Lackeitel"*—German for lackey.

The gathering of Wehrmacht stars sat ramrod straight and listened intently as the fuehrer began speaking. As Hitler's recitation became more impassioned, his face turned crimson and tiny beads of perspiration dotted his forehead and upper lip around his black brush mustache. Around the room, armed SS guards kept a sharp watch on the high-ranking officers, who did not dare to even reach in their pockets for a handkerchief for fear that such a move might be interpreted as pulling out a pistol.

"It is evident that the Anglo-American landing will and must come," Hitler declared. "How and where it will come, no one knows for sure. At no place along our long shoreline is a landing impossible, in view of the Allies' control of the sea. The enemy assault must be liquidated within a few hours. Under no circumstances must it be allowed to last longer than a matter of a few hours or, at most, days. This would prevent the reelection of Roosevelt who, with luck, will finish up somewhere in jail. Churchill, too, has grown old and tired and would be finished, because the Anglo-Americans could never launch another invasion."

Earlier that day, Colonel Alexis von Roenne, the stiff-necked chief intelligence officer of Fremde Heere West whose job was to discern the Western Allies' order of battle (the designation and location of enemy units), sent an urgent message to the Oberkommando der Wehrmacht: "It is now established that General George Patton, who is highly regarded for his proficiency, is now in England."

Lieutenant General George Smith Patton, Jr., a swashbuckling old cavalryman, was the centerpiece of Fortitude South, the deception scheme designed to suggest that the Anglo-Americans would invade the Pas de Calais. Baron von Roenne's information had been obtained from the Double-Cross Committee's "first vio-

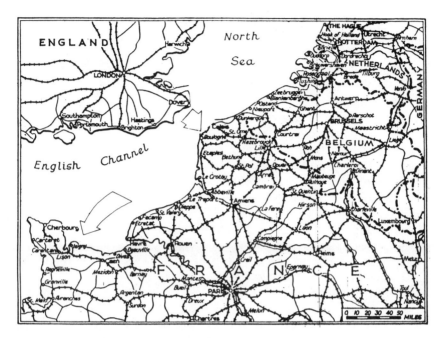

2. Real invasion site (left arrow) and FUSAG hoax (right arrow).

lins,'' who had been sending truthful reports about seeing Patton at various places in England in recent days.

Quicksilver was the code name for an element of Fortitude South. It would fabricate an entire Allied army group (two or more armies), supposedly commanded by George Patton and consisting of some 1 million men. This powerful dummy force would assemble in a wide triangle in southeastern England, directly across the Strait of Dover from the Pas de Calais.

Directly concerned with masterminding Quicksilver were two British officers of the Committee of Special Means (CSM), Colonel Roger F. Hesketh and Colonel J.V.B. Jervis-Reid. Hesketh was the millionaire son-in-law of the Earl of Scarborough, and Jervis-Reid was a graduate of Emmanuel College, Cambridge. Both men possessed boundless energy, enthusiasm and ingenuity.[1] Known as the First United States Army Group (FUSAG), Quicksilver was intended to pin down the powerful German Fifteenth Army along the Pas de Calais on D-Day and beyond, while Allied troops stormed ashore and built up a strong beachhead 170 miles to the southwest in Normandy.

Quicksilver had its beginning in the United States late in November 1943. At that time, J. Edgar Hoover's FBI agents had taken into custody a Dutch native named Walter Koehler, who claimed that he had worked for the German kaiser as a spy in World War I, had been recruited by emissaries of Wilhelm Canaris to be an Abwehr agent during the current conflict, and had been sent to the United States to gather secret information. However, Koehler declared, he had had a change of heart and now was eager to be a double agent for Uncle Sam.[2]

In order to prove his sincerity, Koehler handed over to the FBI men his two secret codes given to him by his Abwehr controllers and the radio with which he was to transmit messages from New York City to Hamburg. J. Edgar Hoover accepted the offer and christened Koehler with the code name Albert van Loop.

There was no chance for van Loop to betray the FBI. For the 52-year-old, heavyset Dutchman was held under guard in a third-rate hotel in Manhattan while a pair of FBI agents skilled in wireless transmittal imitated the "turned" Abwehr spy. Working from a secluded hideout on Long Island, not far from New York City, the two G-men (as they were called) established radio contact with Hamburg, using van Loop's secret ciphers.

Van Loop's reports to Hamburg were a carefully concocted blend of truths (on insignificant matters), half-truths, and outright lies. More than 120 messages would be sent to Hamburg by van Loop's FBI imitators, with the real double agent being unaware of the mischief that was being done in his name to the cause of the Third Reich.

Abwehr controllers were no doubt delighted to learn from van Loop that he had obtained a job as a night clerk in a New York hotel. This post was especially advantageous, he pointed out, because the U.S. Army had taken over the hotel to lodge officers bound for Europe. In Hamburg, the Abwehr apparently failed to notice that their ace agent in New York City had not identified by name this important hotel, which existed only in the nimble minds of an FBI committee stage-managing the van Loop fraud.

As a result of his position in the hotel, van Loop learned of many troopship sailings (all of them phony), and from the nonexistent army officers (who seemed to be hell-bent on breaking security requirements) van Loop passed along their unit designations—many of which were fictitious and to be used as part of the FUSAG deception stratagem.[3]

A bevy of intelligence officers from the Pentagon worked closely with the FBI in creating the messages to be sent to the Abwehr. So clever were the radio transmittals that they arrived in Hamburg too late for German U-boats to be notified and get into position to intercept the "convoys" or to even vouch for their existence.

By March 1944, tens of thousands of "live" American soldiers were pouring into British ports—and so were large numbers of phantom soldiers of FUSAG. The living, breathing GIs became part of the genuine U.S. 12th Army Group, commanded by General Omar Bradley, in southern England, across from Normandy. The phony soldiers "joined" Patton's fictional army group in the southeast, opposite the Pas de Calais.

Despite the machinations involved in creating FUSAG, the wily Germans could not be fooled by phantom divisions alone—there would have to be a whirlwind of activity and invasion preparations in southeastern England. So

FUSAG actually was activated, with its initial headquarters in Bryanston Square, London. Its dummy components included nine divisions of the U.S. Third Army and two divisions of the Canadian First Army.

The Double-Cross Committee's Treasure, Garbo, and Brutus rapidly sent Hamburg reports on the Canadian 4th Armored Division at Aldershot, the Canadian 2nd Infantry Division at Dover, and elements of the U.S. Third Army in Suffolk and Essex. Hamburg apparently gave no serious thought about how a handful of agents could so rapidly penetrate strict Allied security measures and identify and locate these FUSAG units.

Genuine commanders were named to FUSAG formations. If the Allied phantom force threatening the Pas de Calais was to be fully credible to Adolf Hitler and his high command, the names of these FUSAG leaders would have to be leaked. The Wehrmacht had an entire section devoted to keeping track of enemy commanders and often compiled extensive biographies on each one, his strengths, weaknesses, tendencies, and tactical capabilities. If the Germans did not recognize a single name among the FUSAG leaders, their suspicions would deepen and Quicksilver might be wrecked. Only a few names of the FUSAG generals were leaked. As clever as Garbo, Brutus, and Treasure were, it could have demolished the entire Quicksilver deception had a neatly compiled list of all FUSAG commanders arrived at the Abwehr station in Hamburg.

The artful dodgers of Quicksilver selected George Patton to lead the phantom army group because the Germans clearly regarded the armored genius as America's most gifted and audacious combat commander. Patton was the key to pinpointing Allied intentions for the *Grossinvasion*, the Oberkommando der Wehrmacht was convinced.

Tall, trim, devout, and at the same time profane, General Patton had mixed feelings about his Overlord assignment. On the one hand, he was despondent because he would not be leading an army on D-Day. If he had his choice, Patton would be the first Allied soldier to storm ashore. On the other hand, the 59-year-old general relished the role of intrigue to which he had been assigned. "I'm a goddamned natural-born ham!" he told aides.[4]

Patton played his role to the hilt, dashing to and fro around England while presuming to lead Army Group Patton (as the Germans came to refer to the phony unit). With his ramrod-straight posture; lacquered helmet liner; a total of 15 stars gleaming from his headgear, shirt collar, and shoulders; boots polished to a high gloss; an ivory-handled revolver on one hip, roaring profane commands, Patton would have been difficult to miss for even the most myopic and dull-witted German spy.

Since the success or cataclysmic failure of the Allied invasion might well depend upon Adolf Hitler swallowing the Quicksilver deception hook, line, and swastika, FUSAG became an elaborate masquerade on a colossal scale. Scores of tent cities, just like those actually housing thousands of real troops elsewhere, popped up in southeastern England within sight of the Channel. Every tent was empty and their canvas sides flapped like huge drum skins in the early spring wind. But from the chimneys of scores of field kitchens (also deserted), smoke poured thickly every day, as though phantom cooks had regiments of ghosts to feed.

A party of genuine American engineers would drive near to a peaceful wood; officers would climb out, point, and shout orders. Within a few hours, a track connecting the wood with a nearby road would be built. A few large GI trucks would then drive back and forth, leaving tire marks on the muddy road.

There was nothing in the wood except a few squirrels and rabbits, but from the air, the clump of trees appeared to conceal an ammunition dump, a headquarters complex, or even a battalion of troops. Gossipers in nearby villages who witnessed all the hubbub unwittingly augmented the illusion.

This procedure was repeated many times in the FUSAG region. Real trucks, staff cars, jeeps, and ambulances with huge red crosses painted on their roofs to help identify them from the air moved in convoys around the area, past enormous dumps of jerry-cans (empty but presumably filled with gasoline) and huge piles of ammunition boxes (also empty) ringed with barbed wire fences.

Tricks of camouflage, or *ruse de guerre*, were incredibly imaginative. Liaison and other aircraft were needed to support Army Group Patton, so a few dummy airfields sprang up. Handling that job was Colonel John F. Turner, who was regarded as Britain's foremost camoufleur and an officer of exceptional enterprise.

For the benefit of Luftwaffe night reconnaissance planes, dim illumination, known as Q lights, was placed along each side of the runways, which had been scraped out of the green countryside by bulldozers. Phony recognition beacons were erected. Fake aircraft, constructed of wood and heavy-duty canvas, were put next to the runways. Some planes were haphazardly camouflaged, as though ground crews had ailed to do a competent job.

Sound tracks blared forth the noise of aircraft engines revving, presumably prior to takeoff—just to serenade enemy agents who might be registered at the nearby Swan or the Boar's Head Inn or the White Knight. At night, when a snooping Luftwaffe plane was overhead, salvaged automobile headlights mounted on wheels were dragged up and down the fake airfields, conveying the impression that planes were landing and taking off.

Gifted movie set designers from Shepperton Studios were called in, and they supplied Army Group Patton with tanks, artillery, and trucks—all of inflatable rubber. On one chilly morning in March, Winston Churchill arrived in the FUSAG area on an inspection tour and climbed out of his Humber staff car, wearing his familiar spotted blue bow tie and square-crowned bowler. Smoke from the prime minister's ever-present cigar wafted toward the rows of brown tanks in the adjacent green field. Churchill and the two men with him, Major General Leslie Hollis of the War Cabinet, and Lieutenant Colonel Ronald Wingate, John Bevan's number-two man in the London Controlling Section, began striding toward the first line of tanks.

"A most impressive display of armor," Churchill remarked, drawing on his cigar and smiling impishly. "Yet, so you assure me, Hollis, each of these huge tanks could be vanquished by a bow and arrow?" "That is true, Prime Minister," Hollis agreed. "Or by a boy with a hunting knife."[5]

A week earlier, a farmer reported to a British commander in a village that his bull had wandered into a field of these tanks and madly charged one that seemed to annoy him. The farmer was astonished when the animal's horns ran through one side and the entire tank collapsed. No doubt the bull also was amazed.

A few lumber, wire, and canvas hospitals and warehouses sprang to life. Four hundred or so landing craft, built to transport the assault waves of this fictitious force, clogged various rivers, creeks, and inlets, but they would never put to sea. They were simply skeletons of tubular poles welded together in the form of barges, covered by gray canvas and floated on empty oil drums.

Near Dover, nearly three miles of the Channel shoreline was cleared as a site for a huge oil-storage depot, designed to supply Patton's powerful force once it had charged across the narrow Strait and onto the Pas de Calais. But nowhere was there a drop of oil. Basil Spence, a creative professor of architecture at Britain's Royal Academy, had designed this make-believe facility. Spence used miles of sewage pipes taken from bombed cities and scaffolding, unwanted oil tanks, huts, and broken-down jetties in its construction. A huge wind machine was borrowed from a movie studio and it blew clouds of dust across the scene— from the air, it seemed that work was proceeding at a furious pace.

Photographs of General Bernard Montgomery and King George leaving the heavily guarded gates of the "oil depot" appeared in British newspapers, copies of which were soon on the desks of German intelligence officers in Berlin by way of Lisbon. Despite his gigantic burdens, Supreme Commander Dwight Eisenhower spoke at a dinner honoring the "engineers and construction foremen" that was held at the White Cliffs Hotel in Dover.

At this celebration, the mayor of Dover (who was privy to the masquerade) said how delighted he was to have this new installation in his locale. However, he added, "its precise nature must remain secret until the war is over, but it will bring the borough enormous benefits."

Pictures of Eisenhower speaking at the Dover affair were published in various London newspapers. Captions said that the event took place at "an undisclosed location." Double-Cross case officers for the first violins made certain that the Abwehr in Hamburg knew that the "undisclosed location" was Dover.

British and American fighter planes maintained regular patrols above these dummy sites and installations along the southeastern coast. The pilots were under orders to permit an occasional Luftwaffe reconnaissance plane through to photograph these fake preparations for invasion, but never below 30,000 feet. Above that altitude, the inflatable tanks, trucks, jeeps, artillery pieces, and empty camps would appear genuine. Below it, German cameras might reveal to intelligence evaluators that the entire Army Group Patton was an illusion.

Judging from the letters that flooded newspapers in southeastern England, the massive influx of "foreign" troops was having an enormous negative impact on the citizenry. A retired vicar deplored the "decline of morals" among young British women since American and Canadian soldiers "invaded" Suffolk and Kent and Essex. Another published letter complained about the large number of used prophylactics that were being strewn about southeastern England, especially around the encampments of American paratroopers. Housewives' letters expressed anger over the fact that the many military trucks and jeeps that were racing along the roads were stirring up dust and ruining the washing hanging on the lines to dry. Yet other residents wrote protesting letters about the lack of courtesy being shown by American and Canadian tank drivers to citizens using the same roads in the area. Did these tankers think that they were back in the wide open plains of America's Midwest, or on the vast Canadian prairies, instead of on the narrow roads and streets of heavily populated southeastern England?

All of these newspaper items and letters had been planted by the artful dodgers of Quicksilver. Copies of these newspapers were forwarded to Lisbon by Double-Cross agents and were promptly sent on to German intelligence in Berlin.

Meanwhile, the air over southeastern England crackled with a flood of bogus radio messages passing between nonexistent FUSAG command posts, then down to dummy battalions and companies. These messages were sent in easily breakable codes. When the deceptionists wanted to make certain that a specific piece of information was picked up by the highly efficient German Y-Service (electronic listening posts across the Channel), a "careless" radio operator would send the message in the clear.

This blizzard of simulated radio traffic was handled by the U.S. 3103rd Signals Service Battalion. As soon as it had arrived in England in February 1944, the unit began to analyze genuine radio traffic between other American outfits already in England so that it could create a plausible imitation of normal radio communications within a real army group.

Radio signals over southeastern England leaped in intensity when the phony divisions and regiments carried on extensive training exercises to prepare for assaulting the Atlantic Wall, as indeed genuine American divisions were doing elsewhere in the British Isles. Deception experts had to be careful that these fictitious exercises were conducted with a credible amount of time between each one, and they were often called off when the weather was especially bad—just as the real American units would do.

Signalers of the German Y-Service worked in shifts around the clock in concrete bunkers crammed full of the most delicate radio equipment. Their job was to listen. Each man was an expert who spoke three languages fluently, and there was hardly a word whispered through the ether from Allied sources in the British Isles that they did not hear.

These Wehrmacht signalers were so capable and their equipment so sophisticated that they were even able to pick up calls from radio transmitters in military police jeeps in England more than 125 miles from the Channel coast of northern France. American and British MPs (military policemen), chatting with one another as they directed seemingly endless convoys around Great Britain, helped the Y-Service to compile a list of divisions stationed there. Some of these units were real; others, as in the case of FUSAG, were dummies.

Ultra intercepts disclosed that German intelligence was swallowing the Quicksilver mosaic of deceit. Tangible proof that the deception was obtaining the desired effect came when huge German coastal guns at Cap Gris Nez, on the Pas de Calais, periodically shelled the fake oil refinery near Dover. Other than to frighten the handful of British soldiers on duty there, the periodic bombardments did little damage, since the site was a wasteland. But after each salvo of shells, the Brits lit sodium flares to simulate fires caused by direct hits on "oil tanks."

No ruse de guerre was too bizarre to be implemented by the artful dodgers of deception if there was a chance it would help put across the FUSAG illusion. When a group of British pigeon fanciers expressed a wish to contribute their birds to the war effort, a scheme, code-named Columbia, was concocted based on the fanciers' claim that their pigeons would fly back home instinctively from a distance of a few hundred miles.

Attached to the pigeons' legs were meaningless coded messages that indicated the birds belonged to Army Group Patton. Then the pigeons were dropped by parachute into Belgium, Holland, and the Pas de Calais. The birds were crated in pairs with a note saying that, if released, they would return to England and the underground might find them useful for sending information to the Allies.

Hundreds of pigeons were parachuted along the German-held Channel coast. Only five or six of them returned with messages from resistance groups, and the information they contained was of no great value to Allied intelligence. However, the Germans picked up a few crates of the parachuted birds, plotted the points of impact, and found that the drops were all far east of Normandy.

Operation Columbia was not a total success. One bird reached its loft in England with a note scrawled in German longhand attached to one leg: "Here's your pigeon. We ate the other one."

Elsewhere in support of Quicksilver, British and American operatives in the neutral hotbeds of intrigue—Lisbon, Madrid, Istanbul, Berne, Stockholm—began inquiring in bookshops and other likely sources for copies of Michelin Map 51, which seemed to have suddenly become quite popular. Even when the shops sold out of their limited supplies, customers entered to demand loudly that the maps be ordered for them. Michelin Map 51 was designed for prewar tourists and showed the roads and sight-seeing attractions in the Pas de Calais.

All the while, the devious minds on the Double-Cross Committee hatched schemes to reinforce the FUSAG illusion and to convince the fuehrer that the Pas de Calais would be the invasion target. A British double agent (code-named Mullet) had been fairly high in the insurance world in Belgium with a company that insured many buildings in northern France. When war erupted, the insurance executive, for whatever his reason—Nazi idealism, threats to his family, large sums of money—had agreed to be parachuted into England to report back to Berlin about the status of British arms production and economics.

Aware through the double agents that the Belgian was coming, MI–6 had a reception party on hand to greet him when he came down in his parachute. The Double-Cross gave Mullet the cover of working in a London insurance firm, which fitted in well with his genuine background.

Mullet's case officer sent to Hamburg a report in which the Belgian said a British government department, knowing that he had a great deal of information about buildings and industries in northern France, asked him to supply urgently as much data as he could recall about a certain region—the Pas de Calais. Mullet's Abwehr controller was delighted with this added kernel of information and sent a wireless message praising the Belgian for his effort.

The Double-Cross also cooked up a crucial mission for Dusko Popov, the clever Yugoslavian (Tricycle to the British; Ivan to the Germans). He would be sent to Lisbon and hand over to his Abwehr controller, Major Luduvico von Karsthoff, a phony order of battle for Allied forces assembling in the British Isles. Army Group Patton would be among the units listed.

It would be Popov's most crucial assignment of the war: if the Germans discovered that his documents were fake (or perhaps tortured him to extract the truth), the entire Fortitude deception plan would be unmasked.

Within three hours of his flying into Lisbon, Popov held a treff with von Karsthoff. Feigning keen excitement, he told the Abwehr major that the order of battle had been collected by his (nonexistent) subagents in Britain—Freak, the Worm, Balloon, Meteor, and Gelatine. Suspicious of Popov's document, von Karsthoff branded the information as "warmed-over gossip."

Popov, a consummate actor, reacted angrily and demanded that von Karsthoff send the order of battle to Berlin for analysis. The Abwehr officer complied. Back came an upbeat reply from Colonel Alexis von Roenne at Fremde Heere West: he had seen precisely what the stage managers of Fortitude South wanted him to see—a powerful Allied army group forming in southeastern England.

That same day, March 9, 1944, Colonel von Roenne fired off an urgent message to the Oberkommando der Wehrmacht for relay to the fuehrer: "A *V-mann* [secret agent] dispatch has brought particularly valuable information. The authenticity of the report was checked and proved. It contains information about three [Allied] armies, three army corps and 23 divisions, among which the location of only one need be regarded as questionable. The report confirms our Feinbild [enemy picture]."[6]

Allied deceptionists in London were elated when they read von Roenne's message, which had been intercepted and decoded by Ultra. Then, only a few days later, exultation turned to deep concern when events in Lisbon indicated that the Quicksilver machination was about to be exploded by the Abwehr, now under the control of Reichsfuehrer SS Heinrich Himmler's protégé, Walther Schellenberg.

Johann Jebsen, the disillusioned Abwehr officer in Lisbon whom Dusko Popov had recruited for the British as a double agent, was notified by his German superiors that he was to receive a notable decoration because of the excellent intelligence on the Allied buildup in Britain that he had been receiving from his agent there, Dusko Popov. Jebsen (British code name Artist) would be awarded the *Kreigsverdienstkreuz*, 1st Class, an honor that had been bestowed upon none of the other horde of German agents in Lisbon.

On the appointed day, Jebsen arrived at the German embassy in Lisbon to receive his decoration and was escorted to the office of Aloys Schreiber, a senior Abwehr officer. As soon as he stepped through the door, Jebsen was hit a terrific blow in the face by a husky bruiser and knocked to the floor. When Jebsen regained consciousness, he was interrogated roughly and savagely beaten. Then he was drugged, crammed into the trunk of a long, black automobile with diplomatic license plates, whisked through Spain and France, and taken to Berlin.

John Masterman, the Double-Cross Committee chief, was shocked on learning of Jebsen's fate from Ultra intercepts. Jebsen, the Brit found out, was being interrogated by the SD, and since he had been involved with Popov in the Quicksilver scheme, he might spill everything he knew about the plan under heavy torture.

Masterman breathed a faint sigh of relief when Ultra indicated that Artist's arrest had more to do with his alleged stealing of Abwehr funds, but that was small consolation to the deceptionist. He had to assume that Artist would "sing" and disclose Quicksilver.[7]

So Masterman removed Popov from future involvement in the FUSAG scheme. If Artist told all, the Germans would know that Popov was a double agent, that the wealth of information Popov had passed to the Abwehr was phony, that Army Group Patton was fiction, and that there was no genuine threat to the German Fifteenth Army at the Pas de Calais in the event the Allies struck across the Channel. It would not be until the true D-Day that the Double-Cross Committee and SHAEF would learn for certain that Artist had not blown the whistle on Neptune.[8]

15

A Ghost Army Threatens Norway

When war broke out in September 1939, Colonel R. M. "Rory" MacLeod was military assistant to General Edmund Ironside, chief of the Imperial General Staff. MacLeod had been awarded a chestful of decorations during World War I, and had been so greviously wounded in France that one-third of his skull was fashioned into a silver plate. Despite this physical handicap, MacLeod hoped to get a combat command in the new war.

It was only a few months, however, until the new prime minister, Winston Churchill, jettisoned Ironside, and MacLeod fell into military oblivion. In early 1944, MacLeod was 52 years old and resigned to the view that there was no role for him in the pending invasion of northern France, the greatest operation of its kind in history. It was a bitter pill to swallow for an Old Soldier.

On March 3, 1944, Colonel MacLeod was umpiring war games in the damp and windblown Yorkshire Moors when an aide handed him an urgent telegram from the War Office. Opening the envelope, his face brightened into a broad smile when he read the contents. He was to report immediately to SHAEF planning headquarters at Norfolk House. Eagerly, MacLeod left for London, convinced that he was going to be given an infantry division for Neptune. Reporting to Brigadier Richard Barker, a signals officer for Home Forces, MacLeod was told: "Rory, old boy, you have been selected to run a deception operation for SHAEF from Scottish Command. You will travel to Edinburgh, and there you will represent an army which does not in fact exist."

MacLeod was crestfallen. Instead of a combat command for the Big Show, he felt he was being shuttled aside to Scotland to lead a "play army." Brigadier Barker continued: "By means of fake signals traffic you will, however, fool the Germans into believing that an army does exist and, what is more, that it is about to land in Norway and clear the Germans out of there. The whole scheme is an important part of the coming invasion of France. . . . It is terrifically important that it should be a success."[1]

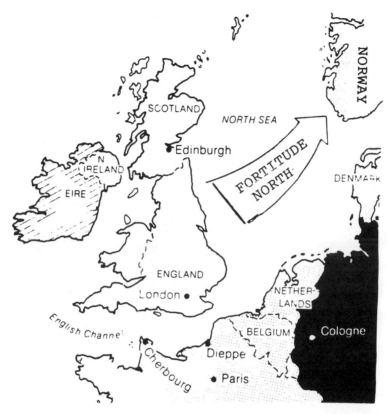

3. Fortitude North.

In order to make Fortitude North plausible, the fictitious Fourth Army assembling in Scotland would have to have a commander of suitable high rank and experience. Chosen for that task was General Andrew "Bulgy" Thorne, who had once been British military attaché in Berlin and was known by many senior Wehrmacht generals. They would expect Thorne to lead some major campaign. Bulgy Thorne, however, would largely be a figurehead; Rory MacLeod would direct most of the day-to-day work, which would consist mainly of establishing a widespread wireless network whose signals the German Y-Service was meant to overhear.

"The Germans are damned good at interception and radio location," Brigadier Barker reminded MacLeod. "They'll have your headquarters pinpointed with a maximum error of five miles. And it won't take them long to do so."[2]

Masking his disappointment, Colonel MacLeod caught a train for Edinburgh and on March 6—only four days after he had been summoned to Norfolk House—he established the ghost Fourth Army headquarters in several rooms under the ramparts of Edinburgh Castle. A great fortress perched on a cliff overlooking

Scotland's capital, Edinburgh Castle housed the country's royal jewels, or *regalia*, in peacetime.

Scotland is a rugged, mountainous country in the northern part of the island of Great Britain. Geographically, it is about the size of the state of South Carolina. Dark clouds often blanket the island, bringing heavy rains, but strong winds from the Atlantic Ocean to the west usually clear the skies quickly.

Within a few days of his arrival, Rory MacLeod had assembled his staff—about 20 British officers who were mostly overage in grade and therefore not candidates for combat duty. A few more elderly majors and young junior officers then established a "corps headquarters" at historic Stirling. Near there, in 1314, Robert Bruce led a Scottish army to a great victory in a war that led to Scotland's independence.

In rapid order, a second dummy corps was activated at Dundee. The third corps to round out the Fourth Army was a genuine headquarters, that of the U.S. XV Corps under Major General Wade H. Haislip, in Ulster. A liaison officer from Haislip's real corps was assigned to MacLeod at Edinburgh Castle.

Rory MacLeod soon learned that creating an entire field army—even a phony one—was no simple task. He complained to Norfolk House that the right people were not being sent to him, that is, officers fully qualified to set up a convincing wireless network. SHAEF quickly solved that problem.

Then there was the matter of security. Did the Germans have genuine spies on the loose in Scotland? If so, they could soon explode the Fourth Army illusion. Soon civilians in Scotland became curious about the strange activities. It required eight officers and 24 radio operators to simulate the wireless traffic of a single division. How could their presence be explained?

Colonel MacLeod arranged for rumors to be spread that the radio operators were involved in a series of large-scale training exercises all over Scotland. It was a logical cover story: MacLeod indeed had been involved in genuine maneuvers of that kind. It was hoped that citizens would not begin wondering where all the soldiers were that were supposed to be taking part in these training operations.

The radio operators were sworn to secrecy, then told frankly that they were involved in a clandestine mission to deceive the Germans on the true date and target of the Allied invasion of northern France. Upon their skills and dedication could depend success or a bloody debacle on the shores of northern France, MacLeod stressed.

Compounding Colonel MacLeod's problems, SHAEF several times altered the Fortitude North scenario. This meant that his limited staff had to waste precious time by rewriting their wireless scripts.

MacLeod also was bedeviled by nagging problems with the genuine units borrowed to give added substance to the phantom army. Commanders of these real formations, which were training in nearby Ireland and in Scotland for actual combat roles in Overlord, either failed to grasp the significance of their assigned part in Fortitude North or agreed to cooperate in the scheme only when it did not conflict with their own preparations for battle.

So great were the difficulties that MacLeod, fearful that the deception operation on such a large scale could not be organized by his small staff in the limited time remaining before the true D-Day, suggested to SHAEF that the ghost force in Scotland be but a single corps. That proposal was promptly rejected: an entire field army would be needed to make Fortitude North plausible.

The Fortitude North scenario would suggest to German intelligence that one corps of Fourth Army would invade northern Norway and two corps would go ashore in southern Norway. The assaults would be launched early in June—at the same time as the true Normandy invasion. These fake assault forces would sail from wide bays called the Firth of Clyde, near Glasgow, along whose banks such famous ships as the *Queen Elizabeth* and the *Queen Mary* had been built, and the Firth of Forth on the eastern coast.

Haislip's genuine U.S. XV Corps, which consisted of the real 2nd, 5th, and 8th Infantry Divisions, was in training in northern Ireland for Overlord, but the Fortitude North script called for it fictitiously to reinforce the Norway invasion by sailing from Belfast, Mersey, Rosyth, and Invergordon.

Within one month, the ionosphere over Scotland was crackling with wireless messages in easily broken code. The massive electronic sham was code-named Skye. The Fourth Army contacted "corps," "corps" spoke to "divisions," "divisions" communicated with "regiments," and "regiments" transmitted orders to "battalions." As the weeks passed, Rory MacLeod "formed" four infantry divisions, an airborne division, an armored brigade, and scores of other units—a ghost army of some 250,000 men with their own tactical air force and 250 tanks and armored combat vehicles.[3]

Back in London, Brigadier Barker had predicted that the Germans quickly would locate the Fourth Army's headquarters from wireless interception. That discovery came much sooner than anyone had thought, however. Three days after the first wireless message was sent, a Messerschmitt fighter plane zoomed low over Edinburgh Castle with all guns blazing and pumped streams of bullets into the old structure. No one was injured in the Fourth Army's first, and only, "combat action."

The radio plan was highly sophisticated; it had to be plausible to German eavesdroppers across the English Channel. Creating only the major dummy formations would not be sufficient to fool the German Y-Service and intelligence evaluators. Subordinate units in support of the Fourth Army had to be assembled in Scotland. Among these fake units were the 303rd Antiaircraft Regiment, the 87th Field Cash Office (the phantom soldiers had to be paid), the VII Corps Postal Unit (to mail troops' letters and to receive them), a Film and Photographic Section, the 405th Road Construction Company of the Royal Engineers, and the 55th Field Dressing Station (to treat the large number of "casualties" that would result from an invasion of Norway).

All wireless messages had to have a logical link with the type of activity being simulated. Signals sent by the 87th Field Cash Office had to be concerned with pay and allowances. Likewise, messages from the 55th Field Dressing Station would have to deal with drugs and medical supplies.

Tucked in among the blizzard of wireless messages being picked up by German electronic listening posts were ones subtly pointing to Norway as the Fourth Army's target. "Captain H.R.L. Smith will report immediately to such-and-such a place for ski training," one signal would say. "II Corps Car Company urgently needs handbooks on servicing engines in cold climates and high altitudes," another would declare.

Calculated leaks to the press and radio strengthened the deception. Scottish newspapers told about football matches among units of the Fourth Army. A BBC reporter spent an entire day with the II Corps in the field—a difficult assignment since there was no II Corps. A major of the Fourth Army married a member of the women's auxiliary of the VII Corps, or so reported a local newspaper.

Wily German wireless-intelligence evaluators would need more than a rash of electronic signals over Scotland to be convinced that the Fourth Army was actually assembling there. Wireless fraud, after all, had been a British deception ploy since the North African battles with Field Marshal Erwin Rommel in 1940 and 1941. Further confirmation would be needed. So the Double-Cross sent two "second violins," code-named Mutt and Jeff, into action.

Mutt and Jeff had been captured as soon as they waded ashore from a seaplane on Moray Firth in northeastern Scotland in April 1941. Both were quickly turned, and their codes and radios were used to send back carefully contrived messages to their Abwehr controllers in Hamburg. Jeff's fake assigned cover was that of an officer in the Norwegian army in Scotland, although at the time of Fortitude North, he was actually in jail for suddenly becoming "difficult." Mutt became a fictional "farm manager" for a wealthy landowner in Scotland; he was in reality under guard in comfortable quarters in London.

When German intelligence began receiving indications that a new Fourth Army was assembling in Scotland, Mutt and Jeff's German controllers radioed instructions for them to snoop around the region and report back on what they had seen and heard.

Mutt—or rather his Double-Cross controller—radioed Hamburg with word that a Russian colonel named Budyenny had flown to Scotland and paid a visit to Edinburgh Castle. Mutt's report was to suggest to German intelligence that Budyenny had come to coordinate a joint British-American-Soviet attack on Norway. He also reported that the British II Corps headquarters was located at Stirling.

Jeff, through his case officer, told Hamburg that "hundreds, maybe thousands" of soldiers were in Scotland, and he described their shoulder patches. Since the Fourth Army was a new formation, the Germans had no record of such a patch, which added to the authenticity of Jeff's wireless report.

While Mutt and Jeff were prowling fictitiously around Scotland, German controllers were contacting two of their best agents in England, Arabel (Garbo) and Ivan (Tricycle) and asking for information on a new Fourth Army in Scotland. Arabel, who seemed to be everywhere in the British Isles, was shortly on the air to tell Hamburg that a Soviet military mission had recently called on General Bulgy Thorne at Edinburgh Castle, thereby confirming Mutt's earlier report.

The Royal Navy played an important role in the wireless deception. Two naval forces were simulated congregating in the Clyde estuary—Force V and Force W, which were supposed to carry the genuine British 52nd Division and fake 58th Division to Norway. Force V began sending radio messages in mid-April suggesting that it had 38 ships. Force W had 35 make-believe ships.

Uncoded radio messages deliberately disclosed to the Germans that these two phony naval forces were engaged in embarkation and disembarkation exercises and that these operations were being carried out at Scottish locales similar to the Norwegian fjords. Late in April, real shipping began to assemble in the broad Firth of Forth on the east coast, opposite Norway, and these vessels would eventually total 71. Royal Air Force fighter squadrons flew regular protective cover over this genuine collection of ships, but purposely allowed an occasional Luftwaffe reconnaissance plane to slip through and photograph the extensive shipping in the Firth of Forth.

Meanwhile, Garbo reported to Hamburg that he had assigned his crack sub-agent, Benedict, to spy on the British naval exercises that were taking place in the Firth of Forth. Garbo radioed his German controllers that Benedict, who was a creature of case officer Tommy Harris' fertile imagination, had been instructed to check into an inn at Methil, on the eastern coast of Scotland, and to remain there for six weeks.

Benedict was equal to the task. Within two days, he reported to Garbo that he had taken a trip to Dundee, on the east coast, and had spotted the (genuine) British 52nd Lowland Division and another unit wearing shoulder patches of a shell on a dark background. That night Garbo relayed Benedict's report to Germany and added, "This insignia is completely unknown to me." There was good reason for spies like Benedict and Garbo not to recognize the shoulder patch: It had been created only recently by British Colonel Roger Hesketh of the Committee of Special Means (CSM).[4]

Benedict also reported in the days ahead that he had traveled across Scotland to Greenock, the port for Glasgow on the Firth of Clyde, and had witnessed a large naval force conducting assault exercises. Eagle-eyed as always, Benedict noted that the troops involved were clad in arctic clothing, presumably the type that would be worn in the frigid climate of northern Norway.

Now Garbo, through his case officer Tommy Harris, put forth to Hamburg his opinion that the Allies might be planning not one, but two major operations to hit at about the same time—an assault against the Pas de Calais and another against Norway, across the North Sea from Scotland.[5]

In the meantime, scores of fighter planes and twin-engine bombers—all of them constructed of wood and canvas—began to pop up on airfields around Scotland. Skilled camoufleurs had erected them under the veil of night when their activities were less likely to be detected by German reconnaissance aircraft.

London began peppering Allied agents—real and fictional—in Norway with urgent requests for information about the topography and Wehrmacht units stationed there. Again, these messages were transmitted in code that could be broken readily by the Germans. These inquiries were discreet, as would be expected, but not too discreet. They asked about the snow levels in the higher elevations of Norway and whether the bridges spanning deep gorges would hold the weight of a medium tank. What distance a day could troops of the crack SS mountain division Prince Eugen be expected to travel on an urgent mission? Had the Wehrmacht in Norway been equipped with special winter clothing or boots that might prolong the troops' endurance in bitterly cold weather?

Late in April, Garbo, that "dedicated Nazi," no doubt delighted his controllers in Hamburg when he advised them that he had been offered a job that would put him in touch with much of what was taking place in the British Isles—as translator for the chief of the Iberian (Spain and Portugal) subsection of the Ministry of Information. There he would be at the knee of Brendan Bracken, the information minister and confidant of Winston Churchill. Bracken, of course, was privy to Great Britain's top secrets.

However, Garbo (through his case officer Tommy Harris) told Hamburg that he was stricken with a major conscience conflict. He was nauseated by the "idea of betraying the fuehrer by working for the British." Since he could still obtain high-grade intelligence without working for the hatred British, should he accept the position?

Apparently aghast at the thought that the conscientious Garbo was about to toss away an intelligence coup that had fallen from the heavens, his German controllers reacted swiftly. Garbo must forget his scruples and take the job. He responded that his mind was now at ease and that he would start work at the Ministry of Information in two days.[6]

Now Garbo would be more valuable to the Third Reich than ever, and it was but a short time before he started bombarding Hamburg with top-secret information he had picked up from Brendan Bracken and his aides. An occasional kernel would be truthful.

Brutus (Polish Captain Roman Garby-Czerniawski; Armand to the Abwehr) also had exciting news for Hamburg—at least his case officer did. Brutus actually was on flight duty with a Polish Air Force squadron based in England, but his case officer told the Germans by radio that he had been assigned to General George Patton's headquarters as a liaison officer between FUSAG and the Polish military leadership in London.

Brutus' Double-Cross case officer had selected this routine job for him because, while he would have access to many secrets, he would not be privy to the really important information the Germans might ask him to obtain and which SHAEF would not want to disclose. Brutus' case officer waited for two weeks to give him time to get settled in at FUSAG; then he began radioing the FUSAG order of battle at his regular midnight transmittals. Brutus sent only part of the information at any one time because, if he stayed on the air too long, British wireless monitors might pick up his signal, he reminded Hamburg.

Unknown to the imaginative orchestrators of Quicksilver and Skye, the deceptions received a boost from Colonel Alexis von Roenne, chief of Fremde Heere West. It had been the practice of the FHW to pass its intelligence evaluations to Walther Schellenberg's SD, with which the FHW had been involved in a bitter conflict to prove to the fuehrer that each was the more capable agency for ferreting out Allied invasion intentions.

Confident that it was better qualified to analyze incoming information than was the FHW, the SD invariably cut in half FHW estimates of the number of Allied divisions in Britain. Adolf Hitler thought the estimates reaching his desk had come from Baron von Roenne, whose evaluations he held in high regard. But the reports were von Roenne's Allied strength estimates cut in half by the SD.

Acting on the halved estimates, the fuehrer in March and April 1944 withdrew divisions from the West for employment on the Russian front. This turn of events deeply disturbed von Roenne, who thought that the forces along the Atlantic Wall should be strengthened rather than thinned out. Reports received by the FHW from Brutus and Garbo confirmed wireless intercepts, Luftwaffe reconnaissance flights, and other sources that a powerful Army Group Patton was being assembled to bolt across the Channel at the Pas de Calais.

Although a Schwarze Kapelle conspirator, von Roenne was dedicated to inflicting heavy casualties on the Western Allies so that when Hitler was eliminated, Schwarze Kapelle leaders would have leverage in seeking a negotiated peace with the United States and Great Britain. Consequently, he decided to take a drastic course of action (one that would eventually cost him his life). Knowing that the SD would halve the estimates in the FHW reports, von Roenne began grossly exaggerating Allied strength in Britain. When his figures reached the fuehrer, after having been sliced in half by SD, the resulting numbers would reflect an accurate assessment.

After receiving Brutus' phony Allied order of battle in late April, von Roenne submitted a false report that stated the Allies had 90 ground divisions and seven airborne divisions available in the British Isles. Actually, there were 32 infantry and armored divisions and three airborne divisions.

Then a curious twist of fate emerged. The SD, for unknown reasons, put its mark of approval on the greatly exaggerated estimate of 97 Anglo-American divisions instead of cutting the figure in half. The report was forwarded to Hitler who, thinking it had come from von Roenne, accepted the information as accurate. Thus, the continuing feud between rival German intelligence agencies gave credence to the myth of General George Patton's phantom FUSAG and General Bulgy Thorne's ghost Fourth Army.

16

Connivances in Stockholm

While the machinations of Fortitude North were in full swing, the wheels of Plan Graffham were set in motion by the Allied artful dodgers. Graffham was a means to add color and substance to Fortitude North by launching strict demands against the government of Sweden, a neutral country that shares an 800-mile border with Norway on the Scandinavian peninsula.

The focus of Graffham would be on Stockholm, Sweden's capital and largest city (about 650,000 people), which lies on a dozen islands in the eastern part of the country. Stockholm is known as "the Venice of the North" because of its many waterways.

In late March 1944, Victor Mallet, the British minister in Stockholm, was called back to London, presumably for consultations. Actually, it was the curtain raiser of a finely orchestrated scenario in which Mallet would return to Stockholm and insist that the Swedish government make several concessions. These would include the right of Allied aircraft to refuel in Sweden after operating over "enemy territory"—meaning Norway. Other demands included facilities at Swedish airports to make minor repairs to Allied aircraft, permission to send a British expert to consult the Swedes about transport between Norway and Sweden in the event of a German withdrawal from Norway, and permission for Allied reconnaissance planes to fly over Sweden.

Victor Mallet was instructed to stretch out the negotiations with Swedish officials as long as possible to perpetuate the deception. In the event the Swedes rejected the demands out of hand, Minister Mallet was to keep up the ploy by paying calls at the Swedish Foreign Ministry on any pretext he could concoct.

The Graffham deception was a team effort in which Great Britain, the United States, and the Soviet Union all had roles to play, although the British, in the jargon of the stage, would be the top banana.

As soon as Victor Mallet returned to Stockholm in early April, he called on Erik Boheman, the secretary-general to the Ministry of Foreign Affairs, and laid the Allies' demands on the table in plain, unvarnished language. This began a bout of diplomatic sparring that would go on for weeks—just as Graffham had dictated.

Boheman, as expected, promptly rejected the demand for using Swedish air space for Allied reconnaissance planes to photograph defenses along the Swedish-Norwegian border. Boheman pointed out, quite logically, that in so doing, the Allies would be photographing Swedish defenses as well. However, Boheman hinted, if Allied aircraft were to violate Swedish air space along the border, they would run no risk of being shot down by Swedish antiaircraft gunners. That was not the response that Graffham was looking for. Covert connivance on the part of Sweden would do no good in the deception plan; what was desired was Swedish cooperation that would be obvious to the Germans.

In the days ahead, Victor Mallet paid regular calls at the Swedish Foreign Ministry, as did his colleagues in Stockholm, the American Herschel Johnson and the Russian Madame Sofia Kollontay. There was no need for secrecy, for the artful dodgers who created Graffham knew that each act and word in the Stockholm melodrama would be funneled to Berlin within 48 hours.

Source of this intelligence pipeline into the Oberkommando der Wehrmacht was a clever operative named Karl-Heinz Kraemer. A lawyer turned Abwehr agent, Kraemer had been involved in intelligence missions against the British since 1942, when he was operating in Cairo. Beginning in mid–1943, he had been doing business in Stockholm.

Kraemer had evolved a technique that would provide Berlin with the highest-grade intelligence from inside the British Isles by tapping the secret services of neutral nations which maintained agents in England. Kraemer's most productive contacts were Count J. G. Oxenstjerna and Major S. E. Cornelius, the Swedish naval and air attachés in London.[1]

Both were highly competent in science and technology, enjoyed the complete trust of the British, and gained periodic access to British military facilities. Oxenstjerna and Cornelius would have been mortified to learn that their comprehensive reports were being copied by an officer of the Swedish intelligence staff in Stockholm and slipped to the crafty Karl-Heinz Kraemer.

To conceal the true method he was using to obtain these Swedish intelligence reports and to protect his cohort in Stockholm, Kraemer created several code names to indicate that his sources were actually agents in England. His principal fictitious spy in London was Hektor, who Kraemer identified to the Abwehr as "a highly placed official" in Winston Churchill's headquarters.

Kraemer told his Abwehr bosses that Hektor was madly in love with a "beautiful London society woman" code-named Josephine, who was his postbox in England. Neither Hektor nor Josephine existed except in Kraemer's creative mind, but he extracted hefty sums of money from the Abwehr to keep them operational.

Throughout the second half of 1943, Kraemer, through the theft of Count Oxenstjerna's and Major Cornelius' reports to Stockholm, provided the Abwehr with genuine and highly accurate intelligence on British aircraft production, the arrival of American convoys, the locations of major ammunition dumps, and Allied strategic plans.

Then, in about November 1943, Karl-Heinz Kraemer was unmasked by the British. Allen Dulles, the OSS station chief in Bern, and Allied agents in Lisbon obtained evidence proving that Josephine and Hektor were ghost agents and that Kraemer was actually getting his information on Great Britain from the Swedish intelligence officer in Stockholm.

Instead of disclosing their hand, John Bevan and his London Controlling Section (LCS) decided to, in essence, "turn" the unknowing Count Oxenstjerna and Major Cornelius. They were permitted to continue their visits to British military facilities, but, through some unknown connivance, their reports to Stockholm were sprinkled by the LCS with phony but plausible bits of information to indicate that the Allies intended to invade Norway in June 1944.[2]

Meanwhile, Victor Mallet and Herschel Johnson kept the heavy-handed pressure on the Swedish government. On April 6, the two colleagues made a joint call on Secretary-General Boheman and sternly demanded that a British transport expert be permitted to come to Sweden and study the country's transportation system. This was necessary, it was explained, in the event of a German withdrawal from Norway.

A few days later, Boheman informed Mallet that his government agreed to that proposal and the transport expert, Brigadier Cecil Manton, rushed to Stockholm from London. Manton proved to be a skilled actor. He held long, detailed discussions with officials of the Swedish National Railways, inquiring about locomotives, rolling stock, bridges, and the condition of tracks—knowing full well that this information was useless.

As part of the Graffham deception plan, British Air Commodore John Thornton was "promoted" to the exalted rank of air vice marshal and virtually smuggled into Sweden. The rank was phony and was intended to impress the Swedes (and the Germans) with how serious the current discussions were.

Thornton had obtained a diplomatic visa under the guise of inspecting the office of the British air attaché in Stockholm. However, as intended, it became obvious to Swedish officials that the "air vice marshal" had far more significant things on his mind. An engaging man, he hit it off well with General Olaf Nordenskiöld, head of the Swedish air force. Thornton even confided to the general—"highly confidentially, of course"—that the Allies intended to invade Norway.[2]

At this stage of Graffham, British Major Derrick Morley, one of John Bevan's men in the London Controlling Section who was in Stockholm to stage-manage the deception scheme, felt that it was now time to "stop scaring hell out of the Swedes" with stiff demands. Instead, Morley suggested, they should be given an offer to buy 12 Spitfire fighter planes without having to make concessions in return. The Swedes, Morley knew, were eager to beef up their air force.[3]

Mallet was enthusiastic over the proposal and even suggested raising the ante to 200 Spitfires. Such an action, if carried out, would certainly make Adolf Hitler nervous, Mallet declared. A mere promise, however, would not be satisfactory: the Spitfires actually would have to be delivered so German agents could see them. These Spitfires, whether numbering 12 or 200, might convince Hitler that something was afoot in Scandinavia, that the Swedes had made a secret deal with the Allies.

Nonetheless, the idea was rejected by the British Foreign Office and Air Ministry. With Overlord approaching, every warplane that could fly would be needed for the operation.

In the meantime, Sweden was gripped by war jitters. Perhaps aided and abetted by leaks from Graffham operatives, Swedish newspapers reported that American and British engineers were inquiring about Swedish rolling stock and roadbeds and that British air officers were inspecting the runways at Swedish airfields. Anxiety heightened after Stockholm newspapers and radio warned civilians to dig air-raid shelters and to store up food, fuel, medicine, and electric lightbulbs.

Graffham had Stockholm rumor mills grinding furiously. One story making the rounds in the upper social circles was that a British air vice marshal was in Sweden to arrange for the landing of Allied aircraft. The wife of Christian Gunther, the Swedish minister of foreign affairs, confided to friends that her husband believed that the Allies were preparing to invade Norway and Denmark. Norwegian men, rumor had it, were being flown from Sweden to Great Britain so they could participate in the pending liberation of their homeland.

Meanwhile, as a component of Graffham, the Allies launched an intense economic warfare campaign against the Swedes, intended, in part, to convince them (and German intelligence) that an invasion of neighboring Norway was looming. Mounted against the unfortunate Swedes was a series of direct threats and intimidations: if Sweden hoped to take its place in a postwar council of nations, it would have to cease giving aid and comfort to Germany. These stratagems included secret negotiations, economic pressures and financial skulduggery, and use made of the power and prestige of British and American bankers and tycoons.[4]

Kicking off the Graffham economic warfare campaign was a blunt speech made in New York City by U.S. Secretary of State Cordell Hull on April 9. Hull, a Tennessee mountaineer who had fought as an army captain in the Spanish-American War, stressed that the U.S. government intended to take a hard line with neutral nations in general, and Sweden in particular, in the postwar world.[5] Since John Bevan had heavy influence over what British and American officials said and did with regard to Bodyguard deceptions, it was likely that he had a hand in the timing and thrust of Secretary Hull's speech, which was widely reported in global media.

Rolled out as weapons in the economic assault against the Swedish government were the American Proclaimed List and the British Statutory List, both of which consisted of the names of German, Allied, and neutral citizens and officials who gave aid and comfort to the enemies of the two countries. Those on the blacklists would be treated as economic lepers after the global conflict ended. Neither Americans nor Britons could do business with them. Their ships and airplanes would be liable to seizure.

America and Great Britain also demanded that Sweden halt the export to Germany of iron ore, machine tools, and ball bearings, the tiny circular items absolutely essential to the production of airplanes, tanks, and a wide variety of weapons. The Third Reich could not produce enough ball bearings to build the accoutrements of war, so it had to import them from Sweden.

As a ploy to convince the Germans that an invasion of Scandinavia was pending, John Bevan and his cohorts in the London Controlling Section proposed a devious scheme to rig the Stockholm stock market and bring a sudden rise in the price of long-moribund Norwegian securities. German intelligence, the British knew, kept close track of the world's stock markets.

After weeks of wrangling, the British Treasury, which had grown depleted after four and a half years of all-out war, finally agreed to provide 30,000 pounds for the rigging scheme. At first, the LCS was going to do the stock manipulations from London, but that proposal was cast aside because the relevant Norwegian stocks were not quoted in the principal British newspapers' financial sections. So, after consultations with a few top London bankers sworn to secrecy, it was decided to do the rigging in Stockholm.

It soon became known in Europe's financial centers that unidentified speculators, apparently British, were buying up the dormant Norwegian stocks and bonds. Of the ten issues targeted by the schemers of the LCS, six went up, and four showed no change or fluctuated slightly. It was hoped that this movement on the Norwegian stock market would come to the attention of German intelligence and convey the impression that the Allies really did intend to invade Scandinavia.

As part of Graffham's economic warfare campaign, Stanton Griffis, an agent of Bill Donovan's OSS, flew to Stockholm to meet secretly with Swedish industrial kingpins to coerce them into halting shipments of huge amounts of ball bearings to Germany. Multimillionaire Griffis was an old friend of General Donovan, and they had served together in key posts in the Calvin Coolidge and Herbert Hoover administrations in the late 1920s and early 1930s. Donovan had been in the Justice Department when Griffis was a roving U.S. ambassador in Europe. When Griffis had returned to Washington, D.C., from his periodic jaunts through the capitals of Europe, he invariably met with Donovan, giving him the latest information and asking his opinions before he reported to the president.

Stanton Griffis was no novice in the cloak-and-dagger business. Bill Donovan had sent him into Finland in December 1942 to organize an espionage network in that strategically important country. On his arrival in Helsinki, Griffis was shunned by the Finnish government, which had been caught between a rock and a hard place. The Nazis were using Finnish territory as a base for operations against Russia, and the Finns were becoming increasingly fearful of full-scale occupation by the Wehrmacht. High officials in Helsinki, therefore, were reluctant to offend the Germans by an overt display of friendship with the United States. Despite these obstacles, along with the fact that he was under Gestapo surveillance, Stanton Griffis organized a spy network, not only in Finland but also in neighboring Sweden.

Now Griffis would be aided in his ball-bearing mission by OSS staffers in Stockholm who had opened their espionage shop in the fall of 1942. The station chief was Bruce Hopper, a Harvard professor of government, who virtually had been smuggled into the Swedish capital. He had crossed the Atlantic from New York to Liverpool, England, in a whale cruiser and was flown to Sweden by the Royal Air Force from a secret air base in Scotland.

The 50-year-old Hopper's chief of operations in Stockholm was Wilho Tikander, an attorney from Chicago, and his assistants included Taylor Cole, a Duke University political science professor; Richard Huber, a Washington, D.C., economist, and Walter Surrey, a New York City attorney. From the first day in Sweden, Hopper and his team had been engaged in a running battle with the striped-pantsed diplomats in the State Department.

American diplomats always had looked on OSS operations as some sort of satanic practice. In Stockholm and other neutral capitals of Ankara, Madrid, Lisbon, and Bern, the assignment to the American embassies of OSS officers under diplomatic cover met with strong resistance from the tradition-bound, staid career professionals of the State Department.

The lone OSS appointment to which the State Department did not object was that of a vivacious editor of *Vogue* magazine who had been assigned to Stockholm as a "fashion attaché." She diligently promoted American clothing designed in Sweden while secretly working with the Danish underground on behalf of the OSS.

Back in late 1942, another woman, Therese Bonney, an American free-lance war correspondent and habitué of Paris society, had been recruited by the OSS; she soon learned firsthand how antagonistic the State Department was toward Bill Donovan's agents. During the war between tiny Finland and the Soviet Union in 1939 and 1940, Bonney had established a close personal friendship with Field Marshal Baron Carl von Mannerheim, Finland's military and political strongman, because of her sympathetic stories. So in late 1942, her OSS instructions were to persuade the Finns to abandon their role as a "co-belligerent" (but not a full-fledged ally) of Nazi Germany in battling the Russian army.

Under cover of a reportorial assignment from *Colliers*, a large-circulation American weekly magazine, Therese Bonney reached Helsinki where she immediately was tailed by Gestapo agents. Nonetheless, she managed to arrange a covert meeting with Baron von Mannerheim. Although she failed to convince the marshal to break with Adolf Hitler, she did obtain a wealth of information about Finland's military apparatus and the extent of Nazi penetration into the Finnish government.

On her way back to Washington, D.C., to report to General Donovan, Bonney paid a short visit to the U.S. embassy in Stockholm to see a State Department official of long acquaintance. She revealed nothing of her OSS connection, but subtly asked her diplomat friend his opinion of Donovan's secret agency. Glancing around furtively as though Donovan had a spy tailing him, the State Department official confided: "I can always smell an OSS officer. We never give them any help."[6]

About a year later, in 1943, the British embassy in Stockholm was caught with egg on its face when a Swedish gangster was convicted of sabotaging German shipping and admitted that he had been working for the Special Operations Executive (SOE), the agency created by Winston Churchill with the mission of "Raising hell behind German lines." So the State Department's Herschel Johnson, a native of the state of Georgia, was determined to prevent similar behavior by the OSS in his bailiwick of Stockholm.

In March 1944, Johnson was horrified to learn that an OSS agent in Stockholm, Vic Shaho, a Minnesota railroad union executive, had arranged for Swedish transport workers to launch a strike against *SKF*, a huge Swedish firm known to be secretly shipping ball bearings to Germany. Johnson hit the ceiling over this "underhanded maneuver" and threatened to have Shaho and his OSS assistants kicked out of Sweden unless the strike was called off. It was.

Now, in April 1944, Stanton Griffis was making preparations for his secret confabulations with Swedish industrialists. Griffis was chairman of the board of New York City's Madison Square Garden (the site of countless major sports events), owner of Brentano's nationwide book chain, and a top executive of Paramount Pictures. He arrived in Stockholm under the cover of being a Paramount talent scout. Griffis was beseiged by a bevy of shapely, starry-eyed beauties, several of whom he signed to worthless Hollywood contracts. All this commotion helped to validate the OSS agent's masquerade.

Paramount Pictures held large quantities of foreign funds in many European capitals, and the OSS was ready to put this money to good use. With checkbook in hand, Griffis met secretly with leaders of the Stockholm business hierarchy in an effort to buy all of *SKF*'s ball-bearing exports to the Third Reich. The Swedes rejected the highly generous financial offer, declaring that an Allied invasion of Europe was merely a propaganda hoax and that the war would continue for years.[7]

Undaunted, Stanton Griffis persevered and through a judicious mixture of blacklist threats, promises of compensating Allied commercial orders, and businessman-to-businessman persuasion, the Swedes finally came to heel. They withdrew insurance from all ships entering German ports, and shipments of ball bearings, iron ore, and machine tools to the Reich were gradually halted.[8]

In spite of frequent clashes with Herschel Johnson and other State Department nabobs in Stockholm, Bruce Hopper, the 50-year-old Roosevelt New Deal liberal and OSS station chief, and his agents pulled off some innovative and politically delicate machinations. Hopper's office became a listening post for Russian activities, and mild forms of espionage against Uncle Sam's Soviet allies were not only condoned but encouraged by Calvin Hoover, the OSS official in Washington responsible for Swedish operations.

Hoover, a Duke University economist, had spent several years in Russia during the early Joseph Stalin era on an academic research project and had returned home with a bitter dislike for the Communist dictatorship. So when he had the opportunity to strike a blow at the Soviet regime he despised, he took it.[9]

Despite repeated efforts by the Americans and British to obtain information on the Soviet armed forces, Moscow had consistently stonewalled the requests. So Calvin Hoover had the satisfaction of having his OSS agents secretly purchase both the Russian army's order of battle and the register of the Soviet navy from Finnish military officers in Stockholm.[10]

Now, in early spring 1944, there were unmistakable signs that the Allies were preparing to launch something big. Swedish government and military officials cast their eyes toward Norway and waited with anxiety for the Anglo-American blow to hit.

South of Sweden in Germany, Adolf Hitler and his generals also had taken notice of the rash of activities the Allies had been conducting in Sweden and of the buildup in Scotland of General Bulgy Thorne's Fourth Army. In late April, orders went out from Berlin for the six Wehrmacht divisions in Norway to go on an alert status.

17

Tightening the Security Lid

Staid old London had survived 2,000 years of brutal wars, deadly plagues, and disastrous fires. It had stood unflinching under the devastating Luftwaffe blitz during the Battle of Britain in 1940. Now, in the early spring of 1944, the city of 3 million people was engulfed by an olive-drab tidal wave of American servicemen. It seemed that the young newcomers from across the Atlantic outnumbered the Londoners, whose cinemas, hotels, restaurants, dance halls, and pubs were swamped by GIs.[1]

These Americans were a strange lot, indeed. They munched chewing gum, loudly sang songs with ridiculous titles like *Hut-Sut Rawlson on the Rillera* and *The Flatfoot Floogie*, called men they did not know "Mac," and spoke a curious language known as "jive." Many loved to jitterbug, which, to most conservative Londoners, was akin to frogs hopping about on a hot griddle.

Flat, warm British beer was only one of many local customs that the Yanks taught themselves to endure. They were stunned to find that the British drive on the "wrong"—that is, left—side of the road. And they learned to eat fish and chips out of last week's newspaper.

GIs rapidly discovered that England and the United States were two nations separated by a common language. The Americans found that a copper was a penny, not a policeman, that a vest was not an outer garment but an undershirt. And an American billeted in a boardinghouse learned not to burst out laughing when his landlady promised to "knock him up"—that is, awaken him—in the morning.

GIs in London on pass slept most of the day and spent nights in the pubs and clubs that stayed open until 7:00 A.M. Even in the blackouts, throngs of pedestrians surged up and down the streets. "Ladies of the night" were in countless doorways, holding lighted cigarettes so the Americans would know they were there. When a customer was hooked, the ensuing encounter was concluded on the spot. The Yanks called them "Piccadilly Commandos."

Even on their best behavior, the Yanks created tensions. An American private earned nearly five times more money than did his British counterpart, and he spent his pay freely on British women. British soldiers considered this to be unfair competition.

By British standards, the Americans were rich. Jealousies and conflicts, heightened by emotional strains and sharply contrasting economic levels, erupted between GIs and Tommies. London's quaint pubs were usually the battle zones where fistfights, supported by furniture and empty whiskey bottles, broke out. With the strains of *Roll Out the Barrel* providing background music on record players, American and British servicemen sought to settle their disputes. These were the same warriors who would soon be fighting shoulder to shoulder against a common foe—the Wehrmacht.

Londoners—indeed natives all over England, Scotland, Wales, and Ulster—were perplexed by the habits of these Americans, who scrawled on rocks, on walls, in lavatories, and on seemingly unreachable places, "Kilroy was here!" Brits never found out for sure who Kilroy was, where he came from, what he did, or why anyone would be so awed by him as to write his name all around the British Isles.

At any given time, there were some half-million military men and women from Allied and neutral countries on leave in or posted to London. They represented about 60 nations. A kaleidoscope of uniforms of every conceivable color and design had become so commonplace that London civilians, hurrying about their business, had long since ceased giving these uniforms even a fleeting glance.

A London newspaper hatched a scheme to dramatize the security risk inherent in this maze of multinational military garb. A reporter was dressed in a genuine Luftwaffe colonel's uniform, and for six hours, in broad daylight, he strolled through the crowds that packed Piccadilly Circus and Trafalgar Square in the heart of London. No one paid any attention to the "Nazi officer."

Under the giant statue of Admiral Lord Horatio Nelson standing atop a tall column in Trafalgar Square, the imposter halted an occasional pedestrian to inquire in a thick Teutonic accent for directions to Whitehall, a broad avenue whose buildings contained the War Office, the headquarters of the British army and navy. Nearby stood the simple brick building at 10 Downing Street that was the official residence of Prime Minister Winston Churchill.

Since the outbreak of war, the British government, newspapers, BBC, clergymen, and headmasters had harangued the public to be vigilant for German spies, saboteurs, and intruders of every stripe. Yet, none of those whom the "Luftwaffe colonel" asked for directions, including a bobby, revealed any suspicion.

When the fake German colonel's newspapers hit the streets with blaring photographic spreads about the caper, loud howls erupted from the hallowed chambers of Parliament as members demanded that something be done to tighten security. Actually, with millions of strangers and even stranger vehicles jamming the major cities, towns, and the countryside alike, there was no surefire means for airtight security—a fact that especially haunted tall, husky U.S. Brigadier General Thomas J. Betts.

As the deputy chief of intelligence at SHAEF, Betts was largely responsible for Overlord's security, a facet of military operations that goes hand-in-glove with deception and that could mean success or failure for the looming invasion. It was a heavy burden, and it had taken its toll on Betts in sleepless nights and fearful days. "I feel like I'm 44 years of age going on 95!" he confided to a friend.

By mid-April 1944, hundreds of American and British officers were privy to the innermost secrets of Overlord—including the projected D-Day and the locale of the invasion. They were known as Bigots, which took its curious name from the stamp "To Gib" that had been imprinted on the papers of officers traveling to Gibraltar for the invasion of North Africa in November 1942. To confuse the Germans (and Allied personnel not in the know), the "To Gib" letters had been reversed.

Being inducted into the Bigot "fraternity" required passing an intense security check in the United States and Britain. Did the candidate drink to excess? Did he have a mistress who might betray secrets if the relationship grew sour? Was he homosexual and therefore a possible target for blackmail? Did he have a reputation for talking too much? Even after one became a Bigot, his conduct was subjected to ongoing surveillance.

Only a Bigot could see secret documents marked Bigot in large red letters. He had a special pass to enter certain offices which others could not enter, however high their ranks. When one Bigot spoke to another Bigot over the wire, a special green telephone equipped with a "scrambler" was used, so that the conversation would sound like gibberish to hostile wiretappers.

On occasion, the Bigot procedure, as it was called, had unintentional comedy overtones. When a Bigot, unsure of another officer's security status, would ask, "Are you a Bigot?" the second man, unaware that there was such a thing as a Bigot, would fix him with a quizzical stare as if to reply: "Why on earth are you asking me if I'm prejudiced?"

General Tom Betts watched over his Bigots like an anxious mother hen. But there were a few hundred of them, and not all could be "chaperoned" all the time. How could he be certain that an ugly duckling had not infiltrated his sizeable brood? And how could Betts be sure that one too many drinks might not lead to loose talk in hotels, bars, restaurants, and other public places?

Betts' security worries seemed to be endless. What was to keep the Germans across the Channel from sneaking into his yard and snatching a Bigot from under the general's protective wing? For four years, black-faced British commandos had been slipping across the dark Channel at night to make raids and bring back prisoners for interrogation. Why couldn't the Germans do the same thing?

It would be a simple task, Tom Betts knew, for a bold leader like hulking, scarfaced Otto Skorzeny, the "Most Dangerous Man in Europe," to pick a few of his SS stalwarts who spoke passable English and clad them in genuine American or British uniforms taken from POWs. As Betts envisioned the scenario, Colonel Skorzeny and his band would be brought by submarine at night to a carefully selected point off the coast of southern England. They would silently slip into inflated rubber boats, row to shore, and capture as many Allied officers as they could before heading back to the waiting submarine.

Betts knew that such a raid would be far simpler than Skorzeny's daring rescue of Adolf Hitler's old crony, Benito Mussolini, from an Italian mountaintop fortress a year earlier. Although England had a relatively short coastline, it was impossible for every yard of it to be strongly patrolled around the clock.

General Betts shuddered from the thought of the intelligence bonanza one or more lightning-like raids would produce for the Germans. Few lower-level Bigots knew all the secrets of D-Day, but wily German intelligence evaluators could piece together a fairly accurate Feindbild of Allied troop concentrations, thereby pointing to Normandy as the likely invasion target.

Then there was a delicate security matter that was whispered around SHAEF as "the Russian problem." In April 1944, Major General Brocas Burrows, chief of the British military mission to Moscow, reported to London that Premier Stalin was demanding that the precise date and locale of Overlord be made known to him. Weeks earlier, a decision had been reached by President Roosevelt and Prime Minister Churchill that the Russians would be told only the approximate date of Neptune in order to coordinate the massive Red Army summer offensive and pin down as many Wehrmacht divisions as possible on the Eastern Front.

British leaders and deceptionists were especially leery of confiding anything to the Russian ambassador to England, a stoical figure the Brits had dubbed "Frogface." His name was Feodor Tarasovich Gousev, and he had honed his diplomatic skills as a butcher in a seedy Moscow grocery store as a young man. Gousev, British intelligence knew, had risen to a high post in the NKVD (Russian intelligence).

Despite Ambassador Gousev's demands, some of them subtle, others blunt, that the Anglo-Americans disclose details of Overlord and Plan Bodyguard, he would not be told where the invasion would hit. However, Gousev did prove useful in the Quicksilver scheme. Straight-faced British and American officers briefed him in detail about General Patton's ghost army group in southeastern England that would launch the principal assault. Consequently, General Burrows in Moscow was instructed to inform Stalin only that D-Day would be two or three days before or after June 1, 1944, depending on weather conditions.

Stalin was not satisfied with that reply and wanted more details. General Burrows was ordered to keep his mouth shut. So the military mission chief could plausibly deny that he was privy to Overlord secrets, he and his assistants were forbidden to return to London. Actually, Burrows was a Bigot.

No one was above the thick veil of security that hovered over the British Isles. Security was an almighty law unto itself. Although Supreme Commander Dwight

Eisenhower was Bigot Number 1, he was not immune to surveillance from those charged with protecting the secrets of D-Day.

Allied security officers were confronted by a situation so delicate that not even Eisenhower himself could be advised of it. The target of the security worry: Kay Summersby, a former fashion model in her early thirties. Although a citizen of Ireland, she held a lieutenant's commission in the American Women's Army Corps (WAC). The reason for the intense concern was that divorcee Kay Summersby and General Eisenhower had formed a very close relationship. Since mid–1942, she had been the supreme commander's chauffeur, confidant, and social companion.

It was an open secret in SHAEF that Eisenhower was infatuated with the willowy, vivacious Kay Summersby. Even while wrestling with monumental problems of Overlord, the supreme commander had written to Chief of Staff George Marshall that he was planning to divorce his wife of 25 years, Mamie, to marry his female aide.[2]

Never was Lieutenant Summersby's loyalty, discretion, or integrity under question by SHAEF security officers. Although Eisenhower had cut through red tape and neatly skirted tradition to secure a commission in the U.S. Army for a foreigner, army regulations specifically disqualified her, as a citizen of Eire, from any contact with Overlord information. Yet daily she was at Eisenhower's side and heard the most secret matters being discussed.

Security officers were concerned particularly about what might happen if the supreme commander and his ladyfriend were to break up prior to D-Day. What, if anything, would be the reaction of Kay Summersby if she became a woman scorned? That prospect sent shivers up the spines of those charged with maintaining D-Day security. But there was nothing they could do about the situation— except to pray that Cupid continued to smile on the couple.[3]

Meanwhile, SHAEF security officers were haunted by the fact that Great Britain was an open and democratic society, one steeped in liberal tradition, and therefore a country where German agents were free to roam largely unhampered. Although the British secret service and Scotland Yard had rounded up scores of Hitler's spies early in the war, no one knew how many remained at large, if any.

Nine months earlier, the congenial British general, Frederick Morgan, who had been in charge of Overlord planning prior to Eisenhower's arrival, had impressed upon Winston Churchill that it would be simple for a spy to deduce the direction of the cross-Channel attack merely by trekking up and down the southern coast to see where the bulk of the forces were concentrated. Morgan had wanted the south coast to be forbidden to civilian visitors.

The prime minister had been aghast at the thought of restricting the movement of civilians and rejected General Morgan's request on the grounds of democratic principles. Morgan had interpreted this response to mean that Churchill and his Cabinet were merely trying to avoid irritating the people for political reasons. "If we fail," Morgan had remarked dryly to his staff, "there won't be any more British politics!"[4]

Now, with D-Day edging inexorably closer, Allied generals and deceptionists alike focused once again on the fact that a lone Nazi agent wandering around southeastern England could detect in a day or two that Army Group Patton was a monumental fraud. In that event, the Oberkommando der Wehrmacht could ignore the threat to the Pas de Calais and concentrate its best troops in the next most logical invasion site—Normandy.

At the same time, there was a group in London numbering some 450 persons, who were patriotic, ethical, well meaning—and potentially dangerous to Overlord security. These were the war correspondents, American, British, and Canadian, all of whom were plagued by a demon of their species, a constant hunt for news.

Censorship was so strict that there was no danger of the operational plan for Neptune being plastered on the front pages of the *New York Times*, *St. Louis Post-Dispatch*, or the *Daily Mail* of London. The security danger lay in the fact that there was nothing to prevent newsmen and women from traipsing around the southern coastal regions in their searches for stories. It was quite conceivable that they might piece together scraps of information gained from personal observations and inquiries that would permit them to form a reasonably accurate idea of the invasion plan. This eventuality would be particularly logical should they spot the fake vehicles, weapons, tanks, equipment, and ammunition stockpiles concentrated across from the Pas de Calais by the artful dodgers of Quicksilver.

Nightly in the teeming, smoke-filled pubs of Fleet Street, the heart of London's publishing empire, scores of reporters bellied up to the bars and conducted combined exercises in future Allied strategy as they consumed their lukewarm ale and bitters. As the hour grew late, these sessions often grew quite loud.

The security danger in these pub "war games" resulted from the fact that members of foreign diplomatic staffs frequented these same watering holes. Their job was to secure information for their governments, and what better way to accomplish that mission than to overhear experienced journalists who had inspected the coastlines and military installations?

SHAEF security officers, especially the British, were haunted by the memory of Rogerio de Magalhaes Peixoto de Menezes, who arrived in London in July 1942 to take up his job as a diplomat at the neutral Portuguese embassy. Menezes was young, handsome, personable and, fortunately for the Allies, stupid and lazy.

Menezes had carried with him to London several bottles of invisible ink and a code that had been given to him in Lisbon by Abwehr agents. His intelligence reports were to be shipped back to Lisbon in the sacrosanct and inviolable Portuguese diplomatic pouch. The 26-year-old Menezes, it developed, could have qualified as the world's worst spy. Most of the information he dispatched to Lisbon was culled from London newspapers, mixed with random gossip he collected in pubs, where he caroused away most nights.

After a few months, Menezes became even too lackadaisical to use the diplomatic pouch and sent his reports by ordinary mail to the "letter boxes" he had been assigned in Lisbon by the Abwehr. British secret service agents in the

Portuguese city discovered these addresses, a detection that led to his arrest in London.[5]

The lesson drawn by the Menezes affair was clear to SHAEF officers charged with protecting Overlord's secrets: a diplomat working for the Germans could not be unmasked unless he was dumb enough to give himself away. How many of the foreign diplomats hanging around the pubs and listening to Allied newsmen discussing theoretical invasion strategy would be as ignorant and lazy as Rogerio Menezes?

Winston Churchill, who had himself once been a reporter, warned General Eisenhower of the dangers involved with newsmen having full freedom to roam the British Isles and suggested that action be taken to limit their travels, especially in southern England (where the genuine Neptune assault forces were concentrating) and in southeastern England (the base of Patton's phantom army group).

Eisenhower was skewered on the horns of a dilemma—"freedom of the press" versus the security of Overlord. So the supreme commander handled the delicate situation by asking American and British journalists not to speculate in any way about where and when the invasion would hit. Then he instructed his staff to treat reporters with respect—and "don't tell them a damned thing!"

Early in April, as the security lid continued to be tightened on the British Isles, General Bernard Montgomery wrote an urgent communication to Eisenhower asking that he use his extraordinary influence to prod the British government into declaring a ten-mile-wide strip along the southern and southeastern coasts of England to be a forbidden zone for outside civilians.

Eisenhower agreed and took up where General Frederick Morgan had left off in frustration in mid–1943. Ike wrote to Winston Churchill: "It will go hard on our consciences if we were to feel, in later years, that by neglecting any security precaution we had compromised the success of [Overlord]." Such was the enormous power that had been placed in Ike Eisenhower's hands that, only four days later, Churchill and his Cabinet issued a decree, establishing the coastal forbidden zone.

Unknown to the Allied deception masterminds, that unprecedented ruling provided a bonus by confusing Adolf Hitler still further about invasion intentions. The fuehrer told his generals: "These Anglo-Saxon demonstrations seem ludicrous to me. The latest reports of their unreasonable regulations, these security measures and so on. Normally such things aren't done when an operation of that kind is planned. . . . I can't help thinking that it's just an impudent posture, that [the invasion] is all an insolent bluff!"[6]

Hard on the heels of his request to seal off the coastal regions, Dwight Eisenhower moved to plug another glaring security loophole—the neutral nations' diplomats in London. Their reports to their governments could easily fall into enemy hands—and did so on occasion. SHAEF also recognized that there were men on the embassy staffs in London who were pocketing healthy fees for feeding sensitive information to the Germans.

Ike pulled no punches. He "requested" the complete suspension of communications from diplomatic representatives in London, except those of the United States, the Soviet Union, and the British Dominions. Churchill promptly granted that request; in fact, he may have suggested that Eisenhower make it. Transmission or receipt of coded wireless messages by the foreign legations also was forbidden.

Embassies were advised that diplomatic pouches would be opened and their mail inspected, censored, and possibly confiscated. Regular incoming mail would be intercepted and examined; telephone lines would be tapped. No member of a diplomatic delegation or his family or servants would be permitted to leave England. A few embassies were told that their officials were not free to travel outside London without specific permission.

England in reality was now an island unto itself. These restrictions were an unprecedented violation of the historical traditions of international diplomacy. Some 50 million English men, women, and children, along with 2 million American and other Allied soldiers, were cut off from the rest of the world.

18

A High-Level Epidemic
of the Jitters

If the Germans obtain as much as forty-eight hours warning of the location of the assault, the chances of success are small. And any longer warning spells certain disaster.

—General Frederick Morgan
Architect of Invasion Plan

Dwight David Eisenhower, always cheerful and upbeat in public, was undergoing the torments of the damned. Each day the supreme commander had to make decisions that would deeply influence not only Overlord but the future of the war. Piled on top of this enormous burden was the fact that Eisenhower had to conduct prolonged arguments with those whose views did not coincide with his own—the U.S. chiefs of staff, the British chiefs of staff, the combined chiefs of staff, Field Marshal Alan Brooke, and Winston Churchill. All the while, General Eisenhower knew that the ultimate success or failure of Overlord rested on his individual judgment.

Since his arrival in London's Grosvenor Square in mid-January 1944, the supreme commander had to weld a SHAEF team whose British and American generals held traditional rivalries going back to the Revolutionary War of 1776. Many American commanders viewed the British as condescending, while most British generals considered the Americans to be arrogant and "newcomers to war."

Wartime coalitions historically had been ripped apart by jealousies, friction, and nationalistic goals, so German Propaganda Minister Joseph Goebbels cleverly tried to drive a wedge between the British and Americans as they prepared to leap the English Channel. One of Goebbels' jingles, which gained considerable circulation among GIs in Britain, was: "England is willing to fight to the last American."

Through the subtle connivance of Field Marshal Brooke, who had long held Dwight Eisenhower to be an inept and inexperienced strategic planner, the supreme commander was surrounded by a phalanx of British officers. Eisenhower's deputy was Air Marshal Arthur Tedder: General Bernard Montgomery, a folk hero in Britain after his victories over Erwin Rommel and his Afrika Korps in the North African desert, was in charge of Allied ground forces for Overlord; and sharp-tongued Air Marshal Trafford Leigh-Mallory was in command of Allied tactical air forces.

It was through Dwight Eisenhower's character, personality—including his world-famous broad grin—and his conduct as an impartial supreme commander that SHAEF rapidly functioned with the smooth efficiency of a major commercial corporation, one where national or personal rivalries were muted.

Early in April, two SHAEF colonels, one American and the other British, got into a violent dispute. Eisenhower sent for the American. "Colonel, I can understand how two dedicated men working alongside one another in a stressful situation could get into an argument," Eisenhower said. "I can even understand a situation in which you called him a son-of-a-bitch. But I refuse to accept your calling him a *British* son-of-a-bitch!" Within 24 hours, the American colonel was heading for the Zone of the Interior (the United States) to spend the remainder of the war shuffling papers and counting paperclips.

In the pressure-cooker climate, there were bound to be personality conflicts and verbal clashes at the high levels of SHAEF. One of these bitter arguments occurred in mid-April and threatened to undermine Allied solidarity.

General Bernard Montgomery was presiding at an airborne planning session at his 21st Army Group headquarters at St. Paul's School, a large, red-brick Gothic building that stood beside the road leading to Heathrow airport outside London. Curiously, Montgomery had attended St. Paul's as a youth. Fireworks were touched off when Air Marshal Trafford Leigh-Mallory made a startling proposal: cancel the parachute and glider assault by the U.S. 82nd Airborne and U.S. 101st Airborne divisions behind Utah Beach, where the untested American 4th Infantry Division would storm ashore.

If one of the five assault beaches were more critical than the others, it had to be Utah, at the base of the Cherbourg peninsula on the far west of the Neptune region. Known as the Ivy Division, Major General Raymond O. Barton's 4th was to drive northward after landing and help seize the port of Cherbourg, the invasion's primary objective.

"I cannot approve your airborne plans," Leigh-Mallory told General Omar Bradley, who commanded American ground forces. "Your losses will be far more than what your gains are worth. I cannot go along with you." Bradley was stunned. "Very well, sir," the low-key American replied, "If you insist on cutting out our airborne attack, then I must ask that we eliminate the Utah assault. I am not going to land on that beach without making sure our airborne people have the four causeway exits behind it."

Now it was Leigh-Mallory's turn to be stunned. After a moment of awkward silence, he responded, "Then let me make it clear. If you insist upon the airborne operation, you'll do it in spite of my opposition." The air marshal turned to Montgomery: "If General Bradley insists upon going ahead, he will have to accept full responsibility for the operation." Bradley flushed with anger and quickly cut in: "That's perfectly okay. I'm in the habit of accepting full responsibility for my operation."[1]

Bernard Montgomery, who for two years had had his share of clashes with British and American generals alike, now found himself in the unaccustomed role of peacemaker. Monty rapped for order and declared: "Gentlemen! Gentlemen! That's not at all necessary. I'll accept responsibility."[2]

With his avalanche of worries and concerns, General Eisenhower no doubt was most haunted by the specter of Adolf Hitler and his Oberkommando der Wehrmacht pinpointing the true landing beaches in Normandy. Was it logical to presume that such a gargantuan operation could be kept "hidden"? The supreme commander's security outlook was hardly uplifted when he received an appraisal of expected German reactions to Overlord from Bernard Montgomery's 21st Army Group: "Whatever further assaults our cover plan [Bodyguard] may lead [the Germans] to expect elsewhere and however effective our jamming of enemy radar, the enemy's appreciation that we are going to assault Normandy will harden until on D-Day plus 1 they will be certain." If that prognostication were not a large enough jolt, Montgomery's intelligence chief went on to say: "I am certain that when you carry out Neptune, you will have against you more panzer divisions than you will find comfortable."[3]

As preparations for Overlord became steadily more hectic, demanding, and nerve-wracking, Eisenhower was beginning to show signs of the enormous strain. Only his intimates knew that he had been undergoing secret medical treatment for an eye that was inflamed and sore, resulting in blurred vision on occasion, and was also being treated for ringing in his ears. Most nights, as only his close friend and naval aide Commander Harry C. Butcher knew, the general was so exhausted he could hardly undress and get into bed. Even then, he was haunted with visions of seemingly insolvable problems, knowing as he fitfully drifted into slumber that his ordeal would resume with the approach of dawn.

No detail in Overlord planning was too small to find its way to the supreme commander. He had even been forced to settle a low-level dispute over the amount of toilet tissue to be taken ashore on the first day of the invasion. Buck-passing halted at Dwight Eisenhower's desk.

Intensifying the deep misgivings of Eisenhower (and no doubt all high-ranking SHAEF officers) was a series of frightening security breaches that might tip off Adolf Hitler and his generals about the place and approximate date of Overlord. Early in April, word was received from the railroad stationmaster in Exeter, in southwestern England where genuine Neptune divisions were training, that a briefcase had been found in a passenger compartment of a train. In the container were a number of papers stamped "Bigot." A security officer rushed to the station to retrieve the briefcase.

In London on a warm day, windows were opened in a stuffy third-floor office where Bigot papers were conveniently stacked on a windowsill. A sudden gust of wind blew the appears outside, and as horrified officers watched, they fluttered into the street. There were ten sheets of paper—only nine of them recovered.

At about the same time, an American paratroop officer browsing through the bookstalls of a London store spotted a volume entitled *Paratroopers*. His curiosity piqued, the officer picked up the book and saw that its author was Major F. O. Mischke, who, it developed, was a Czechoslovakian belonging to a unit of the Free French forces in England.

Thumbing through the pages, the American noticed that they contained a factual summary of German airborne operations during the war. Suddenly, his heart skipped a beat when his eyes fell on a full-page map that was designed to illustrate a chapter on a hypothetical Allied airborne assault that would spearhead an invasion of France across the English Channel. Mischke's map showed the Allied parachute and glider forces dropping and landing in three zones, which were almost precisely where the U.S. 82nd Airborne and 101st Airborne divisions would come down in Normandy in the genuine D-Day operation. The third zone was only a few miles off the true American airborne landing.

SHAEF's hierarchy broke out with a severe case of the willies over Mischke's book. Intelligence officers were convinced that the volume already was being scanned by the Oberkommando der Wehrmacht in Berlin. An intense secret investigation of Major Mischke's background disclosed only that he was a patriotic Czech who had fled his country after it was overrun by the Germans in order to continue the fight against Nazism from England.

This clean bill of health for the author of *Paratroopers* did little to relieve SHAEF anxieties. The haunting question was: Would the Germans consider the theoretical airborne assault in Normandy as described by Major Mischke in his book an incredible Allied security leak and pack Normandy with additional troops, guns, and tanks?

No German radio broadcast during the invasion buildup threw such a scare into the Allied high command than did the one made by the turncoat Englishman, William Joyce, on April 21. Using the pseudonym "Lord Haw-Haw," Joyce boasted over Radio Berlin: 'We know exactly what you intend to do with those concrete units. You think you are going to sink them on our coasts in the assault. Well, we are going to help you boys. We'll save you the trouble. When you come to get underway, we're going to sink them for you.'[4]

Clearly Lord Haw-Haw was referring to the portable harbors code-named Mulberries, one of the most closely guarded secrets of the war. Some 20,000 men labored for nearly nine months to build the two gigantic Mulberries. It required nearly 80 merchant vessels to bring in the 2 million tons of concrete, steel, and other materials required by the project.

Months earlier, Adolf Hitler had told his generals: "If we can keep a major port out of the hands of the Allies in England, we can defeat any attempt to gain a foothold on continental Europe." Then the fuehrer proclaimed several major ports in France and the Low Countries "fortresses" and required their German commanders to sign declarations that they would defend the ports "to the last man and the last bullet" and then destroy the harbor facilities to render them useless to the invaders.

Across the Channel, Eisenhower's strategists had reached the identical conclusion that Hitler had reached: unless the invaders could seize a major port to rapidly bring in troops, guns, tanks, ammunition, fuel, and rations in huge quantities, the Allies would be in danger of withering on the vine and being cut to pieces by panzer divisions converging on the Normandy beachhead. So SHAEF planners focused on Cherbourg, an ancient, heavily fortified city situated in a bowl near the center of the north coast of the peninsula that jutted like a sore thumb into the Channel.

Hitler's hopes for an Allied invasion debacle and a subsequent negotiated peace with the Americans and British lay in his belief that amphibious assault troops would smash directly at a major port bristling with big guns and concrete bunkers. However, the Allies would go ashore at a region in Normandy that was devoid of a major port and therefore less heavily defended.

Until American troops going ashore on Utah could fight their way 20 miles northward and seize Cherbourg from the rear (which would require an estimated two weeks), forces in Normandy would have to be supplied over the open beaches. Plans called for the floating Mulberries to be towed across the Channel by every available tug in England and anchored off the Neptune shores.

The two Mulberries were engineering miracles. They would consist first of an outer breakwater make up of great steel floats. Next would come 145 huge concrete caissons in various sizes which were to be sunk butt to butt to make an inner breakwater. The largest of these caissons would have antiaircraft guns and crews, and when being towed would look like a five-story building lying on its side. Beyond the Mulberries a line of concrete-loaded ships would be sunk as an additional breakwater.

Within these man-made harbors freighters could unload into barges ferrying back and forth to the beaches. Smaller ships could discharge their cargos at huge steel pierheads where waiting trucks would carry them to shore over floating pontoon bridges.

Had the Germans, as indicated by Lord Haw-Haw's broadcast, really discovered the secrets of the Mulberries? If the enemy had learned the truth, they might penetrate the Allied strategy and shift troops from Cherbourg to the open beaches.

In order to head off panic, the supreme commander contacted the Pentagon in Washington with an urgent request for 50 Coast Guard cutters. They were to escort the Mulberries while they were being towed at one mile per hour across the Channel after D-Day, and if the huge structures should be bombed and sunk by the Luftwaffe, the cutters were to fish the crews from the water.

Ultra, at Bletchley Park north of London, was ordered to try to discover how the Germans knew that the Mulberries were being built at several locales along the coast of southern England. In so doing, Ultra intercepted and decoded wireless messages sent from Berlin to Tokyo by General Hiroshi Baron Oshima, the Japanese ambassador to the Third Reich.

Oshima, who was both a capable soldier and a skilled diplomat, had taken two tours of the Atlantic Wall, from the Netherlands to the Spanish border. The first one had been in the fall of 1943, and the last one in April 1944. After the final tour, Baron Oshima was briefed on estimates of Allied intentions by Field Marshal Gerd von Rundstedt at OB West.

During the briefing, the Ultra intercepts disclosed, von Rundstedt had mentioned, almost in passing, that two large concrete structures were being built on the coast of southern England, but added that German intelligence had identified them as antiaircraft gun towers. Generals at SHAEF issued enormous sights of relief.

Also in April, 54-year-old Major General Henry J. F. Miller, a West Point classmate and long-time friend of Eisenhower, was among the guests at a London dinner party for American Red Cross nurses. Host for the lively affair was Major General Edwin L. Sibert, intelligence chief in the U.S. European Theater of Operations (ETO). Miller, a Bigot who had an impeccable record and was regarded as a highly capable officer, was the quartermaster for the U.S. 9th Air Force.

General Sibert's party took place in the public dining room of Claridges, the stylish London hotel that was a hangout for the leading lights of the American and British forces and their guests. With a bevy of awed Red Cross women gathered around him, General Miller declared that the invasion would hit before June 15, 1944. Sibert overheard the astonishing remarks. So did other American officers. Early the next morning, Sibert reported the gross security breach to General Omar Bradley, who also was furious and promptly relayed the report to Eisenhower.

After a crash investigation, the supreme commander reduced General Miller to the rank of lieutenant colonel and ordered him sent back to the Zone of the Interior "on the next boat." Miller vigorously declared his innocence, but Eisenhower stuck to his guns.

There were those among the American officer corps who claimed that Eisenhower had acted rashly and with unjustified harshness. General Bradley, known to the press as Omar the Tentmaker, was not one of them. "Had I been in Ike's shoes," Bradley declared, "I would have been no less severe."[5]

Hard on the heels of the "Miller affair," Eisenhower was hit by another security-leak blockbuster. A deputy to British Brigadier Lionel Harris, head of SHAEF'S telecommunications department, lost the communications plan for Neptune while going to his suburban London home by train from Waterloo station.

Eisenhower, who, when angered, had a vocabulary that could make a muleskinner blush, hit the ceiling. He grew more furious when Harris' aide admitted that he had no idea where he may have lost the plan, which was as bulky as a

New York City telephone book. Nor could the offender say why he had been taking home the Bigot document. Brigadier Harris ventured the opinion that his subordinate had been imbibing.

Losing the plan could compromise Overlord, for it contained details of the wireless networks and codes to be used in Neptune. If it fell into the hands of German agents and reached the Third Reich, skilled intelligence analysts could deduce the approximate strength of the Allied invasion force and get a line on the time and place of the operation.

Two days later, the frantic Brigadier Harris received a telephone call from an officer at Scotland Yard, the headquarters of the Metropolitan London Police. He said that a briefcase belonging to a British officer at Norfolk House, the Overlord planning center, had been turned in to Scotland Yard by a taxi driver who found it in his cab after discharging a passenger at Waterloo station.

Inside were a number of papers marked "Top Secret" and "Bigot," the Yard man said in a casual tone, and they seemed to having something to do with wireless operations. If the documents were of importance, the police sergeant added, he could send someone to Norfolk House with the briefcase the next day, but there was no one available at the time to run the errand.

Greatly relieved, Brigadier Harris instructed the policeman to hang on to the briefcase, and Harris himself hotfooted it across St. James Park to Scotland Yard and picked up the crucial Neptune communications plan. Rumors circulated that a bottle of whiskey was also in the briefcase.

A short time later, British Air Chief Marshal Trafford Leigh-Mallory, commander of the tactical air forces for Neptune, complained to General Eisenhower that an aide to Admiral Harold R. "Betty" Stark, chief of U.S. naval forces in Europe and a top Neptune planner, had been guilty of a flagrant security breach. While attending a party given by a wealthy Portsmouth brewer, the accused American naval captain had blabbed in public the details of Neptune, including the locale, assault force strength, and dates. Eisenhower promptly contacted Admiral Stark, and two days later, the indiscreet naval officer was on a slow boat for the United States. Writing to his boss, General George Marshall in the Pentagon, Eisenhower said the affair had given him "the shakes" and that he would "willingly shoot the offender himself."[6]

As soon as one security leak was plugged, another one raised its head. A British colonel at a convivial gathering in London told guests that his men had been training for weeks to assault a fortified position—one located in Normandy. General Eisenhower, through his British deputies, came down hard on the colonel. He was demoted and removed from his command.

In Chicago, 4,000 miles from London, employees in a post office opened a badly wrapped package and pulled out a collection of documents marked "Bigot." A postal official rushed the papers to Sixth Army headquarters in Chicago, where a general and three colonels inspected them. They found that the documents disclosed the Normandy invasion beaches, the strength of the assault force, and the approximate date of the operation.

Army counterintelligence and the FBI promptly launched a probe and found that the address, on Division Street, was in a neighborhood that was home to many German immigrants. The addressee was questioned, and she identified the handwriting on the package as that of her brother—who was an Army sergeant assigned to General Eisenhower's headquarters. The sergeant and his sister were of German ancestry—but so were 11 million other loyal Americans.

In London, the sergeant was questioned extensively and put under great pressure. Time after time, he gave the same response: he had been working constant 14-hour days and was worn out and worried about his sister, who was ill. The Bigot documents were supposed to have been sent to the Division of Transportation in Washington, so he must have written her Division Street address without realizing what he was doing.

The matter was left at that. But there were eight post office employees in Chicago and at least four officers at Sixth Army headquarters who knew the D-Day secrets. The FBI warned each one that any loose talk on their part could result in tragic consequences for their country. Then a tail was put on each postal employee. But how could a post office worker be kept from engaging in idle conversation?

Then came the biggest security fright of all. Near midnight on April 27, nine German E-boats slipped out of the harbor in Cherbourg, the Normandy port where, in peacetime, carefree passengers debarked from such famed cross-Atlantic luxury liners as the *Queen Elizabeth*, the *Normandie*, and the *Queen Mary*. Swift and armed with torpedoes and heavy machine guns, the E-boats were on a routine patrol of the English Channel.[7]

Unknown to the skipper of the E-boat flotilla, a large convoy of Allied vessels, many crammed with men of the U.S. 4th Infantry Division, was burrowing through the dark swells on its way from Torquay and Plymouth to Slapton Sands, a long, flat beach on the southern coast of England. The flotilla was engaged in exercise Tiger, the final dress rehearsal for the genuine assault on the Normandy beach code-named Utah. On board were the actual units to be employed in the real thing, as well as such innovative secret weapons as "swimming" Sherman tanks and rocket boats.[8]

When the Tiger convoy was some 15 miles off Slapton Sands, there was a tremendous explosion in the center of the formation and a brilliant orange flame shot into the black sky. A 5,000-ton LST (landing ship, tank), loaded with troops, appeared to leap out of the water. It had been struck by a torpedo fired by one of the Cherbourg E-boats that had slipped in among the Allied ships.

The LST caught fire, then exploded. In an instant, 151 of the 282 troops and 94 of the 165 sailors on board were killed outright or tossed into the water where they drowned. As the men in a nearby LST looked on in horror, their craft also was caught in the center by a torpedo; in moments it was blazing from bow to stern, and then it exploded, killing 310 of the 354 soldiers and 114 of the 142 sailors on board.[9]

Survivors reported E-boats sweeping the waters with searchlights and cruising among the wreckage before dashing for home. Had the E-boats fished living Americans out of the water? If so, the Germans would find means to loosen tongues.

SHAEF was shocked by the disaster, which could tip off the Germans about the time and place of *der Grossinvasion*. "It scared the daylights out of us," Colonel Gordon Sheen, chief of the SHAEF security branch, recalled.

Tension at high levels grew more severe when it was learned that ten Bigot officers were among the missing. General Tom Betts, who was undergoing the torments of the damned, rapidly organized a fishing expedition for the corpses. Scores of craft searched and dragged the waters off Slapton Sands. Since the current was moving away from shore and out to sea, Betts knew that large numbers of the 700 missing men would never be found. But only the ten Bigots were being sought.

It was a macabre operation. As each corpse was plucked out of the Channel, eager hands inspected it for Bigot credentials. Five were found, then six. The "fishermen" kept casting their nets. They reeled in the seventh, the eighth, and the ninth. Each was stiff in his lifebelt. As the hours rolled past and the final body could not be found, Betts and his men were frantic. Was the greatest invasion in history to be postponed or canceled because of one missing corpse? Finally, the English Channel gave up the final body. Tom Betts, a placid, determined giant of a man, had recovered his ten Bigots.[10]

In the meantime, tense conferences were held at SHAEF, and serious consideration was given to altering drastically the Utah Beach amphibious and airborne assault. Concerns deepened when, one week after the E-boat attack, Ultra intercepts revealed that Field Marshal Erwin Rommel was rushing two extra German divisions, both specialists in antiparatrooper duty, into the Cherbourg peninsula, site of Utah Beach.

Was this German troop deployment just a coincidence, a hunch by the wily Rommel? Or had he acted as the result of information extracted from Americans fished alive from the Channel waters off Slapton Sands? After much study and reflection, General Eisenhower decided that Neptune would proceed as planned. Reflecting the anxiety that was simmering at SHAEF, the supreme commander wrote his old friend, Lieutenant General Brehon Somervell, chief of the Army Services of Supply, in Washington:

> As time goes by, tension grows and everybody gets more on edge. This time, because of the stakes involved, the atmosphere is probably more electric than ever before. . . . We are not merely risking a tactical defeat—we are putting the whole works on one number.[11]

19

Behind Enemy Lines

Gut-wrenching tension was not limited to Allied leaders and forces in the British Isles. Early in May 1944, Field Marshal Erwin Rommel wrote to his wife Lucie-Maria back in Herrlingen: "I can't take many more big [inspection] trips . . . because one never knows when the invasion will begin. I believe only a few more weeks remain until things begin here in the west."

In the Normandy village of La Madeleine, close to Utah Beach, the Feldgrau were whooping it up and applauding a visiting troupe of actors from Berlin. Suddenly, the master of ceremonies burst onto the stage and called out: "How much longer are we going to sit on this keg of dynamite?" The rafters rocked with laughter. Humor, dry "inside" humor, concealing a specter of which each soldier was aware—the powderkeg could explode at any minute.

Far to the east of La Madeleine, Allied bombers, day after day, were pounding General Hans von Salmuth's Fifteenth Army manning the Atlantic Wall along the Pas de Calais. There the German soldiers grimly joked that the ideal place for a rest cure was in the zone defended by the Seventh Army in Normandy. Far fewer bombs had fallen there.

The deluge of explosives being rained on bunkers, troop concentrations, coastal batteries, airfields, fuel dumps, and panzer parks in the Pas de Calais was part of Quicksilver IV and V, subplots of Bodyguard to reinforce the illusion that George Patton's dummy army group would hit at the Pas de Calais.

Dwight Eisenhower and other SHAEF planners knew that getting a sizeable force ashore in Normandy did not mean success for Overlord. The first four or five weeks would be critical, for the Germans could be expected to rush reinforcements from throughout Europe to northwestern France. So in mid-April 1944, the supreme commander approved an aerial stratagem code-named Transportation, of which Quicksilver IV and V were components.

Short and simple, the bombing scheme was intended to destroy the French railroad system and, in military jargon, to isolate the battlefield. The plan was created by Solly Zuckerman, a British anatomist, at the request of Air Chief Marshal Trafford Leigh-Mallory, a commander of tactical air forces for Neptune.

Zuckerman was aided by a French railroad official, whose code name was Pierre Moreau. In a cloak-and-dagger scheme that rivaled fictional spy thrillers, Moreau and his wife, who was seven months pregnant, slipped out of their home in Lyon, France, 250 miles south of Paris, on April 2. The couple, at the risk of their lives, were taken in tow by SOE agents, driven through blacked-out streets patrolled by German military police to an isolated pasture outside Lyon. Carrying only the clothes they were wearing, the Moreaus climbed aboard a waiting Lizzie, as the British called Lysanders, small, maneuverable airplanes capable of landing and lifting off in short spaces.

For more than two years, the SOE had been conducting nighttime "set down" and "pick up" shuttle service to the Continent in order to infiltrate and bring out secret agents. The Lizzies were part of the Moon Squadron, which was based at secret Gibraltar Farm north of London.

Pierre Moreau and his wife had a difficult time squeezing into the two-seater Lysander. The pilot sat in one seat. In order to provide room for one passenger, the Lizzies had been stripped of guns, armor, and other equipment. Laboriously, the French rail official wedged himself into the second seat and his wife managed to wriggle onto his lap.

Moments later, the shadowy figures on the dark pasture froze. Off in the distance and heading toward them were three or four sets of headlights. Frenchmen were not allowed to drive at night; these vehicles had to be German. Suddenly, the Lizzie's engine revved, and the strident noise seemed as if it would carry for miles.

Slowly at first, the Lizzie trundled along the bumpy turf as the pilot and the Moreaus silently prayed that a ditch or sturdy fence was not looming ahead of them. Then the craft gained speed and was airborne and the Royal Air Force pilot set a course for England. Glancing back over his shoulder, Moreau caught a glimpse of the menacing headlights which still seemed to be moving toward the pasture.

The danger was far from over. Using only a map held in his lap and illuminated periodically by a thin shaft from a flashlight, the pilot was guided by whatever landmarks—villages, roads, rivers—he might detect in the darkness. The lumbering plane would have to avoid Luftwaffe night fighters, ack-ack guns, and searchlights on the German-held Channel coast. In case the Lizzie developed engine trouble or was riddled by bullets and disabled, there would be no chance for those aboard to parachute to safety—the craft was flying too low and the pilot and the Moreau couple were shoehorned in so tightly that they could not budge in an emergency.

Hardly a word was spoken during the flight. As was the Moon Squadron's practice, the pilot never knew the names of those he picked up in German-occupied territory. One thought haunted the pilot on this particular flight—it would be a hell of a time for Madame Moreau to give premature birth to her child.

Despite the potential for disaster, the Lizzie touched down routinely at Manston just past midnight, and the shadowy forms of MI–6 men emerged to greet the newcomers. The Frenchman and his wife, near exhaustion from anxiety and the intense discomforts of the long flight, were ensconced in Brown's Hotel on Piccadilly. They devoured a sumptuous meal, bathed, and fell into deep slumber.

Snatching Pierre Moreau from under the noses of the Germans had been a bonanza for SOE and MI–6. As a lifelong key official of the French railway system, he knew as much as any man about the network, and German transportation officials had briefed him extensively on its use in the event the Anglo-Americans were to invade. Moreau also brought with him a priceless asset: three handbooks on the current operation of the French railroad system.

After the Moreaus had been refreshed, Solly Zuckerman arrived at their suite in the Brown's Hotel and the two men labored around the clock to hatch the Neptune air-bombing plan. It called for the destruction of 80 railroad targets in northwestern Europe in the period of time leading up to D-Day, scheduled for the last week in May.[1]

Winston Churchill and his War Cabinet were violently opposed to the bombing plan when they were told that it might result in 20,000 French and Belgian citizens being killed and perhaps 60,000 injured. The prime minister promptly called President Roosevelt, pointing out that ''such a mass slaughter of civilians'' would breed French ill will for the United States and Great Britain for perhaps decades.

Roosevelt consulted with his joint chiefs of staff, then told Churchill that he was not prepared to impose restrictions on SHAEF commanders that might jeopardize the success of Overlord or add significantly to Allied casualties. Roosevelt had the last word and on April 26 the massive bomber strikes began.

Allied pilots and crewmen in England knew that the bombing campaign to isolate the Neptune battlefield would be a bloody one. Although the Luftwaffe had been reduced in numbers, its pilots were still full of fight, particularly so now that the Fatherland was being threatened with invasion. And the Channel coast in France, Belgium, and the Netherlands was studded with antiaircraft batteries.

At one American bomber base near London, a magazine advertisement by an aircraft manufacturer in the United States was pinned to the blackboard in an orderly room. The ad showed an Army Air Corps machine gunner, his eye staring fiercely through the back-sight of his weapon, which he was aiming at a swarm of Focke-Wulf 190 fighter planes. The caption blared: ''Who's afraid of the Big Bad Wulf?''

It was classic Madison Avenue prose. But the GI crewmen, who faced sudden death every day over Europe, had a more realistic outlook. Scrawled across the magazine advertisement in large red letters were the words ''We are!'' Every flying officer on the base, including the commander, put his signature on the ad, then the whole lot was sent, without comment, to the manufacturer.[2]

As yet another means to suggest to the German high command that the Pas de Calais was the invasion target, the American and RAF squadrons began dropping two curtains of bombs. One was along the Seine River between Paris and the Channel, where 36 rail and road bridges were sent plunging into the water. Other bridges were wiped out along the Albert Canal in Belgium. Not only would these two curtains of destruction, one to either side of the Pas de Calais, drastically hamper the German Fifteenth Army should it try to move westward on D-Day or afterward to assist the Seventh Army in Normandy, but the bombing pattern would also, it was hoped, suggest to Wehrmacht intelligence that the Allies were trying to isolate the Pas de Calais in preparation for an assault by General Patton's fictitious army group.

Meanwhile, the RAF Fighter Command and the U.S. Ninth Air Force vastly increased reconnaissance flights over German-held territory. Three times as many flights were over the Pas de Calais as over Normandy. The reconnaissance pilots were not briefed in advance about which was the real invasion target, but it was implied that the Pas de Calais would be the target in case they were shot down and "interrogated" by the Germans.

Wireless traffic by Allied air forces in England was heightened significantly in order to keep the efficient German Y-Service flooded with messages to be intercepted and decoded. Most of the messages were meaningless. This heavy wireless traffic would be kept going continuously through the many major amphibious and other exercises that were being held in the British Isles and would be similar to the real radio signals that would fill the ether just before and on D-Day. Ideally, when Neptune forces were ready to plunge across the Channel, the Y-Service, straining to keep abreast of the torrent of Allied air forces wireless traffic, would conclude that it was just another large-scale exercise (such as the one at Slapton Sands).

Aware that the Luftwaffe could spare aircraft only for periodic reconnaissance flights over the British Isles, the Quicksilver deceptionists broadcast many messages intended to give the illusion that the bulk of Allied air power was concentrated in the flat fields of southeastern England—in the FUSAG area—while the genuine squadrons in the midlands and southwestern England remained on radio silence and communicated by telephone and courier.

The air battles over northern Europe to pave the way for the invasion and to deceive the fuehrer on its locale were prolonged and bitter. During the six weeks leading up to D-Day, the Allies launched in excess of 20,000 missions and paid a frightful toll: 12,000 killed, wounded, or missing, along with 2,000 planes.

However, the Luftwaffe in Europe had been virtually wiped out. This situation led to Wehrmacht infantry veterans counseling young recruits moving into the Atlantic Wall: "If you see a white airplane, it's an American; if it's black, it's British; if you don't see any planes, it's the Luftwaffe!"

Beginning early in May, the Americans and British accelerated air and sea missions to supply and arm the resistance groups in northern France, Belgium, and the Netherlands. None of those involved in the task were told that the true invasion would hit Normandy, but briefers dropped hints that the target was the Pas de Calais. At any rate, twice as many missions were directed at the Pas de Calais.

The Allied brain trust knew that there were some 60 French underground *réseaux* (networks), but if they were to be fully effective in support of Neptune, they would have to be heavily reinforced with weapons, ammunition, and supplies. There was also a need to infiltrate scores of spies into the German-held coastal regions to report back on Wehrmacht activities.

So during the spring of 1944, Wild Bill Donovan's OSS agents and Major General Colin McV. Gubbins' SOE men and women were pouring clandestinely into France. They parachuted from airplanes, slipped ashore from PT (patrol torpedo) boats and submarines, and crossed the rugged Pyrenees Mountains from Spain on foot. A few agents even crept into France from the Third Reich.

The OSS, as a relatively new and inexperienced organization, leaned heavily on the expertise of the SOE, which had been engaged in covert warfare since 1940. Colin Gubbins, a 49-year-old Scotsman, was regarded as Britain's foremost expert on guerrilla and unorthodox warfare. Most of his military career had been spent in special means—sabotage, deception, intrigue. After World War I, Gubbins had fought in Russia against the Bolsheviks and later with the Irish rebels and had been sent to deal with insurrections in India. He had authored several handbooks on guerilla tactics, and his views were blunt and to the point: "the way to handle an informer is to kill him."

By May 1, 1944, Gubbins had perhaps 1,000 British and French agents plying their trade in France, while the OSS had some 350 American and 500 French agents working behind German lines. The American and British spies were sheltered by a network of "safe houses" and other underground hideouts where they could eat, sleep, and set up their radio transmitters as the *Maquis* (French resistance fighters) kept vigilant watches.

In April alone, 52 OSS agents parachuted into France, and seven of them suffered major injuries from broken ankles to a broken back. Men engaged in the dangerous game of parachuting as espionage agents into France did not have a monopoly on courage. Women spies, as with their male counterparts, had to depend upon their courage, steel nerves, and resourcefulness.

One of the female OSS agents dropped into France in April was Virginia Hall, who previously had lost a leg in an automobile accident, but she badgered the OSS to send her into Nazi-occupied France. Adding to the normal perils, she was well known to the Gestapo from a previous sabotage mission. When she parachuted into France, her artificial leg had been tucked under one arm to prevent its damage on crashing to earth.

Despite her physical handicap, Hall was a human dynamo. She helped organize the French underground and on occasion joined with her fighting men on sabotage and ambush missions. She even helped to blow up a bridge and to derail a troop-carrying train. She kept in radio contact with the OSS in London and provided information on German activities. The communications function was particularly hazardous due to the constant enemy electronic surveillance.

These Allied secret agents carried out specific assignments or free-lanced behind German lines. One pair of OSS men, working near La Bourget airport outside Paris, pilfered the plans of two secret war production plants and rushed the drawings to London by Lysander aircraft pickup. Within 48 hours, Allied bombers leveled one target, an explosives factory which, an OSS agent declared, "went up with one hell of a bang." A week later, the second facility, a refinery producing oil for the Wehrmacht, was bombed out of existence.

Among the intruders fighting a shadow war in France were three-man Allied teams known as Jedburghs. (Jedburgh was an area in Scotland where the Scots, several centuries earlier, conducted guerrilla warfare against the British.) Each Jedburgh team consisted of an American OSS or British SOE officer along with a Dutch, French, or Belgian officer and a radio operator. They had been picked for their sound judgment, courage, leadership qualities, and skill in guerrilla tactics.

In order not to pinpoint Normandy in the likely event that members of the Jedburgh teams would be captured and forced to talk, the shadow-war units were parachuted or landed by PT boats and submarines at locales from the Brittany peninsula in northwestern France all the way eastward to the borders of Belgium and the Netherlands.

Equipped with jeeps, bazookas, machine guns, grenades, and other weapons— all parachuted from Allied airplanes—the Jedburghs were trained to organize French underground warriors into basic hard-hitting 32-man units that rapidly could break into eight-man teams, each self-sufficient and capable of espionage, handling explosives, or fighting with rifles and automatic weapons. They blew bridges, blasted rail lines, ambushed convoys, harassed German units in hit-and-run raids, and acted as the eyes and ears in France for Overlord planners and commanders.

All the while, the Jedburghs and their French guerrillas were risking their lives on faith in the Allied cause alone. None ever had the slightest clue that the invasion would hit in their region or that their actions would contribute to the success of Overlord. Scores of them would never live to see D-Day.

Early in May, Lieutenant Commander Ray Guest paid a visit to PT-boat Squadron 2 at the Channel port of Dartmouth. Prior to the war, Ray and his brother Winston had been widely known as high-goal players representing the Meadowbrook Club polo team on the north shore of Long Island, New York.[3] Ray Guest was one of Bill Donovan's OSS bluebloods, and he had a zest for action. In recent times, Guest had been posted to London where he worked with the British to organize spy-running and underground-supply sorties across the Channel.

Leader of Squadron 2 was Lieutenant Commander John D. Bulkeley, who had electrified the free world in March 1942 when he rescued General Douglas

MacArthur in a PT boat from Japanese-surrounded Corregidor, a tiny rock fortress in the mouth of Manilla Bay in the Philippines. Bulkeley's exploits during those black early days after Pearl Harbor brought him the Congressional Medal of Honor, national fame, and the moniker "Wild Man of the Philippines."[4]

Commander Guest came with orders for Squadron 2: it would land OSS spies and supplies for the underground on the coast of France. Unknown to Bulkeley, he and his PT boaters also were playing a role in Fortitude South, the deception to suggest that the Pas de Calais was the invasion target. For while Bulkeley's boats were slipping spies and supplies ashore in Normandy, speedy British motor torpedo boats were conducting similar operations in the Pas de Calais, in Belgium, and in Holland.

Most of the Allied spies being sneaked into northwest Europe by boat were not told where the invasion would hit—except for those landing at the Pas de Calais who received hints that the invasion would strike there. If the poor devils were captured and force to talk, they would no doubt disclose that fact.[5]

In London in mid-May, 36-year-old Brigadier General James M. Gavin, who would lead parachute elements in the U.S. 82nd Airborne Division into Normandy five hours before H-Hour for the amphibious forces, strolled into the lobby of London's fashionable Claridges hotel. Known to his tough paratroopers as "Slim Jim," Gavin was the youngest American army general since the Civil War.

Back in July 1943, Gavin, then a colonel, led the first major American parachute assault, leaping into Sicily at the head of his men. After the six-week battle against German and Italian forces that ensued, Gavin happened to run into General George Patton on a high hill overlooking the Mediterranean; the famed armored commander warmly congratulated the parachute officer for his outfit's achievements. Now, through a sea of humanity in Claridges, General Gavin spotted George Patton—a total of 15 stars gleaming from his cap, shirt collar, and shoulders—walking toward the front door.

"Hello, Gavin," Patton called out loudly in his high-pitched voice. "How in the hell are you?" The two men shook hands and engaged in brief conversation. All eyes in the lobby were on Patton. Finally, Patton continued toward the door, then turned, and nearly shouted, "See you in the Pas de Calais, Gavin!"

Unaware that Patton was playing a role in Quicksilver to mislead the Germans about the true invasion locale, officers in the lobby cringed over this shocking security violation. George Patton never could keep his mouth shut.[6]

While George Patton was dashing madly around Great Britain, "playing Sarah Bernhardt," as he quipped in reference to the legendary actress, General Hans Cramer, a leader in Erwin Rommel's once vaunted Afrika Korps before it was destroyed in Tunisia a year earlier, was confined to a prisoner-of-war camp in Wales. By May 1944, Cramer was in failing health. Despite the looming invasion, Allied authorities decided to repatriate the German general to the Third Reich through a program administered by the Swedish Red Cross.

Accompanied by two British officers (who were agents of the Double-Cross

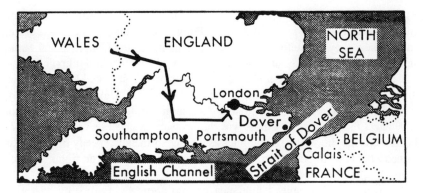

4. Route taken by General Hans Cramer's escorts.

Committee), General Cramer was driven from Wales eastward across England toward London. The route took the German directly through the genuine assembly area for the invasion in southwestern and southern England, and Cramer's eyes bulged as he saw the massive buildup of troops, tanks, warplanes, armor, and artillery.

The talkative British escorts, friendly types, carelessly let slip that they were going through the Dover region of southeastern England, where Patton's ghost army group was supposed to be concentrating for the leap over to Calais. Since British road signposts had been removed, and the names of towns and railroad stations had been obliterated in 1940 in anticipation of a German invasion, General Cramer had no way of knowing otherwise.

Reaching London, the former Afrika Korps leader was introduced to General George Patton, who was identified as "the commanding general of FUSAG." Patton hosted a dinner for the German general and invited several U.S. corps and division commanders. It was one of those acts of medieval knighthood chivalry among men of arms that had seldom been seen in the current war and for good reason. Mixed in with the Americans' conversations were fleeting references to the Pas de Calais.

In subtle ways, George Patton, always the gracious host, alluded to the great difficulties the Wehrmacht had encountered back in 1940, when Hitler planned to cross the Channel from France and conquer virtually defenseless Great Britain. He remarked that enormous strides had been made in amphibious assaults since then—implying to Cramer that he was about to put those new techniques to use.

Forty-eight hours later, General Cramer sailed on the white-painted Swedish ship *Gripsholm* and landed at a German port on the Baltic. He rushed to Berlin where he reported to the high command on what he had seen and heard in England in recent days. Cramer promptly was sent to Hitler's mountaintop retreat at Berchtesgaden in the Bavarian Alps where he told the same story to the fuehrer: the Anglo-Americans had massed a powerful force under General Patton across from the Pas de Calais. Since this scenario dovetailed nicely with Hitler's views, largely formed from Bodyguard machinations, he readily accepted Cramer's eye-witness report as accurate. It apparently had been a master coup by the Double-Cross. How could the fuehrer and his high command conceivably distrust or doubt the accuracy of a highly decorated German general who had seen it all with his own eyes?[7]

In the meantime, the Royal Engineers' master camouleur, Colonel John Turner, and his illusionists, had completed work on misleading lighting schemes that stretched along much of the Channel coast of England. These displays were to suggest to the Germans that there were heavy concentrations of troops and vehicles in the FUSAG area in the southeast. Typically, John Turner and his men used great ingenuity in devising the deceptive lighting scheme. But the problems were many and diversified—from having to work in sectors that had been saturated with land mines to cantankerous cows that insisted on either crushing equipment or trying to eat it. "Those cows are very unladylike!" Colonel Turner complained."[8]

By mid-May, the decoy-lighting job was done. In Cornwall, a valley was damned and flooded, and lights played on the water to simulate a nearby harbor that was jammed with real landing craft that would be used to carry genuine troops to Normandy. It was hoped that, if the Luftwaffe appeared, bombardiers, confused by the deceptive lighting, would drop their lethal loads on the dummy harbor.

In the FUSAG area, several ports and railheads were provided lights that were dim enough to seem realistic to high-flying German night bombers but that would reveal clearly that a beehive of activity was in progress there. The idea was for the Luftwaffe to waste its bombs on the FUSAG ports where no genuine Neptune movements were taking place.

Colonel Turner and his camouflage experts set up 65 deceptive lighting schemes, including 12 misleading displays on the FUSAG coast across from the Pas de Calais and 23 decoys to divert German bombers from the real Neptune embarkation docks.

All the while, numberless other plots and subplots of Bodyguard were continuing to unfold. Field Marshal Gerd von Rundstedt, at OB West, was monitoring closely the reports sent from London by the double agent Garbo. Von Rundstedt was especially eager to learn of the whereabouts of the crack British Guards Armored Division, whose capable leader, Major General Allan H. S. Adair, would be in the vanguard of any major Anglo-American operation, the field marshal was convinced. While real British armored divisions were skipping into genuine Neptune assembly areas in southern England under the strictest radio silence, the Guards Armored Division was moving from Yorkshire to Hove in Sussex to join General Patton's dummy army group—or so Garbo's Double-Cross case officer wirelessed Hamburg.

Garbo told his Hamburg controllers in a series of wireless reports that while the Guards Armored Division was on the road, the luggage of various units had become mixed, resulting in widespread confusion and angry officers. It was hoped that the German Y-Service would aim its sensitive electronic equipment toward the FUSAG assembly area in southeastern England. There it could eavesdrop on uncoded, expletive-dotted conversations between Guards Armored Division generals and colonels concerning their supposedly strayed luggage.

Actually, the Y-Service would be picking up British corporals and sergeants masquerading as generals and colonels, and they were speaking over a wireless net set up in the FUSAG area to impersonate radio traffic of the Guards Armored Division. Actually, General Allan Adair and his outfit were far to the west, under radio silence in the real concentration areas of General Bernard Montgomery's genuine 21st Army Group.

20

Vendetta and Copperhead

As the climactic day neared, Bodyguard's experts cranked up the deception machine full speed. They flooded their German counterparts with a deluge of false, true, half-true, and unfalteringly conflicting information that it would have taken the enemy an eternity just to sift out.

Special copies of books were printed containing matter that should have been eliminated by the censors. These books hinted at Allied invasions of Norway, southern France, and the Balkans. In one book, an author billed as a military expert ventured the view that the entire Allied buildup was but a sham; that Franklin Roosevelt, Winston Churchill, and Joseph Stalin had agreed at the Teheran conference that the Third Reich could be brought to its knees by bombing alone.

Magazines and technical journals published articles (concocted by the deceptionists) describing scores of new and projected developments for the Anglo-American war machine. Other articles, in what appeared to be a flagrant lapse of security, discussed in detail invasion training and equipment. Still others had experts (who were making no more than educated guesses) debating where and when the invasion would take place. One "expert," who had been coached by the deception artists, was confident that he knew the looming grand strategy: the Allies would return to Europe through the Balkans and were projecting a big buildup in England in order to keep Wehrmacht divisions pinned down in northwest France.

Hundreds of highly technical diagrams and charts and hundreds of "authentic" pictures published in London's Fleet Street press showed military activities under captions such as "Big Day Nears."

Letters began to arrive in neutral Eire from Irish citizens in Great Britain with amazing amounts of information which, it was hoped, would ring true to German agents. Here and there in the letters, in order to add authenticity, passages were blacked out just to show that the official censors were on the job. It was doubtful whether any secret operatives had as harrowing and frustrating experiences as the Germans in Dublin who had to sort out the mountain of "facts" with which they were being deluged and send it on to Berlin by means of miniature transmitting sets.

As speculation about a looming invasion began to mount in the press and on radio in Great Britain and the United States, Britain's Political Warfare Executive (PWE) and American and British diplomats around the world intensified a misleading campaign of rumors to support the fiction of Bodyguard. The diplomats, in Most Secret messages delivered by couriers, even had scripts to guide them.

At cocktail parties or other social functions at embassies in Madrid, Lisbon, Ankara, Stockholm, or Bern, an American diplomat would remark to one from a neutral nation: "Don't breathe a word about this, but that damned Winston Churchill is botching things up. The invasion might be postponed because he's demanding that the operation be in the Balkans."

Elsewhere around the perimeter of Nazi-held Europe, there was a sharp increase in mayhem that, it was hoped, would alarm Adolf Hitler and intensify his confusion about the time and place of the Allied invasion. In Scandinavia, a series of hit-and-run raids by British Commandos struck the coast of Norway, and the huge German battleship *Tirpitz*, camouflaged and in hiding under the bare mountains of Alta Ford in northern Norway, was bombed heavily by the RAF.

In Sweden, Allied demands that the government there provide air bases for "forthcoming operations" grew much tougher, as though an urgent matter had to be settled. Actually, the Allies were in no hurry for an agreement: Operation Graffham called for stretching out negotiations until D-Day and beyond. Next door in Finland, heavy pressure was put on Field Marshal Carl von Mannerheim and figurehead President Risto Ryti to withdraw from the country's alliance with Adolf Hitler.

This Bodyguard threat to Scandinavia was not lost on Adolf Hitler. He not only kept his divisions in place but rushed reinforcements to Norway. By mid-May, there were 13 army divisions, 58,000 Luftwaffe members, and 89,000 naval personnel hunkered down in Norway a total force of 372,000 men. They were destined to sit out a nice quiet war waiting for the onslaught from Scotland by General Bulgy Thorne's phantom Fourth Army.

Planted rumors were rife in Romania, Bulgaria, and Hungary that underground uprisings would soon be launched. Reading a distinct threat to the Balkans through the Cicero machinations and the suggested mounting of an invasion force in the Mediterranean by Dudley Clarke's A-Force deceptionists, Adolf Hitler began pouring in divisions, including *Fallschirmjaeger* (paratrooper), mountain, and panzer troops—a total of 25 divisions that would be sitting idly hundreds of miles from Normandy on D-Day and beyond.

Meanwhile, SHAEF intelligence concluded that the Germans were about to write off the possibility that the Anglo-Americans might be preparing to launch a major operation against the western French coastline in the Bay of Biscay. If that were true, the Wehrmacht could ignore the defense of the Atlantic coast and rush Major General Wend von Wietersheim's elite 11th Panzer Division from the Bordeaux region northward to help smash the Allies' Normandy beachhead. The 11th Panzer was the only armored reserve in southern France and, like all Wehrmacht tank formations, could not be committed or moved without the specific approval of the fuehrer himself.

Consequently, Colonel Dudley Clarke was ordered to launch Ironside, a deception plan that would suggest the Western Allies indeed were getting ready to storm ashore along the Bay of Biscay, with the principal objective being the major port of Bordeaux. Playing a key role in Ironside would be a young Argentinian woman whose British code name was Bronx. In 1942, she was visiting her father who was connected with the Argentine embassy in Vichy, France. There she was approached at a cocktail party by an Abwehr officer working undercover, and he suggested that she go to England as a spy for the fuehrer.

The young woman accepted the proposal and left for Britain by way of Madrid, where she slipped into the British embassy under a veil of darkness and told all. MI–6 agents took her in tow and saw that she was escorted to London, where she was held for several weeks by suspicious security officials.

Finally, the Argentinian was cleared and turned over to the Double-Cross Committee, whose artful dodgers put her to work early in 1943. They provided her with secret ink and concocted the information she sent to her German controllers. The Abwehr was delighted with her work and paid her a monthly retainer of 25 pounds ($120), a tidy sum at the time, plus expenses and an occasional bonus for exceptional reports.

Before leaving the Iberian peninsula to go to England in late 1942, the young woman, as directed by the Abwehr, established a personal account in the Bank of the Holy Ghost in Lisbon. Now she sent her secret-ink letters to the Abwehr through that Portuguese financial institution (which apparently had a German agent on its staff). In December 1943, the Germans, who had become increasingly nervous about an Allied invasion along the Bay of Biscay, provided Bronx with a special code that would permit her to send urgent information to Lisbon by commercial telegram. If Bronx learned anything about an Anglo-American invasion, she was to telegraph a request for funds to the Bank of the Holy Ghost: 100 pounds sterling meant that the invasion would hit in northern France, 125 pounds indicated that the Bay of Biscay was the target, 150 pounds the Mediterranean coast of southern France, 175 pounds the Balkans, 200 pounds Greece, and 250 pounds Scandinavia. If the woman discovered the month of the invasion, she was to indicate that by mentioning in her cable the time when she needed the requested funds.

Meanwhile, Dudley Clarke and his A-Force, by various special means, began leaking the fictitious operations plan for an invasion along the Bay of Biscay. It called for the assault to be launched on June 7, 1944—about a week after the genuine landing in Normandy.

The Ironside threat suggested that three assault and seven follow-up divisions would invade the Bordeaux region from west coast ports in the British Isles and from the United States. Bordeaux, to the military mind, would be a plausible invasion objective. Lying on the Garonne River about 60 miles inland from the Atlantic Ocean, Bordeaux is one of France's chief commercial centers and its natural harbor can handle a large amount of shipping.

The phony Bay of Biscay assault plan called for a wide array of warships, troop-carrying transports, landing craft, and mine sweepers. A British brigade was to seize airfields at Cozes and Medis, a few miles inland, and aircraft from carriers would land there to continue air operations.

A-Force requested Anglo-American bomber commands in Britain to provide tangible evidence to support the Ironside fairy tale by actually pounding key targets along the Bay of Biscay, which would be the case if the invasion were genuine. The request was denied, with the explanation that the project would require at least 850 bombers to be realistic and that no aircraft could be spared from the bombing of the French railroad system in northern France.

Next, the Double-Cross Committee was called on to use its turned agents to bulwark the Ironside fantasy. That request was also rejected: the credibility of the "first violins" could not be jeopardized by their sending the Germans information that might be recognized as phony. However, the Double-Cross decided to inject Bronx into the Ironside scheme, for she was one of the first violins involved in the Pas de Calais deception. On May 15, she cabled the Bank of the Holy Ghost: "Send 125 pounds quickly. I need it for my dentist." In the German code that had been given her, this message meant: "Am certain the Allies will land on the Bay of Biscay within one month."

The ambitious fiction of Ironside was doomed to die a natural death. With the absence of hard physical evidence—Allied naval ships and heavy bombers—the deception was ignored by Adolf Hitler and his generals.

At the same time Ironside was playing to an empty theater in Berlin, Allied deceptionists launched Vendetta, an operation intended to keep the German Nineteenth Army in southern France pinned down along the 300-mile Mediterranean coastline between Spain and Italy—some 500 miles from Normandy—on D-Day and beyond. Led by General of Infantry Friedrich Wiese, who was regarded by his colleagues as a capable tactician, the Nineteenth Army consisted of 11 divisions.

Unlike Ironside, which had been described by Dwight Eisenhower's chief of staff, Walter Smith, as being "very thin," Vendetta would be a positive threat with a large amount of physical evidence to support the illusion of a pending assault on the Mediterranean coastline. Dudley Clarke and his A-Force hatched a fictitious plan with real operations which German intelligence could not fail to notice. Since the Allies planned to launch Operation Dragoon, a genuine assault of the French Riviera about two months after D-Day in Normandy, many troops, planes, and ships already were available in the Mediterranean to give substance to the Vendetta sham.

Commander of the fictitious Vendetta force was Major General Alexander M. Patch, who was the actual leader of the genuine U.S. Seventh Army with headquarters in Naples, Italy. Fifty-four-year-old Sandy Patch was a logical choice to command Vendetta: he had distinguished himself as a combat leader in two wars.[1]

General Patch's authentic headquarters was in the Flambeau Building in Naples. A-Force agents launched a whispering campaign in sleazy waterfront bars and in fashionable hotels that Patch and his planners were putting the finishing touches on an expedition that would hit the Mediterranean shoreline around June 10 (days after the true D-Day in Normandy).

Unlike George Patton, Sandy Patch customarily shied away from publicity, but through the manipulations of Dudley Clarke and his men, photographs of Patch began popping up in newspapers in southern Italy. Captions usually stated that he was in Naples to prepare for a secret operation.[2]

An intricate shipping program was conceived for Vendetta. Convoys sailing from England were timed so as to give the impression that an exceptionally large number of ships were steaming through the narrow Straits of Gibraltar in the western Mediterranean at about the same time when vessels would be expected to load assault troops in North Africa had Vendetta been genuine. Gibraltar butted against the southern Spanish border from which vantage point Nazi spies reported on the comings and goings of ships passing through the Straits.

In what would seem to be a shocking violation of security, three British convoys, numbering in excess of 120 ships, passed through the Gibraltar Straits in broad daylight during the last week of May. Presumably, the ships were bound for embarkation ports on the southern shore of the Mediterranean. Once darkness had blanketed the region, however, the ships reversed course, joined a westbound convoy, retraced their route back through the Gibraltar Straits, and returned to England.

Meanwhile at Draguignan, a town 16 miles inland from the French Riviera, 44-year-old Pierre Aumont had long been the target of many natives who believed that he was too friendly with the German troops who regularly visited his cafe. There the homesick soldiers of the Third Reich would gulp copious amounts of *vin*, loudly sing the lilting ballad *Lili Marlene*, and engage in convivial conversation with the jovial Aumont far into the night.

Aumont provided a sympathetic ear to the Feldgrau's complaints about a pompous new colonel or other real or imagined grievances. The husky, red-haired Aumont was a shameless excuse for a Frenchman, some of his neighbors snarled.

It was past midnight in early May 1944 when Aumont padlocked his cafe and strolled for a half-mile to his modest home, where his wife and two teenage sons had long been in bed. Silently, he tiptoed down the steps into the basement, and by the dim glow of a lighted candle he pawed at a large pile of potatoes and pulled out a radio receiver and transmitter. Moments later he established contact with a small A-Force unit in Italy.

For more than two years Aumont had been chief of the local *reseau* (underground cell) of General Charles de Gaulle's *Armée Secrete*, and he had risked his life almost nightly to send terse reports on General Friedrich Wiese's Nineteenth Army. Most of his factual information came from talking to the Germans whose tongues had been loosened by the wine he served them.

Huddled in his basement, Aumont received electrifying news over his radio: a large American and British force would invade southern France within a month. The false news was part of Vendetta. Within a few days, a pending Allied invasion was a matter of common knowledge along the Riviera—and it was hoped that word would reach the ears of German intelligence officers.

In the meantime, the genuine U.S. 91st "Powder River" Infantry Division, an untested outfit commanded by Major General William G. Livesay, was camped around the major port of Oran in Algeria, on the southern shore of the Mediterranean Sea. This 14,000-man unit would play a major role in Vendetta. Livesay put the Powder River boys through strenuous amphibious training, and it was leaked that the division would spearhead a looming invasion of southern France. The division's preparations included the intense study of maps of the targeted coastline and of aerial photographs taken of that region.

Special booklets titled *A Guide to Southern France* were printed and distributed to the men of the 91st Infantry Division. Dudley Clarke's agents made certain that a few of these booklets about Oran were purposely left for the eyes of Nazi spies. For hours on end, the GIs sat in classrooms and were given short courses on basic French words and on the local customs of the French Riviera region.

A month later, after the Vendetta sham had run its course, the 91st Infantry Division was shipped from Oran to Italy, where it fought with great distinction. Unaware that they had been engaged in a major decoy operation in Oran, the Powder River soldiers groused unkindly about the mentality of army brass who evidently thought that the method for preparing the division to fight in Italy was to give its members French language lessons and have them study maps of southern France.

As a means to strengthen the Vendetta threat to southern France, an operation code-named Royal Flush was put into action. The American and British ambassadors to Spain jointly paid a visit to General don Francisco Gómez Jordaña, the Spanish foreign minister in Madrid. The diplomats requested the use of facilities at the Mediterranean port of Barcelona, only 60 miles southwest of the southern French border, for the evacuation of Allied casualties in what they described as "impending operations."

While this conference was in progress, lesser British and American diplomatic figures circulated in the extensive dock system in Barcelona. They approached Spanish foremen with questions about the port's capacity for handling incoming ships, berthing arrangements and, most important, housing that could be used for surgical and nursing people. Within 48 hours, it became common knowledge in Spanish government circles that the Western Allies were preparing to launch a major assault against southern France and hoped to convert the Barcelona dock complex into a huge hospital facility.

For nearly six months, Generalissimo Francisco Franco steadily had been extricating himself from his longstanding alliance with Adolf Hitler. Now, with signs generated by Royal Flush indicating that powerful Allied blows were to strike soon, the Spanish dictator was almost eager to grant the diplomatic request to provide all Barcelona dock facilities and personnel for handling some 2,000 Anglo-American casualties. When the war was over, Francisco Franco had no intention of being on the outside looking in at the councils of the victorious Allies.

Meanwhile, late one morning in early May 1944, the telephone rang at the desk of Lieutenant M. E. Clifton James in the Royal Army Pay Corps office in Leicester, England. "This is Colonel Niven of the Army Kinematograph section," a pleasant voice said. "Would you be interested in making some army films?" Lieutenant James immediately recognized the voice of the caller: the renowned movie star David Niven. "Yes sir," James replied. "I most certainly would." "Good," Niven responded. "Come to London for a screen test as soon as you can."[3]

James replaced the receiver. He had been a stage actor for 25 years before volunteering his services as an entertainer when the war broke out. Instead, he was given a commission in the Pay Corps, where, by his own admission, he was a "royal misfit." Now, perhaps the mistake was going to be corrected. Maybe he would be cast in some sort of army film with David Niven himself.

That was the beginning of one of the war's most bizarre deception schemes. Code-named Copperhead, the machination was designed to strengthen Vendetta. On reporting to a certain location in London, Clifton James was taken in tow by MI–5 agents and received the shock of his life: he had been chosen to act as a double for General Bernard Montgomery.

Lieutenant James already was aware that he bore a striking resemblance to the famous British general who would lead Allied ground forces in the genuine Normandy invasion. His picture had once appeared in the London *News Chronicle*, posed in a beret and captioned: "You're wrong—his name is Lieutenant Clifton James."

Six weeks earlier, Lieutenant Colonel J.V.B. Jervis-Reid, the number-two man on SHAEF's Committee of Special Means, happened to see that newspaper photograph, and he conceived the scheme for James to impersonate General Montgomery. On closer scrutiny, it appeared that the plan was doomed to failure. Montgomery was a teetotaler and James, it was discovered, had periodic bouts with John Barleycorn and lost most of them.

What's more, there was a sharp personality difference between the general and his would-be impersonator. Montgomery was arrogant and self-assured, while James came across as meek, uncertain, even introverted. The CSM decided to pursue the project anyway.

Under the direction of A-Force, Clifton James (as the general) would be paraded around Gibraltar and Algiers. The idea was to pile up evidence that Monty—the likely commander of Overlord ground forces—had left his post in England for a different part of the world. This scheme was to suggest that the cross-Channel invasion was not imminent, despite the feverish activities that were taking place in the British Isles, or that Montgomery had come to command the southern France invasion.

James promptly broke out with a severe case of stage fright. He had been a teenaged private in World War I and had retained a schoolboy fear of senior officers. Now he was to impersonate the greatest British general of them all.

The first move was to separate Clifton James from both his bottle and his wife. Then, hour after hour, the need for total secrecy was pounded into his head by his deceptionist stage-managers. Any action that might betray him as a Monty double could unmask the entire Vendetta deception and conceivably jeopardize Overlord. James became even more jittery, and he was leery of talking to anyone—even his MI–5 coaches.

"You should look on all this as a play in which you are starring for the benefit of Adolf Hitler and his generals," James was told. "We have to hoodwink the German high command."

In the days ahead, James was tutored relentlessly for his role of a lifetime. Endlessly it seemed, James studied newspaper photographs and watched newsreels of the general. MI–5 officers drilled him in hundreds of details of the impersonation, including Monty's idiosyncrasies, of which there was no shortage. When the real Montgomery was contacted by MI–5 and asked if there were any peculiarities about his diet that James should know, the general snapped: "Certainly not! I take no milk or sugar with my porridge. That's all!" At meals, James learned, Monty never once mentioned war. Instead, he chatted buoyantly with his staff about birds, animals, and flowers.

Finally, as a sort of graduation test, the Army Pay Corps lieutenant was assigned to Montgomery's staff in the guise of an Intelligence Corps sergeant, and for several days he watched the general like a hawk, trying to catch his fleeting expressions, his characteristic walk with hands clasped behind his back, and the way he pinched his cheek when thinking. Finally, James was convinced that he could impersonate Monty, as far as voice, gestures, and mannerisms went. Fortunately for the masquerade, both men had the same relatively short, wiry build.

Next, the Pay Corps officer was taken to Myer and Mortimer, military tailors in London, and was outfitted in an elegant battledress with the scarlet gorgets of the Imperial General Staff, epaulets holding a general's crossed swords, five rows of decorations ribbons, a black beret, a gold chain and fob, and a few handkerchiefs with the initials BLM. A makeup artist, sworn to secrecy, trimmed James' mustache a shade, brushed up his eyebrows to make them bristle like Montgomery's, and applied a touch of makeup to have his temples appear slightly grayer. MI–5 officers beamed over the finished product. The likeness between General Bernard Montgomery and Clifton James was amazing.

The stage show was ready for the grand tour. One haunting specter gripped the MI–5 coaches: since Monty never drank or smoked or even permitted others to do so in his presence, what if James were to get hold of a bottle before his public debut as Montgomery and come out reeling and reeking of alcohol?

Meanwhile, far to the south, A-Force agents were busy planting rumors around the Mediterranean that Montgomery might be coming to take command of an invasion of southern France.

At 6:30 P.M. on May 25, 1944, the curtain rose on the Copperhead extravaganza. Clifton James donned his general's battledress and black beret with its Armored Corps badge. Followed by a real brigadier, two real captains, and two phony aides, James strolled briskly out the door to his waiting Rolls-Royce, which was flying Monty's pennant.

A large crowd had gathered and a rousing cheer echoed across the landscape. James flashed the brilliant Monty smile and the famous Monty salute. Shouts of "Good old Monty!" rang out. Paced by two motorcycle policemen and trailed by three cars with assorted military functionaries, the Rolls drove through the streets of London where cheers and shouts greeted the legendary folk hero.

At Northolt airport, there were more crowds. MI–5 undercover men strolled through the gathering and passed remarks that the general was bound for North Africa. The imposter boarded Prime Minister Churchill's private airplane and moments later took off on the overnight flight to Gibraltar.

Neither of James' aides (who were actually A-Force men) was aware that he had concealed a pint flask of gin in his handbag. After those on board had settled for the night, James went to the toilet in the rear of the plane. Minute later, an escort missed him and hurried to the rear—just in time to find James swigging the bottle. Half of the flask was empty.

When the airplane was but two hours from Gibraltar, James was still inebriated. If he arrived in Gibraltar in that condition, the entire stratagem would be blown. So a crash program was initiated to sober him up. Treatments included forcing him to vomit and holding his face to the icy slipstream coming through the plughole in a cabin window. Then James was slapped, massaged, and finally stripped naked and doused with cold water.

When the four-engine aircraft landed at Gibraltar, "General Montgomery" was quite sober. After brief welcoming ceremonies and review of the guard of honor, James was driven through the streets of Gibraltar town while throngs of Spanish civilians—including at least one German spy—watched the procession. There were more crowds at Government House where Ralph Eastwood, governor general of Gibraltar and an old friend of Montgomery, smiled and held out his hand: "Hello, Monty, it's good to see you again." Eastwood had been briefed on just enough of Copperhead to put on a convincing act. Inside Government House, General Eastwood stared in astonishment at James. "I can't get over it!" he exclaimed. "You *are* Monty!"

That evening, Eastwood gave a small party and introduced "Montgomery" to a pair of prominent Spanish bankers, one of whom was believed to have connections with Walther Schellenberg's SD. "General Montgomery," a talk-ative chap, twice let slip remarks about "Plan 303," presumably code for the pending invasion of southern France. Each time, General Eastwood, playing his role to the hilt, tugged gently at James' sleeve and he abruptly changed the subject.

The A-Force men hovered over Clifton James like mother hens, alert to make certain that he did not reach for the cocktails that servants were carrying around the room on trays. That night, after searching James' luggage for alcoholic contraband, they locked him in his bedroom and stood guard outside the door.

"Montgomery's" departure from Gibraltar was much like his arrival. Bayonets flashed in the sun and a flight of Spitfires zoomed low overhead, dipping their wings in salute.

In order to buy time for a sizeable crowed to gather, the scenario called for the prime minister's airplane to develop a minor engine gremlin. Eastwood and James went to the airport restaurant for a cup of tea and within earshot of Spanish employees, "Montgomery" began talking once more about the mysterious Plan 303. When the pair departed, James had left behind a handkerchief embroidered with the initial BLM.

Twenty-four hours after James had reached Gibraltar, German intelligence in Berlin knew of his presence. Orders were flashed to German agents throughout the Mediterranean: "At all costs, find nature of Plan 303."

When James' airplane touched down at Maison Blanche airfield in Algiers, he was greeted by hulking General Henry M. Wilson, Allied commander in the Mediterranean. After the usual pomp and circumstance attendant to the arrival of a distinguished warrior, James was driven to the ornate St. George Hotel and ensconced in a plush suite once occupied by General Dwight Eisenhower when Algiers was his headquarters.

For the next few days, there were official receptions, guards of honor, bogus pep talks to troops, cheering crowds of civilian spectators—no doubt with Ger-man agents among them. James' car sped to and fro as though he were heading to urgent meetings. British intelligence reported that the Algiers region was buzzing with talk about the presence of the famous General Montgomery.

Suddenly, "Montgomery" vanished from the Mediterranean. His job was done—and A-Force did not want to stretch its luck. Dressed in his Royal Army Pay Corps lieutenant's uniform, Clifton James was smuggled out the back door of Jumbo Wilson's headquarters at night, flown to Cairo, put up in a small room under guard, and kept there for three weeks, until after the Normandy invasion.[4]

21

Electronic Spoofing

Although the intricate maze of Bodyguard connivances appeared to be misleading Adolf Hitler into keeping his armed forces widely dispersed, SHAEF was confronted with a seemingly insolvable problem: how could a mighty invasion fleet of 5,000 vessels be "hidden" as it plowed for ten hours across the English Channel to Normandy? On the Far Shore in France and Belgium were 92 sites equipped with an entire array of sophisticated ground radar—*Mammuts*, *Wassermans*, *Würzburgs*, *Freyas*, and *Seetakts*. Their job was to keep watch on Channel shipping.

Marquee players in this electronic melodrama were Reginald V. Jones, a 33-year-old wizard on the MI–6 scientific intelligence staff, and his long-time colleague, Robert Cockburn. The two scientists had been working together since the spring of 1940, when Reichmarschall Hermann Goering's vaunted Luftwaffe tried to bring Great Britain to its knees by a bombing blitz of unprecedented ferocity.

During those black hours for England, Jones discovered by piecing together scraps of information found in crashed Heinkel bombers that the Germans had developed a radio beacon they called *Knickebein* (Crooked Leg), a revolutionary electronic guidance technique. With this new technology, the Luftwaffe was able to pinpoint British cities at night with a high degree of accuracy, while RAF bombers often got lost over Germany while trying to locate their targets in the darkness. Unless countermeasures were created, England's doom could be sealed.

On June 21, 1940, an urgent meeting was called at 10 Downing Street to discuss the alarming Knickebein threat. Young Reginald Jones found himself seated among the high and the mighty of the British empire, including cigar-chomping Winston Churchill. Jones presented a lengthy briefing on the Knickebein, and when the session was over, he had been given the green light to try to develop a radio countermeasure (RCM) to neutralize the Knickebein.

Under Cockburn, a team of scientists plunged into the task. Cockburn commandeered diathermy sets from scores of hospitals and used them to distort the Knickebein beams with sound. Then the team developed equipment that transmitted its own radio beam (code-named Aspirins) that jammed the Knickebein transmission.

Aspirins proved highly successful, as the garbled Knickebein signals confused Luftwaffe bomber crews, causing some aircraft to fly in circles through the black skies of England while seeking their target. One Heinkel, out of gas after a night of circling, crash-landed on a Channel beach in southern England in the belief that it was coming down in France.

Along with the selfless heroics of a few hundred pilots of Air Marshal Hugh C. T. "Stuffy" Dowding's Fighter Command, Reginald Jones, Robert Cockburn, and other unheralded scientists had thwarted Adolf Hitler's goal of crushing England.

Now almost four years later, Jones, Cockburn, and their colleagues were confronted with another monumental challenge: "blinding" the Germans so that they could not "see" the approaching Neptune fleet.

First, three Ping-Pongs, complex electronic direction finders that Cockburn and his associates had created, were set up along the southern coast of England. These devices produced fixes on the 92 German radar sites along the Far Shore. After the sites had been pinpointed electronically, their existence was confirmed by RAF reconnaissance flights.

By early May 1944, Reginald Jones had developed a comprehensive picture of the entire enemy radar network in northern France. But this mosaic had to be updated daily. Radar sets, particularly mobile ones like Würzburg and Freya, could be moved rapidly, then put into operation within a few hours of their arrival at a new locale.[1]

Then began the difficult and perilous task of putting out the cyclops-like "eyes" that would be staring at the Neptune invasion fleet. Early one morning, a flight of 12 RAF Typhoons arrowed across the Channel as though heading for inland targets in Belgium. Suddenly, the swift fighter planes dove earthward and at treetop height raced toward the huge Wasserman early warning radar site perched on the Belgian coast near Ostend.

The Typhoons launched rockets and strafed the facility, then altered course and headed for England. Glancing back, the pilots were disappointed: the 130-foot Wasserman tower was still standing erect and presumably operational.

Reaching their home base, the Typhoons were refueled, loaded with machine-gun bullets and rockets, and at 4:00 P.M. that same day, they lifted off again for the Ostend facility to finish the job. Several more rocket hits were scored, but the seemingly indestructible tower remained defiantly standing.

Crestfallen, the RAF pilots, who had flown through a torrent of German flak around the Wasserman site, returned home, convinced that they had failed. However, the blast of the rockets had so severely damaged the tower's turning mechanism that the aerial could not be traversed and remained rigid—and useless—in the upright position. The entire aerial structure had to be tediously dismantled and repaired, and the Wasserman would still be out of operation on D-Day.

In the three weeks prior to D-Day, American and British bombers and fighter bombers flew thousands of sorties against the German radar network on the Far Shore, knocking out most of those facilities. Among the targets bombed out of existence was the headquarters of the German electronic monitoring network in northern France, at Urville-Hague near Cherbourg. Ninety-nine RAF heavies blasted that complex installation off the map.

In a curious new twist in electronic warfare, and as a component of Fortitude South, 16 of the 92 German radar sites were deliberately spared in the bombing campaign. Robert Cockburn and other British scientists were perfecting a variety of ruse de querre to spring on the enemy when the invasion fleet sailed. It was hoped that the surviving German "eyes" on the Far Shore would report to OB West that two large Allied convoys (actually two ghost fleets) were bound for the Pas de Calais at the same time that the real sea armada was making for Normandy.

Creation of these ruses began during late April—two months prior to D-Day—when Cockburn arranged to have captured Würzburg, Seetakt, and Freya radar sets moved from the Royal Aircraft Establishment (RAE) at Farnborough in Hampshire to Tantallon Castle, a crumbling old landmark perched on a height overlooking the Firth of Forth in Scotland. These German radar devices had been in British hands since February 1942, when British paratroopers, under Major John D. Frost, had jumped into the French coastal town of Bruneval, wiped out a Wehrmacht garrison, dismantled a Würzburg, and brought it back to England by boat for study by Reginald Jones and other electronic wizards. Since that time, the German radar arsenal at RAE had been updated by items captured during fighting in North Africa and Italy.[2]

While Würzburg had been at the RAE, it was called by its original German designation, *FuSE.62* (*Funk-Sender Empfänger 62*). When papers were prepared for shipment of the Würzburg to Tantallon Castle, a typographical error listed the 3,000-pound piece of equipment as "Fuse Type 62." When Cockburn's men tried to haul the Würzburg through the main gate at Farnborough, the guard refused to allow it to pass: he was suspicious that the Würzburg was being stolen, possibly by German agents.

A hassle erupted when the guard turned a deaf ear to the pleas of the Würzburg escorts. Then a security officer was summoned and the dispute was settled. The conscientious guard had seen the "Fuse Type 62" on the papers and knew that a fuse did not weigh anywhere close to the one and a half tons of the Würzburg.[3]

In a nondescript building below the ramparts of historic Tantallon Castle, Robert Cockburn, Joan Curran, and a few scientists from the Telecommunications Research Establishment (TRE), began creating a ghost fleet technique. Centerpieces for the scheme were an ECM known to the British as Window and to the Americans as Chaff and another called Moonshine.

Back in 1942, Joan Curran developed Moonshine, a device that could be installed in airplanes and ships. It received the pulse sent out by enemy radar stations and sent it back to them in magnified form, producing an "echo" similar to that from a 10,000-ton ship. Moonshine never had been used since then, so the Germans would be unfamiliar with the device.

In early 1943 Curran headed an electronic research team that discovered if strips of aluminum foil were dropped from a bomber stream in large quantities at intervals, they would devastate German radar defenses. Window (or Chaff) blacked out enemy radar screens, snarled direction-finding equipment, and created so many false "echoes" that confused German operators gained the impression that not one, but thousands, of Allied bombers were in flight. It became impossible to identify specific objects.

On the night of July 23, 1943, a mighty force of 791 RAF bombers was winging toward the major port of Hamburg, in northern Germany, and would make the initial combat test of the new electronic warfare weapon. At a designated point, each of the bombers began releasing a batch of 2,000 aluminum foil strips at one-minute intervals.

With the approach of the Hamburg-bound bomber force, German radar defenses were thrown into chaos. Frantic radar operators reported that 12,000 aircraft were in the stream. Radar-controlled searchlight beams leaped wildly about the black sky, and antiaircraft guns, directed by radar, filled the night with bursting shells aimed at echoes, not real bombers. Luftwaffe night fighters, which relied on radar to lead them to the intruding bombers, chased about the air in confusion. Twelve RAF planes were lost in the raid—a percentage rate far below normal losses in similar missions over the Third Reich.[4]

Now, with D-Day edging inexorably closer, the Tantallon Castle research team conceived an intricate electronic scheme to make it appear on German radar that two large Allied fleets, each deployed over an area of 256 square miles, was approaching, when in reality, only a few Moonshine-equipped launches and 16 bombers dropping Window would be involved.

Each ghost fleet would have a line of launches spread across a front 14 miles wide. Their task would be to jam the German coastal radar stations but just enough to confuse their pictures. Another line of launches would be abreast some ten miles to the rear of the jammers. Each of these launches would tow a Filbert, a 29-foot-long balloon with a Moonshine built inside it, and tow another float with a Filbert.

High above the launches would be RAF bombers (eight to each fleet), which would drop Window at the rate of 12 bundles per minute. These aircraft would fly oblong patterns, parallel to the shore. To make the dummy fleet appear to be advancing at eight miles per hour on German radar screens, every seven minutes the bombers' oblong patterns would move forward for a mile.

In order to inject realism into the electronic spoof, other RAF bombers, equipped with Mandrel jammers, would be circling nearby. These aircraft would be strategically positioned so that German radar could barely "see" through the cracks in the jamming blanket and detect the phantom fleets.[5]

Such a large concentration of ships certainly would not be a silent one. So Robert Cockburn and his colleagues created another elaborate ruse. Once the ghost fleets halted ten miles from shore, real smaller boats armed with powerful amplifiers would begin blaring out prerecorded sounds of a landing force debarking: the shrill noise of bosuns' pipes, warships' bugle calls, commands being shouted, the rattles of chains lowering landing craft, and their incessant banging against the sides of the transports after reaching the water.

These noises had been recorded during the actual Anglo-American invasion at Salerno, Italy, in September 1943. It was hoped that the Feldgrau on shore would hear the sounds and report that a major amphibious assault was about to be launched.

All of this electronic spoofery was yet only theory. So early in May—four weeks before D-Day—Cockburn and his associates were ready for a realistic test. In a task akin to having teeth extracted, Cockburn finagled the services of two RAF squadrons of Stirling and Lancaster heavy bombers. The Air Ministry wanted every airplane that could fly for Neptune and was hardly enthused about sidetracking aircraft for testing some electronic hoax. Only through the intervention of Winston Churchill, who reveled in special means stratagems, were the bombers made available to Cockburn.

The electronic scientists also managed to pry loose the Canadian destroyer *Haida* and several RAF sea-rescue launches. Then Cockburn and a few colleagues paid whirlwind visits to the RAF squadrons, briefed them on the test, and arranged for crewmen to begin rehearsing the patterns they were to fly.

Finally, Cockburn selected a British radar site at Flamborough Head as the target of his experiment. The radar equipment there was the nearest British equivalent to the Würzburg. No one at the Flamborough Head station was informed in advance of the pending test.

On the appointed day, the Stirlings and Lancasters winged over the designated area at a precise speed and altitude, dropping bundles of Window at exact intervals. At the same time, the destroyer *Haida* and several launches, all trailing Filberts, sailed into the test area on the Firth of Forth. As earlier directed, the vessels "Moonshined" the Flamborough Head radar. When all this was done, the combination of Window, Filbert, and Moonshine created a blizzard of blips on the British radar screens.

Flamborough Head operators were stunned. This was the largest collection of vessels they had ever "seen"—or so they thought—and it was bearing down on them at eight miles per hour. The ghost-fleet concept passed its test with flying colors—but would it really spoof the Germans when it was time for the real thing?

In London, Colonel John Bevan, the deception genius and chief of the LCS, was delighted with the electronic creation of Robert Cockburn, Joan Curran, and their colleagues at Tantallon Castle. After consultation with his staff, Bevan approved two electronic deceptions code-named Glimmer and Taxable. These operations would make it appear to German radar on the Far Shore that two great fleets were approaching the French coast, one heading for Boulogne and the other for Calais, both sites being in the Pas de Calais. All the while, the genuine fleet was sailing toward the Bay of the Seine in Normandy, 150 to 200 miles to the west.

While John Bevan and other deceptionists were including Glimmer and Taxable into Fortitude South, Cockburn and his team were putting the final touches on another ingenious electronic scheme which, it was hoped, could confuse and confound German commanders during the early hours of D-Day to help gain that slight edge that could mean the difference between success or failure of the Allied airborne assault.

Centerpieces of this machination were realistic rubber dummies, about half-human size and garbed in paratrooper uniforms, boots, and helmets, which would be dropped at midnight from airplanes flying at about 400 feet. On landing, the dummies would emit the harsh sounds of battle: the sharp crack of rifle and pistol shots, the staccato chatter of automatic weapons—all prerecorded. A few real British paratroopers would jump at the same time, and after reaching the ground, they would switch on powerful amplifiers that would send other pre-recorded battlefield noises echoing across the landscape: human shouts, moans, thuds, loud curses, cries for help. These genuine parachutists also would release a chemical that created the pungent smell of detonated explosives. The code name for this stratagem was Titanic.

Meanwhile on May 30, with D-Day at hand and men of the 82nd and 101st Airborne divisions sealed into camps of long rows of pyramidical tents at scattered airfields in southern England, Air Marshal Trafford Leigh-Mallory paid a call on General Dwight Eisenhower to protest one final time the "futile slaughter of these two fine American airborne divisions."

Twice in recent weeks, Leigh-Mallory had been overruled while trying to have the American airborne assault behind Utah Beach canceled. It appeared to furious American generals, notably Omar Bradley, who would command the Utah assault, that Leigh-Mallory had dedicated himself to preventing the Americans from inflicting a catastrophe upon themselves. Bradley declared that the British air marshal was laying the foundation to prove himself "right" if U.S. paratroopers and glidermen were chopped down in wholesale numbers among the tangled hedgerows and apple orchards of Normandy. "You can expect seventy percent casualties among American glider troops and fifty percent among parachute troops," the 51-year-old air marshal insisted. It was a frightening prediction to be dumped onto Eisenhower's already sagging shoulders at virtually the final hour.

The implication to be drawn from Leigh-Mallory's contention was mind-numbing. If the air marshal, billed as SHAEF's expert on such matters, turned out to be accurate and Eisenhower permitted the American airborne assault to proceed, then the slaughter of the 82nd and 101st would result in disaster for the Utah amphibious landings. And that would mean that the seizure of the invasion's primary objective, the crucial port of Cherbourg 20 miles north of Utah, would be impossible.

Without a major port to bring in reinforcements and mountains of supplies, the two American, one Canadian, and two British assault divisions landing by sea at Utah and on the Calvados Coast to the east would be cut off from the large harbor and left to flounder on the shore like a huge beached whale. There would be a monumental Allied debacle possibly leading to a negotiated peace with Adolf Hitler.

Grim-faced and worried, the supreme commander retired to his private house trailer to ponder Leigh-Mallory's viewpoint. It was his decision to make, and his alone. Eisenhower anguished for more than an hour, reviewing over and over each step in the Neptune plan. Then he rose from his chair, smothered the tenth cigarette he had smoked during the past hour, returned to his office and placed a call to Air Marshal Leigh-Mallory: The American airborne attack would proceed as planned.[6] If Eisenhower had made a faulty decision, even Robert Cockburn's rubber paratroopers could not prevent a catastrophe.

Invasion Fever

Supreme Commander Dwight Eisenhower had at his beck and call the mightiest ground, sea, and air force ever assembled for an invasion. More than half of his 3 million soldiers were American, while British and Canadian troops jointly totaled 1 million. Free French, Belgian, Czech, Polish, Dutch, and Norwegian contingents made up the remainder of the juggernaut.

Overlord was backed by the combined industrial muscle of the United States and Great Britain. For nearly two years, the most intense study, planning, and projections had been poured into the invasion by the most brilliant military minds in the Allied world. Yet Eisenhower was at the mercy of a demanding master he could not influence: the capricious English Channel weather.

On May 17, Eisenhower picked one of three days in June 1944—the fifth, sixth, or seventh—for D-Day. SHAEF meteorologists, headed by Group Captain John Stagg of the Royal Air Force concluded that critical weather requirements for Neptune could be expected for Normandy on those days.

Darkness would be required to conceal the flight of 18,000 paratroopers from England to Normandy, but then the visibility provided by a midnight-rising moon would be needed to perform their mischievous deeds once they had landed. About four hours later, shortly after dawn, a low tide would be necessary so that assault craft carrying the first waves of amphibious troops could avoid being skewered by the thousands of obstacles that Field Marshal Erwin Rommel had planted just offshore which were covered at high tide.

Group Captain Stagg, a Scotsman who had earned a fine reputation in his field, warned that the chances were ten to one against Normandy having perfect weather conditions on any one of those three days. Against this dark backdrop, Eisenhower picked June 5 for D-Day.

If bad weather forced a postponement, the assault could be launched the next day. But if the landings on the sixth had to be canceled again, convoys already at sea would have to return to port and the problem of refueling the ships might prevent an invasion on the seventh. If it became necessary to move D-Day ahead again, the invasion might have to be delayed until July.

Such an eventuality would mean that 150,000 assault troops had detailed knowledge of Neptune. They would have to laboriously disembark and be locked up incommunicado for nearly a month—if such a feat were possible. Almost certainly, the big secret would be leaked to the Germans.

Equally alarming, the incredible maze of Bodyguard plots and subplots, which seemed to have hoodwinked the fuehrer and his generals on the time and place of D-Day, would collapse like a punctured balloon. For six months, all the deception schemes had been based on the premise that the Anglo-Americans would launch a major invasion *somewhere* in the first few days of June, so the web of deceit that was partially to cloak Neptune would no longer apply.

Creating a largely new Bodyguard-like plan would be an impossibility. There was not nearly enough time. Nor could the same scenarios be repeated and effective. So when the Allies stormed ashore in Normandy at a later date, there would be minimal deceptions to mask their intentions and a holocaust could ensue. A long postponment was "too bitter to contemplate," Ike Eisenhower told his aides.[1]

Late in May, England was gripped by invasion fever. The dusty roads and narrow-gauge rail lines heaved and groaned under the weight of the war juggernaut edging southward toward the ports along the English Channel. Seaborne assault troops, grim and burdened under heavy weapons and equipment, marched into coastal assembly areas called sausages because of their oval shapes on high-level military maps.

Southern England had become a huge arsenal. Concealed in the woods were mountains of shells, bombs, and ammunition. Stretching northward for nearly 100 miles, bumper to bumper, were trucks, jeeps, ambulances, half-trucks, tanks, and armored cars. In the greenery of hundreds of pastures were huge stocks of earth-moving equipment, from excavators to bulldozers, all intended to reshape the Normandy countryside. Nearly 1,000 new locomotives and some 20,000 tanker cars and freight cars clogged the rails—they would replace the destroyed French railroad equipment once the Neptune beachhead was firmly established. In excess of 125,000 hospital beds foretold the butchery expected on the far shore. So staggering was this arsenal of weapons, equipment, and supplies that a standard joke among GIs was that the British Isles would sink into the sea were it not for their being kept afloat by the barrage balloons that saturated the cities and landscape to discourage low-flying Luftwaffe aircraft.

Hundreds of miles from the English Channel on May 23, an American platoon probing German defenses near Valmontone, Italy, captured a headquarters armored car concealed in an olive grove. Documents found in a cabinet were rushed to U.S. Lieutenant General Mark W. Clark's 15th Army Group headquarters in the ornate Royal Palace in Casterta.

Analyzed by intelligence officers and A-Force men, the papers proved to be a blockbuster, confirming that Bodyguard deception stratagems had largely been a success—at least so far. Adolf Hitler, the documents disclosed, had stretched his Wehrmacht to the breaking point all around the perimeter of his Nazi empire trying to thwart real and fictitious Allied invasions.

There were but the equivalent of nine divisions in the Third Reich, and most of them were kept in the vicinity of Berlin to stamp out any rebellion by the German people or the Wehrmacht officer corps (about which the fuehrer had been hearing a great amount of rumors). About 167 German infantry and panzers divisions were in the East trying desperately to stem the advance of the Russian army, while another 24 divisions were battling Mark Clark's 15th Army Group (the U.S. Fifth and British Eighth armies) among the towering Apennines in Italy. However, nearly 150 other German divisions were defending Norway, Denmark, the Netherlands, Belgium, the Balkans, and southern France against the phony Bodyguard invasions, the captured Valmontone documents revealed.

A week after the GI patrol had seized the top-secret Wehrmacht papers, Ultra provided solid evidence that the fuehrer had swallowed the Fortitude and Quicksilver fairy tales. On May 30, Baron Hiroshi Oshima held a long conversation with Hitler at Berchtesgaden, and the Japanese ambassador's report to Tokyo was intercepted at Bletchley Park and decoded. Its contents were eyepoppers. The fuehrer had confided to Oshima that there were 92 to 97 Allied divisions, including eight airborne, in Great Britain—the precise Bodyguard scenario. Actually, there were 33 infantry and armored divisions and three airborne divisions. Hitler also was convinced, the Ultra intercepts disclosed, that while the Anglo-Americans might launch an elaborate feint against Normandy, Brittany, or the Netherlands, the main invasion would hit at the Pas de Calais.

At OB West, Field Marshal von Rundstedt seemed to have been influenced by the Fortitude South chicanery of having the Allied air forces drop two bombs on the Pas de Calais for every one dropped on Normandy. On May 29, von Rundstedt, saying that he had studied enemy bombing patterns in France, notified Berlin that the Allied main thrust would be in the Pas de Calais.

The Old Prussian did not intend to be caught with his epaulets down, so he covered all bets. It also was possible, he included in his report, that the Allies might land in Brittany, the Cherbourg peninsula, or near the French border with the Netherlands. It may well have galled the aristocratic field marshal to know that he was in lockstep with "that Bohemian corporal" in a strategic sense.

Meanwhile, another German field marshal, Erwin Rommel, had performed an about-face with regard to the locale of the Allied invasion and withdrew from the chorus of German generals harmonized with the fuehrer that the Pas de Calais would be the principal target. Five months earlier, Rommel also had subscribed to military logic and thought the Allies would plunge across the narrow Strait of Dover against the Pas de Calais, but he had become convinced that the main invasion actually would be in Normandy.

It was not unusual that Erwin Rommel found himself out of tune with the German general corps aristocracy, who did not consider the teacher's son to be their equal, although he outranked most of them. It rankled them that he had risen meteorlike in only three years from colonel to the dignity of field marshal, a leap that smacked of favoritism. Rommel was regarded as an upstart, so they were not surprised when he tiptoed out of the Pas de Calais chorus.

In late May, Rommel reported to the high command:

> From the Allied point of view the number one objective is to get firmly ashore.
> . . . This is improbable on the Pas de Calais coast, which is strongly defended, but possible on the Normandy coast which is barely fortified.[2]

Field Marshal Rommel did now know *when* the Allies would strike, but he was so confident that the invasion would hit at Normandy's Cherbourg peninsula and along the Calvados coast just to the east that he urgently submitted his shopping list to the Oberkommando der Wehrmacht in Berlin. He requested that the three crack armored divisions being held inland (under the direct command of the fuehrer) be released to him. He proposed moving the 12th SS *"Hitler Jugend"* Panzer Division into the Cherbourg peninsula, only 30 minutes from what the Allies called Utah Beach; for the Panzer Lehr Division to displace forward to Bayeux, 20 minutes from Omaha and 30 minutes from the Canadian beach; and for the 21st Panzer Division to get closer to the coast at Caen, a half-hour from the two British beaches.

The Desert Fox also asked for a brigade of 24 *Nebelwerfer* (large six-barreled mortars whose shells exploded with terrific impact) to be positioned north of Carentan behind Utah Beach. Then Rommel requested of Reichmarschall Hermann Goering, commander of the Luftwaffe, the services of the 3rd Antiaircraft Corps, which was dispersed all over France. Its 24 batteries, all equipped with deadly accurate, multipurpose .88-millimeter guns, would be placed in the Cherbourg peninsula and provide murderous fire against intruding paratrooper transport planes. This was the precise region where Major General Matthew B. Ridgway's battle-tested 82nd Airborne and Major General Maxwell Taylor's green but eager 101st Airborne were to descend in the early morning darkness of D-Day.

Rommel argued that if the three armored divisions were held in reserve until the invasion struck, awesome Allied air power would chop them to pieces before they could move forward to the point of attack. Therefore, he declared, if the invasion were to be defeated, the three panzer divisions would have to be lined up along the coast.

Now the green monster of envy reared its ugly head in the high levels of the German command. Rommel, the legend whose homefront popularity equaled that of the fuehrer, had gained far too much of the limelight in the Fatherland. Hermann Goering, obese, flabby-jowled, vain, and now addicted to wearing rouge and lipstick on occasion at his castle north of Berlin, flatly turned down the request for the 24 antiaircraft batteries, even though they were not being utilized.

Adolf Hitler bluntly declined to release the critical panzers to Rommel or to move them forward to the Normandy coast, or to give Rommel the Nebelwerfer brigade that he wanted so desperately. Rommel would have to make do with the resources available to him.

In the meantime, tens of thousands of American, British, Canadian, and French troops were confined to their sausages near Torquay, Plymouth, Portland, Dartmouth, Southampton, Portsmouth, and other Channel ports. When they entered the sausages, the soldiers had not known their destination. They were issued maps that gave no clues: the rivers of Normandy had been given Russian names and Caen was called Warsaw. There were extensive marshes and swamps on these maps (the region behind Utah Beach), but they were not identified, causing conjecture that the target was Norway.

Then they were shown photos of the real breaches where they were to land. These pictures had been taken from sea level and revealed the coast sections exactly as the men would see them from approaching landing craft. The photos were so clear that the soldiers could make out the faces of the Feldgrau they would soon have to kill to seize strong points along the Atlantic Wall.

Finally, on June 1, those fighting men who would storm five beaches and drop from the air onto and behind German positions were briefed in detail on Neptune—Normandy was the target; D-Day was June 5. French invasion money was issued to each man. Hundreds of field security and military police ringed the sausages with orders to shoot to kill anyone trying to get out.

Two thousand dedicated men of the U.S. Army's Counterintelligence Corps (CIC) worked tirelessly all over southern England, plugging possible leaks of the big secret. They also quietly took into custody an innocent British carpenter who inadvertently popped into a headquarters room whose walls were lined with top-secret invasion maps.

Despite these unprecedented measures, SHAEF was rocked by an alarming security breach. Freshly printed French ''invasion money'' turned up in pubs in Torquay and two other coastal towns. Should word of this special currency reach the eyes or ears of German agents, it would be a tip-off that the operation was about to be launched and that the target was northern France.

Eisenhower was horrified and ordered a prompt investigation. Frantic sleuthing by the CIC produced no results, other than to turn up more invasion currency. CIC agents concluded that an unknown number of assault soldiers, alone or in pairs, had risked being shot by guards, wriggled under fences at night, and rushed to the closest town for one final fling of what the Americans called B and B (booze and broads).

Across the Channel at OB West in Saint-Germain, Field Marshal Gerd von Rundstedt was poring over air-reconnaissance reports that showed heavy nighttime road traffic in southwestern England across from Normandy. Drivers appeared to be careless about leaving their vehicle lights on. Von Rundstedt felt that this ''carelessness'' was an Allied ploy to convince him that the landings would come in Normandy rather than at the Pas de Calais.

Each day, von Rundstedt's staff officers carefully were marking Anglo-American units on a huge wall map of England, largely using information provided by German agents controlled by the Double-Cross. These marking showed heavy concentrations of divisions in southeastern England (figments of Quicksilver and Fortitude South deceptionists' imaginations), while only a portion of the genuine Neptune divisions were shown in southern and southwestern England.

At the same time, Field Marshal Erwin Rommel, at his headquarters in tiny La Roche-Guyon (French population: 532), was scanning these same Luftwaffe reconnaissance reports. His interpretation of them was far different from that of his nominal boss, von Rundstedt. Rommel noted that daylight reconnaissance planes were allowed to fly over southeastern England (in the FUSAG region) without heavy opposition form the RAF, but when German aircraft tried to reach the Channel ports in southern and southwestern England, they were driven off by swarms of British fighter planes before they could take pictures. These critical clues to Allied intentions reinforced Rommel's view that the invasion target was Normandy. Why else would the RAF be so touchy?

In recent days, Dwight Eisenhower had established his Overlord headquarters in Southwick House, a commodious mansion perched on a hill overlooking the Channel city of Portsmouth. On the evening of May 30, the harried supreme commander summoned his righthand man, General Walter Smith, who bustled importantly into his office. "Okay, Beetle, send it out!"

"It" was the code phrase *Exercise Plus Six*, which was flashed to all Neptune commanders. This told them that D-Day would be six days hence, on June 5.

Twenty-four hours later, Group Captain John Stagg, the chief SHAEF meteorologist, called on Eisenhower with grim news. After consulting with outlying weather-reporting stations in the Atlantic, Stagg said that the weather forecast for the fifth, sixth, and seventh was "not good."

In the meantime, General Tom Betts, the SHAEF security chief, was a deeply worried man. For months, only a relative handful of Bigot officers were privy to the date and place of Neptune. Even then, there had been terrifying security breaches. Now, perhaps 150,000 people in England (mainly those sealed in the sausages) knew the big secret.

On June 1, Betts learned about the most recent security breach. A young British junior officer, who was serving as liaison between SHAEF headquarters at Portsmouth and London, made a short detour during one of his regular trips and visited his parents. As they listened in astonishment, their son told them that the invasion would hit in Normandy on June 5.

After the officer left, neighbors learned of his shocking disclosures, notified authorities, and the son was placed under arrest. He would be dealt with after Neptune.

On Friday, June 2, time was running out for General Eisenhower to decide whether to proceed with D-Day on the fifth, or postpone it for 24 hours. He called a conference of his top commanders for that night.

Meanwhile that day, John Stagg consulted by telephone with outlying weather reporting stations far out in the Atlantic, and all of them agreed that weather disturbances were forming there. Data kept pouring into Stagg's office from these outposts, but the information was confused and uncertain.

Prior to that night's crucial conference, Captain Stagg met with his Meteorological Committee, which included his deputy, U.S. Army Air Corps Colonel D. N. Yates; weathermen from Allied ground, sea, and air forces; the British weather ministry; and the U.S. weather service. A wrangle erupted. Some members of the committee were positive that turbulent weather would not strike the Channel in the next few days; others were convinced that a violent storm would be raging during that period.

Stagg was worried. If at Eisenhower's conference in one hour he presented the views of those forecasters who predicted that the weather would be calm and cloud cover minimal, the supreme commander might launch the invasion only to meet disaster in a Channel lashed by high, angry waves and an overcast that would ground the Allies' powerful air force. If he predicted stormy weather, Eisenhower might have to postpone the invasion for a month or longer.

In the austere conference room at Southwick House, a grim Ike Eisenhower snapped, "Well, Stagg, what have you got for us this time?" Captain Stagg replied that the weather situation for the next few days was "potentially full of menace," and he forecast heavy clouds and strong westerly winds over the Channel until at least June 6 or 7. After deliberating with his commanders and their chiefs of staff, Eisenhower decided to postpone his "Go" or "No-Go" decision for another 24 hours.

Arising shortly after dawn on Saturday, June 3, Dwight Eisenhower peered out the window of his trailer, which was nestled in a clump of trees two miles from Southwick House. He frowned. After days of bright sunshine, the sky was murky. The trailer, which the supreme commander called "my circus wagon," was a long vehicle resembling a moving van. Three tiny compartments served as living room, bedroom, and office.

Later that morning in a conference at Southwick House, Eisenhower and his commanders were briefed by John Stagg, who expressed the guarded opinion that a violent storm expected to pound the English Channel the next day *might* subside on June 6 or 7. The supreme commander had to issue a "Go" or "No-Go" order for a June 5 assault, because some Allied convoys were so far from the landing beaches that they would have to shove off that same night to reach Normandy in time for H-Hour. Eisenhower postponed D-Day for 24 hours.

Beetle Smith promptly flashed the code phrase *Ripcord 24*, indicating that the assault had been moved ahead 24 hours. Several convoys were already at sea, and most of them reversed course in the storm-pitched Channel and headed back to England. However, word failed to reach the Royal Navy commodore in charge of a convoy of 124 ships carrying elements of the U.S. 4th Infantry Division bound for Utah Beach.

In the Operations Center in Southwick House, a bevy of solemn Royal navy officers awaited the latest word on the recalled convoys. Two Wrens, using a traveling stepladder, every few minutes moved colored markers on a gigantic chart of the English Channel that covered an entire wall, plotting the current position of each flotilla.[3]

Staff officers from several Allied services watched the procedure in silence, masking the knots that had been twisted in their stomachs. The waves were angry, and the wind in the Channel was blowing in 30-miles-per-hour gusts. As the clock ticked on, the officers present seemed to relax slightly, for the chart showed that the convoys were edging orderly into British ports.

But where was the errant convoy? Had it been confronted by a German naval force? Had it become lost? Desperate efforts to reach the convoy by radio were fruitless, so RAF Walrus seaplanes took off to search for the missing groups of vessels. Flying through rain squalls and handicapped by limited visibility, the pilots finally spotted the quarry. One plane swooped down nearly to deck level over the command ship and dropped a canister with an official coded message, ordering the convoy to return to port. However, the container missed its target and plunged into the angry sea. Then the pilot circled, scrawled his own note in plain English, put in it another container, zoomed over the ship, and pitched the canister. This time the aim was true.

Although the message was rushed to the bridge, the convoy plowed on toward Normandy, now only 70 miles away, as the Royal Navy commodore in charge pondered the authenticity of the message from an unidentified pilot of a seaplane with RAF markings. Perhaps the Luftwaffe had a captured British aircraft of this type in its inventory, and this curious maneuver could be a diabolical German trick to disrupt the invasion.

Finally, the uncertain convoy commander broke radio silence to contact Allied authorities at a port in southern England, and his vessels reversed course and returned to their base. Now another nagging specter beset SHAEF: Had Luftwaffe reconnaissance planes seen the convoy, crammed with assault troops, steaming hell-bent for the shores of Normandy?

Storm devils were shrieking over the English Channel just past 6:30 A.M. on Sunday, June 4, when Group Captain John Stagg rushed through the torrential downpour from his tent to the Southwick House weather center. Weather charts provided a ray of optimism: Stagg interpreted them to indicate that there might be a 36-hour break in the storm on June 5 and 6.

At the same time, Dwight Eisenhower left his trailer in the woods and was heading for Southwick House in an olive-drab staff car driven by WAC Lieutenant Kay Summersby. Deep in thought, the supreme commander hardly spoke a word, for this would be one of the most significant dates of the 20th century. Eisenhower would be forced to decide whether the pent-up man-made hurricane that was the Anglo-American war machine would be hurled against the Atlantic Wall on June 6 or whether the dangerous alternative of a month's postponement would be put into effect.

Within minutes at the morning session of the Meteorological Committee, a heated squabble erupted and continued to rage for three hours. Some members expressed themselves as "positive" that turbulent weather would remain over the Channel for the next few days, while others, including Stagg, discerned a brief surcease in the storm patterns on June 5 and 6.

Night was beginning to pull its cloak over England when John Stagg hurried across the Southwick House grounds for a critical 9:30 P.M. conference with the top SHAEF brass. This had been the most nerve-wracking day of his life. His spirits were not materially raised when he passed a well-meaning friend who called out: "John, they'll string you up from the nearest lamppost if you don't read the omens right!"[4]

Minutes later, Stagg was briefing Eisenhower and 12 of his senior commanders in the Southwick House library, a large, comfortable room with a conference table covered by a green baize cloth. Heavy blackout curtains hung at the windows. A strained silence fell over the room as Stagg began speaking. Anxious eyes were glued on him. What was decided in that room within the next 30 minutes could well alter the future course of the war in Europe.

Carefully weighing his words, the group captain sketched the weather picture for the past 24 hours, and then he quietly said, "Gentlemen, there have been some rapid and unexpected developments in the situation." Almost in unison, the brass seemed to lean forward slightly, listening intently. Earlier, Stagg had decided not to advise the SHAEF leaders of the bitter dispute at the weather committee meeting on the theory that Eisenhower already was heavily burdened.

A shifting weather front had been spotted, which, Stagg said, would move into the Channel within the next few hours and result in a gradual clearing over Normandy. These improving conditions would begin the next day and continue to about noon on D-Day, June 6. After that, the weather would begin to deteriorate again.

Stagg predicted that around midnight of June 5–6, the wind would not be strong enough to interfere with the delivery of paratroopers and glidermen, that cloud conditions on June 6 would permit accurate air strikes, and that the Channel would be sufficiently calm for accurate warship bombardments of the Normandy beaches.

As the meteorologist concluded the briefing, the room was hushed in utter silence. Then a rapid discussion ensued with each officer asked to comment. Beetle Smith was for launching the attack on June 6. General Bernard Montgomery was decisive—"Go!" Air Marshal Arthur Tedder, deputy supreme commander, was cautious, settling for pronouncing a Tuesday assault as "chancy." Air Marshal Leigh-Mallory doubted that the air force could operate effectively in the cloud cover Stagg had predicted.

Deliberations were over. Others could, and did, equivocate. Eisenhower had the burden of saying "Go" or "No-Go." Outside, Mother Nature was playing an eerie, soul-wracking background overture—howling winds that rattled the shutters on Southwick House and pouring rain that splattered against the windows of the conference room.

Finally, Dwight Eisenhower spoke softly, but firmly: "I am quite positive that we must give the order. . . . I don't like it, but there it is. The question is, how long can we hang this thing out on the end of a stick and let it hang there? . . . I don't see how we can do anything else. . . . Let's go!"[5]

D-Day was set: Tuesday, June 6. H-Hour: 6:30 A.M.[6]

By unleashing the most powerful invasion force that mankind had known, Dwight Eisenhower had crossed the Rubicon. There could be no turning back. Of such magnitude was the invasion apparatus that neither the supreme commander nor any mortal could halt its inexorable move toward Normandy. Now, the plan had taken over.

At the same moment that Eisenhower was issuing his fateful order, some 200 miles to the south in Paris, Vice Admiral Theodor Krancke, the German naval commander in the West, was dispatching his estimate of the situation to Berlin. It was Krancke's job to alert the land forces to the approach of an Allied invasion fleet.

For six months, Krancke had made a comprehensive study of Anglo-American amphibious warfare tactics and concluded that the seaborne assault would hit during darkness under a full moon, at high tide to permit landing craft to sail over beach obstacles, and at or adjacent to a major port. Krancke, a capable and experienced officer, perhaps had been influenced by the ongoing reports of the Double-Cross Committee, for he was totally wrong on all counts.

While a few thousand Allied ships and boats were preparing to sail from ports in the British Isles, Krancke said in his report on the night of June 4: "It is doubtful if the enemy has yet assembled his invasion fleet in the required strength."

23

Threshold of a Mighty Endeavor

H-Hour Minus 25 Hours. Shortly after a storm-swept dawn on June 5, 1944, Colonel John Turner, the British camouflage wizard, hurried into Southwick House in response to an urgent summons. SHAEF officers were deeply concerned over the fact that a crucial component of Fortitude South had gone awry; there was a danger that the Germans might be tipped off in the final hours that Army Group Patton was an elaborate hoax and rush the Fifteenth Army from the Pas de Calais to Normandy.

Scores of the hundreds of inflatable rubber boats and landing craft in the harbors, rivers, and estuaries of southeastern England—vessels that were supposed to carry Patton's phantom force across the Strait of Dover—had been punctured, deflated, and torn loose from their oil-drum moorings by the storm and were sagging badly.

Colonel Turner relieved anxious minds. If Luftwaffe reconnaissance planes were kept above 30,000 feet by the RAF patrols, the drooping dummy craft would still appear realistic in photographs

H-Hour Minus 24 Hours. Walther Stroebe, a Luftwaffe colonel who was chief meteorologist for German forces in the West, forecast disturbed weather over the Channel for the next several days. He predicted winds of Force 7 at Cherbourg and Force 6 at the Pas de Calais, with a cloud base of 900 to 1,800 feet— conditions that ruled out Allied aerial bombardment of beaches or paratroop operations. Since the current storm had lashed the Channel into a frothy frenzy with waves of seven to nine feet, amphibious operations would be impossible for the next several days. So certain was Stroebe and his top aide, Major Ludwig Lettau, of their weather findings that they gave their officers the day off on June 5 to take in the sights and fleshpots of Paris.

Neither Stroebe nor Lettau had the means to spot an alarming danger signal: conditions in the Atlantic had changed abruptly and a new front bringing improved weather was heading toward the Channel. Unlike SHAEF meteorologist John Stagg, Stroebe had no far-reaching network of weather stations, well-equipped weather ships, or aircraft far out into the Atlantic.

H-Hour Minus 23 Hours.   Driven by his longtime chauffeur, Daniel, Field Marshal Erwin Rommel was speeding across France in the back seat of his Storch. After reading Stroebe's current weather report, he left La Roche-Guyon an hour earlier to spend a day with his wife, Lucie-Maria, and their 15-year-old son, Army Private Manfred Rommel, at the family's modest frame home in the hillside village of Herrlingen, outside Ulm in southern Germany.

Rommel had an urgent personal reason for wanting to get home and, therefore, was thankful for the raging storm that was lashing the Channel. June 6 was Lucie-Maria's birthday. Officially, the Desert Fox was en route to *Adlerhorst*, Adolf Hitler's retreat on towering Obersalzburg near Berchtesgaden to make one final appeal to the fuehrer to release the three panzer divisions being held far inland.

H-Hour Minus 21 Hours.   Field Marshal Hugo Sperrle's Luftwaffe headquarters in Paris issued its daily intelligence report: "The enemy is still trying, by every trick in the war of nerves, to prevent us from discovering his invasion plans."

H-Hour Minus 18 Hours.   Outside Paris, Field Marshal Gerd von Rundstedt was enjoying a leisurely luncheon with his son, a young army lieutenant, at his favorite dining spot, Coq Hardi. Earlier that day, the elder von Rundstedt had sent to Berlin his estimate of the situation: "As yet there is no immediate prospect for the invasion."

H-Hour Minus 16 Hours.   In his chalet at Berchtesgaden, Adolf Hitler was holding a lengthy conference with his war production genius, 39-year-old Albert Speer. The topics discussed were methods for smokescreening the Rhine River bridges and the building of diesel trucks. No mention was made of a looming invasion.

H-Hour Minus 14 Hours.   Every ship (3,323 British and Canadian and 2,110 American) was at sea or at its assigned berth or moored in harbors, rivers, and creeks along southern England. Squat, gray-painted transports were crammed with grim fighting men. Each in his own way was steeling himself for the ordeal that lay just over the horizon. Most felt that they were being offered up as human sacrifices on the altar of Neptune.

Many scrawled brief "final" letters to loved ones. Others exchanged addresses of wives, parents, or girlfriends back home, "just in case you make it tomorrow and I don't." Some read pocket-sized Bibles or held rosaries as their lips moved almost imperceptibly in prayer. Most simply lay on their bunks, stacked four deep, silent and alone in their thoughts.

A few of the young warriors were unperturbed by the specter of pending doom on the Far Shore. One of these rare exceptions was 20-year-old Karl Kaupert, a squad leader in the U.S. 87th Mortar Battalion. Reclined on a bunk, he engaged in his favorite diversion—reading *Dick Tracy* and *Secret Agent X–9* comic books.[1]

H-Hour Minus 13 Hours.   At his headquarters in the road-junction town of Carentan at the base of the Cherbourg peninsula, not far behind Utah Beach, Lieutenant Colonel Friedrich August von der Heydte, the 34-year-old commander of the elite 6th Parachute Regiment, was puzzled by a report that 20 Alsatian soldiers, conscripted into his unit by force to perform logistical duties, had vanished.

Since it would be difficult for 20 French deserters to hide indefinitely in a region packed with German soldiers, Baron von der Heydte, a professor in international law in peacetime, concluded that the local underground had tipped them off that the Germans would soon be far too occupied to search for them.

Concerned by the implications he had drawn from this event, von der Heydte recalled several of his companies that were inland on maneuvers. Despite assurances from Wehrmacht weathermen that an invasion was impossible for the next day, the paratroop commander told aides that he had "an uneasy feeling."

H-Hour Minus 12 Hours.   Like a huge hydra-headed monster, its tentacles reaching into Plymouth, Dartmouth, Torquay, Portland, Southampton, Portsmouth, and 17 other ports, the invasion fleet began to uncoil. Thousands of vessels, ticketed for the initial assault, edged into the English Channel and rendezvoused in a five-mile-radius area, nicknamed Piccadilly Circus, south of the Isle of Wight. In a marvel of intricate planning and seamanship, involving minute-to-minute traffic patterns, the ships sorted themselves out and each one took a predetermined position with the convoy bound for the particular beach to which it had been assigned.

Slowly, ponderously, the armada, the largest by far ever assembled, steamed southward—21 convoys headed for the American beaches at Utah and Omaha and 39 convoys steered for the British and Canadian beaches at Sword, Gold, and Juno. It was a fantastic cavalcade, a seemingly endless array of ships in every shape and size.

Packed with 150,000 assault troops, guns, tanks, ammunition trucks, jeeps, and supplies were swift new transports, rusty old freighters, coastal steamers, weather-beaten tankers, and scores of shallow-draft landing craft. Many of the vessels were trailing barrage balloons intended to discourage strafing and bombing by low-flying Luftwaffe planes.

Overhead, hundreds of Allied fighter aircraft crisscrossed the murky sky, hovering over the fleet like mother hens over their broods. Escorting the convoys was a colossal array of some 700 warships—mainly sleek destroyers, corvettes, and gunboats.

H-Hour Minus 11½ Hours.   At tension-gripped Southwick House, General Pinky Bull, SHAEF's deception chief, was handed a wireless bulletin that sent shock waves reverberating through the Allied high command. The signal originated from a Brissex intelligence team, one of the 100 two- and three-man parties that had parachuted deep into France in April to keep an eye on railroad junctions through which the three panzer divisions being held in reserve would have to pass to reach Normandy.

The Brissex undercover agents sending the urgent report had been keeping an eye on the Panzer Lehr Division near Orleans. Led by Lieutenant General Fritz Bayerlein, a grizzled, tough, and unflappable veteran of fighting in North Africa, the Panzer Lehr could wreak havoc with Neptune forces before they got tanks and artillery ashore.

British Brigadier General E. J. Foord, chief of the Brissex operation, said in his bulletin to Pinky Bull that his agents had spotted flatcars being loaded with tanks in the railroad yard at Orleans and that it appeared the Panzer Lehr was ready to move out. But to where?

Bull promptly contacted Ultra at Bletchley Park. If the Panzer Lehr were indeed moving out, the air over Orleans should be saturated with wireless signals. Ultra reported that there was no unusual radio activity. But had the crafty General Bayerlein imposed radio silence to mask his division's intentions?

H-Hour Minus 11 Hours.   At Cherbourg, the main objective of Overlord, Rear Admiral Walther Hennecke, commander of German naval forces in Normandy, was told by an aide that the powerful radar station at La Pernelle had detected unusually heavy activities in the Channel. Hennecke, who for months had been enjoying the finest French wines and living the comfortable life of a commander long submerged in the sedentary existence of an occupying authority, was mildly concerned by the report and called in his weather officer.

High seas, bad visibility, and strong winds made it highly unlikely that even a few of the sturdiest of ships could make it across the Channel, Admiral Hennecke was assured. After ordering the customary nightly patrol of the Channel by a squadron of his Cherbourg-based E-boats canceled, Hennecke returned to his adjacent ornate villa where he was hosting a champagne party for his officers and their wives or French girlfriends.

H-Hour Minus 10½ Hours.   Out in the English Channel on the transport USS *Bayfield*, Major General J. Lawton "Lightning Joe" Collins strolled around the deck, weaving his way through the throng of troops. The 48-year-old Collins was commander of the U.S. VII Corps, elements of which would assault Utah Beach. Darkness was starting to blanket the Channel as the peppery, silver-thatched general glanced skyward, puzzled by the tranquility that continued to reign, even though this monstrous fleet was bearing down on the fuehrer's Fortress Europe. Where was the Luftwaffe? It was inconceivable to him that the

German air force would fail to discover this armada.[2] Lightning Joe Collins would have breathed easier had he known that the Luftwaffe that day had sent out only one reconnaissance aircraft to probe for Allied activity—with orders to scour the sea off the coast of Holland.

The collective intricate machinations of Bodyguard over many months were paying enormous dividends.

H-Hour Minus 10½ Hours.   Major General Hans Speidel, a bespectacled intellectual who was Field Marshal Erwin Rommel's chief of staff, admired his boss but did not share his passion for frugality and early nights. So with the Desert Fox at home in far-off Bavaria, Speidel threw a small dinner party at the Chateau de La Roche-Guyon in the steep hills overlooking the winding Seine River.

Among those present at the convivial affair were Speidel's brother-in-law, Ludwig Horst, and Ernst Juenger, a philosopher, author, and good friend of Rommel. Conversation centered around Adolf Hitler, for all of those present were members of the Schwarze Kapelle, the conspiracy to oust or assassinate the fuehrer.

Over glasses of champagne, they discussed a 20-page document that Juenger had drafted at the request of Rommel, a paper that the field marshal planned to use as a basis for peace negotiations with the United States and Great Britain.

H-Hour Minus 10 Hours.   Ground crews at scores of American and British air bases in England finally learned the reason why tons of white paint had been delivered to them a day earlier. In what may have been the largest ''crash'' paint job in history, the crews were instructed to put three broad white stripes on the wings and fuselages of all Allied aircraft—10,000 of them—before daybreak.

This procedure would enable friendly planes to be more easily distinguished in the air from those of the enemy in the expected aerial confusion on D-Day. The order had been held up until the last possible minute so that the Luftwaffe would not be able to duplicate these new markings.

H-Hour Minus 9 Hours.   In London, Prime Minister Winston Churchill, keen and energetic at age 70, was spending the evening in his underground suite at Storey's Gate, drinking brandy with his secretary and confidant, Jock Colville. The British Bulldog was uncommonly silent, even brooding. More than most, he realized that all the cards were now on the table. After five years of brutal conflict, Britain was committing everything in its arsenal and dwindling manpower. If the invasion failed, it could not be repeated.

The prime minister knew how much was riding on the special means techniques he himself had set into motion four years earlier after the British military disaster at Dunkirk. If the enormous amount of meticulous planning, manpower, money, and deception skills that had gone into Bodyguard for the past six months had failed to hoodwink Adolf Hitler, then the beaches of Normandy would soon run red with British, American, and Canadian blood.

Elsewhere in London, Field Marshal Alan Brooke poured out his deep inner concerns to his diary: "I am very uneasy. At the worst it may well be the most ghastly disaster of the whole war. I wish to God it were safely over."[3]

H-Hour Minus 7½ Hours.   In London, Charles de Gaulle, a six-foot-seven-inch general who had proclaimed himself head of the Free French after escaping to England following the fall of France in 1940, was fuming in the mansion he had been assigned by SHAEF. With British security men discreetly surrounding the villa and tapping his telephone line, de Gaulle was virtually under house arrest.

Short and simple, Churchill, Roosevelt, Eisenhower, and other Anglo-American leaders did not trust de Gaulle. Most D-Day secrets were kept from the 53-year-old Frenchman, much to his anger and humiliation. It was decided, however, that his presence was needed in London at the time history's most perilous military operation was about to be launched, to add his implied authority to SHAEF's orders to the French underground.

On the previous day, General de Gaulle was invited to Southwick House where Dwight Eisenhower explained Neptune in the broadest terms. Then the French leader was taken to the sacrosanct war room, where the really important items and information had been tucked out of sight.

The supreme commander performed his act beautifully. He showed de Gaulle some top-secret maps—which had been so sanitized that they made no sense to Eisenhower, much less to the Frenchman. Never overburdened by humility, de Gaulle presumably did not want to admit that he failed to understand the maps. Then, almost casually, Eisenhower lied that the landings in Normandy were diversionary, that the main invasion would hit at the Pas de Calais under General Patton. It was a Fortitude South ploy by the supreme commander who was following a prepared script.[4]

H-Hour Minus 7½ Hours.   Suddenly, nearly all of the major German headquarters in Normandy lost their generals and staff colonels. After waiting for darkness as a shield against marauding Allied warplanes, one by one they left by automobile for Rennes, in adjacent Brittany, where Colonel General Friedrich Dollman, the silver-haired leader of the Seventh Army, had scheduled a *Kriegsspiel*—a war-map exercise. Its theme was: "Enemy landings in Normandy preceded by paratroop drops."[5]

H-Hour Minus 7 Hours.   At Southwick House overlooking blacked-out Portsmouth, whose harbor was now virtually devoid of ships, General Pinky Bull flashed an historic signal—"Adoration from 0200"—a crucial component in the Fortitude South scenario. Wireless activity in the ghost army group region opposite the Pas de Calais was to be stepped up dramatically at the same time that thousands of American and British paratroopers would be bailing out into the dark unknown over Normandy at 2:00 A.M. on D-Day.

H-Hour Minus 6½ Hours. In the dark Bay of the Seine, all was eerily silent. A swarm of PT boats was shepherding a few score minesweepers toward Utah Beach, where assault elements of the U.S. 4th Infantry Division would storm ashore at dawn. Leading the crucial operation to clear the way for hundreds of assorted ships and boats to follow was Commander John Bulkeley, the Congressional Medal of Honor recipient.

The slow, ugly-duckling minesweepers, the unsung heroes of many earlier American invasions around the world, swept channels clear of mines all the way from south of the Isle of Wight right up to the sands of Utah. (Similar operations were taking place at the other four Allied landing beaches.)

Bulkeley was not privy to Bodyguard secrets, but he and others in the spearhead flotilla would be among the first to discover if the elaborate deception schemes of the past six months would result in the German defenders being taken by surprise.

Unaware that Admiral Hennecke had canceled Channel naval patrols that night because of the storm-swept sea, Bulkeley was puzzled by the fact that the 15 to 20 E-boats known to be based in nearby Cherbourg had not charged out to challenge the minesweeping flotilla. And he was astonished that the Barfleur lighthouse, one of the world's tallest and most brilliant beacons, on the northeastern tip of the Cherbourg peninsula, was shining brightly. Was this powerful beam splitting the night a predesignated signal to German forces that the invasion was about to hit Normandy? As the sweepers plodded up and down the nine-mile length of Utah Beach clearing mines, the shore batteries did not open fire at the swarm of ducks squatting virtually under the Germans' noses.[6]

H-Hour Minus 6 Hours. At scores of airfields in the Midlands, Lincolnshire, and Devon, the ear-splitting roar of aircraft engines told that the big airborne parade was being launched. Thousands of tough American and British paratroopers, keyed up and tense, were crammed sardinclike into 1,058 transports. Towed gliders that hauled men, field pieces, jeeps, and ammunition joined the sky procession bound for Normandy.

H-Hour Minus 5½ Hours. In Saint-Germain, OB West was nearly silent. Von Rundstedt, after fortifying himself with cognac, had climbed into bed at 10:00 P.M. Early in the morning, the Old Prussian intended to take his lieutenant son to the Normandy coast to see the vaunted Atlantic Wall. General Bodo Zimmerman, OB West's erudite operations officer, was also fast asleep. Colonel Wilhelm Meyer-Detring, OB West's intelligence officer, was on overnight leave in Paris.

As the clock tolled midnight, the duty officer in the war room had on ear phones and was listening to the regular communiqué from Berlin over a miniature wireless receiver. It was depressing news. Rome had fallen a day earlier to General Mark Clark's GIs.

H-Hour Minus 5 Hours.   At the underground command post of the London Controlling Section, where countless decisions had been reached during the Bodyguard campaign, Colonel John Bevan, the deception mastermind, and his number-two man, Lieutenant Colonel Ronald Wingate, were keeping a nightlong vigil. There were unspoken visions of an Allied apocalypse in Normandy after dawn. If Fortitude South and Quicksilver were successes, chances were good that the debacle would be avoided.

Bevan and Wingate, calmly and dispassionately, reviewed the long and intricate campaign to hoodwink Adolf Hitler on the time and place of the invasion. But what had they left undone? What had they done that they should not have done? John Bevan and Ronald Wingate had no way of knowing that, as the result of Bodyguard machinations and meteorologist John Stagg's educated divining of weather conditions, no one—not Adolf Hitler, Gerd von Rundstedt, Erwin Rommel, Friedrich Dollman, Theodor Krancke, or anyone else in the Wehrmacht—had the foggiest notion that an Allied juggernaut was bearing down on Normandy.

24

D-Day Decoys and Deceptions

June 6, 0010 Hours. Standing in the open door of a Stirling bomber and shivering from the chilly blasts of air, British Lieutenant Noel Poole, a bank clerk in civilian life, could see most details on the Norman landscape, which was bathed in the rays of a late-rising moon. Poole, a member of the elite Special Air Service (SAS), was leader of a three-man party known as a Titanic, a stratagem to focus the Germans' attention on the landing of hundreds of rubber paratrooper dummies and away from genuine airborne drops.

Lieutenant Poole bailed out, banged his head on the tail of the Stirling, and floated semiconscious toward the earth when his parachute opened automatically. Poole crumpled into a pasture about five miles west of Saint-Lô, at the base of the Cherbourg peninsula. Still dazed, he could hear vague thuds as his SAS comrades landed nearby.

After reclining in the dewy grass until the cobwebs had cleared from his head, Lieutenant Poole located the small pigeon crate that the Stirling air crew had pitched out in a parachute after him. By the pale light of the moon, he scrawled a brief message outlining the situation, clamped the signal to a tiny cylinder on the pigeon's leg, and released the bird. Ten hours later, a policeman in Buckinghamshire, England, found the pigeon strutting along a rural road. Lieutenant Noel Poole was the first armed Allied fighting man to reach Normandy.

0016 Hours. Two hours in front of the main body of the 101st Airborne Division, Colonel Joel Crouch was at the controls of a C–47 carrying Captain Frank L. Lillyman and a stick of his pathfinders. Altogether, 11 sticks of his Screaming Eagle trailblazers would mark out with lights three paratrooper DZs (drop zones) and one LZ (landing zone) for gliders behind Utah Beach.[1]

Lillyman was suffering intensely and had been for three days. In order not to miss the big show, he had concealed the fact that he had badly torn leg ligaments in a practice jump four days earlier, an injury that can take weeks to heal.

Standing in the door and braced to jump, Captain Lillyman saw the green light flash on in the cabin, and out he went, a big, black cigar clenched in his teeth. Behind him leaped the rest of the stick. Frank Lillyman was the first armed American to reach Normandy.

0021 Hours. Hard on the heels of Noel Poole's SAS group, 15 other three-man Titanic parties jumped into Normandy at some 15 scattered locales behind the Atlantic Wall. Crewmen in other Stirlings flew over and dropped scores of dummy paratroopers. Their chutes opened automatically.

As soon as the rubber figures hit the ground, hundreds of tiny bombs, much like Roman candles, zoomed Very lights and flares into the dark sky. At the same time, the cracks of hundreds of rifles and the clatter of submachine guns echoed across the countryside—simulators created by Robert Cockburn and his electronic wizards.

Working independently, the Titanic parties rapidly set up black metal boxes and flipped switches. Blaring out were the harsh sounds of mortar and bazooka explosions, shouted orders, and cries for medics. To the perplexed Germans, it must have sounded as though large numbers of Allied paratroopers had dropped and that violent firefights had erupted all the way from the Cherbourg peninsula eastward for 60 miles to Caen.

0034 Hours. At the Luftwaffe Y-Service in northern France, the duty officer grew uneasy. His concern was based on the previous interception of many American Mercury broadcasts. Mercurys were weather intelligence flights, and what worried the Y-Service officer was that the Americans usually made these flights in daylight because they bombed only during the day. Why were Mercury flights being made at night during the past 48 hours? There could be only one explanation: the Americans were about to launch a major nighttime air operation—possibly the invasion.

So suspicious did the circumstances look to the Y-Service duty officer that he scrambled a few Luftwaffe night fighters, and they were airborne by 41 minutes after midnight. Fortunately for the Allies, the German interceptors were vectored between Amiens in France and Deelen in Holland. Had they patrolled to the west, they would have stumbled onto the massive skytrains carrying American and British paratroopers to Normandy. No doubt swarms of hungry Luftwaffe night-fighter pilots would then have risen to feast on the plodding, unarmed C–47s, resulting in an Allied air debacle of colossal proportions.

0050 Hours. In Cherbourg, Admiral Walther Hennecke's champagne party broke up hastily when a bulletin was received from Luftwaffe headquarters in Paris that ''50 or 60 two-engined planes'' were swooping in from the west over the Cherbourg peninsula. Nervously, Hennecke confirmed to Paris that paratroopers were dropping, but that most of them were ''straw'' dummies.

Moments later, another urgent message from Paris thundered into Hennecke's bunker headquarters, reporting that a sizeable force of parachutists had dropped near Bayeux, just inland from the Calvados coast of eastern Normandy. Actually, only a few Titanic rubber dummies had landed there.

0055 Hours.   At Saint Germain, OB West's acting intelligence officer, Major Max Doertenbach, telephoned General Hans Speidel, Rommel's chief of staff, at La Roche-Guyon, seeking information on the rash of red spots marking paratroop landings on his map. Speidel, who was still entertaining his fellow Schwarze Kapelle conspirators, replied that the reported parachutists were "probably bailed-out bomber crews."

0100 Hours.   Two ghosts fleets, designed to draw the Germans' attention away from the real Neptune sea armada heading for the Bay of the Seine far to the west, were bearing down on the Pas de Calais. Three Moonshine RAF sea-air rescue launches and six other small boats were bound for Cap d'Antifer (Operation Taxable), while 50 miles farther eastward one Moonshine launch and eight other boats were steering toward Boulogne (Operation Glimmer).

As anticipated, German radar sites—deliberately spared from bombing for this illusion—discovered the Glimmer and Taxable "fleets," which were approaching at eight miles per hour, the same rate of speed a genuine naval force would advance.

Operators in the launches observed German radar signals on their cathode ray tubes, switched on their transmitters, and "Moonshined" the enemy sites. The electronic cat-and-mouse game was on. During the next three hours, scores of German radar signals were received by the launches, and the enemy transmissions were bounced back in highly amplified form.

Each launch also carried radio transmitters, which exchanged prerecorded orders simulating the preparations for a rocket barrage on the Pas de Calais shoreline. This wireless traffic was not coded, so the German electronic ears along the coast could easily pick it up and understand it.

Over these collections of tiny boats flew the Stirlings and Lancasters, weaving their complex patterns and strewing Window. All the while, the airplane-boat tandems were edging closer to Cap d'Antifer and Boulogne.

The entire fleet decoy operations were fraught with peril for the participants. Each man knew that he was "bait." If Luftwaffe night fighters were to rush up, the relatively slow heavy bombers would become machine-gun fodder, for they were loaded from cockpit to tail with tons of Window. With this great amount of cargo on board, it would be doubtful if the crew could escape a watery grave should a Stirling or Lancaster be shot down. If swift, heavily armed E-boats were to dash out to confront the two "fleets," the plodding little launches would probably be blasted out of the water within minutes.

When the twin phantom flotillas reached their stop lines ten miles off the Pas de Calais, RAF planes swooped in and blanketed the region with thick smoke, a standard technique in genuine amphibious assaults. Then, with the first hint of dawn, loudspeakers bellowed the prerecorded sounds of an invasion force debarking. Even though the launches edged within only two miles of the beaches, the almost gale force wind may have kept the Germans from even detecting these sounds.

A critical factor the Allied deception artists had counted on—the fog of war—may have contributed to at least partial success for Glimmer and Taxable. A single young German draftee huddled before his radar screen would "see" through the jamming what appeared to be a large enemy fleet, and he and other excited operators along the Pas de Calais would pass along their sightings to superiors. These hazy preliminary reports would climb up the chain of command in the West and eventually evolve into "confirmed facts" and become broad arrows signifying invasion forces on situation maps at many Wehrmacht headquarters.

0205 Hours. High in the moonlit sky, a flight of 31 Lancasters and Flying Fortresses was soaring eastward above Amiens, France. Crewmen were pitching out thousands of pounds of Window (Chaff) that would make it appear on German radar that a large bomber stream was headed for the Third Reich. This was a decoy force whose mission was to draw German focus away from the 1,058 lumbering transport planes carrying paratroopers to Normandy, far to the west.

Many of these four-engine bombers in the decoy flight were equipped with radar-jamming transmitters known as Cigars. These Cigars were to blot out surviving radar stations in northern France. At the same time, jamming transmitters on the ground in southern England handled enemy frequencies that the airborne Cigars could not reach.

In Britain, the Kingsdown electronic monitoring station intercepted a German air controller ordering all night fighters in the region to scramble and vector on the decoy bomber flight. A few intercepted the deception force, and one Lancaster was shot down while its crew was tossing out a bundle of Window.

0206 Hours. While Luftwaffe night fighters in northern France were off chasing the small decoy flight of bombers toward Germany, thousands of American and British paratroopers were bailing out over Normandy without a single transport plane being lost to enemy aircraft. However, heavy flak, gusty winds, darkness, and pathfinder units landing far from their DZs all contributed to a chaotic situation.

Maxwell Taylor's 101st Airborne was scattered over an area of some 17 by 28 miles on the Cherbourg peninsula. Without two hours, nearly 1,500 of the 101st Airborne's 6,600 paratroopers were dead, captured, drowned, or seriously injured.

Three 82nd Airborne parachute regiments under Brigadier General "Slim Jim" Gavin were likewise sprinkled all over the Cherbourg peninsula—and beyond. Some 40 miles deep into France from the nearest 82nd Airborne DZ, 23-year-old First Sergeant Leonard A. Funk and his stick bailed out so far to the enemy's

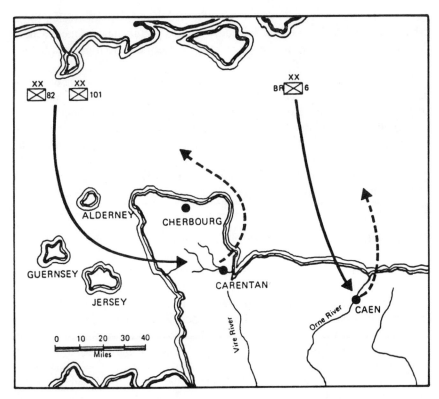

5. Flight routes of airborne divisions.

rear that German vehicles were driving on occasion with headlights blazing, and Feldgrau were sauntering around villages, presumably on overnight passes. It would require a 21-day trek, touch-and-go all the way, including several firefights, before Leonard Funk and his men would reach an outpost of the U.S. 90th Infantry Division.[2]

Drownings took a particularly heavy toll among troopers of the 82nd Airborne. Burdened with up to 90 pounds of weapons and gear, they plunged into swamps and flooded areas and were dragged under as they struggled to free themselves from parachute harnesses.

Soon Wehrmacht command posts all over the Cherbourg peninsula and beyond were receiving reports that large groups of American paratroopers were marauding the region, ambushing German patrols and motorcycle couriers, shooting up vehicles, planting road mines, and attacking isolated machine-gun and antiaircraft battery positions.

These ''large groups'' of American paratroopers were mainly pairs and tiny bands who, on finding themselves alone and far from their true drop zones, went into business for themselves. Bold and resourceful by nature and by training, they struck swiftly and with surprise, then melted into the night to strike again at some other locale.

As it developed, the wide dispersal of the two U.S. airborne divisions proved to be an unexpected deception bonanza that no Bodyguard genius could have even conceived. This wildly exaggerated reporting caused German leaders to conclude that at least six Allied airborne divisions had descended from the clouds.

Fifty miles east of the true American DZ and LZs, 4,256 paratroopers of Major General Richard Gale's British 6th Airborne Division were dropping over a large region, victims of enemy flak that dispersed flights, navigational errors, and angry winds. Some fell as far as 30 miles from their DZs. The mission of Gale's Red Devils, as they were known, was to prevent German panzers from plunging into the side of the invasion bridgehead.

0209 Hours.   At his command post near Caen, Lieutenant General Edgar Feuchtinger, commander of the battle-tested 21st Panzer Division, received reports that paratroopers (the British 6th Airborne) had dropped only a short distance away. His formation had as a nucleus old hands of Erwin Rommel's vaunted Afrika Korps and in excess of 125 heavy tanks.

Had the 21st Panzer jumped off at once, it could no doubt have inflicted a bloodbath on the lightly armed Red Devils, who had no tanks, artillery, or antitank guns. General Feuchtinger alerted his command to strike, then did nothing. Like all panzer divisions in France, the 21st could move only with the implicit approval of the fuehrer—who was asleep at Berchtesgaden 600 miles away.

0210 Hours.   At Saint-Lô, the telephone jangled impatiently on the desk of General Erich Marcks, commander of the MXXXIV Corps. The scholarly Marcks, who had left a leg on the Russian front, picked up the receiver. Colonel Wolfgang Hamann, acting commander of the 709th Division, was calling from Valognes, some 15 miles south of Cherbourg.

"There are enemy parachutists near Varreville and at Sainte Marie-du-Mont," Hamann reported. "A second group is west of the Carentan-Valognes road on both sides of the Merderet River, and on the road to Sainte Mère-Église. The 919th Grenadier Regiment is holding prisoners from the USA 101st Division Airborne."[3]

Grimly, Erich Marcks replaced the receiver. Now there was no doubt in his mind: "*Der Grossinvasion* is on!" The Allies would never waste an elite airborne division in a diversionary operation.

0212 Hours.   Just north of what the Allies called Utah Beach, a company of Germans was guarding a coastal battery at Saint Marcouf. *Oberleutnant* Hermann Grieg dashed excitedly into the company CP (Command Post) after returning from a patrol.

"Herr Kapitaen," Grieg blurted out, "we came under fire from enemy paratroopers!" Having been assured only hours earlier that the weather and tide conditions would not allow an invasion for at least two weeks, the captain scoffed: "Nonsense! There can't be any paratroopers!"

The captain played it safe, however, and sent out a 22-man patrol, heavily armed with Schmeisser machine pistols and grenades, to scout the surrounding swamps. A half hour later, Lieutenant Grieg's patrol returned to its base with four American prisoners—all of them 101st Airborne Division.

The German officers were astonished when they inspected the equipment taken from the paratroopers: compasses in jacket buttons and silk scarves with maps printed on them. Even the fields where the *Rommelspargel* (Rommel's asparagus; antiglider poles) had been planted only a few days earlier were accurately marked, as were German machine-gun posts—a mute tribute to the men and women of the Centurie underground.

0216 Hours.   At Bordeaux on the Atlantic seaboard of western France, Admiral Theodor Krancke, naval commander in the West, took a telephone call from Kriegsmarine headquarters in Cherbourg and was told of American paratroopers landing near the big gun battery at Saint Marcouf. Krancke, who was in Bordeaux on an inspection trip, promptly telephoned his headquarters in Paris and learned that the radar network was nearly out of action in the Bay of the Seine area (where Neptune was hitting). However, the net was functioning spottily along the Pas de Calais (as Fortitude South had intended).

0221 Hours.   At the LeMans headquarters of Colonel General Friedrich Dollman's Seventh Army, charged with the defense of Normandy and Brittany, Major General Max Pemsel, the chief of staff, received a telephone call from General Marcks at Saint-Lô. A large number of paratroopers were dropping all over the Cherbourg peninsula, he told Pemsel. Since General Dollman was in Rennes for the Kriegsspiel, Pemsel flashed an urgent order, putting the Seventh Army on full-alert status.

0225 Hours.   At Bletchley Park north of London, Ultra officers were alarmed by the absence of German radio activity in northern France. History's mightiest naval invasion armada was barely 20 miles from the Norman shore, the moonlit sky over Normandy was awash with thousands of parachutes, scores of gliders packed with fighting men were crash-landing in the fields of the Cherbourg peninsula and along the Orne Canal to the east, and 1,327 RAF bombers were pounding fortifications and installations up and down the shoreline of Normandy and the Pas de Calais. Much of the sky along the coast reflected an eerie orange glow as countless fires raged out of control.

Where were the *Schnellboote*, those speedy craft with the enormous sting, the kind that had wreaked havoc on the 4th Infantry Division convoy of Slapton

Sands in late April? Where was the Luftwaffe? Where were the vaunted *Unterseeboote* (submarines)?

0231 Hours.   Nervous tics were rampant at SHAEF battle headquarters at Portsmouth. None of this made sense. Why hadn't the big coastal guns opened fire on the swarms of minesweepers and their escorts that had crawled up and down the five landing beaches for hours? Did the Germans really have terrifying secret weapons, as Adolf Hitler had boasted, to inflict a single devastating counterstroke while the assault waves were going ashore? Was the powerful beacon shining at Pointe de Barfleur to be suddenly extinguished as a signal for the Wehrmacht to spring the most monumental trap in military history?

SHAEF and Ultra had no way of knowing that German commanders in France were virtually paralyzed by confusion and indecision. Their tactical visions were clouded by the Bodyguard machinations: the Titanic rubber dummies, the Glimmer and Taxable ghost fleets, the decoy force of Window-pitching Allied bombers headed for the Third Reich, and the sophisticated enemy radar jamming. Contributing to this chaotic German situation were the unintentional wide dispersal of American and British paratroopers, the grossly flawed weather predictions by Wehrmacht meteorologists, and the fog of war.

Compounding German confusion and indecision were the misconceptions of Fortitude South, which had inflicted upon Adolf Hitler and his generals (except for Erwin Rommel) the deep-set conviction that the main invasion would be launched by Army Group Patton against the Pas de Calais, and that any Allied operation in Normandy would be a diversion.

0251 Hours.   In his ornate villa on the edge of the park at Saint Germain, Field Marshal Gerd von Rundstedt was sound asleep. An adjutant awoke him with news of the heavy airborne assault and reports that engine noises—hundreds of them—could be heard out in the Bay of the Seine, off Normandy. The Old Prussian was grumpy. No doubt this flap was just another false alarm, an Allied ruse to keep the Wehrmacht off balance and jumpy.

Seated at his desk and stroking his unshaven chin, von Rundstedt pondered the situation and decided to play it safe. Turning to his chief of staff, Bodo Zimmerman, the field marshal issued instructions for him to send an urgent message to Adolf Hitler's headquarters at Berchtesgaden:

> If this is actually a large-scale enemy operation, it can only be met successfully if immediate action is taken. This involves commitment on this day of all the strategic reserves, including 12th SS Panzer, 21st Panzer, and Panzer Lehr Divisions. . . . If they assemble quickly and start early they can enter the battle on the coast during this day.[4]

Gerd von Rundstedt was far too wise an old owl to be cast as the scapegoat by the fuehrer should a German disaster ensue in Normandy. Confident that his message had covered him, he returned to his quarters to shave and await developments.

0306 Hours.   At Berchtesgaden, Lieutenant Colonel Fritz Friedel, the duty officer in General Alfred Jodl's command post, scanned the urgent signal from Field Marshal von Rundstedt. Friedel had no intention of disturbing the sleeping Jodl. There had been such a rash of false alarms of enemy landings (generated by Fortitude South) in recent weeks that there was no reason to believe that this was anything more than another inaccurate report, or merely a commando raid. Friedel sent back a formal acknowledgment of von Rundstedt's message (to protect himself), then returned to reading a book on Frederick the Great, Adolf Hitler's idol.

0309 Hours.   In Bordeaux, Admiral Theodor Krancke received a report that originated from a listening post along the Calvados coast in Normandy: "Large landing craft detected lying seven miles offshore, indicating unloading activity." Now Krancke was convinced that a major assault was about to hit Normandy. He telephoned Admiral Hennecke in Cherbourg to send a squadron of E-boats to probe the Channel waters, ordered three destroyers to prepare to sail, and set into motion procedures for a squadron of submarines to go to sea and engage the enemy.

Hardly had he issued this stream of orders when the Fortitude South deception hoaxes began to cloud his vision. More reports reached him of two large convoys off the Pas de Calais coast, near Boulogne, and at Cap d'Antifer. These were the Taxable and Glimmer ghost fleets with their electronic machinations.

Krancke ordered a few E-boats at Dieppe to investigate the two Pas de Calais plots. They did so, then returned to port, and the skipper said he had seen nothing. Had he gone a mile or two farther into the Channel, the E-boat commander would have run head-on into 25 to 30 defenseless launches playing the recorded sounds of a debarkation.

0310 Hours.   Since midnight, Dwight Eisenhower had been pacing nervously the floor of his caravan in the Portsmouth woods, chain smoking and gulping cup after cup of coffee. No one is more forlorn than a senior commander waiting for scraps of information to filter in from an operation he has set into motion. Eisenhower's only companions were his aides, Commander Harry Butcher and Lieutenant Kay Summersby. The minutes and then the hours crawled past in almost total silence.

0405 Hours.   Ten miles off Omaha Beach, Captain Ettore V. Zappacosta, a company commander in the battle-tested 1st Infantry Division, was among the packed humanity waiting on the dark deck of a transport ship. These were the men who would go in first, who would have nothing between them and the bristling machine guns of the Atlantic Wall other than the buttons on their shirts.

Captain Zappacosta had made earlier amphibious assaults in Operation Torch (North Africa), Operation Husky (Sicily), and Operation Avalanche (Italy), and he knew that a combat infantryman is a fugitive from the law of averages. Only hours earlier, he had confided to a friend in the stifling hold of the ship that he felt his luck would run out on Omaha Beach.

Burdened with heavy gear, weapons, and ammunition, the Big Red One infantrymen were nervous and tense. Old friends grimly shook hands. There were whispers of "Good luck!" and "See you on the beach!" Suddenly, muted loudspeakers called out the order that all the silent men dreaded yet knew was bound to come: "Now hear this—board your landing boats!"[5]

In other transports off Omaha and Utah, identical scenarios were taking place. H-Hour for both beaches was 6:30 A.M. On a ship carrying the Omaha first wave of the U.S. 29th Infantry Division, Platoon Sergeant Roy Stevens struggled through the soldiers waiting on the dark deck in search of his twin brother. He finally found him and the brother extended his hand. "No," Roy Stevens said solemnly, "we will shake hands at that crossroads in Normandy like we planned!" Roy would never see his brother again.

0415.   Along a bluff overlooking the broad expense of sand known on Allied maps as Omaha, General Hellmuth Kraiss' veteran 352nd Infantry Division was dug in. It was a dominant defensive alignment that tactical leaders only dream about. For if the Allies were foolish enough to land here, German gunners on the heights could pour deadly fire downward into their ranks, much like shooting fish in a barrel.

While awaiting developments, Kraiss received an urgent bulletin that Allied paratroopers had landed in force to the south. So he sent his 915th Regiment, riding in old French trucks and peddling bicycles, through the sleeping villages and along the narrow, winding lanes of the *bocage* with orders to wipe out the enemy parachutists. Unknown to General Kraiss, the sky intruders were but two Titanic parties and a few genuine British paratroopers who had been dropped far from their DZ.

0423 Hours.   Lieutenant Colonel Edward "Cannonball" Krause, a battalion commander in the 82nd Airborne, and 108 of his heavily armed men, their faces blackened by charcoal, were stealing into the dark outskirts of Sainte Mère-Église, five miles west of Utah Beach. They discovered that the German garrison had pulled out, but not before it had wreaked havoc upon several 82nd Airborne troopers whose misfortune had been to parachute directly into the marketplace where enemy soldiers were congregated. Dead parachutists, still in their harnesses, hung from trees, shot before they reached the ground.

Colonel Krause headed for the town hall, pulled out an American flag that his division had flown over Naples after capturing that Italian city the previous fall, and ran Old Glory up a flagpole. Saint Mère-Église was the first town in Normandy to be liberated from the Wehrmacht.

0438 Hours.   In his war room at OB West, Field Marshal von Rundstedt was furious over the failure of Adolf Hitler, "that Bohemian Corporal," to release the panzers to him. He was unaware that the Fuehrer was sleeping soundly. Knowing that these elite armored formations had to be rushed to the Channel shore, the Old Prussian decided to act first and face Hitler's wrath later.[6]

0442 Hours.   Von Rundstedt sent orders for Brigadefuehrer SS Kurt Meyer, a blond, handsome officer who commanded the 12th SS Panzer Division near Caen, to rush half of his force to the Calvados coast to wipe out a large force of paratroopers that had landed there. Meyer, the youngest of German generals at age 34, had been personally decorated by the fuehrer for his slashing panzer attacks against the Russians. Now he rushed toward the Channel with elements of his division, only to find that the "large paratrooper force" was actually the Titanic rubber dummies.

0548 Hours.   An eerie stillness caressed the Bay of the Seine off Utah, Omaha, Gold, Juno, and Sword beaches. As the first hint of dawn began to shatter the black sky into irregular patterns of light, the ghostly hulks of thousands of Allied ships were faintly visible to the naked eye. Ears were cocked for the ominous sounds foretelling the arrival of the Luftwaffe. Any German bombardier could hardly miss, so numerous were the floating targets. It was the proverbial calm before the storm.

25

Bombs, Bullets, and Broadcasts

An ear-splitting roar pierced the tranquility along the Neptune coast of Normandy, echoing for miles across the turbulent Channel. Six hundred Allied warships, their huge guns belching orange and black clouds, hurtled salvo after salvo of shells toward German bunkers, coastal artillery batteries, and strong points. Each gun on each ship had specific targets, many of which had been identified by the Centurie underground network. It was 5:52 A.M. on June 6, 1944.

Anything that could float—battleships, cruisers, destroyers, gunboats—was blasting away. Off the three British beaches, the battlewagons *Ramillies* and *Warspite*, veterans of countless actions, lobbed tons of explosives from their powerful 15-inch guns. Off Omaha, the huge battleships *Arkansas* and *Texas*, each with five 14-inch, six 12-inch, and six five-inch guns, pumped out nearly 600 shells in less than 30 minutes.

Lieutenant Robert Arras, a gunnery officer on the *Texas*, wondered if the ship "was going to shake to pieces and sink bit by bit," because it was trembling almost constantly from the recoil of the big guns.[1]

Fifteen minutes after the naval gunfire was unleashed, a conveyor belt of 2,493 RAF and U.S. Eighth Air Force heavies—Lancasters, Flying Fortresses, and Liberators—began droning overhead at 11,000 feet. In one Fortress, Lieutenant Frank L. Betz, a navigator in the American 379th Bomb Group, felt his heart racing from the excitement of knowing that he was involved in one of the major endeavors of all time. Through breaks in the fluffy layer of clouds, Betz looked down and gasped at the panorama of "wall-to-wall ships" squatting offshore from the landing beaches.[2]

Then came the swift fighter-bombers—Mustangs, Spitfires, and Thunderbolts—7,406 of them. Their invasion markings—white stripes on wings and fuselages—were prominent to both friends and enemies. Like avenging hawks, they swooped down to unload their lethal cargos and strafe the beaches and targets for three miles inland.

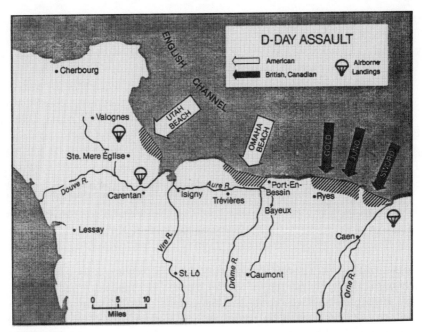

6. D-Day assault.

While the Higgins boats loaded with the first waves were less than one mile off Omaha, a force of 329 bombers flew toward the bluffs overlooking the beach. On the crown of the heights and along its forward slope were eight concrete bunkers with 88-millimeter guns, 35 pillboxes with various artillery pieces or automatic weapons, 35 rocket-launching sites, 18 antitank guns, and nearly 100 machine gun nests. Bombardiers were hampered visually by the cloud layers and, fearful of hitting American troops in the Higgins boats, dropped more than 12,000 bombs from one to three miles inland. The heights above Omaha hardly had been scathed.

Elsewhere along the Neptune beaches, the earth-shaking deluge of explosives was uninterrupted hell for the Germans. Inside the command bunker at Strongpoint W–5 on Utah Beach, Lieutenant Arthur Jahnke tried to calm his frantic men. Many of them went berserk. They screamed and hollered, thrashed around on the floor, pressed hands over eyes and ears as if to shut out the nightmare that had engulfed them. Others merely lay still on the sand or in the bunker, staring sightlessly into space as the torrent of bombs and shells exploded around them. Only the periodic blinking of their eyes distinguished them from the dead.

Lieutenant Jahnke, who had been under heavy bombardments in Russia but had never experienced anything as horrendous as this, was near despair. Above the man-made thunderclaps, he shouted to a sergeant next to him: "It looks as though God and the entire world has forsaken us!"[3]

At the same time the defenders of the Atlantic Wall were enduring hell on earth, Alfred Jodl awakened routinely at 6:00 A.M. at his OKW headquarters in Berchtesgaden. After the duty officer briefed him on overnight reports concerning heavy activity in the skies over Normandy, Jodl was informed that Field Marshal von Rundstedt had ordered the 12th SS Panzer to head for the Calvados coast (where British, Canadian, and French troops would soon storm ashore). Jodl was furious. He ordered Major General Treusch Baron von Buttlar-Brandenfels to telephone Bodo Zimmerman at OB West and read him the riot act for the Old Prussian's "arbitrary action."

Buttlar-Brandenfels, in a tone a drill sergeant might use to a recruit, ordered the panzers to be recalled and for von Rundstedt to wait the fuehrer's decision on the three armored divisions. When General Zimmerman warned that the looming amphibious landings might succeed unless the panzers were committed promptly, a bitter dispute resulted.

"*You*, Herr Zimmerman, are in *no* position to judge," barked Buttlar-Brandefels from his far-distant perch in the make-believe world of the fuehrer's retreat on the Obersalzburg. "Besides, the main landing is going to come at an entirely different place [the Pas de Calais]." It was striking evidence that Hitler was still dancing to the tune orchestrated by Fortitude South.

Meanwhile in the flaming cauldron of Normandy, the fearsome Allied bombardment ceased abruptly. It was precisely 6:25 A.M. An eerie silence descended over the vast sweep of shore, which was enveloped by a choking pall of smoke, dust, and haze. Churning toward Utah and Omaha were swarms of Higgins boats carrying the Americans of the first waves.

Most were violently seasick from the bucking and pitching craft that had taken them on the 90-minute trek through the angry Channel swells. Some were covered with vomit. Many were using their helmets to bail out water to keep their craft from being swamped. All were drenched to the skin from the merciless sprays. Knees felt weak from fear, even jelly-like. Despite the chill, perspiration dotted foreheads.

Led by 59-year-old Brigadier General Theodore "Teddy" Roosevelt, the son of a former president of the United States, the 600 men in the first wave stepped off lowered ramps of their 20 boats into waist-deep water, waded ashore, and edged up to the protective embrace of a seawall. Only two or three German shells, fired from mobile batteries far inland, exploded on the beach to protest the arrival of the invaders.

Scores of GIs, who had been convinced they would never live to reach Utah, were astonished by their good luck. "What the hell's going on?" a soldier called out in disbelief.

Ten miles to the east of Utah behind Omaha Beach, veterans of General Hellmuth Kraiss' 352nd Division had fingers on triggers and hands on artillery lanyards as they peered down at the Big Red One and 29th Infantry Division first waves that were coming toward them. Orders were for the grenadiers to hold their fire until the landing craft had almost reached the beach. It was a classic ambush.

On came the Higgins boats. Four hundred yards away . . . 300 yards . . . 200 . . . 100. Except for the throaty purr of the engines, it was deathly silent.

Suddenly from the bluffs, scores of high velocity 75- and 88-millimeter guns began pouring flat-trajectory fire into the helpless men in the Higgins boats, which had ground to a halt 70 yards from the beach. The flight of the shells was faster than sound, so the swishing noise of the projectile's trek was heard an instant before the sharp crack of the muzzle blasts.

German mortar and artillery pieces, on and behind the cliffs, joined in the deadly serenade. Tremendous explosions along the shore sent gushers of water and sand reaching into the sky. Streams of machine-gun bullets, sounding like swarms of angry bees, ricocheted off the water and caused fiery sparks where they struck the landing craft's steel hides.

A cacophony of sound scourged the shoreline as the Higgins boat ramps, groaning and squealing in protest, were lowered and men leaped into water nearly up to their necks. Hundreds of Americans began struggling forward through the heavy surf. Captain Ettore Zappacosta, the battle-hardened 1st Infantry Division company commander who had a premonition that his luck would run out on Omaha, was the first out of his craft. A hail of bullets whistled past his head. After he had waded about ten yards, Zappacosta yelled, "I've been hit!"

A short distance behind the captain, medic Thomas Kenser shouted, "Hang on! I'm coming!" But Ettore Zappacosta disappeared below the surf. His luck indeed had run out.

While the first waves at Omaha were being chopped to pieces at the water's edge, follow-up units tried to get onto the beach in the face of the torrential rain of shells and bullets. Many of those wading through the surf were only nicked by machine-gun slugs, but weakened by shock and fear, they were unable to keep their heads above water and perished. Some men with superficial wounds dragged themselves onto the beach, where they collapsed from exhaustion, and were overtaken by the raging surf and drowned.

Still they came. Wave after wave of frightened Americans. The three-mile stretch of Omaha mirrored the most horrible scenes from Dante's *Inferno*. Black, oily smoke from burning jeeps, tanks, and bulldozers drew a curtain over the agony on the shoreline. The pungent smell of cordite from exploding shells assaulted nostrils. Pandemonium, carnage, and death reigned. Hundreds of corpses, mutilated and grotesque, piled up on the beach or drifted back and forth in the surf. Soon the white froth of the water was mixed with the red of GI blood.

Hundreds of other Americans, alive but terrified, lay prostrate shoulder-to-shoulder in the sand. Many prayed, some out loud, others to themselves, as the crescendo of German shells burst around them and ceaseless fusillades of machine-gun fire riddled their ranks. Above the din could be heard piercing screams as white-hot shell fragments hacked off a man's arm or the side of his face.

While a debacle of major proportions was shaping up at Omaha, assault elements of Lieutenant General Miles C. Dempsey's British Second Army were battling their way ashore at Sword, Juno, and Gold, a 20-mile stretch between the village of Le Hamel on the west to Quistreham. Due to tide conditions, H-Hour was at 7:30 A.M., an hour later than at the American beaches.

Although the assault against Sword, Juno, and Gold had been bloody, the fighting was relatively brief. Follow-up waves were amazed to find that a few sniper shots and an occasional burst of a long-range artillery shell were the only signs of German resistance. Tommies and tanks rapidly plunged inland.

Hundreds of miles from the flaming Normandy beaches, the early morning mist draped the mountain peaks around Berchtesgaden like a wedding veil. Admiral Karl Jesko von Puttkamer, Adolf Hitler's naval advisor, was awakened shortly before 5:45 A.M. and told of reports from OB West that "some kind of landing" was taking place in northern France.

Admiral Puttkamer discussed the situation with General Alfred Jodl, and they debated whether to notify the fuehrer, who was still sleeping in his retreat on the Obersalzburg overlooking Berchtesgaden. For two hours they talked, while a rash of alarming bulletins poured in from OB West. Jodl and Puttkamer could not bring themselves to disturb Hitler.

Shortly after 9:00 A.M. (8:00 A.M. German time) Jodl and Puttkamer listened to the BBC broadcast news from London: "Under the command of General Eisenhower, Allied naval forces, supported by air forces, began landing armies this morning on the northern coast of France."

Jodl and Puttkamer stared grimly at one another. It was now clear that the fuehrer would have to be told. But who dared to awaken him with this grave news? In the tradition of all armies since the beginning of warfare, the sticky task was bucked down the chain of command to Hitler's adjutant, Major General Rudolf Schmundt.

Schmundt tapped lightly on the fuehrer's bedroom door. Hitler and his mistress, Eva Braun, were sleeping soundly. After persistent raps, the fuehrer came to the door in his nightshirt, and Schmundt broke the news. Schmundt was startled to see that Hitler was exuberant. "At last we are going to meet our real enemies face to face!" the fuehrer cried.[4]

Hitler told Schmundt to summon his two closest military advisors, Alfred Jodl and Field Marshal Wilhelm Keitel, and prepared to leave for the Berghof's conference room. Eva Braun reminded him that a nightshirt might not be the most appropriate garb in which to meet with his top generals.

Typically, Jodl and Keitel said virtually nothing until they discerned what tack the fuehrer would take. Hitler was irritated. "Well, is it or isn't it the invasion?" he kept repeating.[5]

In this most critical of wartime conferences, Jodl and Keitel forgot to bring up the fact that Field Marshal von Rundstedt was desperately seeking the release of the panzers to drive the invaders back into the sea.

Eleven miles off blood-soaked Omaha on the heavy cruiser USS *Augusta*, General Omar Bradley, outwardly a portrait of serenity, was wracked with anguish. The assault on Omaha had been stopped cold. Now he was faced with a grueling decision: should Omaha be written off as a failure, abandoning perhaps 2,000 survivors on the beach, and should succeeding waves be diverted to Utah or the British beaches? It was 9:05 A.M.—H-Hour plus 155 minutes.

Then the gods of battle took a hand. The sun came out and the winds blew, clearing away the haze, smoke, and dust from the scene of the carnage. Allied fighter-bombers swooped down on German positions along the bluffs and on artillery positions to the rear, bombing and strafing. Warships, now able to see the targets clearly, moved in perilously close to blast the enemy along the heights with flat-trajectory shells. There was a noticeable slackening of fire from the cliffs.

By 10:00 A.M., large numbers of GIs had clawed, scratched, and fought their way to the top of the bluffs. A colossal debacle, one that could have jeopardized the entire invasion, had been averted by a hair's-breadth. The triumph at Omaha had an enormous price tag—some 2,450 dead, wounded, or drowned.

Although it was not planned in advance, Bodyguard machinations had played a significant role in preventing the Omaha assault from being a prodigious catastrophe. General Helmuth Kraiss had two of his regiments on the cliffs. Had his third regiment been on the firing line instead of many miles away chasing Titanic rubber paratroopers, the scales might have been tipped in favor of the Wehrmacht.

At Bletchley Park that historic morning, Ultra officials were especially alert to pick up an order from the fuehrer: "Initiate Case Three." That was the code signal for General Hans von Salmuth to begin rushing his Fifteenth Army, the strongest in France, from the Pas de Calais westward to Normandy, only a one-day road march away under normal conditions.

Allied forces were ashore, but in some places they were hanging on by their fingertips. Whether they remained in Normandy during these early critical hours of the invasion would depend greatly on Fortitude schemes continuing to unfold. So even as savage fighting was raging on and behind the Neptune beaches, John Bevan and his colleagues in the London Controlling Section launched Topflite, the code name for a series of broadcasts and public statements by top Allied leaders. Topflite's purpose was to reinforce Adolf Hitler's viewpoint that Normandy was but a diversion and to cause him not to initiate Case Three.

The scripts for these Allied leaders had been painstakingly created weeks earlier by Bodyguard strategists, and the entire verbal scenario had been coordinated to be cohesive and to convey subtly to monitoring German intelligence that a second prodigious blow was about to strike the fuehrer's Fortress Europe.

At 10:00 A.M. that day, even as Americans were clambering up the bullet-swept cliffs at Omaha Beach, a prerecorded statement by Dwight Eisenhower was broadcast over the BBC. The supreme commander referred to the Normandy landings as an "initial assault" and said that "the first great obstacle has been surmounted," implying that a sledgehammer blow would soon hit elsewhere.

Eisenhower dropped other second-assault hints. "The present battle is a mere beginning," he declared. "We have gained only a foothold. . . . Through the opening thus made, and through others yet to come, the flood of our fighting strength must yet to be poured." Then, with an eye toward keeping scores of Wehrmacht divisions pinned down in the Balkans, the Mediterranean, and Scandinavia—far from Normandy—the supreme commander said, "the Nazis will be forced to fight throughout the perimeter of their fortress stronghold."[6]

Bent on strengthening Fortitude North, the intricate ploy to keep German forces waiting idly in Scandinavia in anticipation of an invasion by General Bulgy Thorne's ghost Fourth Army in Scotland, Bodyguard deceptionists arranged for Eisenhower to be followed on the BBC by 72-year-old King Haakon VII of Norway. The popular monarch barely had escaped capture when the Germans invaded his country in April 1940, and he had established a government-in-exile in London.

King Haakon, too, spoke of an "initial landing," and he encouraged the 50,000 members of the Norwegian resistance not to allow their hatred of the Nazis to provoke them into "premature acts," an insinuation that the resistance should wait for a looming invasion of Norway.

Next, Belgian Prime Minister-in-Exile Hubert Pierlot took to the BBC microphone and, to inject yet another ingredient into the Fortitude witch's brew, he described Normandy as a "preliminary operation" and hinted that Allied landings would soon take place in Belgium.

As a flourishing grand finale to this D-Day psychological warfare strategy in support of Fortitude, the Allied big guns—Franklin Roosevelt and Winston Churchill—were unlimbered. In a 15-minute broadcast to the American people from the White House, the president declared, "The Germans appear to expect landings elsewhere. Let them speculate. We are content to wait on events"—inferring a second invasion.

At noon, the prime minister appeared in the House of Commons. After praising the fighting skills of Allied soldiers in Italy who had captured Rome the previous day, Churchill, always the master showman, paused long moments for dramatic impact, then told the House what it had already learned from the radio: "During the night and early hours of this morning the first of a series of landings in force on the European Continent has taken place."[7]

A few minutes later, Churchill slipped in another Fortitude-oriented remark: "There are already hopes that actual tactical surprise has been attained [in Normandy]. We hope to furnish the Germans with a succession of surprises during the course of the fighting."[8]

At noon on D-Day, Fortitude deceptionists received a healthy boost from an unexpected source—Foreign Armies West, Colonel Alexis von Roenne's intelligence branch in the OKW. In his bulletin to the fuehrer, von Roenne painted an Allied strategic picture that dovetailed precisely with Hitler's own views: "While the Anglo-Saxon landing on the coast of Normandy represents a large-scale operation, the forces employed comprise only a relatively small portion [of the available enemy divisions]. Of the 90 [divisions] in southern England only 10 to 12, including airborne troops, appear to be participating so far."

Then Baron von Roenne, a leader in the Schwarze Kapelle conspiracy, cautioned the fuehrer: "Not a single unit of the First United States Army Group [FUSAG, General Patton's phantom command], which comprises around 25 large formations, has so far been committed. . . . The same also holds true of the 10 to 12 combat formations in Scotland [the dummy Fourth Army]." Von Roenne concluded his D-Day assessment by declaring: "This suggests that the enemy is planning a further large-scale operation in the Channel area, which one would expect to be aimed at the Pas de Calais."[9]

When darkness enveloped embattled Normandy on D-Day, Adolf Hitler's "impregnable" Atlantic Wall had been breached: 57,506 American and 72,215 British and Canadian soldiers and hundreds of tanks were ashore. General Eisenhower and SHAEF breathed deep sighs of relief; so effective was Bodyguard that some 2,500 Allied soldiers had lost their lives, and total casualties were fewer than 12,000. Secretly, SHAEF had predicted that 10,000 Allied troops would be killed in the initial assault and some 50,000 others wounded.

For the Germans, D-Day ended as it had begun—in confusion and uncertainty. Officers at OB West were listening to the regular midnight war summary over Radio Berlin. In a broadcast from "the Normandy Front," German war correspondent Heinz Priet candidly declared that the Wehrmacht had been "caught napping." Captain Ludwig Sertorius, the Third Reich's leading military commentator, predicted that other Allied landings might be made in the Pas de Calais "with a sudden stab for Paris."[10] When the 15-minute newscast was concluded, Radio Berlin followed its format of many months by playing a record of musical star Maria von Schmedes singing *Another Beautiful Day Draws to a Close*.

26

The Invasion Remains in Jeopardy

Shortly after 9:00 A.M. on June 7—D-Day plus 1—General Bernard Montgomery, the ground commander, was holding the first high-level conference for Neptune in Europe, on board the HMS *Faulknor*, which was anchored off the invasion beaches. Present were General Miles Dempsey and General Omar Bradley, leaders of the two assaulting armies. A thin veil of concern hovered over the wardroom, for nowhere had Neptune succeeded as planned, and the Allies' toehold on Hitler's Fortress Europe was wafer thin.

Although Bodyguard had been highly instrumental in catching the Wehrmacht off guard, the Germans were resisting in most locales with typical tenacity. Field Marshal Erwin Rommel, who had returned from his home in Herrlingen, Ultra learned, had in northern France nearly 1 million men and some 1,500 panzers. If he could concentrate forces to mount a full-blooded counterattack, the invaders might be hurled back into the sea.

Making the Allied outlook even more ominous was the crucial supply situation, which was behind schedule, and the weather was expected to grow more violent and halt or slow the unloading on the open beaches or at the tiny fishing villages.

Overlord strategists long had recognized that unless the invaders could swiftly seize a major port to rapidly bring in troops, guns, tanks, ammunition, fuel, and rations, the Allies would be in danger of withering on the vine and being cut to pieces by a Wehrmacht converging by land into Normandy.

Overlord's eyes were on Cherbourg, an ancient, heavily fortified port situated in a bowl near the center of the north coast of the Cherbourg peninsula and some 22 miles from Utah Beach. Not until Cherbourg was seized and its excellent harbor facilities put into operation would Neptune be secure on the Continent.

Two years earlier, Adolf Hitler had reached that identical conclusion. So he had proclaimed Cherbourg and several major ports in northern France and the Low Countries "fortresses" and required their German commanders to sign declarations that they would defend the coastal strongholds "to the last man and the last bullet" and then destroy the harbor to render it useless to the invaders.

While Allied soldiers were fighting doggedly to expand the five beachheads and the Feldgrau were desperately trying to throw the invaders back into the Channel that morning of June 7, an array of Nazi commentators took to Radio Berlin. Joseph Goebbels, the clever propaganda minister, explained to the German homefront the reason for the Allied operation: "[President] Roosevelt needed invasion success to win his [November] reelection campaign."[1]

Then Goebbels unleashed a long-prepared anti-invasion blast directed at the French. Its theme was "don't help the British and Americans, for you will be sorry when all of your country is handed over to the Russian Bolsheviks by Roosevelt and Churchill."[2]

Two other German broadcast commentators provided tangible evidence that Adolf Hitler and his high command had swallowed the Bodyguard bait: that Normandy was but a large-scale diversion and the main blow would be struck at the Pas de Calais. Lieutenant General Kurt Ditmar, a foremost Reich military analyst, told the German people: "It may be taken for granted that the size of Montgomery's forces already operating on the Normandy coast are only a fraction of the Allied divisions held in reserve in England."[3] Captain Ludwig Sertorius dismissed the whole Normandy beachhead operation as a "nibble," and implied that the entire "meal" would be served in the Pas de Calais.[4]

Through Ultra intercepts, aerial reconnaissance, the French underground, and Brissex spy teams, SHAEF swiftly learned that Hitler released the Panzer Lehr, 12th SS, and 21st Panzer divisions to Rommel and they were already pushing up toward the Normandy front. Other German formations, including paratroop and panzer, were heading toward the beachhead from Brittany and central France. In excess of 550 Luftwaffe fighter-bombers were ordered from the defense of the Reich to bases near Normandy.

An all-out effort was launched by the Allies to halt the flow toward the battleground of these German reinforcements. Trains, truck convoys, and panzer columns were sabotaged, ambushed, and harassed by French Maquis (resistance fighters), Jedburgh teams, and special units. Every Allied warplane that could fly bombed, strafed, and rocketed.

Bodyguard connivances were employed to slow down these German troop movements. In the dark hours of June 7, Erwin Rommel's headquarters received an urgent bulletin from the field: "Three hundred Allied transport planes have dropped hundreds of paratroopers about seven miles east of Saint-Lô." Rommel immediately sent orders for German units, which were on the way from Brittany to Omaha Beach, to rush instead to the drop site and wipe out the Allied paratroop force. After losing 48 hours in their trek to Omaha, the sidetracked German formations discovered that the large Allied parachute force was actually a few score Titanic rubber dummies that had been dropped by three transports, not 300 of them.[5]

Under normal conditions, it would have required these reinforcements a week to reach Normandy. But stalled repeatedly by the heavy blows they were receiving, it would take three weeks for the trek. So SHAEF's most haunting concern remained the German Fifteenth Army along the Pas de Calais. These forces were the only reinforcements available to Rommel that could reach Normandy in time to have an impact on the raging battle, which was still touch-and-go.

Consequently, Allied deceptionists spun a web of machinations that were intended to be viewed by the Wehrmacht as identical to the genuine activities conducted by the Anglo-Americans just prior to the Normandy invasion. In mid-afternoon on June 7, a French voice on the BBC began broadcasting to the underground in the Pas de Calais an incoherent stream of *messages personnels*—all of them fake. For the Germans had such thick troop concentrations in the Pas de Calais to meet the looming threat from the dummy Army Group Patton that there were few resistance cells in that region. However, to monitoring Wehrmacht intelligence officers, this flood of coded messages to the underground in the Pas de Calais, combined with real signals sent to highly active underground groups elsewhere in northern France, could be a tip-off that Army Group Patton was nearly ready to cross the narrow Strait of Dover.

OSS and SOE teams were parachuted into the Pas de Calais, and British submarines and motor torpedo boats were seen cavorting off the Pas de Calais shore. The German Y-Service was permitted to hear greatly intensified wireless traffic in Patton's ghost army group—after which the chattering suddenly fell silent, a telltale sign that a major operation was imminent.

Colonel John Turner's camouflage magicians discreetly illuminated with dim lights the ports of southeastern England to convey to Luftwaffe reconnaissance aircraft that ships were being combat-loaded at night. To mask these nonexistent troop embarkation operations from prying Luftwaffe eyes in daylight, ships laid thick smokescreens along the Dover coast. Minesweepers, escorted by PT boats, churned out of harbors along the Strait of Dover and went through the motions of clearing paths through the minefields in front of Calais and Boulogne.

To reinforce these deceptions, Brutus, one of the Double-Cross' first violins, radioed an urgent signal to his Abwehr controller in Paris. At least Brutus' case officer did—Brutus himself (Polish Flight Officer Roman Garby-Czerniawski) was fighting with an RAF squadron. Dated June 8, Brutus' message said that he had seen "with my own eyes the Army Group Patton embarking" in southeastern England. Patton had at least 50 divisions in his force, Brutus added, with five of them being airborne.

In London on the night of June 8, John Bevan, Ronald Wingate, and their colleagues in the London Controlling Section at Storey's Gate were eagerly listening to Captain Ludwig Sertorius, the Nazi commentator, broadcasting over Radio Berlin. Sertorius pointed out that "none of the more than 50 divisions at Eisenhower's disposal have been used yet. . . . But they may be within the next few days—in the region opposite Dover [the Pas de Calais]." John Bevan and his artful dodgers broke out in smiles. So far, the German high command appeared to be accepting as gospel Fortitude's Army Group Patton preaching.

Early on the morning of June 9—D-Day plus 3—both von Rundstedt and Rommel desperately were pleading with General Jodl for the fuehrer to release the Fifteenth Army sitting idly in the Pas de Calais. It would never be clear who issued the order, but the Fifteenth Army was turned over to Rommel, and elements began rolling toward Normandy that same afternoon.

In the meantime that day, in support of Brutus' message on the previous day, Garbo (German code name Arabel) dispatched a lengthy summary of Allied intentions to General Erich Kuhlenthal, the Abwehr official in Madrid:

> Request following report be urgently submitted to OKW for immediate attention.
> Sources do not repeat do not believe Normandy landing is main thrust of Anglo-American invasion.
> V372 Liverpool reports large concentrations U.S.A. armored still held his area. V373 estimates at least 35 divisions are awaiting orders in Scottish lowlands. V377 traveled by train saw elements of 20 divisions in stretch 15 miles south of York.
> So far not a single soldier of FUSAG [Army Group Patton] has been engaged. Strongly suggest Normandy landing is purely diversional.[6]

Garbo's summary was yet another masterpiece of his Double-Cross case officer, Tommy Harris. Perhaps it was the crown jewel in his galaxy of deceits and deceptions inflicted by Garbo (the Spaniard Juan Pujol) on the Oberkommando der Wehrmacht for nearly two years. During the roughly eight months of the Fortitude campaign, 62 of the trusted Arabel's (Garbo's) reports were quoted in German intelligence summaries.

At Foreign Armies West in Berlin on June 9, Colonel Alexis von Roenne was sifting through the eyewitness reports sent in by Brutus and Garbo, along with a mass of other eyepopping intelligence collected from aerial reconnaissance of southeastern England and Y-Service monitoring. A half-hour before Adolf Hitler's regular noon conference with his generals, von Roenne telephoned Colonel Friedrich-Adolf Krummacher, Hitler's personal intelligence officer.

Speaking in his staccato fashion, von Roenne severely criticized the release of the Fifteenth Army for the Normandy front, stressing that he had high-grade information that the enemy was about to launch a large-scale operation from southeastern England. Impressed, Colonel Krummacher assured von Roenne that he would present his views to the fuehrer at noon "with all the emphasis at my command."[7] At the conference, Adolf Hitler listened impassively to the presentation of von Roenne's points, and he said he would wait until his midnight conference to decide whether to recall the Fifteenth Army advance forces bound for Normandy.

Late that afternoon, General Jodl showed the fuehrer the contents of a wireless signal that had just arrived from Kuhlenthal, the Abwehr bigwig in Madrid. It was an evaluation of the views of "my agents" in England—all of whom were controlled by the Double-Cross. "After considering the massive concentration of troops in southeastern England which are taking no part in the present operation, I have come to the conclusion that the [Normandy] operations are a maneuver," Kuhlenthal declared. "Its purpose is to entice our reserves into the bridgehead in order that the decisive assault can be launched at another point."[8]

At his midnight conference on June 9–10, the fuehrer, perhaps influenced by the Fortitude ploys of the past three days, performed an about-face. He ordered the Fifteenth Army to halt its move to Normandy (where its presence might tip the scales in favor of the Germans) and to remain in the Pas de Calais. When Field Marshals von Rundstedt and Rommel received Hitler's order before dawn, each knew that the Battle of Normandy—and perhaps the war—had been lost.[9]

By June 10, the Allies had failed to expand their Normandy enclave as swiftly as the Neptune planners had envisioned. On the eastern flank, British and Canadian troops were engaged in a bloody slugfest with panzer formations that refused to budge from in front of Caen (population 55,000), the world-renowned center for modern art. "Lightning Joe" Collins' U.S. VII Corps was locked in a yard-by-yard struggle to drive westward from Utah and cut the neck of the peninsula before turning north to capture the port of Cherbourg. Colonel Friedrich von der Heydte's tough 6th Parachute Regiment was clinging to the key road center of Carentan, preventing a linkup of Utah and Omaha forces.

In Berlin on June 11—D-Day plus 5—Reichsfuehrer SS Heinrich Himmler, the one-time chicken farmer and now the second most powerful figure in Nazi Germany, directed Ernst Kaltenbrunner, chief of the SD (the SS security service), to send Arabel (Garbo) a message of congratulations:

Attention Arabel:

Reichsfuehrer SS Himmler has directed his warm appreciation to Arabel. All reports received in last week from Arabel undertaking have been confirmed without exception and are to be described as especially invaluable.

Arabel's reports had been "confirmed" by other Double-Cross "first violins."[10]

Normandy had turned into a slaughterhouse. Smothering Allied air power, artillery battalions placed almost hub-to-hub, and big naval guns from warships offshore were chopping the Feldgrau to pieces. A distraught Erwin Rommel confided to his wife in a letter that he was losing the equivalent of a regiment a day. Gasoline, oil, and ammunition shortages began to plague Rommel. Because of Bodyguard intrigues, most of these battlefield necessities were stored in the Pas de Calais.

The Allies, too, were suffering heavy casualties. Word had filtered down from the fuehrer to the lowliest Feldgrau: "Don't give up a foot of ground!" Even though Maxwell Taylor's 101st Airborne Division seized bomb- and shell-battered Carentan after a bloody altercation with Baron von der Heydte's paratroopers and the Neptune beachheads were linked into a solid front, the invasion remained in jeopardy. Neptune plans called for Collins' VII Corps to capture the port of Cherbourg on June 13—D-Day plus 7—but on June 14, his tanks and infantrymen were still 20 miles away.

In order to take the heavy pressure off the Americans, Bodyguard strategists put into play a simulated assault against the western coast of the Cherbourg peninsula, near Granville, 30 miles southwest of Carentan and well behind Rommel's lines. Code-named Accumulator, it was a hastily conceived ploy.

On June 13, Canadian destroyers *Haida* and *Huron* sailed from England. Through electronic manipulations and Filberts, the two ships were supposed to represent a fleet of landing craft and other vessels. Knowing that the German Y-Service would be monitoring the "invasion flotilla," radio operators on the destroyers, when they were about 50 miles from the Granville coast, broke radio silence to flash word to England that a landing ship had developed engine trouble. This mishap, it was explained, had forced that craft to reduce its speed to ten miles per hour, thereby delaying the entire operation. *Haida* and *Huron* wireless operators and those at a base in England chattered for nearly three hours as, reading from previously prepared scripts, they revised a plan of attack.

Then the plot went awry. An American reconnaissance pilot flew over *Haida* and *Huron* and, unaware of Accumulator, radioed his base in the clear that he had spotted two unidentified warships steering a course toward the western shore of the Cherbourgh peninsula. No doubt the pilot's report was intercepted by the Y-Service, and it convinced the Germans that the landing was phony, for Ultra found no indication of enemy reaction to the threat behind Rommel's lines.

Allied deception agencies continued to launch schemes to keep the German high command jittery and uncertain. On the morning of June 14, a BBC broadcaster "happened" to single out the Strait of Dover in a weather report: "Fickle weather in the Strait changed again last night—for the better. After a day of intermittent rain and mist, with high wind, the sun came out in the afternoon and there has been a steady improvement of conditions. By this morning, the Channel had subsided considerably and visibility is good over the horizon toward Calais." This seemingly innocent report was a reminder to the antsy Germans that weather conditions and tides were right for Army Group Patton to cross the Strait of Dover.

A day later, a SHAEF spokesman broadcast over the BBC a new warning to Belgians, Netherlanders, Danes, Norwegians, and citizens of northern France for "fishermen now in port to remain there and any still at sea to return to port immediately. . . . Failure to do so may cause danger to fishermen and will hinder operations of the Allied forces."[11] This fake warning, too, was intended to imply to the Germans that Patton was ready to strike. Actually, the flamboyant American general was finalizing plans for moving his genuine Third Army headquarters to Normandy under top-secret wraps.

A few days earlier, Garbo had radioed his German controllers that U.S. Army Chief of Staff George Marshall and General Henry "Hap" Arnold, commander of the U.S. Army Air Corps, had flown from Washington to visit George Patton and his army group before it departed for the Pas de Calais. In fact, the two Pentagon generals, along with other members of the Anglo-American Combined Chiefs of Staff, had come to England to be on hand should there arise the need to make a "crucial decision"—that is, the withdrawal of Neptune forces if the invasion proved to be a catastrophe.

Now, to bulwark Garbo's already solid credibility with the German high command, Bodyguard deceptionists felt it was important to put the spotlight on Marshall and Arnold to make certain that the enemy was convinced that they were indeed in England. So in a flood of media publicity and pomp and circumstance, King George VI received the two highest-ranking American generals in an audience at Buckingham Palace in London on June 14.

Allied deceptionists knew that massive bombings and shellings, French underground sabotage, and confusion caused by the fog of war had turned the efficient Wehrmacht communications network in northern France into what General Guenther Blummentritt at OB West would call an *ungeheuerer Kladderadatsch* (monstrous mess). Therefore, on June 14, fictitious reports intended to confuse the Germans about Allied operations and take some of the heat off the hard-pressed British and Americans in Normandy were planted in newspapers around the world.

Said to have originated in neutral Spain, these stories disclosed that Allied Commandos and Rangers, equipped with jeeps, light tanks, and antitank guns, had parachuted and landed in gliders deep behind Rommel's lines on "airfields prepared by French patriots." To inject an added touch of authenticity to the phony report, it was stated that "there was no Allied confirmation of these rumors."

A day later, a broadcast over Nazi-controlled Vichy (France) radio seemed to confirm that the Wehrmacht high command had swallowed yet another Bodyguard ploy designed to help pin down German divisions in southern France. Quoting an unidentified "Berlin military spokesman," Radio Vichy declared that "important Allied shipping movements have been observed in the Bay of Biscay off Gascony, near the French-Spanish border"—400 miles south of the Normandy battleground. The German spokesman pointed out that Gascony had flat, sandy beaches, ideal for an amphibious landing but added that "it is too early to say whether the shipping movement is a feint or a prelude to a new invasion." Actually, Fortitude's "first violins" were the source of the "Allied shipping" fairy tale.

27

Rommel Seeks a Secret Peace

In far-off Berchtesgaden on the night of June 26, a grim-faced General Alfred Jodl handed a wireless bulletin to the fuehrer: Lieutenant General Karl Wilhelm Dietrich von Schlieben, the hulking commander of Fortress Cherbourgh, and Admiral Walther Hennecke had surrendered to GIs of Joe Collins' VII Corps after a bitter fight for the crucial port, Neptune's main objective.

Hitler was livid. "A disgrace to the uniform and the lowest form of German general!" he ranted about von Schlieben.

At Army Group B headquarters at La Roche-Guyon, Field Marshal Rommel and his staff dined in almost total silence that night. The fall of Cherbourg had slammed shut the door on any chance of driving Anglo-American forces back into the sea.

On this beautiful summer evening, Rommel was clearly choking from emotion—sorrow for his Feldgrau who were being slaughtered in Normandy, bitter anger that those at the top around the feuhrer were endeavoring mightily to place the blame squarely on Rommel's tenacious soldiers for the Normandy disaster, and anguished that he could not do more to rid his beloved Fatherland of the man he was convinced was bringing the Reich crashing down in utter ruins—Adolf Hitler.

Erwin Rommel's deep frustrations also were rooted in Hitler's dogged determination to direct the battle of Normandy from his perch on the Obersalzburg, 600 miles from the front. "My functions are so restricted by Hitler that any sergeant-major could carry them out," Rommel would tell his 15-year-old son, Manfred. "He interferes with everything and turns down every proposal we make."[1]

Even worse for Rommel, the fuehrer and the sycophant generals at his elbow continued to be mesmerized by the Fortitude fantasies, apparently putting their full faith in the reports of the Double-Cross agents in England. Arrogantly convinced that their military judgment was far superior to that of von Rundstedt and Rommel, Hitler and his crowd followed eagerly the activities of George Patton, who the turned agents reported was dashing about England like a whirling dervish.

Despite the devastating loss of Cherbourgh, Rommel still hoped to inflict such massive casualties on the Anglo-Americans that they would be receptive to the peace feelers he planned to extend to them on his behalf. So Rommel invited the fuehrer to visit La Roche-Guyon for a conference. If, at that time, Hitler refused to release the idle Fifteenth Army to him, Rommel would have the fuehrer arrested by soldiers loyal to the field marshal.

At this stage of the war, Adolf Hitler (with ample reason) was suspicious of all his generals with the possible exception of Alfred Jodl and Wilhelm Keitel. Therefore, suspecting a plot, the fuehrer rejected the invitation but agreed to meet with Rommel at a bunker command post near the French city of Soissons. There, on June 27, as GIs were mopping up a few diehard Germans in Cherbourg, Rommel and Gerd von Rundstedt confronted Hitler.

For 30 minutes, Erwin Rommel spoke of the courage of German fighting men in Normandy and how the enormous Allied firepower had chopped divisions down to battalion size. He told of the great strength of the British and American formations and of how German intelligence continued to send him conflicting reports. Above all, Rommel tried to impress upon the fuehrer, who sat impassively toying with pencils, that the capture of the U.S. V Corps and VII Corps operational plans proved that Normandy was truly the *coup de main* invasion.

After a break for lunch, Rommel returned to the attack, frustrated by the fact that his pleadings were making no impression on Hitler. Unless the Fifteenth Army were released to him promptly, Rommel exclaimed, Normandy was lost. Did the fuehrer really believe that Germany could still win the war?

Hitler tensed, his face contorted. "Look after your invasion front, Herr Rommel," the fuehrer snapped angrily. "And don't bother about the continuation of the war!" Erwin Rommel's personal fate was sealed at that moment.

A crestfallen Rommel returned to La Roche-Guyon. Hans Speidel, his dedicated chief of staff and fellow Schwarze Kapelle conspirator, noted that the field marshal was both depressed and convinced that action had to be taken promptly to rid Germany of Adolf Hitler. Rommel began to form a plan whereby General Speidel and Lieutenant General Karl-Heinrich von Stuelpnagel, military governor of France and a descendant of the Prussian military aristocracy, who had been plotting against the fuehrer since 1938, would sneak across the battle lines to negotiate an armistice.

Rommel's terms would provide for the withdrawal of German armies in the West to the Siegfried line on the Reich border, and in return, the Anglo-Americans would cease bombing German cities. On the Russian front, the Wehrmacht would continue the struggle. Meanwhile, the fuehrer would be "removed from the picture" (by the Schwarze Kapelle).

Erwin Rommel, professional soldier, displayed his political naivete by telling his fellow conspirators that "my friend [Bernard] Montgomery" would grant a "separate peace," as though the British general were empowered to engage in such a move. Unconditional Surrender was the stance taken a year earlier by the Big Three—Roosevelt, Churchill, and Stalin.[2]

While Erwin Rommel was plotting to obtain an armistice in the West, George Patton, the Allied general the Germans feared most, flew "secretly" onto a landing strip behind Omaha Beach on July 6. Several hundred American soldiers were on hand to cheer the bold buccaneer, who promptly launched into a speech. "I'm going to lead you to Berlin," he declared. "And when we get there, I'm going to personally shoot that goddammed paper-hanging son-of-a bitch Hitler!"[3] Howls of laughter echoed across the green pastures.

George Patton's presence in Normandy was a morale shot in the arm for GIs and many American commanders alike. Seven weeks after the Allies had stormed ashore, the invaders were stalled not far from the D-Day landing beaches. Nearly one and half million American, British, and Canadian troops and their weapons and equipment were bottled up in the narrow confines of the Cherbourgh peninsula and along a thin strip of the Calvados coast in front of the ancient city of Caen.

During the first two weeks of July at the base of the Cherbourg peninsula, the savage fighting in the swamps and hedgerows north of the strategically crucial town of Saint-Lô raged relentlessly. "The most monstrous bloodbath, the like of which I have not seen in eleven years of war," exclaimed the German commander in the sector, Lieutenant General Dietrich von Choltitz. American gains, if any, were measured in yards; a half-mile advanced was hailed as a major tactical achievement. At that rate, it would require decades to reach Berlin.

For centuries, the flatlands of the lower Cherbourg peninsula had been divided and subdivided into small pastures by means of thick earthern walls. Many of these walls were eight to ten feet high, and long, snakelike roots packed the dirt together much as reinforcing steel would strengthen concrete.

A thick, thorny growth of trees, bushes, and brambles crowned each wall. The earthern mounds furnished ideal protection for defenders and the tangled vegetation provided natural concealment. Tough and motivated, the outnumbered and outgunned Feldgrau burrowed into the thick hedgerow walls, and armed with a formidable array of machine guns and *Panzerfauste* (rocket launchers) took a frightful toll among American attackers.

At cemeteries behind the lines, the bodies of young GIs, each shrouded in a mattress cover, were stacked in long rows awaiting interment by grim-faced burial details. By July 20, General Bradley's First Army had suffered more than 61,000 casualties since D-Day, 11,258 of those being killed.

As the dogfaces (as American soldiers called themselves) and the Feldgrau were slaughtering one another in the swamps and hedgerows, massive blood-letting also was taking place along the eastern sector of the beachhead where the British and Canadians had been stalled since D-Day. Fearful of a breakout toward Paris by Lieutenant General Miles Dempsey's Second Army, Rommel had congregated most of his available panzer forces to shield Caen.

George Patton had not been told by SHAEF that an American breakout from Normandy was in the works, nor that he would lead a powerful armored thrust that, it was hoped, would drive all the way to the doorstep of the Reich—or beyond. So for two weeks, Patton paced about like a caged tiger at his Third Army headquarters in an apple orchard near Nehou in the Cherbourg peninsula, far behind the front lines. Old Blood and Guts, as his troops called him, was itching to get into action; he had been "in the doghouse" since the previous autumn in Sicily when he had slapped a soldier whom he suspected of malingering.

Patton had been given no specific assignment after reaching Normandy, and he growled to aides, "My destiny in this goddamned war is to sit here on my ass and watch cider apples grow!" George Patton was what the news correspondents called "good copy." He could be counted on to spit out some offhand remark that, a few hours later, would appear in bold headlines in the States—sometimes plunging the outspoken and opinionated general into hot water.

Aware of Patton's anger and frustrations over having to "watch the cider apples grow" while other Americans were fighting, a bevy of reporters asked him what he would do to break the stalemate if he were in command in Normandy. Flicking the ash off his cigar, Patton could not resist a candid off-the-record reply. "I'd line up my tanks on a narrow front and in a couple of days we'd go through the Krauts like shit through a goddamned goose. We'd head for Avranches [35 miles to the south] and from there burst out all over France," he explained. Patton, as was his wont, paused briefly for dramatic effect, then added, "Of course that would be too bold for some. We'd never do it with that little fart in charge!"

Reporters knew the identity of "that little fart"—British General Bernard Montgomery. Patton and Monty long had been arch foes, hardly able to exchange civilities when meeting.

George Patton soon would learn that the view he had expressed to reporters was the precise operational plan for Cobra, the code name for the looming breakout.

George Patton's presence in Normandy created a serious problem for Quicksilver deceptionists. How could a general wearing a tailored, brass-buttoned jacket, pink jodhpurs, highly polished riding boots with spurs; carrying a riding crop; accompanied by a pet bulldog terrier named Willie; and with 15 large silver stars blazing on his lacquered helmet liner, shirt collar tabs, and shoulders be kept secret from the Germans? Concealing Patton's presence was a task akin to hiding an approaching tornado.[4]

It was feared that German intelligence in a matter of days, perhaps hours, would learn that Patton was not commanding an army group preparing to smash at the Pas de Calais from Dover but was in charge of a single army (the Third) in Normandy under Omar Bradley. That revelation would puncture the long-nourished Quicksilver fairy tale that the fuehrer still believed.

Allied deceptionists concluded that the solution to the thorny matter was to "demote" George Patton. Word was leaked to the Germans (mainly through the "first violins") that the volatile and often bellicose Patton, who long had been afflicted with foot-in-the-mouth disease, had perpetrated yet another indiscretion, and Dwight Eisenhower had demoted him to command of a single army.

Patton's "demotion" would require a successor to lead the dummy army group in England, and General Lesley J. McNair, the 61-year-old chief of Army Ground Forces, was rushed from Washington for that purpose.

General McNair was hardly enthused by his paper tiger role. When he had conferred with Chief of Staff Marshall before departing Washington, he had not been told his specific assignment, other than it was a "vitally important one." Marshall could not run the risk that someone in the Pentagon might inadvertently leak the nature of McNair's mission in England.

Like every professional officer, McNair yearned for a combat command—perhaps a field army under Omar Bradley. So when McNair met with Dwight Eisenhower at Southwick House on July 15, the three-star general departed in a fit of white-hot anger after learning that he would merely be a decoy.[5]

Meanwhile, in Berlin, Baron Alexis von Roenne continued to insist that the Anglo-Americans would yet deliver a sledgehammer blow at the Pas de Calais. Nearly every day through July, he bombarded various Wehrmacht headquarters with "reliable information" that the Allies had more divisions in Great Britain than they had in Normandy and that these uncommitted formations were backed by powerful air and naval forces. The sources of von Roenne's "reliable information" were the Double-Cross first violins. In order to keep the German high command confused and uncertain, Allied deceptionists touched off Rosebud, whose function was to strengthen the fantasy that a million Allied soldiers under Lesley McNair were still in southeastern England awaiting the go sign to assault the Pas de Calais. Rosebud's theme was that McNair was being leashed until the German high command foolishly sent the Fifteenth Army to Normandy, leaving behind but a skeleton force to defend the Pas de Calais.

Rosebud was to convey to German intelligence that three great assault fleets—code-named Mike, Nan, and Fox—were congregating in harbors, rivers, and estuaries in southeastern England. The same rubber or timber and canvas assault craft that had been used in Fortitude South were employed in this scheme. There were warnings to the Germans from Double-Cross agents, the clatter of wireless chatter, a large increase in radio messages to Pas de Calais' largely nonexistent underground cells, and stepped-up reconnaissance flights over the Pas de Calais.

British and American warships in southern England bolted from one port to another, indicating urgent preinvasion business. Rosebud introduced a new twist: the creation of an entire tactical air force, which, Double-Cross agents advised the Germans, had been brought in from the United States to support the Pas de Calais invasion. Actually, this new tactical air force consisted of hundreds of rubber airplanes, which, when inflated and installed near the runways at a score of airfields, looked just like the real things to Luftwaffe photographic pilots flying at 30,000 feet.

Meanwhile in the German camp, momentous events were occurring. On July 7, the fuehrer sacked Gerd von Rundstedt and replaced him as commander-in-chief-West with Field Marshal Hans Guenther von Kluge, whom some Germans called "Clever Hans." The stocky, 61-year-old von Kluge had been a Hitler favorite when conducting a "victorious defense" as commander of Army Group Center in Russia for two years.

Von Kluge arrived at Saint-Germain with spirits high and a firm resolve that the Allies could yet be soundly defeated in Normandy. Within days, the "hero of victorious defense" became totally disillusioned. The Feldgrau were being mindlessly butchered in a hopeless cause instead of being pulled back to a natural defense line along the Seine River or even to the German border. Von Kluge's order from the fuehrer had been *"Starre Verteidigung!"* (Stand fast!). Consequently, Field Marshal von Kluge joined the Schwarze Kapelle conspiracy and entered a pact with Erwin Rommel to seek a negotiated peace with the Western Allies independently of Hitler.

On July 17, the gods of battle intervened in the Normandy conflagration. Shortly after 6:00 P.M., Erwin Rommel and two aides were speeding along a French road on the way back to La Roche-Guyon after visiting the front. Suddenly, two RAF fighter-bombers zoomed in at treetop level and riddled the Mercedes with 20-millimeter shells. The driver was killed and the car went out of control and smashed into a ditch, tossing the unconscious Rommel onto the road. Ironically, the episode had taken place near the town of Montgomery, the name of Rommel's long-time battlefield foe.

The field marshal was rushed to a civilian hospital in nearby Livarot, then on to a Luftwaffe medical center outside Bernay. German doctors found that Rommel had a fracture at the base of the skull, two fractures of the left temple, and his left cheek bone had been crushed. He had a severe concussion, his left eye was badly damaged, and his scalp had been ripped open. The Luftwaffe doctors gave him little chance to live.[6]

Three nights later on July 20, Field Marshal von Kluge strode wearily into his office at Saint-Germain after an exhausting and gloom-ridden day conferring with his battle commanders along the Normandy front. The pudgy von Kluge's eyes promptly focused on a document marked *Blitz Geheim* (literally, lightning secret) that had arrived only minutes earlier. Hurriedly tearing open the envelope, the field marshal read the message and slumped into a chair, an expression of disbelief etched into his pale face. The Schwarze Kapelle had struck. Adolf Hitler was dead.

For two hours, von Kluge discussed the momentous development with his chief of staff, General Guenther Blumentritt, who was aware of, if not an active participant in, the anti-Hitler conspiracy. Colonel Klaus von Stauffenberg, the decorated young count, had placed a bomb next to the fuehrer while he was conducting a conference at Wolfsschanze, outside Rastenburg, East Prussia.

Von Kluge observed to Blumentritt that his first action should be to secure an armistice with the Americans and British in Normandy to halt the bloodshed on both sides. Minutes later, a telephone call came from Field Marshal Wilhelm Keitel at Wolfsschanze. Keitel said that the fuehrer was the target of a bomb blast, but that he was "alive and only slightly injured." The OKW chief stressed that von Kluge was to take orders from no one but Hitler or Heinrich Himmler, the Gestapo and SS chief.

An ashen-faced von Kluge thoughtfully replaced the receiver. No doubt he shuddered inwardly to think he had almost leaped too soon and exposed himself as a Schwarze Kapelle conspirator. It was nearly midnight when von Kluge dictated an urgent message: "To the Fuehrer. Thanks to a merciful act of Providence, the infamous and murderous attempt against your life, Fuehrer, has miscarried. On behalf of the three branches of the Armed Forces entrusted to my command, I send you my congratulations and assure you, my Fuehrer, of my unalterable loyalty."[7]

On July 23, General Omar Bradley met with a group of newsmen at his command center of canvas and caravans shoehorned into an apple orchard behind Omaha Beach. The First Army commander made a solemn promise: give him three hours of good flying weather any forenoon and he would burst out of the Normandy *bocage* "like a rocket."

Bradley's plan was code-named Cobra. Rather than mount another maximum effort by infantrymen to forge out of Normandy, slashing yard by bloody yard through the hedgerows in frontal assault with four corps abreast, Cobra would concentrate enormous firepower in a tiny rectangle of countryside along the Saint-Lô–Périers road, a few miles west of the key road center of Saint-Lô. The Cherbourg peninsula's largest, with a peacetime population of 11,000, Saint-Lô had been captured by American forces on July 18 and was now a pile of pulverized rubble.

The targeted rectangle was three-and-a-half miles long and one-and-a-half miles deep. Cobra would kick off with some 2,500 heavies, mediums, and fighter-bombers saturating the rectangle with more than 60,000 bombs, after which artillery would drench the same locale with 140,000 shells. Then three infantry divisions, closely packed on the north side of the dividing road, would advance immediately into the pulverized triangle and clean up whatever resistance survived. Swarms of tanks from three armored divisions would then bolt through the yawning gap and dash southward—all the way to Avranches.

In the meantime, Ultra intercepts made it known to SHAEF that Field Marshal von Kluge felt convinced that the British at Caen would make the looming maximum effort to break out of Normandy, and he deployed most of his panzer formations in that sector, some 50 miles east of where Cobra would strike. So Allied deceptionists reinforced von Kluge's tactical viewpoint by a series of ploys.

British and American warships were sent into the waters off Le Havre, east of Caen. As anticipated, this maneuver was promptly reported to German intelligence. The Allies also greatly increased air reconnaissance in the vicinity of Caen, a telltale factor also noted by the Wehrmacht. A rash of French underground sabotage actions suddenly erupted along the northern coast of France, and German intelligence was fed clues that indicated a large Allied airborne force was preparing to land behind German lines near Caen.

George Patton, meanwhile, became even more angry and frustrated after Omar Bradley briefed him on Cobra and gave no indication that the Third Army commander would play a role in its execution. Patton recognized the breakout operation as virtually the same one that he had expounded to newsmen off-the-record: concentrating tanks on a narrow front, bombarding the Germans, and going through them like "shit through a goose."

With Cobra ready to be launched when the murky weather cleared, General Patton relieved his frustrations by lashing out at American generals in his personal diary:

Neither Ike [Eisenhower] nor Brad has the stuff. Ike is bound hand and foot by the British and doesn't know it, poor fool. . . . Bradley and [Lieutenant General Courtney H.] Hodges are such nothings. . . . I could break through in three days, if I commanded.

A Monstrous German Debacle

Early on the morning of July 25, an important matter was being thrashed out at the highest levels of government in London: should the Anglo-Americans take up where the Schwarze Kapelle had failed and try to kill Adolf Hitler by aerial bombing? Through Ultra, the fuehrer's presence was constantly pinpointed, almost minute by minute.

It was decided not to make the effort for fear of tipping off the Germans to the fact that their Engima code had been broken. "Besides," commented Winston Churchill, flicking an ash from his long cigar, "they might put some other Nazi in there who is even worse than Herr Hitler. With the Fuehrer at the helm, we can't lose the war!"[1]

Three hundred miles south of London that same morning—D-Day plus 49— the battlefront along the road linking Saint-Lô and Périers seemed to be haunted. Except for a few sporadic rifle shots, it was eerily silent. Here and there, crows and sparrows cawed and flew gracefully from bush to tree. Crickets chirped in the lush greenery. It was as though a degree of sanity had been restored to a world gone mad.

Dug in along the south side of the road was General Fritz Bayerlein's first-rate Panzer Lehr Division, which had suffered heavy losses in the bitter fighting among the tangled hedgerows, but which remained an aggressive fighting force. Bayerlein's 5,000 grenadiers (infantrymen) were unaware that they were perched on a patch of ground that Allied commanders had selected to be wiped off the face of Normandy.

Lieutenant Hans Uehler of Bayerlein's 902nd Grenadier Regiment was worried. Why had the slaughterhouse suddenly become so quiet? Even American artillery, which had been firing almost incessantly since D-Day, was muted.

Suddenly, the tranquility was shattered. One of Uehler's lookouts shouted, *"Feinde Flugzeuge!"* *"Feinde Flugzeuge!"* ("Enemy aircraft! Enemy aircraft!"). It was a familiar warning, yet neither Uehler, a lawyer from Leipzig, nor other German fighting men in Normandy ever got accustomed to it. It meant approaching death and mutilation.

Lieutenant Uehler whipped out his binoculars and peered into the sky toward the north. Thunderstruck, a chill surged through his body. As far as Uehler could see, there was an endless stream of four-engine aircraft coming from the north—and they were winging directly toward him.

The lieutenant turned to look at those of his Feldgrau who were nearby. His eyes met their dull stares, cold with terror. He presumed his eyes looked the same to them.

Now the skies were filled with the mighty drone of the first wave of Liberators and Flying Fortresses. Soon there was the eerie, whistling sound of hundreds of bombs plummeting through space, then a steady drumfire as they exploded on the terrified Germans like a string of giant firecrackers.

On came the seemingly endless sky armada. The tortured earth shook and trembled from the rat-a-tat-tat of explosives. It was as though a gigantic super-natural force had taken hold of a few miles of Norman countryside and was shaking it in vengeful anger. Entire German systems and their occupants were wiped out. Panzers were crushed, bodies were tossed high into the air, minefields exploded, messengers were blown off motorcycles, and artillery and machine-gun positions vanished.

One of Lieutenant Uehler's 20-millimeter automatic guns, deeply dug in, was hurled 100 feet into the air, then plunged to earth a twisted, blackened chunk of metal. Grenadiers, clinging desperately to the bottoms of foxholes, were driven out of their senses by the torrential rain of bombs. They bled profusely from the mouth, ears, and nose. Many leaped from cover and scrambled around in circles, babbling incoherently. An enormous pall of smoke and dust blanketed the targeted rectangle.

Slowly, almost imperceptibly, the mild breeze shifted, and the immense cloud of smog began to drift over American positions. Soon the arrow-straight road was covered by the pall, and bombardiers at 15,000 feet could not distinguish the red smoke of American artillery-shell markers from the bright flashes of exploding bombs. Now it was the Yanks' turn to be terrified: thousands of "friendly" bombs came screaming down on them.

After two hours, the last bomber droned off into the distance. The carnage had been horrendous on both sides of the road. More than one-third of Bayerlein's Panzer Lehr had been killed; a few thousand were wounded. Hundreds of others had been reduced to moron status, unable to function. Only 11 of the division's 126 tanks were operable.

North of the road, all three divisions of Joe Collins' VII Corps, which were to spearhead the Cobra ground assault, received heavy casualties from the "friendly" bombs. Leland Hobbs' 30th "Old Hickory" Division had been es-pecially devastated: 111 men killed, 490 wounded, and 182 others suffering from combat shock. Raymond Barton's 4th Infantry Division, veterans of D-Day but now filled with a few thousand replacements, and Manton Eddy's 9th

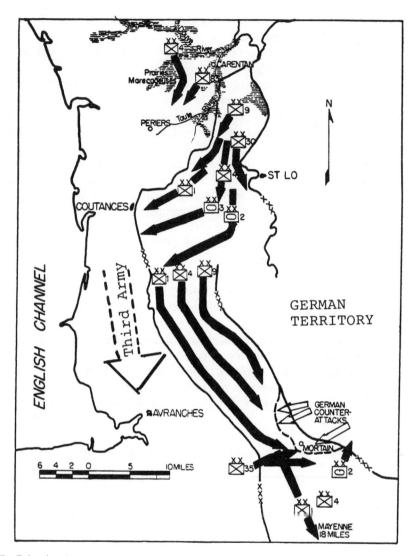

7. Cobra breakout.

Infantry Division, which had helped to capture Cherbourg, had been badly chewed up by the bomb "shorts."

These American assault troops, dazed, demoralized, and many still badly shaken from their ordeal, were rallied by company commanders, lieutenants, and platoon sergeants. They shouldered packs and picked up rifles, BARs (Browning Automatic Rifles), machine guns, mortars, and bazookas. Forming into attack formation, the GIs pushed across the Saint-Lô–Périers road into the pockmarked Rectangle of Death, which stank with the acrid fumes of cordite from exploding bombs and shells.

Joe Collins' corps bogged down, far short of the day's key objectives, the road centers of Marigny and Saint-Gilles, about two miles to the south. Gloom was thick at Allied headquarters. Cobra was to have been the Sunday punch, but it had fizzled. The outcome of the Battle of Normandy was still in doubt.

It had been the longest day of General Fritz Bayerlein's life. At his command post four miles to the rear of his Panzer Lehr Division, he had to stand by helplessly as his formation virtually vanished under a cascade of American bombs and artillery shells. In late evening, a German staff car pulled up and a stern-faced lieutenant colonel, clad in a spotless dress uniform, boots shined to a high gloss, strode into Bayerlein's office in an old chateau.

The visitor said that he had been sent by Field Marshal von Kluge with a direct order: the Saint-Lô–Périers road was to be held at all costs. A pall of silence fell over the room. Bayerlein, a veteran of the North African campaigns, flushed with anger. Finally he spoke in a low tone. "Hold at all costs? May I ask with what?"

The impeccably groomed staff officer replied firmly: "Herr General, I am passing on to you a direct order from Feldmarschall von Kluge. Not a single man is to leave his position along the Saint-Lô–Périers road!"

For long seconds, Fritz Bayerlein glared at the emissary. Then he moved within inches of the man's face and shouted, "You may report to the Feldmarschall, Herr Oberstleutnant, that not a single one of my men left his post. They're all holding their ground! They're all dead! Do you understand? *Dead*!"[2]

That same night a tiny group of American officers huddled around a freshly dug grave in an apple orchard behind Utah Beach for the secret burial of General Lesley McNair, who only recently had succeeded George Patton as leader of the phantom army group across from the Pas de Calais. McNair had been at a forward observation post to view Cobra's air bombardment and had been killed by "shorts."

Reporters were not told that a senior general had been killed in action.

At the urgent behest of Allied deceptionists, Dwight Eisenhower swiftly contacted George Marshall in the Pentagon, and Lieutenant General John L. de Witt was rushed in from Washington to take command of the dummy army group at Dover.

Brutus, a "first violin," through his controller, leaped into action. A wireless message was sent to Hamburg stating that he had just learned that General Lesley McNair, whom he described as commander of the First United States Army Group, had been killed in Normandy. "McNair had gone there to consult with General Montgomery and to inspect the German coastal defenses," Brutus explained. "Here at FUSAG this loss is considered very serious. It is thought that a successor will be appointed immediately to command the FUSAG operation."[3]

Skies over Normandy were clearing early on the morning of July 26 when hordes of American tanks, belching, clanking, and trailing spiraling plumes of dust, plunged into the breach in the German lines and barreled southward. The collective roar of the iron monsters was deafening as it echoed across the Norman landscape.

Seventy-two hours after the Cobra rocket swooshed through the huge gap in the German lines, a cohesive front no longer existed in Normandy. Now there was a wild melee between fleeing bands of dispirited and confused Germans and surging American tank-tipped task forces. Gone were the Wehrmacht's proud symbols of yesteryear—the battle streamers and bugles, the highly polished boots, the stern Prussian discipline, the swagger.

Early on the morning of July 29, Field Marshal von Kluge was on the telephone to General Alfred Jodl at Wolfsschanze. "Herr Jodl," the commander in the West cried, "everything here is *eine Riesensauerei* [one hell of a mess]!"[4]

That afternoon Adolf Hitler finally realized that the Patton–McNair–de Witt army group in southeastern England was a monumental fraud and that no more Channel landings would be made by the Allies. Fortitude had finally worn thin. So, nearly eight weeks after D-Day, Hitler authorized von Kluge to pull divisions from the Fifteenth Army in the Pas de Calais and rush them to Normandy to help stem the American tidal wave. It was too little and too late.

Hitler was furious over the Cobra breakthrough. He ranted to Keitel and Jodl that the Anglo-Americans seemed to anticipate every move the Wehrmacht had made during the war. A traitor or traitors in the German general staff or signal corps was betraying the Third Reich, the fuehrer stormed.

Hitler would remain unaware that a "traitor" was indeed responsible for tipping his hand to the Anglo-Americans—a "traitor" north of London named Ultra.

Early on August 2, Dwight Eisenhower summoned his naval aide, Commander Harry Butcher, into his office. Butcher, the peacetime radio network executive, was greeted by the famous Eisenhower smile. These were heady days at SHAEF. "If Ultra is right, we are to hell-and-gone in Brittany and slicing 'em up in Normandy!" the supreme commander enthused.

Minutes later, Eisenhower received confirmation that a Third Army combat team under Colonel Bruce Clarke had roared into Rennes, 40 miles southwest of Avranches in Brittany, during the night.[5]

When rampaging American spearheads reached Avranches, Omar Bradley sensed a fantastic opportunity to trap two entire German armies, the Seventh and Fifth Panzer—within a matter of days. Outwardly a professional, mild-mannered type, Bradley had chosen a "riverboat gambler" strategy. He was elated over the thought of inflicting on the Wehrmacht in Normandy a disaster on a scale that would surpass the fuehrer's catastrophe at Stalingrad the year before when Field Marshal Friedrich von Paulus' Sixth Army was encircled and surrendered to the Russians.

Bradley instructed George Patton to extend his westward thrust into Brittany and at the same time to send spearheads knifing eastward to get behind SS General Paul Hausser's Seventh Army and General Heinz Eberhard's Fifth Panzer Army. On reaching Le Mans, 100 miles southeast of Avranches, Patton's flying columns were to alter their course and charge northward to Argentan to form the southern jaw of a gigantic trap.[6]

Meanwhile, General Henry D. G. Crerar's Canadian First Army, attacking southward from the Caen region, would advance to Falaise, about ten miles north of Argentan, forming the northern jaw of the trap. Patton's and Crerar's converging forces would then link up, pocketing the bulk of the Seventh and Fifth Panzer armies.

In order to buy the 72 hours Patton would need, General Bradley conceived a masterful deception plan that was given the innocuous label "Tactical Operation B." The scheme was intended to encourage the fuehrer into believing that Patton's goal was to seize Brittany. Tactical Operation B's theme was as ancient as warfare itself: feign that an army is in big trouble while launching an attack.

Colonel David I. Strangeways, commander of R-Force, the deception group at Bernard Montgomery's headquarters, and Colonel William H. Harris, leader of Bradley's Special Plans Branch, in cooperation with the Double-Cross Committee, would stage-manage Tactical Operation B. A phony scenario was developed rapidly for the benefit of Adolf Hitler:

> The American forces in Normandy were hard-pressed for supplies because Cherbourg had been so badly damaged it was not yet operational. So it was crucial for Patton to capture three of the Brittany ports before Eisenhower could even consider heading his forces eastward in the direction of Germany.
>
> However, Patton's two divisions in Brittany, the 4th Armored and 6th Armored, were stalled, short of supplies and needing more infantry and artillery in order to seize the crucial ports.[7]

Armed with this scenario, Double-Cross agents Brutus and Garbo, through their case officers, began flashing bulletins to their German controllers scraps of information that indicated the Americans seriously had overextended themselves and that Eisenhower's main concern was halting Lüttich and providing backup forces for Patton, who was bogged down in Brittany. (Actually, Third Army tank-infantry task forces were running wild in Brittany and hell-bent for Brest, Lorient, and other ports.)

Garbo wirelessed to the Reich: "General Bradley has ordered daring General Patton to clean up his situation by sending adequate infantry and artillery forces into the [Brittany] peninsula immediately to capture the ports Saint-Malo, Brest, Lorient, and Saint-Nazaire in order to bring in badly needed supplies." Hardly had Garbo's controller in Germany received this crucial intelligence than reinforcements for the presumably stalled Patton rolled through Avranches and on into Brittany—but they numbered only 1,300 men. They were members of the

U.S. 23rd Headquarters Special Troops, who were trained and equipped for large deception operations that would suggest the rapid movement of several divisions. Fake unit numerals of nonexistent divisions were painted on the vehicles of the 23rd Headquarters Special Troops, and the soldiers wore phony shoulder patches—ploys to fool at least two German stay-behind spies known to be operating wireless sets in Avranches and in Saint-Malo.

After reaching Brittany, the Special Troops split into companies, each one heading toward a port where they would "reinforce" American armored units that were supposed to be stalled in those locales. Through ceaseless radio chatter between nonexistent units, one company, simulating an entire armored division, rushed toward Saint-Nazaire; another company impersonated an armored division bound for Saint-Malo; while a third company made wireless noises like an infantry division bound for Brest, at the tip of Brittany.

This blizzard of wireless messages in the dummy American divisions was intended to be picked up by German electronic listening posts and coerce Adolf Hitler into believing that Patton was bogged down in Brittany. Meanwhile, Patton's genuine spearheads were galloping eastward, hell-bent for Le Mans and Alençon.

Near midnight on August 11, Adolf Hitler finally recognized that his two armies in Normandy were in danger of being encircled by American, Canadian, and British troops. So he gave Field Marshal von Kluge permission to withdraw eastward toward the natural defensive barrier of the Seine River.

But it was too late. Tactical Operation B had provided Omar Bradley with the 72 hours he needed, and on August 13, Patton's spearheads and Crerar's Canadians, converging from the south and the north, had virtually linked up near Falaise, 70 miles east of Avranches. Guenther von Kluge's worst nightmare became a reality—his Seventh and Fifth Panzer armies were caught in a huge Allied trap.

It was a monstrous German debacle. Nearly all of the Seventh and Fifth Panzer armies were bagged or destroyed. Some 10,000 Feldgrau had been killed in the pocket, perhaps 25,000 wounded and 50,000 captured. A few German units, mainly elite SS troops, had escaped before the trap snapped shut. One bedraggled Felgrau, his head swathed in a dirty, blood-soaked bandage, looked wearily at an American military policeman at the gate of an improvised POW enclosure and seemed to be speaking for the Wehrmacht in Normandy: "*Alles kaputt! Alles kaputt!*"

The Battle of Normandy was over.

Adolf Hitler and his high command had been outwitted and outgeneraled. Bodyguard, the greatest hoax that mankind has known, passed into history.

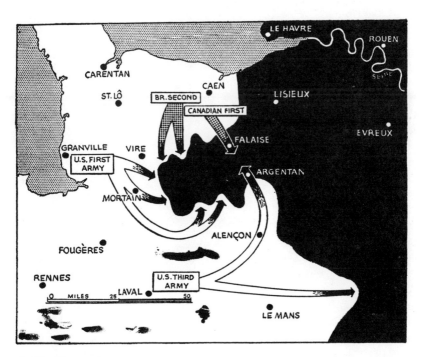

8. The Normandy trap.

Notes

CHAPTER 1

1. In that era, press and newsreel photographers were bound by an unwritten code not to take pictures of President Franklin Roosevelt when he was being physically assisted.

2. Prime Minister Winston Churchill suggested the code name Overlord for "this majestic operation."

3. Viscount Alanbrooke, *Diaries* (London: Collins, 1957–59), vol. 2, p. 74.

4. Forrest C. Pogue, *George C. Marshall* (New York: Viking, 1963), vol. 3, p. 297.

5. Ibid., p. 305.

6. During the World War II Battle of the Bulge in December 1944, Otto Skorzeny led a force of English-speaking German soldiers wearing American uniforms. They infiltrated American lines and created a great amount of confusion and concern.

7. Alanbrooke, vol. 2, p. 286.

8. Iran announced its neutrality when World War II broke out. Since Iran's Trans-Iranian Railway was needed to send arms and supplies to Russia, England and the Soviet Union sent troops to invade and jointly occupy Iran. Later, American soldiers helped in the occupation.

9. Stanley Lovell, who was in charge of research and development for the OSS during World War II, was the primary source of C–12's activities.

CHAPTER 2

1. Winston S. Churchill, *The Second World War* (Boston: Houghton Mifflin, 1948–54), vol. 3, p. 331.

2. Lord Moran, *The Diaries of Lord Moran* (Boston: Houghton Mifflin, 1966), p. 148.

3. Fleet Admiral William D. Leahy, *I Was There* (New York: McGraw-Hill, 1950), p. 205.

4. Lord Moran, p. 141.

5. Ibid., p. 144.

6. U.S. Secretary of State Cordell Hull was ill and could not attend the Teheran conference. Harry Hopkins was acting informally in his place.

7. Leahy, p. 207.

8. Ibid., p. 208.

9. Jael was the original code name for the Bodyguard plan.

10. According to ancient Greek legends, the Trojan horse was a huge wooden animal loaded with Spartan soldiers. The Trojans (residents of the city of Troy) were told the horse was gift for the goddess Athena. When the wooden animal was brought inside the the massive walls of Troy, the Spartan soldiers got out at night and opened the gates. The Spartans stormed into Troy and conquered it, ending a ten-year war.

11. Sir Ronald Wingate, *Not in the Limelight* (London: Hutchinson, 1959), p. 185.

12. Leahy, p. 202.

13. Churchill, vol. 5, p. 338.

14. Ibid., p. 339.

15. Ibid., p. 345.

16. Dwight D. Eisenhower, *Crusade in Europe* (New York: Doubleday, 1948), p. 206.

17. Ibid., p. 207.

18. Alanbrooke, vol. 2, p. 106.

CHAPTER 3

1. Brigadefuehrer SS is equivalent to a United States one-star general.

2. On the night of May 10, 1941, Rudolf Hess, the number-three man behind Adolf Hitler and Hermann Goering, bailed out of a Luftwaffe fighter plane over Scotland and told the British that he had come as a self-appointed peace emissary to ''save humanity.''

3. Walther Schellenberg, *The Schellenberg Memoirs* (New York: Harper, 1956), p. 137.

4. It never would be known what evidence Admiral Canaris had about Heinrich Himmler.

5. Mata Hari (born Gertud Zelle in the Netherlands) was an exotic dancer who was executed by the French as a German spy in 1917.

CHAPTER 4

1. Reinhard Gehlen, *The Service* (New York: World, 1972), pp. 128–29.

2. Allen Walsh Dulles was the brother of J. Foster Dulles, who served as U.S. Secretary of State in the Dwight Eisenhower administration. After the war, Allen Dulles became the first director of the Central Intelligence Agency (CIA), the successor to the OSS.

3. Allen W. Dulles, *Secret Surrender* (New York: Harper & Row, 1966), p. 179.

4. After the war, Allen Dulles described Fritz Kolbe as ''an intelligence officer's dream, undoubtedly one of the best [spies] any intelligence service ever had.'' In early 1945, Kolbe escaped to Switzerland, one step ahead of the Gestapo.

5. Kim Philby, *My Secret War* (New York: Grove, 1968), p. 103.

6. Ibid., p. 104.

7. Schellenberg, p. 371.

8. Felix Kersten, *The Kersten Memoirs* (New York: Macmillan, 1957), p. 194.

9. Anthony Cave Brown interview with Allen Dulles, 1974.

10. Elysea Bazna was "discharged" as the British ambassador's valet in April 1944, seven weeks before D-Day in Normandy. He thought he was a rich man, as the Germans had paid him the equivalent of $1 million or 300,000 British pounds. However, the money was counterfeit, and Bazna died broke years later.

11. Gilles Perrault, *The Secret of D-Day* (Boston: Little, Brown, 1965), p. 171.

12. Allen W. Dulles, *Germany's Underground* (New York: Macmillan, 1947), p. 142.

13. Ibid., p. 145.

CHAPTER 5

1. Adrienne's last name was thought to be Molnar.

2. Apparently the relationship between Adrienne and Wilhelm Hamburger did not endure.

3. Generaloberst was equivalent in rank to a United States four-star officer.

4. Ladislas Farago, *The Game of the Foxes* (New York: McKay, 1971), p. 603.

5. Ibid.

6. Digging a tunnel under the Strait of Dover had long been considered, but both France and England secretly feared that the excavation might be used by invading armies.

CHAPTER 6

1. Field Marshal Gerd von Rundstedt held a post roughly similar to that of General Dwight D. Eisenhower, but the German had only a fraction of the Allied leader's authority.

2. Paul Carell, *Invasion: They're Coming!* (Boston: Little, Brown, 1964), p. 49.

3. Perrault, p. 178.

4. Alfred Knox did not live to see the full exploitation of Ultra. He died at the age of 60 in 1943.

5. An aide to Rear Admiral John Godfrey was Lieutenant Commander Ian Fleming, who would win postwar fame as the novelist creating James Bond, the British supersleuth.

6. Ewen Montagu, *Beyond Top Secret Ultra* (New York: Coward, McCann & Geoghegan, 1978), p. 46.

7. Ibid., p. 48.

8. Farago, p. 595.

9. Ibid., p. 596.

CHAPTER 7

1. In 1947, the Spanish *Cortes* (National Congress) named Francisco Franco chief of state for life with the right to appoint his successor when he retired.

2. Lieutenant Colonel Klaus von Stauffenberg actually planted the bomb.He was identified as a Schwarze Kapelle conspirator.

3. After the war, Otto John became head of the West German equivalent of the Federal Bureau of Investigation or Britain's Scotland Yard. John defected to the Soviet Union in 1953.

4. Bruce Page, *The Philby Conspiracy* (New York: Doubleday, 1968), p. 159.

5. After the war, Kim Philby continued to pass British secrets to the Russians. In

1961, when he was about to be arrested as a Soviet spy, he fled to Moscow and made his home there.

6. Nicholas Rostov ("Ernst") moved his residence to Moscow.

7. Erik von Auenrode (Karsthoff) reportedly was killed by Russian troops in Austria in 1945.

8. Gertrude "Trudy" Körner was killed in a bombing raid on Berlin in early 1945.

9. Leonard Mosley, *The Druid* (New York: Atheneum, 1981), pp. 52–53.

CHAPTER 8

1. Alanbrooke, vol. 1, pp. 527–28.

2. Dwight Eisenhower diary, Eisenhower Library, Abilene, Kansas, p. 1063.

3. British Major General Frederick Morgan, a 49-year-old artillery and armored officer, had been developing a plan for the cross-Channel attack since July 1943. His title was Chief of Staff Supreme Allied Command (designate), shortened to COSSAC. That group was dissolved when SHAEF was established in January 1944.

4. Lieutenant Colonel William H. Baumer eventually would retire as a two-star general.

5. Charles Cruickshank, *Deception* (New York: Oxford University Press, 1979), p. 115.

6. Ibid., p. 119.

7. John R. Deane, *The Strange Alliance* (New York: Viking, 1947), p. 148.

8. Subsequent events would lend credence to the suggestion that the Soviets merely signed the Bodyguard agreement with the intention of doing little or nothing toward being involved in assigned deceptions.

CHAPTER 9

1. The 1940 Hollywood movie *The Fighting 69th* starred James Cagney and Pat O'Brien. George Brent played the role of William Donovan.

2. Unvouchered funds is a certain amount of money allowed by Congress to be spent by a president at his discretion without any accountability.

3. Charles Lindbergh, *Wartime Journals* (New York: Harcourt, Brace, Jovanovich, 1970), p. 573.

4. Joseph Goebbels' remark was quoted in Drew Pearson's column, December 3, 1941.

5. Adolf A. Berle, *Navigating the Rapids* (New York: Harcourt, Brace, Jovanovich, 1973), p. 271.

6. Henry H. Arnold, *Global Mission* (New York: Harper, 1979), p. 206.

7. OSS veterans who later played important roles in the U.S. government included CIA Directors William Casey, Allen Dulles, Richard Helms, and William Colby; Supreme Court Justices Lewis Powell and Arthur Goldberg (who also served as secretary of labor and ambassador to the United Nations); Treasury Secretary C. Douglas Dillon; and presidential advisors Walt Rostow, Carl Kaysen, Douglas Cater, Clark McGregor, and Arthur Schlesinger, Jr.

8. Donald Downes, *The Scarlet Thread* (London: Verschoyle, 1953), pp. 87–97.

9. Fred Israel, *The War Diary of Breckenridge Long* (Lincoln: University of Nebraska Press, 1966), p. 234.

10. Stewart Alsop and Thomas Braden, *Sub Rosa* (New York: Harcourt, Brace and World, 1964), p. 20.

11. Author interview with Robert Parrish.

12. Ibid.

13. Ibid.

14. Dunlap, p. 394.

15. Ibid., p. 421.

16. John "Pappy" Ford continued to direct blockbuster Hollywood movies after World War II.

17. W. Averell Harriman, *Special Envoy to Churchill and Stalin* (New York: Random House, 1975), p. 291.

18. Richard Dunlap, *America's Master Spy* (New York: Rand-McNally, 1982), p. 430.

19. Charles E. Bohlen, *Witness to History* (New York: Norton, 1973), p. 155.

20. Harry Hopkins was one of the most powerful American figures during the World War II era. He died a year after peace came at the age of 56.

CHAPTER 10

1. In the early 1980s, the author visited Erwin Rommel's hometown of Herrlingen. Fame is fleeting. No one could be found who recalled Germany's famed field marshal, much less the house in which he had lived.

2. Twenty-five years later, Manfred Rommel was elected mayor of the large city of Stuttgart.

3. John Keegan, ed., *Who Was Who in World War II* (London: Bison, 1978), p. 172.

4. After World War II, Joachim von Ribbentrop vanished, but was captured, put on trial at Nuremberg, and hanged.

5. Tommy Harris was killed in an automobile accident in January 1964.

6. Elysea Bazna, *I Was Cicero* (New York: Harper & Row, 1962), p. 109.

7. In August 1944, Walther Schellenberg personally arrested his "good friend" Wilhelm Canaris on treason charges. On April 9, 1945, a month before the war's end in Europe, the former Abwehr chief was hanged by the SD.

CHAPTER 11

1. Henry Maitland "Jumbo" Wilson was later promoted to field marshal and in November 1944 he was assigned to Washington, D.C., in charge of the British Joint Staff Mission.

2. The word *Balkan* means "mountain" in Turkish.

3. Anthony C. Brown, *Bodyguard of Lies* (New York: Harper & Row, 1975), p. 495.

4. Acting under the personal orders of Adolf Hitler, SS Colonel Otto Skorzeny and a small team kidnapped Admiral Miklós Horthy after the regent announced Hungary was withdrawing from the war in October 1944. Horthy was taken to Germany, where he was held until the Americans freed him seven months later.

5. Miklós Kallay, *Hungarian Premier* (New York: Columbia University Press, 1954), p. 179.

6. Ibid., pp. 370–71.

7. Ibid., pp. 376–77.

8. Sterling Hayden, *Wanderer* (New York: Knopf, 1963), p. 313.

9. After World War II, Josip Broz (Tito) seized power in Yugoslavia, set up a Communist dictatorship, charged Chetnik leader Draza Mihailovich with crimes against the state, and executed him after a ''trial.''

10. A. Cretzianu, *The Lost Opportunity* (London: Cape, 1957), p. 96.

11. Hungarian Premier Miklós Kallay was arrested in Budapest by SS troops in September 1944. He was put in the Mauthausen concentration camp, survived the war, and died in exile.

CHAPTER 12

1. *Signal* (German army magazine), March 1944.

2. During his final days, Adolf Hitler named Joseph Goebbels to succeed him as German head of state. Goebbels witnessed Hitler's marriage to his mistress, Eva Braun, in a Berlin bunker just before the fuehrer committed suicide in late April 1945. Goebbels shot himself and his wife on May 1, 1945, after poisoning their six children.

3. Omar Bradley, *A Soldier's Story* (New York: Henry Holt, 1951), p. 148.

4. Author's personal recollections.

5. Arthur Bryant, *The Turn of the Tide* (New York: Doubleday, 1957), p. 205.

6. Alanbrooke, p. 397.

7. Richard Collier, *Ten Thousand Eyes* (New York: Dutton, 1958), pp. 138–40.

8. René Duchez had to go underground. He joined the *Maquis* (French resistance fighters) and survived the war. His wife was arrested by the Gestapo, was sent to the Mauthausen concentration camp, and rejoined René after the hostilities concluded in Europe.

CHAPTER 13

1. Mathilde Carré, *I Was the Cat* (London: Four Square Books, 1961), pp. 107–9.

2. Hugo Bleicher, *Colonel Henri's Story* (London: Kimber, 1954), pp. 58–59.

3. Ibid.

4. During the war, Lily Sergeyev told friends that she had an incurable illness and would live for only a year. Twenty years later, in the mid–1960s, she was still hale and hearty.

5. Dusko Popov, *Spy-Counterspy* (New York: Grosset & Dunlap, 1974), p. 66.

6. Ibid., p. 69.

7. John Masterman, who headed the Double-Cross Committee, said long after the war: ''Connoisseurs of double-cross have always regarded the Garbo case as the most highly developed example of their art.''

8. Juan Pujol (with Nigel West), *Operation Garbo* (New York: Random House, 1985), p. 77.

9. Ibid., p. 79.

10. J. C. Masterman, *The Double-Cross System* (New Haven: Yale University Press, 1972), p. 114.

CHAPTER 14

1. Sir Roger Fleetwood Hesketh became a prominent Conservative member of Parliament after the war.

2. Two decades after World War II, Walter Koehler claimed he really had been a triple agent and had badly fooled J. Edgar Hoover. There was no independent confirmation.

3. J. Edgar Hoover, "The Spy Who Double-Crossed Hitler," *American Legion*, May 1946.

4. Robert Allen, *Lucky Forward* (New York: Vanguard, 1947), p. 197.

5. James Leasor, *Nimrod* (Boston: Houghton Mifflin, 1981), p. 23.

6. Sefton Delmer, *The Counterfeit Spy* (New York: Harper & Row, 1971), p. 156.

7. Masterman, pp. 152–54.

8. Johann Jebsen was thought to have been executed in a German concentration camp in April 1945.

CHAPTER 15

1. Delmer, pp. 117–19.

2. Ibid.

3. Operation Skye got its code name from the Scottish island of Skye.

4. Pujol, p. 120.

5. Ibid., p. 126.

6. Delmer, p. 178.

CHAPTER 16

1. Farago, p. 276.

2. When "Vice Air Marshal" Thornton returned to England, the London Controlling Section requested that he keep his temporary rank until Graffham had run its course. The request was refused, and Thornton reverted to air commodore.

3. Cruickshank, p. 135.

4. David L. Gordon and R. J. Dangerfield, *The Hidden Weapon* (New York: Harper, 1947).

5. U.S. Secretary of State Cordell Hull was awarded the Nobel Peace Prize in 1945.

6. R. Harris Smith, *OSS* (Berkeley: University of California Press, 1972), p. 25.

7. Stanton Griffis, *Lying in State* (New York: Doubleday, 1957), p. 203.

8. After World War II, Stanton Griffis was appointed successively U.S. ambassador to Poland, Egypt, Argentina, and Spain.

9. When the Central Intelligence Agency (CIA) Board of National Estimates was established in 1950, Calvin Hoover was one of its members.

10. Calvin Hoover, *Memoirs of Capitalism, Communism, and Nazism* (Durham: Duke University Press, 1965), p. 139.

CHAPTER 17

1. The total population of Greater London, which included suburbs, was about 10 million people in 1944.

2. General George Marshall reportedly threw cold water on Dwight Eisenhower's marital plans, pointing out that divorcing Mamie could skuttle his postwar career.

3. Kathleen McCarthy-Morrogh "Kay" Summersby remained as General Eisenhower's aide until July 1945, when he was called to the United States to embark on a career that took him to the White House. Later Kay Summersby also moved to the United States.

4. Frederick Morgan, *Overture to Overlord* (London: Hodder & Stoughton, 1950), p. 214.

5. Rogerio Menezes was condemned to death by the British. His mother made tearful pleas to King George VI and Winston Churchill, and he was eventually pardoned.

6. Perrault, p. 95.

CHAPTER 18

1. In the fall of 1944, Air Marshal Trafford Leigh-Mallory and his wife were killed in an airplane crash while on the way to India where he was to begin a new assignment.

2. Bradley, p. 217.

3. Brown, p. 459.

4. Edward Ellsberg, *The Far Shore* (New York: Dodd, Mead, 1960), p. 155.

5. Bradley, p. 224.

6. Dwight Eisenhower letter to George Marshall, dated May 21, 1944, Eisenhower Library, Abilene, Kansas.

7. During the weeks before D-Day and during the invasion, American PT boats and German E-boats often had high-speed running gun battles in the Channel.

8. On D-Day, of some 40 "swimming" Sherman tanks that were launched offshore, about 35 of them sank.

9. Author was below on a troop transport in the Tiger convoy, but knew nothing of the disaster until many years after the war. The Tiger dress rehearsal continued as planned.

10. The Tiger disaster was kept a strict secret. Hundreds of those killed were secretly buried on a hill near the site of the E-boat attacks.

11. Dwight Eisenhower letter to Brehon Somervell, Eisenhower Library, Abilene, Kansas.

CHAPTER 19

1. "Pierre Moreau" and his wife remained in England until the Allies liberated Paris in August 1944. Then he resumed his job with the French railway system and eventually retired after 40 years of service.

2. Author interview with U.S. Eighth Air Force veteran Bobby Taylor.

3. Ray and Winston Guest were said to be distant cousins of Winston Churchill.

4. John Duncan Bulkeley remained on active duty until 1989, when he retired as a three-star admiral. He is thought to be the most highly decorated American fighting man in history.

5. John Bevan, the LCS chief, would never admit that agents were deliberately sacrificed on behalf of Bodyguard. However, he once said: "The higher the prize, the higher the cost."

6. Author interview with Lieutenant General James M. Gavin (Ret.), 1988.

7. After the war, Hermann Goering told Allied interrogators that General Hans Cramer had arrived back in Germany with a "defeatist attitude" after seeing the enormous Allied buildup in southern England.

8. Cruickshank, p. 184.

CHAPTER 20

1. Alexander Patch was soon promoted to lieutenant general.

2. Major Alexander M. Patch, Jr., the general's son, was killed in Normandy in July 1944.

3. Reader's Digest, *Secrets and Spies* (Pleasantville, N.Y.: Reader's Digest Association, 1964), p. 352.

4. When Lieutenant Clifton James returned to his regular job in the Royal Army Pay Corps, colleagues speculated that he had been off on a five-week drunk.

CHAPTER 21

1. Author interview with Professor Reginald V. Jones of Aberdeen, Scotland.

2. British Major John D. Frost gained world fame 15 years after the war as the commander of the doomed Red Beret unit that held the Arnhem bridge until overrun by panzers depicted in the Hollywood movie *A Bridge Too Far*.

3. Alfred Price, *Instruments of Darkness* (London: Kimber, 1967), p. 204.

4. The massive RAF raid on July 23, 1943, destroyed three-fourths of Hamburg, which was not rebuilt until after World War II.

5. Price, p. 205.

6. Years later, Dwight Eisenhower said that his toughest decision of the war was giving the green light for the American airborne assault behind Utah Beach to continue as planned.

CHAPTER 22

1. Eisenhower, p. 249.

2. Perrault, p. 179.

3. A Wren was a woman auxiliary, somewhat akin to American WAVES (navy) or WACS (army).

4. J. M. Stagg, *Forecast for Overload* (New York: Norton, 1972), p. 112.

5. Dan Holt, director of the Dwight David Eisenhower Library at Abilene, Kansas, told the author that his facility had on file at least 56 different versions of General Eisenhower's precise words when he gave the "Go" order.

6. The precise H-Hour varied at the five Neptune beaches, depending upon the tide.

CHAPTER 23

1. Sergeant Karl Kaupert received numerous medals and a battlefield commission.

2. Author interview with four-star General J. Lawton "Lightning Joe" Collins, 1984. A few years after World War II, Collins was appointed U.S. Army chief of staff.

3. Alánbrooke, vol. 2, p. 206.

4. General Charles de Gaulle became French president after Paris was liberated in

August 1944, and he served in that post for many years. De Gaulle would never forgive the United States and Great Britain for their humiliation of him prior to D-Day.

5. Adolf Hitler had an exhaustive investigation conducted into why so many of his generals were absent from their posts when the Allies invaded. The fuehrer suspected one or more spies in the headquarters of his Seventh Army in Normandy.

6. Author interview with Vice Admiral John D. Bulkeley (1992).

CHAPTER 24

1. A "stick" is an arbitrary number of paratroopers in one airplane.

2. James M. Gavin retired from the army as a lieutenant general in the 1950s, and a few years later he was appointed ambassador to France by President John F. Kennedy.

3. Cornelius Ryan, *The Longest Day* (New York: Simon & Schuster, 1959), p. 121.

4. Carell, p. 30.

5. Leasor, p. 184.

6. After the war, General Bodo Zimmerman told Allied interrogators that Adolf Hitler had long been aware that Field Marshal Gerd von Rundstedt privately referred to the fuehrer as "that Bohemian Corporal."

CHAPTER 25

1. Author interview with Robert Arras.

2. Martin W. Bowman, *Castles in the Air* (Wellingborough, England: Patrick Stephens, 1984), p. 148.

3. Carell, p. 141.

4. Leasor, p. 188.

5. Ibid.

6. *New York Times*, June 7, 1944.

7. *Times of London*, June 7, 1944.

8. Ibid.

9. Brown, p. 748.

10. *Washington Star*, June 8, 1944.

CHAPTER 26

1. *St. Louis Post-Dispatch*, June 8, 1944.

2. *Chicago Tribune*, June 8, 1944.

3. *New York Times*, June 9, 1944.

4. Ibid.

5. Chester Wilmot, *The Struggle for Europe* (London: Collins, 1952), pp. 298–99.

6. Mosley, p. 210.

7. Delmer, p. 16.

8. Ibid., p. 18.

9. Lieutenant General Bodo Zimmerman, von Rundstedt's operations officer at OB West, after the war wrote about von Rundstedt's and Erwin Rommel's feelings on receiving Hitler's order.

10. Incredibly, MI–5 case officers working closely with Garbo (Juan Pujol) for more

than two years never discovered his real identity until May 1984 when he suddenly emerged from self-imposed obscurity abroad to attend a private reception at the Special Forces Club in London to observe the 40th anniversary of D-Day.

11. *New York Herald Tribune*, June 15, 1944.

CHAPTER 27

1. Erwin Rommel, *The Rommel Papers*, ed. B. H. Liddell Hart (New York: Harcourt, 1953), p. 495.

2. Walter Bargatzky, "Personal Recollections of the 20th of July 1944," dated October 20, 1945, Hoover Institution, Stanford, California.

3. Adolf Hitler was said to have been a wallpaper hanger in his younger days.

4. General George Patton was independently wealthy, and most of his uniforms were custom-made. He was said to have given his army salary to charities.

5. Delmer, p. 235.

6. Field Marshal Erwin Rommel survived his serious wounds, but his role with the Schwarze Kapelle was uncovered. On October 13, 1944, two OKW generals arrived at his home in Herrlingen and gave him two choices: to stand trial for treason or commit suicide with the poison they had brought with them. In order to protect his wife, Lucie-Maria, and his young son, Manfred, Rommel took the poison and was given a state funeral in nearby Ulm.

7. Field Marshal Hans Guenther von Kluge was implicated in the Schwarze Kapelle conspiracy, and on August 18, 1944, he bit into a phial of poison and was dead in moments.

CHAPTER 28

1. Churchill, vol. 5, p. 147.

2. Carell, p. 206.

3. Delmer, p. 245.

4. Carell, p. 208.

5. Colonel Bruce Clarke rose to four-star rank after the war.

6. Omar Nelson Bradley was promoted to five-star rank after the war and became chairman of the U.S. Joint Chiefs of Staff.

7. "The Deceptive Practices of 23rd Headquarters Special Troops during World War II," Study, Aberdeen Proving Ground, Maryland.

Bibliography

BOOKS

Alanbrooke, Viscount. *Diaries*. London: Collins, 1957–59.

Allen, Robert. *Lucky Forward*. New York: Vanguard, 1947.

Alsop, Stewart, and Thomas Braden. *Sub Rosa*. New York: Harcourt, Brace and World, 1964.

Andersen, Hartvig. *The Dark City*. New York: Rinehart, 1954.

Arnold, Henry H. *Global Mission*. New York: Harper, 1949.

Barkus, Geoffrey. *The Camouflage Story*. London: Cassell, 1952.

Bauer, Eddy. *Encyclopedia of World War II*. New York: Cavendish, 1970.

Bazna, Elyesa. *I Was Cicero*. New York: Harper & Row, 1962.

Beesly, Patrick. *Very Special Admiral*. London: Hamish Hamilton, 1980.

Berle, Adolph A. *Navigating the Rapids*. New York: Harcourt, Brace, Jovanovich, 1973.

Bleicher, Hugo. *Colonel Henri's Story*. London: Kimber, 1954.

Bohlen, Charles E. *Witness to History*. New York: Norton, 1973.

Bowman, Martin W. *Castles in the Air*. Wellingborough, England: Patrick Stephens, 1984.

Bradley, Omar. *A Soldier's Story*. New York: Henry Holt, 1951.

Brown, Anthony C. *Bodyguard of Lies*. New York: Harper & Row, 1975.

Bryant, Arthur. *The Turn of the Tide*. New York: Doubleday, 1957.

Bulloch, John. *M.I.5*. London: Barker, 1963.

Butcher, Harry. *My Three Years with Eisenhower*. New York: Simon & Schuster, 1946.

Carell, Paul. *Invasion: They're Coming!* Boston: Little, Brown, 1964.

Carré, Mathilde. *I Was the Cat*. London: Four Square Books, 1961.

Churchill, Winston S. *The Second World War*. 5 vols. Boston: Houghton Mifflin, 1948–53.

Collier, Richard. *Ten Thousand Eyes*. New York: Dutton, 1958.

Colvin, Ian. *Master Spy*. New York: McGraw-Hill, 1951.

Cookridge, E. H. (pseud.). *Inside S.O.E*. London: Barker, 1966.

Cretzianu, A. *The Lost Opportunity*. London: Cape, 1957.

Cruickshank, Charles. *Deception*. New York: Oxford University Press, 1979.

Deacon, Richard. *History of the British Secret Service*. London: Muller, 1969.

Deane, John R. *The Strange Alliance*. New York: Viking, 1947.

De Guingand, Sir Francis W. *Operation Victory*. New York: Scribners, 1947.

Delmer, Sefton. *Black Boomerang*. New York: Viking, 1962.

————. *The Counterfeit Spy*. New York: Harper & Row, 1971.

Downes, Donald. *The Scarlet Thread*. London: Verschoyle, 1953.

Dulles, Allen W. *Germany's Underground*. New York: Macmillan, 1947.

————. *The Craft of Intelligence*. New York: Harper & Row, 1963.

————. *The Secret Surrender*. New York: Harper & Row, 1966.

Dunlap, Richard. *America's Master Spy*. New York: Rand-McNally, 1982.

Eisenhower, Dwight D. *Crusade in Europe*. New York: Doubleday, 1948.

Farago, Ladislas. *The Game of the Foxes*. New York: McKay, 1971.

Ferguson, Bernard. *The Watery Maze*. New York: Holt, Rinehart & Winston, 1961.

Foot, M.R.D. *SOE in France*. London: HMS Office, 1966.

Ganier-Raymond, Philippe. *The Tangled Web*. New York: Pantheon, 1968.

Gehlen, Reinhard. *The Service*. New York: World, 1972.

Gisevius, Hans B. *To the Bitter End*. Boston: Riverside Press, 1947.

Goldston, Robert. *Sinister Touches*. New York: Dial Press, 1982.

Gordon, David L., and R. J. Dangerfield. *The Hidden Weapon*. New York: Harper, 1947.

Griffis, Stanton. *Lying in State*. New York: Doubleday, 1957.

Harriman, W. Averell. *Special Envoy to Churchill and Stalin*. New York: Random House, 1975.

Hayden, Sterling. *Wanderer*. New York: Knopf, 1963.

Hohne, Heinz. *Canaris*. Garden City, N.Y.: Doubleday, 1979.

Hoover, Calvin. *Memoirs of Capitalism, Communism, and Nazism*. Durham: Duke University Press, 1965.

Hull, Cordell. *Memoirs*. New York: Macmillan, 1948.

Hyde, H. M. *Room 3603*. New York: Farrar, Straus, 1952.

Infield, Glenn B. *Skorzeny*. New York: St. Martin's Press, 1981.

Ingersoll, Ralph McAllister. *Top Secret*. New York: Harcourt Brace, 1946.

Irving, David. *The Mare's Nest*. London: Kimber, 1964.

Israel, Fred. *The War Diary of Breckenridge Long*. Lincoln: University of Nebraska Press, 1966.

John, Otto. *Twice through the Lines*. New York: Harper & Row, 1973.

Jones, Reginald V. *The Wizard War*. New York: Coward, McCann & Geoghegan, 1978.

Kallay, Miklós. *Hungarian Premier*. New York: Columbia University Press, 1954.

Keegan, John, ed. *Who Was Who in World War II*. London: Bison, 1978.

Kersten, Felix. *The Kersten Memoirs*. New York: Macmillan, 1957.

Leahy, W. *I Was There*. New York: McGraw-Hill, 1950.

Leasor, James. *Nimrod*. Boston: Houghton Mifflin, 1981.

Leverkuehn, Paul. *German Military Intelligence*. New York: Praeger, 1954.

Lewin, Ronald. *Ultra Goes to War*. New York: McGraw-Hill, 1978.

Lindbergh, Charles. *Wartime Journals*. New York: Harcourt, Brace, Jovanovich, 1970.

Lovell, Stanley. *Of Spies and Stratagems*. Englewood Cliffs, N.J.: Prentice-Hall, 1963.

Maiskii, Ivan. *Memoirs of a Soviet Ambassador*. New York: Scribners, 1968.

Masterman, J. C. *The Double-Cross System*. New Haven: Yale University Press, 1972.

Montagu, Ewen. *Beyond Top Secret Ultra*. New York: Coward, McCann & Geoghegan, 1978.

Moran, Lord. *Churchill: Taken from the Diaries of Lord Moran*. Boston: Houghton Mifflin, 1966.

Morgan, Frederick. *Overture to Overlord*. London: Hodder & Stoughton, 1950.

Morgan, William. *The OSS and I*. New York: Norton, 1957.

Mosley, Leonard. *The Druid*. New York: Atheneum, 1981.

Moyzisch, L. C. *Operation Cicero*. New York: Coward-McCann, 1950.

Page, Bruce. *The Philby Conspiracy*. New York: Doubleday, 1969.

Papen, Franz von. *Memoirs*. New York: Dutton, 1952.

Payne, Robert. *The Life and Death of Adolf Hitler*. New York: Praeger, 1973.

Perrault, Gilles. *The Red Orchestra*. New York: Simon & Schuster, 1969.

———. *The Secret of D-Day*. Boston: Little, Brown, 1965.

Philby, Kim. *My Secret War*. New York: Grove, 1968.

Pogue, Forrest C. *George C. Marshall*. New York: Viking, 1963.

Popov, Dusko. *Spy-Counterspy*. New York: Grosset & Dunlap, 1974.

Price, Alfred. *Instruments of Darkness*. London: Kimber, 1967.

Pujol, Juan (with Nigel West). *Operation Garbo*. New York: Random House, 1985.

Reader's Digest. *Secrets and Spies*. Pleasantville, N.Y.: Reader's Digest Association, 1964.

Reit, Seymour. *Masquerade*. New York: Hawthorne, 1978.

Rommel, Erwin. *The Rommel Papers*. Edited by B. H. Liddell Hart. New York: Harcourt, 1953.

Roosevelt, Elliott. *As He Saw It*. New York: Duell, Sloane & Pearce, 1946.

Ruge, Friederich. *Rommel in Normandy*. Novato, Calif.: Presidio, 1979.

Ryan, Cornelius. *The Longest Day*. New York: Simon & Schuster, 1959.

Schellenberg, Walther. *The Schellenberg Memoirs*. New York: Harper, 1956.

Schlabrendorff, Fabian von. *The Secret War against Hitler*. New York: Pitman, 1965.

Schramm, Percy. *Hitler: The Man and the Military Leader*. Chicago: Watts, 1971.

Schulze-Gaevernitz, Gero von. *They Almost Killed Hitler*. New York: Macmillan, 1947.

Shirer, William. *The Rise and Fall of the Third Reich*. New York: Simon & Schuster, 1960.

Smith, R. Harris. *OSS*. Berkeley: University of California Press, 1972.

Speer, Albert. *Inside the Third Reich*. New York: Macmillan, 1962.

Speidel, Hans. *Invasion—1944*. Chicago: Regnery, 1950.

Stagg, J. M. *Forecast for Overlord*. New York: Norton, 1972.

Stanford, Alfred Boller. *Force Mulberry*. New York: Morrow, 1951.

Stilwell, Joseph. *The Stilwell Papers*. New York: W. Sloane, 1948.

Strong, Kenneth W. D. *Intelligence at the Top*. New York: Doubleday, 1969.

Summersby, Kay. *Eisenhower Was My Boss*. New York: Prentice-Hall, 1948.

Turner, John F. *Invasion '44*. New York: Putnam, 1959.

Warlimont, Walter. *Inside Hitler's Headquarters*. New York: Praeger, 1966.

Wilmot, Chester. *The Struggle for Europe*. London: Collins, 1952.

Wingate, Sir Ronald. *Not in the Limelight*. London: Hutchinson, 1959.

Winterbotham, Frederick W. *The Ultra Secret*. New York: Harper & Row, 1974.

Zuckerman, Solly. *From Apes to Warlords*. New York: Harper & Row, 1978.

GOVERNMENT AND MILITARY PUBLICATIONS

American Historical Association. Committee for the Study of War Documents. *Guides to German Records Microfilmed at Alexandria, Virginia*. 41 vols. Washington, D.C., 1959–65.

Cole, Hugh M. *VIII Corps Operations, Operation Cobra*. Washington, D.C.: Chief of Military History, 1945.

Hansen, Chester B. *Diaries*. Washington D.C.: U.S. Army Military History Institute, 1946.

Hechler, Major Kenneth W. *VII Corps in Operation Cobra*. Washington, D.C.: Chief of Military History, 1946.

Kronman, Mark. *From Normandy into the Reich*. Covert Warfare series. D810S7C66. "The Deceptive Practices of 23d Headquarters, Special Troops during World War II." Study, US Army Material Systems Analysis Activity, Aberdeen Proving Ground, Maryland, January 1978. 2113–23HST–1978.

Military Signals IV. Description of 23d Spec Sig Co at Fort Riley, Kansas.

National Archives and Record Center, Washington, D.C., T-Series:

T–70:	Records of the Reich Ministry for Public Enlightenment and Propaganda
T–73:	Records of the Reich Ministry for Armaments and War Production
T–77:	Records of Headquarters, German Armed Forces High Command
T–175:	Records of the Reich Leader of the SS and Chief of the German Police (Heinrich Himmler)

National Archives and Records Center. *Summary Sheets of Captured German Documents*. Washington, D.C.

Park, Edwards. "A Phantom Division Played a Role in Germany's Defeat." *Smithsonian* 16 (April 1985).

Praun, Albert. "German Radio Intelligence." USAREUR Foreign Military Study P–038, n.d.

Rogge, O. John. *The Official German Report*. New York, 1961. Based on the interrogation of 66 Nazi officials in 1945–46 by a team of the U.S. Justice Department and the FBI.

Rosignoli, Guido. *Army Badges and Insignia since 1945*. London: Blandford Press, 1980.

Staubwasser, Anton. "Army Group B. Intelligence Estimate (6 June–24 June 1944)." USAREUR Foreign Military Study B–782, December 16, 1948. FMS#B–782.

———. "The Enemy as Seen by the High Command of Group of Armies B during the Fighting in Northern France and Belgium (25 July to 16 September 1944)." USAREUR Foreign Military Study B–825, March 1, 1948. FMS#B–825.

Thompson, George Raynor and Dixie R. Harris. *The Signal Corps: The Outcome (Mid-1943 through 1945)*. Washington, D.C.: Office Chief of Military History, 1966. D769A533V.

U.S. Army. 12th Army Group. *Report of Operations (Final After Action Report)*. Wiesbaden, Germany, 1948. 02–12–1948, UHRm.

U.S. Department of Army. *Unit Citation and Campaign Credit Register: DA Pam 672–1, July 1961*.

U.S. Department of State. *The Spanish Government and the Axis: Official German Documents.* Washington, D.C., 1946.

U.S. War Department. Military Intelligence Division. *German Military Intelligence.* Washington, D.C., April 1946. UB250G4U5.

————. *Signal Company, Special, 23d Headquarters, Special Troops: Table of Org & Equip 11–78,* April 14, 1944.

Index

About the Author

WILLIAM B. BREUER landed with the first assault waves in Normandy on D-Day, then fought across Europe. Later, he founded a daily newspaper in Rolla, Missouri, and a highly successful public relations firm in St. Louis, Missouri. He has been writing books since 1982, twelve of which are now in paperback, and eight of which have become main selections of the Military Book Club.